GREEN BAY PACKERS

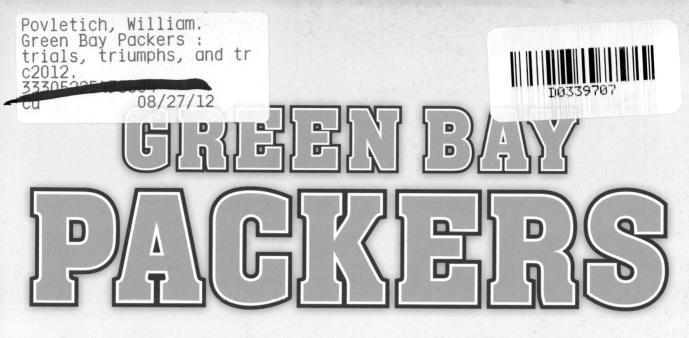

Trials, Triumphs, and Tradition

William Povletich

WISCONSIN HISTORICAL SOCIETY PRESS

Published by the Wisconsin Historical Society Press
Publishers since 1855

Publication of this book was made possible in part by a gift from Hazel Drebus.
Additional funding was provided by a grant from the D. C. Everest fellowship fund.

wisconsin**history**.org

Printed in the United States of America
Designed by Percolator

16   15   14   13   12   1   2   3   4   5

Library of Congress Cataloging-in-Publication Data
Povletich, William.
   Green Bay Packers : trials, triumphs, and tradition / William Povletich.
      p. cm.
   Includes bibliographical references and index.
   ISBN 978-0-87020-497-5 (pbk. : alk. paper) 1. Green Bay Packers (Football team)—
History. I. Title.
   GV956.G7P683 2012
   796.332'640977561—dc23

                                                        2011039253

Green Bay Packers

This book is dedicated to all the George Calhouns, Lee Remmels, Art Daleys, and Bud Leas who've dedicated their careers to reporting on the Packers in the moment. Along the way they've drafted a rich compendium for generations to come. No true history of the Packers could be compiled without referencing their work.

Art Daley (left) and Lee Remmel (right) reporting from the Lambeau Field press box, circa 1966

CONTENTS

FOREWORD

By Bob Harlan

For nearly four decades, I've had the pleasure of serving the greatest sports franchise on the planet: the Green Bay Packers. When I arrived in Green Bay as Dan Devine's assistant general manager in 1971, the business of professional football was growing, but it was nothing like today's financial juggernaut. Back then there might have been fifteen people working in the Packers' front office. Today the Packers employ more than 185 full-time workers and hundreds of part-timers—and that's not counting coaches and players. As the costs of fielding a team have skyrocketed along with revenues, the Packers organization has become much more corporate. But despite these changes, the franchise will always be a small-market team. Being from the smallest city in professional sports, the Packers will always have to compensate with creative revenue sources just to stay competitive against NFL teams from New York, Chicago, and other big cities.

The business of professional football has always fascinated me. While holding a number of front-office positions for the Packers during the 1970s and 1980s, I gained a deep understanding of the importance of preserving what I consider a national treasure. I knew that relying solely on the traditions and championships of decades past would eventually bankrupt the franchise. We had to start winning games in the present.

When I became the Packers' president and CEO in 1989, I made it my number one priority to restore the team's dignity on the field, which began with staying competitive with the rest of the NFL's franchises at the bank. For the next nineteen seasons, the Packers posted one of the best overall records of any team and experienced unprecedented financial success as well—all while maintaining the team's rich history and returning the Lombardi Trophy to Green Bay with our Super Bowl XXXI victory.

For this success I am indebted to both Ron Wolf and Mike Holmgren. I hired Ron in 1991 to resurrect the Packers franchise. By hiring Holmgren, trading for Brett Favre, and signing Reggie White, Ron restored character and dignity to an organization that had only four winning seasons and two playoff appearances in the 1970s and 1980s.

My role with the Packers was a dream job, heading up a company with the most loyal customers in one of the most lucrative businesses in the world. However, I knew building and sustaining Green Bay's elite-franchise status would not come without sacrifice. Difficult decisions had to be made, and I had to stand behind my convictions. I tell people now that the two toughest business decisions I made as president were eliminating the home games played in Milwaukee after 1994 and renovating Lambeau Field in 2003. At first neither decision was totally popular, but I can't imagine what would have happened to the Packers if we had acted otherwise. In the end, none of my worst fears were realized. The fans have since thanked me again and again for the new Lambeau Field, for bringing our Milwaukee friends with us to Green Bay, and most of all for restoring a tremendous sense of pride to the franchise. I've been told that as long as Ted Thompson, whom I hired in 2005, and Mike McCarthy are here, my fingerprints are going to be all over this organization, and if that's true, I couldn't be prouder.

Since entering the NFL nearly nine decades ago, the Green Bay Packers have been celebrated in hundreds of articles, books, and documentaries, many of which have focused on larger-than-life heroes being led to victory by iconic coaching legends. What I admire about *Green Bay Packers: Trials, Triumphs, and Tradition* is its ability to convey the oftentimes overlooked business decisions and behind-the-scenes characters as vital components of the Packers' thirteen NFL championships and financial survival. It takes the dedication and talents of an entire organization, from the front-office staff and locker room personnel to the ticket vendors and custodial staff, to win a championship. William Povletich's book captures how those spirited individuals kept the franchise solvent so our illustrious athletes in green and gold uniforms and coaches in tan fedoras and beige trenchcoats could succeed on the gridiron.

For nearly four decades, I've revered the Packers organization like a family heirloom. In publishing *Green Bay Packers: Trials, Triumphs, and Tradition,* the Wisconsin Historical Society Press, our state's foremost storyteller, ensures that the Packers' true story will be preserved for generations to come. Through scrupulous research, rare photographs, and one-of-a-kind financial records, the book demonstrates a deep understanding of the trials, triumphs, and traditions that indeed make the Green Bay Packers the greatest sports franchise on the planet.

PROLOGUE
The Timelessness of Titletown

The story of the Green Bay Packers has been built on a historical foundation unlike any other in sports. The complete truth about the birth of professional football in Green Bay, Wisconsin, will always be subject to interpretation, since the events can no longer be verified by those who witnessed them. Indeed, the Packers' mythic origins are so shrouded in lore that even former team president Bob Harlan has admitted, "I always tell people that the Packers' story is more like fiction than reality."

But what can't be disputed is that since 1919 the Packers have been both "a community project and a regional religion," as team cofounder Earl "Curly" Lambeau once called them. For generations the team's history has been passed along with the same reverence devoted to sacred family stories.

The Packers exist because dreamers like Curly Lambeau and George Calhoun never questioned whether a little town like Green Bay could compete in the National Football League. When professional football took root in the years following World War I, Green Bay was one of several small-town teams struggling to survive. While other clubs such as the Canton Bulldogs and Pottstown Firebirds vanished from the gridiron landscape, the Packers persevered, despite being on the brink of extinction numerous times. The franchise went into receivership, was sued by a fan, almost went out of business when an insurance company failed, and nearly faded away in the 1950s due to the lack of a modern stadium. Through it all the Green Bay Packers phenomenon lived on—as fascinating as ever. "There is no parallel to the way a small city like Green Bay has been able to remain a vital part of professional football's big league—from the founding of the National Football League to the present," legendary coach Vince Lombardi once said. "There is only one Green Bay. The story of the Packers stands alone."

Today the Packers are woven into every fiber of Green Bay's social fabric. The city brands itself "Titletown USA." Dozens of restaurants and shopping centers are emblazoned in the team's green and gold color scheme. The Main Street Bridge has been christened after Ray Nitschke, and streets are named after such legends as

Favre, Holmgren, White, Starr, and Canadeo. The team's stadium, Lambeau Field, is located at 1265 Lombardi Avenue, across the street from Clarke Hinkle Field and the Don Hutson Center. And the fans are as much a part of the team as anyone who has suited up to play. Playing football in Green Bay "is like playing for a college or university," Don Hutson recalled. "You get to know the fans and they get to know you."

Wisconsin kids are raised as students of the game, born into the Packer Backer lifestyle. Family photo albums include countless images of kids growing up in Packers clothing. From birth, fans are taught to appreciate the past, enjoy the present, and look forward to the future. "If you want to go on a wild goose chase in Green Bay," former coach Phil Bengtson remarked, "ask someone where you can meet the biggest Packer fan in town."

As professional football has evolved into a financial juggernaut—with economic growth that even the most lucrative Fortune 500 corporation would envy—the Green Bay Packers continue to boast one of the most successful stories in sports. With 112,158 stockholders, the Packers are the only professional sports franchise in the United States that is owned by its fans. Born out of necessity, that public ownership structure has since served the club enormously well, creating a Packers community that has rallied around the franchise in its struggling years. "You can't really compare the Packers to any other franchise," Bart Starr has said. "They're totally unique, one of a kind. The success of the Green Bay Packers is now something global."

Regardless of where the team's famous "G" logo appears—from Asia to Africa—the center of the Packers universe will remain its stadium. Lambeau Field is foot-

The Packers Hall of Fame is the perfect conduit for introducing new generations of fans to the unique relationship between the community and its franchise. (COURTESY OF CHIP MANTHEY)

ball's mecca, a shrine that rivals baseball's Wrigley Field or basketball's Boston Garden as host to epic games and legendary players. Hundreds of thousands of loyal fans from all fifty states and more than one hundred countries have made the pilgrimage to pro football's most hallowed ground. The stadium embodies the vision of Curly Lambeau, the hometown boy who didn't want to stop playing his favorite game; the sincerity of the men who supported him; and the fiery civic loyalty that still glows bright in Green Bay. The mystique of the game that was spawned on the dusty gridirons of midwestern industrial towns survives inside the Lambeau Field bowl. "It's not so much what the stadium looks like; it's what happened here that makes this place unique," Bob Harlan has said. "A story like this will never happen in professional sports again."

Inside the Lambeau Field Atrium, the Green Bay Packers Hall of Fame serves as the perfect link between new generations and the legends of yesteryear. As parents escort their children hand in hand through the Hall of Fame, the larger-than-life mannequins clad in muddy jerseys and the memorabilia-filled display cases lure

The Green Bay Packers' future depends on the next generation's dedication, loyalty, and hard work to preserve this American treasure. (COURTESY OF CHIP MANTHEY)

even the most reluctant fan with the same mystical green and gold potion that helped shape a team, a community, and a nation during the past ninety years. By the time the visit is complete, the Green Bay Packers will have won over another lifelong fan.

Behind the Packers' league-best thirteen NFL titles, twenty-one pro football Hall of Fame inductees, and nearly six-digit waiting list for season tickets are the dedicated individuals and the shrewd business decisions that helped the only publicly owned franchise in professional sports survive. Behind every Packer who became a legend on the field—names like Michalske, Adderley, and White—was a Turnbull, Olejniczak, and Harlan, whose dedication to preserving the solvency of the franchise was unwavering. Today the success of the Packers, along with that of the entire National Football League, is reflected in billion-dollar television contracts and record-breaking attendance figures in stadiums across the country. The Green Bay Packers' storied history, like the game of football itself, rose from the obscurity of small-town America into a national obsession.

Green Bay Packers

PIONEERS
of
PACKERLAND

On October 23, 1921, nearly 6,000 fans poured into Green Bay's Hagemeister Park to witness the Packers' American Professional Football Association debut. Facing the Minneapolis Marines, a team composed mainly of World War I veterans and former college stars, the hometown eleven were under tremendous pressure to win. Even though the season hadn't begun, league officials had already publicly doubted if a little town in northern Wisconsin could support a major-league football franchise. APFA president Joe Carr had been kind in his reception of the Green Bay team, but he stressed that if the newcomers were to remain in the professional ranks, they would have to win.

Featuring a lineup that included local favorites Herman Martell, Nate Abrams, Wally Ladrow, and Martin Zoll, the Packers struggled until there was about five minutes left to play. Behind the heroics of Earl "Curly" Lambeau, Buff Wagner, Grover Malone, and Art Schmaehl, Green Bay pulled out a 7–6 victory. The Packers' first win in the APFA that afternoon was the culmination of a journey that a former high school football hero and a career newspaperman had begun just two years earlier.

On Monday, August 11, 1919, Curly Lambeau and George Whitney Calhoun had presided over a group of nearly two dozen enthusiastic young men gathered in the offices of the *Green Bay Press-Gazette*. Although there had been some preliminary talk and planning, that night's decision wasn't announced until three days later. As an unknown scribe for the Packers' 1969 Press Guide would later write, "The big step had been taken. So August 11 is as good a birthday as any. They didn't know it, but that was the beginning of the incredible saga of the Green Bay Packers."

Green Bay was no stranger to football before that meeting. As far back as the 1890s, the city had fielded various clubs that contributed to a thriving football

Early Packers teams were as colorful on the field as their talented players' nicknames, including Boob Darling, Lavvie Dilweg, Red Dunn, Jug Earp, Tiny Cahoon, and Curly Lambeau. (COURTESY OF TOM PIGEON COLLECTION)

LEFT: Starting when he organized the Green Bay Packers with George Calhoun in 1919, Earl "Curly" Lambeau served as the team's quarterback until 1928. (MILWAUKEE JOURNAL SENTINEL)

RIGHT: In the Packers' early years, George Calhoun served as the club's secretary, publicity man, guardian of the ticket gate, and statistician (perhaps the NFL's first). (COURTESY OF CHRIS NERAT)

culture across Wisconsin. Those early teams faced hundreds of men from Milwaukee, Waukesha, La Crosse, Madison, Menomonie, Eau Claire, Rhinelander, Oconto, Fond du Lac, Peshtigo, and Appleton in countless games on dozens of fields across the Badger State. The game itself had become a popular pastime among Green Bay's blue-collar workers who would play and watch games after their shifts at the nearby paper mills and factories. So to those in attendance that August evening, the birth of one of professional sports' most unusual organizations went largely unnoticed. "In 1919, no one in Green Bay considered the latest edition of the Green Bay city team to be anything but just that," author Larry Names recounted in *The History of the Green Bay Packers: The Lambeau Years—Part One.* "Curly Lambeau wasn't starting something new. He was simply the new captain of the aggregation."

Green Bay's strong sense of gridiron pride was rooted in its high school football programs. One of the city's most celebrated talents was Earl "Curly" Lambeau, who lettered in the sport all four years he attended East High School and served as the team's captain during his senior year. After enrolling at the University of Wisconsin–Madison in the fall of 1917, he dropped out less than a month later when the freshman football program was canceled. He returned to Green Bay and worked in his family's construction business alongside his father, Marcel Lambeau, before enrolling at Notre Dame for the 1918 fall semester.

Following a successful season in Knute Rockne's legendary backfield alongside George Gipp—of "win one for the Gipper" fame—Lambeau returned home for the holidays. While there he began suffering from a severe case of tonsillitis. He was forced to wait six weeks for the swelling to subside before doctors could remove his tonsils. By the time Lambeau felt better, he had chosen not to return to Notre Dame for the spring semester, saying too much time had elapsed. He focused his attention and affections on his high school sweetheart, Marguerite Van Kessel, who was still living in town.

With their wedding set for Saturday, August 16, 1919, Lambeau went about finding work in Green Bay. After he was offered a job at the local Indian Packing Company for the modest sum of $250 a month, college became less of a priority for him, and "he had a lingering ache to play football again as the summer of 1919 began to fade into fall," according to former Packers executive committee member John Torinus.

Lambeau's quest to return to the gridiron led him to discuss the possibility of organizing a town team with an old friend, George Calhoun, sports editor of the *Green Bay Press-Gazette*. For the next several weeks, the cigar-chewing Calhoun incorporated stories about a possible new team into the *Press-Gazette*'s sports pages, inviting players to attend a planning meeting on August 11. Like past Green Bay teams, this one would be composed of local men who "just wanted to play for the love of football," Lambeau explained years later. "We agreed to split any money we got and each man was to pay his own doctor bills."

To help cover team expenses, Lambeau convinced his employer, the Indian Packing Company, to pay for twenty football jerseys, a dozen footballs, shoulder pads, and use of the vacant lot next to the plant for practices. "I talked my boss, a man named Frank Peck, into backing a pro football team. I told him it would take five hundred dollars to equip a team and get it through a season," Lambeau said of that first sponsorship agreement. "All they wanted was the name 'Indian Packing Co.' on the sweaters. It was good advertising, and good will for them because they had just come to Green Bay from Providence, Rhode Island."

The 1919 Green Bay Packers went 10-1 against other local town teams. (COURTESY OF THE OTTO STILLER COLLECTION OF THE NEVILLE PUBLIC MUSEUM OF BROWN COUNTY)

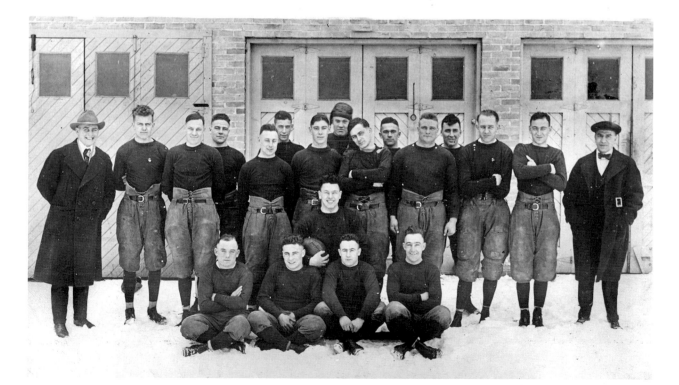

The group of young men met again on Thursday, August 14, to officially organize the club. There, Lambeau was elected team captain, and Calhoun was named the club's manager. Calhoun would also serve as the team's publicity manager, promoting every aspect of the club. While penning numerous impassioned articles about the team in the pages of the *Press-Gazette* during those first few years, Calhoun would refer to the team by several different names, including the Indians on occasion because of the company's sponsorship affiliation, but he referred to them as the Packers for the first time in the *Press-Gazette* the day after the August 14 meeting. "Too bad there isn't a place in the Hall of Fame for characters like Calhoun, who really shared in the fathering of professional football in Green Bay," author Steve Cameron noted in *The Packers! Seventy-five Seasons of Memories and Mystique in Green Bay*. "He worked himself numb creating the Packers out of the city's needs and energies—as he saw them—and almost literally beat the drums until the Packers were known nationwide."

The team arranged to host its first home games at Hagemeister Park. The open field was a prime location for spectators arriving on the Walnut Street streetcar. Fans who drove could sit atop or inside their parked automobiles and watch from behind the ropes that stretched about ten yards behind the playing field. Since Hagemeister Park lacked any sort of seating arrangements or ticket turnstiles, Calhoun walked through the crowds, soliciting donations from spectators by passing the hat. Fans were encouraged to follow the action up and down the field by moving alongside the play as it progressed. With a "50-yard-line" perspective at all times, spectators often spilled onto the field in the middle of a play when things got exciting. At halftime, when each team adjourned to opposite end zones, players sat on blankets strategizing for the next half. Fans were encouraged to form a ring around their huddles, which made for handy windbreaks but all too often led to opinionated fans interrupting the tactical discussions.

Despite the field being 100 yards long with 10-yard-deep end zones, the game was quite different in those early days. Goal posts stood on the goal line, not in the back of the end zone. There were no hash marks. Each successive play began where the last one ended, and when a ball carrier was knocked out of bounds, the ball was placed at the point inbounds where he went out, right along the sidelines. Forward passing was allowed, but with the restriction that the passer had to throw from at least 5 yards behind the line of scrimmage, reducing the possibility of deception. When a pass fell incomplete in the end zone, it was ruled a touchback, with the defenders given the ball on their 20-yard line. Games took about two hours from start to finish, with statistics rarely recorded. Players were much smaller than they are today; linemen weighed between 180 and 220 pounds (with the occasional behemoth reaching 240) and ranged in height from 5'10" to 6'2". Some backs were no more than 5'6" and 150 pounds. Their regulation wool jerseys were often faded and torn, and when it rained the crude, clumsy uniforms doubled in weight. The flimsy leather helmets, which were optional for years, could be folded and shoved into a player's back pocket. Offered little protection, a player retiring with all of his original teeth and a nose that didn't bend in an unorthodox fashion was considered lucky.

On September 14, 1919, the Packers—sporting the Indian Packing Company–sponsored blue and gold sweaters and pants made of coarse tan canvas—played their first organized game against Menominee, Michigan, and won 53–0. Green Bay went on to crush town teams from Marinette, New London, Sheboygan, Racine, and Oshkosh before losing its season finale against Beloit en route to a 10–1 record. Although the original Packers players weren't technically professionals, "the twenty-one 'regulars' divided up the profits. Each man got $16.75," sportswriter Chuck Johnson wrote in *Green Bay Packers: Pro Football's Pioneer Team*. "Not long after, Calhoun bought a new Jeffrey sedan. The players kidded him for some time about 'holding onto the hat' when he passed it for the offering."

Between 1919 and 1922 the Packers played their home games at Hagemeister Park, which was adjacent to the East River near Baird and Walnut Streets and named after the Hagemeister Brewery. (COURTESY OF TOM PIGEON COLLECTION)

Before the Packers began their sophomore season, the Indian Packing Company was sold to the Acme Packing Company, leaving Lambeau with a new boss and the team with a new sponsor. To generate additional revenue and discourage passersby from watching the games for free, "Marcel Lambeau directed volunteers in the construction of wooden bleachers on one side of the Hagemeister Park field; the roughly 200 seats were available exclusively for ticket-holders," author Don Gulbrandsen explained in *Green Bay Packers: The Complete Illustrated History*.

Those who paid fifty cents for a game ticket in 1920 had the pleasure of watching the Packers dominate their scheduled slate of town teams, racking up 227 points to their opponents' 24 that season. "Like so many other successful town teams across the nation, the Packers were going to have to rise above the local fray and compete nationally," author Denis Gullickson chronicled in *Vagabond Halfback: The Life and Times of Johnny Blood McNally*. "In the process, the roster featured fewer and fewer of the local boys." After compiling a 9–1–1 record, the Packers were receiving significant notoriety as a successful town team, only fueling Curly Lambeau's aspirations of joining the upstart American Professional Football Association.

Prior to September 17, 1920, when the APFA was organized in the showroom of a Hupmobile car dealership in Canton, Ohio, professional football was contained for decades as an assortment of local and regional teams scattered across small cities and neighborhoods throughout the Northeast and Midwest. The APFA required a $100 membership fee for each franchise to join, yet no team ever paid. The league's first season was a loosely organized conglomerate of franchises playing as many members as nonmembers. The fledgling association struggled to reverse pro football's growing reputation as a sport associated with blue-collar workers, violence for profit, gambling, and the corruption of young men's morals. The APFA suffered from an overall lack of national interest, despite having named its only nationally recognizable player, Olympic gold medalist Jim Thorpe, as league president. A pro team was lucky if 5,000 patrons showed up at a game. Meanwhile, a major college football contest at the same time would draw as many as 70,000 fans. The APFA's initial struggles did little to dissuade Curly Lambeau, who persuaded his boss, Acme co-owner John Clair, to present Green Bay as a viable pro football franchise. "Spreading the Acme name around the Midwest appealed to Clair as much as the possibility of making money from the team," author Larry Names remarked. "He agreed to apply for a franchise by sending his brother Emmett to the league meeting."

In summer 1921, there was no guarantee their application would be accepted. Green Bay was the smallest town with the smallest surrounding population applying for a franchise. Plus, the American Professional Football Association was in disarray. During the APFA's inaugural season, league president Jim Thorpe was nothing more than a figurehead. When the APFA failed to publish standings, three teams claimed the league championship at the end of the 1920 season. Team owners then elected Joe Carr as the league's new president, hoping his strong credentials as a football businessman—after leading the Columbus Panhandles town team into the APFA the previous year—would help him reorganize the association in time for the start of its second season, just a few weeks away.

After relocating the league offices from Canton to Columbus, Carr focused on cleaning up the game's reputation for allowing college players to play on the professional gridiron. No teams had received punishment during the APFA's first season, when dozens of young men performed for their alma mater on Saturday and played under assumed names in the pros on Sunday. So Carr was swift to establish strict rules stating that college players were not eligible to play in the pros until they completed their education.

Carr also believed that for the league to survive and thrive, franchises from small communities would need to be replaced or relocated to large cities. The theory made economic sense and was key to the APFA's earning national recognition as a major league. Small-city patronage was limited, and civic pride alone could not sustain teams in the new league. But with so much franchise instability, Carr could do little to accomplish the goal during his first year as league president. Of the twenty-one franchises that started the 1921 season, eight dropped out or didn't play enough inter-association games to be recognized as full-fledged APFA franchises.

Despite his doubts that the franchise would survive, Carr granted John and Emmett Clair, the Acme Company sponsors, an APFA franchise in Green Bay on August 27, 1921, for the entry fee of $50. If the Packers were to survive in this unstable environment, local business and political leaders needed to recognize how important pro football was as a means of promoting their city's economic growth

The 1921 Packers finished seventh among twenty-one clubs in the American Professional Football Association (soon to be renamed the National Football League) with a 3–2–1 record. (COURTESY OF THE OTTO STILLER COLLECTION OF THE NEVILLE PUBLIC MUSEUM OF BROWN COUNTY)

When the Packers (seen here in action at Hagemeister Park) joined the American Professional Football Association in 1921, there were between eighteen and twenty-two players on a roster and starters played all sixty minutes of a game. Player salaries averaged between $100 and $200 a game, with a star receiving as much as $400 a game—often paid in cash at the conclusion of each game. (COURTESY OF TOM PIGEON COLLECTION)

and national reputation. To signify that they were part of something bigger, the 1921 Packers began issuing *The Dope Sheet: Official Program and Publication, Acme-Packers Football Team.* Published during the Packers' earliest years by team manager George Calhoun, *The Dope Sheet* helped educate fans on the game with player news, rule descriptions, and promotion of upcoming contests. "Of all the gentlemen connected with dispensing information to the press in the National Football League, Cal probably was the pioneer," sportswriter Arch Ward said in *The Green Bay Packers: The Story of Professional Football*. "He was the first to begin compiling his own team's statistics."

Calhoun was meticulous when it came to cutting out the box scores and statistics for every game played during pro football's infancy, pasting them into notebooks that he updated on a weekly basis. "In the 1950s, a writer by the name of Roger Treat got the idea of

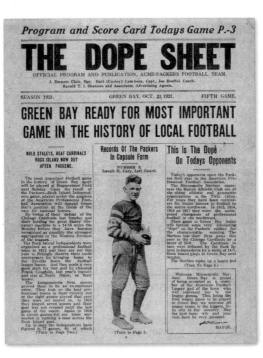

The Dope Sheet, written by George Calhoun, served as the Packers' first official press release and game program between 1921 and 1924. In its inaugural year it listed J. Emmett Clair as the team's manager, Lambeau as captain, and Joe Hoeffel as coach. (COURTESY OF CHRIS NERAT)

compiling an encyclopedia of pro football, and Calhoun's files of all the NFL games became one of Treat's main sources of information," Torinus recalled.

Although Calhoun blazed the path for future football statisticians, he would gloss over who coached the Packers' 1921 squad. At the time, in both the *Green Bay Press-Gazette* and Calhoun's own *Dope Sheet*, Joe Hoeffel was recognized as the team's coach. In fact, the masthead of five separate issues of *The Dope Sheet* in 1921 listed Hoeffel as the Packers' first coach and Lambeau as team captain. Pro football kept few records on the game until 1932, and as the "legend of Lambeau" grew in later years, neither Curly nor Calhoun sought to correct the perception of who coached the Packers in 1921. After all, "he ran everything," future team president Bob Harlan said of Lambeau. "Now, what his title was and what a title meant at that particular time, I'm really not comfortable saying. But he was the one running the show."

Behind Hoeffel and Lambeau, the Packers finished seventh in the now thirteen-team league with a 3–2–1 record in 1921. The Rock Island Independents, Evansville Crimson Giants, and Hammond Pros provided far greater challenges for Green Bay than the Packers' previous town-team foes. When they were scheduled to face George Halas's Chicago Staleys in the 1921 season finale, more than three hundred Packers fans and the twenty-two-piece Lumberjack Band paid almost $10 each to travel by train to Chicago's Cubs Park. During the inaugural contest, the Packers absorbed the rivalry's first "extracurricular" blow when the Bears' John "Tarzan" Taylor sucker-punched Howard "Cub" Buck, breaking his nose. After the towering Buck admonished his attacker in a soft, calm voice, "You're supposed to be a college graduate and a gentleman, you know," never again did anyone associated with either

The Packers' Lumberjack Band (seen here during a 1927 Packers-Bears game) was a fixture at home games from 1921 until they disbanded in 1997. In 1931 they played "Go! You Packers Go!" for the first time; it is still the team's official fight song. (COURTESY OF THE NEVILLE PUBLIC MUSEUM OF BROWN COUNTY)

of the two teams ask their counterparts for an apology or an autograph, as one of professional sports' most heated rivalries was born.

That afternoon the Packers were outplayed in a 20–0 loss. After the game the *Chicago Tribune* boasted that Heartley "Hunk" Anderson and two of his Fighting Irish teammates from Notre Dame had played for Lambeau. The incident escalated when Chicago sportswriters lobbied for Green Bay's expulsion from the APFA as an example to other pro teams aspiring to poach college talent. Less than a year into his regime, "Joe Carr was proving himself a real president who was going to make the new league's rules stick, and the Packers chanced to be the team on the immediate spot," sportswriter Arch Ward recalled.

Although Notre Dame's Anderson also played under an alias for the Canton Bulldogs that season, Carr chose to make an example of the Packers, declaring that their action was not only a violation of the rules but also a breach of trust for the fans. Two months later he revoked the franchise, as documented in the APFA meeting minutes for January 28, 1922: "Again the matter of the Green Bay franchise came up and Mr. Clair (J. Emmett) of Green Bay, after a discussion with the club members, asked the Association to consider the withdrawal of the Green Bay franchise with the apology to the Association. A motion to this effect was made by Mr. Halas and seconded by Mr. O'Toole. Carried." After just one season, the Packers were expelled from the American Professional Football Association.

It was evident the Packers were being made a scapegoat, since Canton received no punishment for breaking the same rule. Because Lambeau had been a schoolmate of Anderson's at Notre Dame and had the best chance of acquiring the star's legitimate services for 1922, "George Halas, owner of the Chicago Bears [who changed their name from the Staleys during the offseason], . . . urged Carr to enforce the league's latent restriction against using college athletes," author Craig Coenen wrote in *From Sandlots to the Super Bowl*. "As soon as the Packer franchise was revoked, Lambeau applied for a new one, but the 'application was held up pending further consideration.' Carr held up Green Bay's new franchise application just long enough for the Bears to sign Anderson."

Five months after submitting the $250 application fee, Lambeau received a blank franchise application form and invitation to attend the upcoming APFA meeting in Cleveland. On June 24 he presented his reinstatement case. Afterward, fellow team owners decided that if Lambeau could put up the $1,000 cash bond—the amount each team was required to post with the league office before play began that fall—Green Bay deserved another chance. The league's bond requirement served as a forfeit guarantee to be confiscated if teams were caught using college players or if a club failed to honor all scheduled games. The steep financial requirement forced nearly one-third of the franchises to drop out because they could not or chose not to pay the guarantee. Lambeau promised to pay the guarantee, and by the end of the meeting he had received his franchise, addressed to the "Green Bay Football Club, E. L. Lambeau of Green Bay, Wisconsin." Curly Lambeau now owned the Packers.

During that same league meeting, the APFA renamed itself the National Football League—a reflection of president Joe Carr's interest in teams thinking of themselves as uniformed members of a larger organization. He also established a standard player contract that included a reserve clause. It was based on the baseball model, which prevented players from jumping to another team by giving teams first rights on players' services for the following season. All player contracts would now be printed and distributed to all the teams in the league. To keep costs manageable, team rosters could only include eighteen players with a total team salary limit of $1,200 per game—which resulted in several teams paying their star players off the books. On the field, Carr required that all uniforms have numbers so fans could identify their favorite players.

■ ■ ■

With the 1922 season approaching, Lambeau's Green Bay Football Club came up with the $1,000 needed for the league deposit—the first team to make good on the requirement—by selling eighty shares of stock at $100 each. The $8,000 in capital was enough to get the team started, but it wasn't enough to sustain the franchise through the entire season. Expenses mounted as team payroll, venue rental costs, and visiting team guarantees (money promised by the home team to an opponent, regardless of the game's outcome or attendance) were determined before kickoff. The sooner the Packers reestablished themselves as winners, the greater the chance they'd start drawing at the gate because, as Lambeau said, "You can't do anything without the people in the stands."

> ## "You can't do anything without the people in the stands."
> —CURLY LAMBEAU

Lambeau didn't like "Packers" as a nickname—especially since the company was no longer sponsoring the team—and he exerted his new authority as Green Bay's owner to distinguish *his* team from the Packers team that had been forced to withdraw from the league the previous season. He debated several choices. "Calhoun used to call us the 'Big Bay Blues' in the *Green Bay Press-Gazette*. We didn't like that name either," Lambeau recalled. He eventually accepted the team's nickname, explaining, "The Milwaukee writers—Ollie Kuechle of the [*Milwaukee*] *Journal* and Stoney McGlynn on the [*Milwaukee*] *Sentinel*—kept referring to us as the Packers and the name stuck."

Although Lambeau had full control of the team in 1922, he couldn't control the weather. A rain-soaked autumn kept attendance down in Green Bay, which resulted in less-than-anticipated revenue. The Packers' first victory of the season, over the

Panhandles on November 5, was witnessed by a sparse crowd, causing their debt to rise. The team anticipated receiving financial relief thanks to a rain insurance policy Lambeau had purchased earlier that year, but the insurance company refused to pay on the claim, saying that the official amount of precipitation was three-hundredths of an inch below policy requirements.

Desperate to keep the team solvent, Calhoun ghostwrote a letter as the Packers to the *Press-Gazette*, pleading for further public support. He wrote the team was $5,400 in debt, with the Columbus game alone having increased the Packers' losses by $1,500. After reading the letter in the newspaper, a longtime friend and former teammate of Lambeau's offered to help keep the team afloat. "Nate Abrams deserves to be recognized as one of the many who helped Curly Lambeau fulfill his dream," author Larry Names proclaimed. "If Abrams hadn't loaned $3,000 to Lambeau's corporation in 1922, the Green Bay Football Club would have folded in midseason."

Despite the generous loan, the Packers were still in dire financial straits. Later that season, when the Bears' George Halas demanded a $4,000 visitor's guarantee, which Lambeau couldn't meet, their game at Hagemeister Park was scrapped. To fill the hole in its schedule, Green Bay hosted the Duluth Kelleys on the Sunday after Thanksgiving. As kickoff approached, another downpour was drenching the field. Again, Lambeau and Calhoun were faced with the prospect of playing in front of empty stands and had to decide if the game should be canceled. They asked the advice of Andrew Turnbull, business manager of the *Green Bay Press-Gazette*. Understanding that the game couldn't be canceled if Green Bay hoped to continue hosting a professional football franchise, Turnbull told them, "You go on with that game if nobody is in the stands. Play it. I don't know where we'll get the money, but we'll get it."

Although fewer than a hundred patrons witnessed the Packers' 10–0 triumph over the nonleague opponent, "Lambeau will tell you that, despite the fact that the Packers did play, won the ball game, and lost $2,200, it was still the finest bit of advice he ever took advantage of in his whole career," sportswriter Arch Ward remarked. "Postponement of this one game might well have sounded the death knell of the Packers."

Knowing that the Packers couldn't afford to cancel any games, under any circumstances, for both financial and public relations reasons, Turnbull promised Lambeau he would back the team through the end of the season. With a 4–3–3 record, the Packers finished eighth in the eighteen-team league, while having amassed a $3,400 debt. In December Turnbull rallied fellow Green Bay businessmen Dr. W. Webber Kelly, lawyer Gerald Clifford, and grocer Lee Joannes to meet him and Lambeau at the Beaumont Hotel's Attic Room. "They knew that a professional football team in Green Bay was a good thing, not just for them but for the whole community, the whole area of northeast Wisconsin and the Upper Peninsula of Michigan," author Larry Names noted. "Lambeau and Calhoun had given Green Bay a way to stand out on the national map, and Turnbull and friends fought to keep their city in plain view of the rest of the nation."

Later dubbed the Hungry Five—a nickname given to them by *Milwaukee Journal* sportswriter Oliver Kuechle based on a popular 1920s radio program—Turnbull, Kelly, Clifford, Joannes, and Lambeau devised a way to keep the team solvent with the creation of the Green Bay Football Corporation. To generate revenue, they would initiate two stock sales. The first saw four hundred fans crowd into the Elks Club on Cherry Street during the spring of 1923. The second was staged later that summer. By selling stock shares that paid no dividends at $5 each, they produced enough capital—$5,000—to guarantee a third season of professional football in Green Bay. The success of the drives prompted the Green Bay Football Corporation to file articles of incorporation with the State of Wisconsin on August 18, 1923. Andrew Turnbull was named team president, and the franchise was to be governed by a five-person executive committee and fifteen-member board of directors. The articles of incorporation further specified that any earnings from the team's disbandment or sale were to be directed to Green Bay's Sullivan Post of the American Legion. "The American Legion supplied the team with volunteers who did all the other chores in return for free admittance to the park," Torinus remembered. "That is how the idea of making the American Legion post beneficiary in the event of dissolution of the corporation occurred."

The reorganization of the franchise gave Green Bay and its fans the ability to keep the Packers solvent while teams in Canton, Hammond, Rock Island, and other midwestern factory towns were folding due to financial instability. "The Hungry Five and their man Calhoun performed within that span one of the greatest missionary campaigns in any sport," Arch Ward wrote. "Civic pride gave birth to the slogan, 'Once a Packer, always a Packer.'"

While preparing for the 1923 season, Curly Lambeau was tasked with finding the team a new home. Their old field, Hagemeister Park, had been chosen as the site of Green Bay's new East High School. Since construction was already under way before the season started, the Packers relocated to Bellevue Park. The new grounds at the end of Main Street were built for baseball and were considered inadequate for football as criticisms arose that the gridiron was too far away from the wooden bleachers. Nevertheless, the Packers averaged more than 3,000 fans per contest that season while attracting fans throughout the Fox Valley and the Door County Peninsula. The increased fan support at Bellevue Park and the Packers' impressive third-place finish with a 7–2–1 record helped the team maintain its stable financial status. When the final accounting came in, "although it was written in red ink,

> "Civic pride gave birth to the slogan, 'Once a Packer, always a Packer.'"
> —SPORTSWRITER ARCH WARD

ABOVE: The Green Bay Packers' board of directors (left to right): Gerald "Jerry" Clifford, Earl "Curly" Lambeau, Andrew Turnbull, Fred Leicht, Lee Joannes, Emil Fischer, Frank Jonet, and Henry "Tubby" Bero (COURTESY OF THE PRESS-GAZETTE COLLECTION OF THE NEVILLE PUBLIC MUSEUM OF BROWN COUNTY)

RIGHT: When the Packers sold stock shares at $5 each in 1923, they produced enough capital to guarantee a third season of professional football in Green Bay. (COURTESY OF THE GREEN BAY PACKERS)

Turnbull had every reason to feel vindicated because the operation had lost only $147.74," according to Names. "The Packers and the Green Bay Football Corporation were headed in the right direction."

· · ·

Pro football's economic success depended on good gate receipts covering team costs, so the Packers began an aggressive season-ticket sales drive as soon as the 1923 season ended. Knowing that a winner on the field didn't guarantee a winner at the bank unless there were fans in the stands, the Hungry Five of Turnbull, Lambeau, Clifford, Joannes, and Kelly started a tradition that Packers management would continue practicing in the ensuing years. They spent the offseason visiting Green Bay's surrounding towns and villages to speak at dinners, schools, club meetings, and anyplace where potential Packers fans might gather, offering box seats for the six home league games and one exhibition game for $15 and grandstand seats for $10. They described how the franchise could promote Green Bay, help build its national reputation, and enhance its economic growth—but only if the Packers stayed competitive, an expensive proposition for any NFL franchise.

Between 1920 and 1924, average game expenses for a competitive team increased more than 33 percent, from $3,700 to $4,950. While the minimum visitors' guarantee continued to rise, so did the cost to enter the league. In 1924 the NFL franchise fee rose to $500. Two years later, both the fee and the forfeit guarantee jumped to $2,500. The growing revenue demands caused several teams in medium-size midwestern communities, such as Racine, Wisconsin; Evansville, Indiana; and Duluth, Minnesota, to fold, becoming nothing more than footnotes in NFL history. Of the twenty-one teams listed in the league's final 1921 season standings, only nine, including the Packers, completed all three campaigns through 1923.

President Joe Carr's increased fees succeeded in eliminating some of the NFL's unstable franchises, but his goal of creating a league filled with nothing but strong, large-city teams was yet to be realized. Pro football was still considered a minor sport compared to college football and baseball in the nation's metropolises, with its small-town teams often faring better than their big-city brethren. The NFL was surviving thanks to the support of working-class citizens in factory towns who saw pro football as a source of civic pride. Yet pride didn't pay the bills, and victories didn't guarantee franchise security. Nothing showcased the league's instability more than its 1922 and 1923 champions, the Canton Bulldogs. After winning twenty-one out of twenty-two games with the only blemish being a tie, the franchise reported a loss of $13,000 and was forced to relocate to Cleveland before the start of the 1924 season.

To combat Carr's perceived bias toward large-city teams, Curly Lambeau attempted to alter the NFL's scheduling process on behalf of small-town teams. Since the league's inception, scheduling was left to individual team owners and favored the wealthier and more successful large-city teams. In advance of the 1924 season, Lambeau suggested the league devise a comprehensive schedule for all franchises, helping to reduce costs and generate more popular interest throughout the league. But as author Craig Coenen explained in *From Sandlots to the Super Bowl*, "Carr and large-city owners refused to accept that change. A balanced and fair schedule for all teams would take the NFL's best attractions away from larger cities and bolster clubs in smaller communities." The Packers were burdened with a schedule that saw them start the season on the road for two games, play at home for five consecutive games, and finish on the road with four more. The team persevered, finishing the 1924 season 7–4, good for sixth place in the eighteen-team league.

In January, at the annual Green Bay Football Corporation stockholders' meeting, Andrew Turnbull announced that the Packers' success on the field translated into the corporation now being solvent. The franchise was free of all debts, including those left over from Lambeau's corporation, which meant the corporation had paid back Nate Abrams while turning its first profit of just $2.20.

Knowing the team couldn't afford to continue hosting games in a minor-league baseball park, the Hungry Five rallied the city of Green Bay and the community's school board to build a new stadium. Adjacent to the brand-new Green Bay East

The Packers enjoyed their home field advantage during their two-year tenure at Bellevue Park, compiling an 8-3-3 record while attracting crowds ranging from 4,000 to 5,000 patrons per game. (COURTESY OF TOM PIGEON COLLECTION)

Beginning in 1925 the Packers played their home games inside City Stadium behind Green Bay East High School. (COURTESY OF TOM PIGEON COLLECTION)

High School, City Stadium was built atop the former site of Hagemeister Park, where the Packers got their start. The football stadium was finished within days of the start of the 1925 season and featured wooden bleachers on both sides of the field with an initial seating capacity of 5,000 to 6,000 patrons. The new stadium would soon be recognized as one of the finest gridiron stages in the NFL. It boasted a high-quality grass playing surface designed for football that benefited from one of the most innovative irrigation and drainage systems of the time. Yet City Stadium lacked most of the amenities of a modern sports park. There were no locker rooms on site, forcing the Packers to change in the East High locker room and visiting teams to dress at their hotel before games. For fans, the lack of restrooms during its first decade of operation often left male spectators to relieve themselves under the wooden stands and prompted many female fans to leave long before a game was over. Despite its shortcomings, City Stadium provided the Packers with a distinct home field advantage in 1925, as they won all six of their games there. The road was not as kind. Their 8–5 record left them in ninth place among the bloated twenty-team league that season, which included new franchises in Pottsville, Pennsylvania; Providence, Rhode Island; Detroit; and New York.

. . .

During the offseason George Calhoun and the *Green Bay Press-Gazette* staff kept Packers fans abreast of the sport's surging popularity. After the 1925 regular season, George Halas contracted college football's most illustrious superstar, University of Illinois's Harold "Red" Grange, to join the Chicago Bears on a nationwide barnstorming tour. The "Galloping Ghost" played nineteen games that winter, attracting enormous crowds, which included a contest between the Bears and Giants at the Polo Grounds that attracted more than 72,000 fans. The national media took notice as the cross-country tour proved to be a priceless marketing tool for pro football. It emblazoned the pro game onto the American consciousness while making Grange the sport's first superstar—and a rich one at that. By the time the barnstorming tour was over, Grange was estimated to have earned $100,000 for his services. His unprecedented contract, during an era when the average pro player made between $100 and $150 a game, guaranteed him $2,000 per game, with an additional 10 percent take on the first $5,000 at the gate, 20 percent on the second $5,000, and 40 percent thereafter. The tour's success proved there was a demand for the pro game and that tremendous amounts of money could be earned promoting it. The NFL had achieved its first moral victory against critics who insisted that professional football was a mongrel sport, certain to fail.

Following the tour, Red Grange's manager, C. C. Pyle, demanded that the Bears pay his client a five-figure salary and grant him one-third ownership of the Bears if they wanted to retain his services in 1926. When the team refused, Pyle retained Grange and approached the NFL for a New York City franchise, arguing the Big Apple could support two teams like Chicago's Bears and Cardinals. When his franchise request was rejected, Pyle started his own league in 1926—the American Football League—with Red Grange as its marquee player.

The new league's grandiose vision of nine teams intended to challenge the NFL in three of its biggest markets: New York, Philadelphia, and Chicago. The AFL looked to the rosters of teams from its established rival for talent. The attempted poaching resulted in NFL clubs increasing their contract offers to players in hopes of preventing them from signing with the new league. While several NFL franchises struggled to retain players, the Packers avoided losing any of their top stars. However, to compensate for the escalating salaries, the team appealed to its dedicated fan base to start purchasing 1926 season tickets early, despite the slight rise in admission prices.

In a further response to Pyle's new league, the NFL expanded to twenty-two franchises before the 1926 season kicked off. The strategy worked; the AFL became a financial lemon. Playing in front of sparse crowds, the new league's weaker franchises began folding, with only four teams—the New York Yankees, the Philadelphia Quakers, the Chicago Bulls, and the Los Angeles Wildcats—completing their schedules. After Philadelphia won the league title with an 8–2 record, the entire AFL folded.

Still, despite having existed for only one year, the AFL had a lasting financial impact on the NFL. The direct competition forced player salaries to spike and prompted league president Joe Carr to convert the NFL into a big-city league. He took aggressive steps toward eradicating the league's growing epidemic of harboring insolvent teams. Several of the NFL's small-town franchises were buckling under the financial pressures brought on by the upstart league. An impatient Carr gave them the choice of dropping out or suspending their franchise. Although the Packers finished the 1926 season in fifth place with a 7–3–3 record and a small profit, the team's existence was in jeopardy.

■ ■ ■

Before the start of the 1927 season, Carr evicted ten franchises from the NFL, including the Akron Indians, Hammond Pros, and Columbus Tigers (formerly the Panhandles)—all charter members. Seven of the dropped franchises were in small or medium-size cities that would never host an NFL club again. After adding the New York Yankees from the defunct American Football League, the NFL streamlined itself into a twelve-team league. Fewer teams meant there were fewer roster spots available for players. The higher concentration of available talent meant salaries would rise in a bidding war among NFL clubs. In Green Bay, the Hungry Five recognized that to compete against the teams with deep pockets in New York and Chicago, Curly Lambeau would need more money. The Packers' executive committee raised the additional revenue through early season-ticket promotions and the sale of the stock, which was still on the books from previous seasons. The team's strong financial standing was further solidified after finishing the 1927 season with a 7–2–1 record, second to the New York Giants, whose 11–1–1 record earned America's largest city its first NFL championship.

When the NFL announced that league-wide attendance had surpassed the half-million mark in 1927, professional football was still benefiting from the popularity built during Red Grange's barnstorming tour two years earlier. Owners claimed the league was at an ideal size, despite fielding only twelve teams. Even after Duluth and Buffalo folded in the months running up to the 1928 season, the league declared that no additional franchises would be allowed into the league for the following season. The NFL was down to ten teams, with only the Packers, Chicago Bears, Chicago Cardinals, and Dayton Triangles remaining from the original twenty-one franchises that had made up the league in 1921.

■ ■ ■

On the eve of the 1928 season, hopes were high in Green Bay that the Packers, who had almost captured their first NFL championship the year before, were on the verge of greatness. After hosting six of their first eight games at City Stadium, the Packers traveled by train for almost a month for five consecutive road games against the New York Giants, Pottsville Maroons, Frankford Yellow Jackets, Providence Steam Roller, and Chicago Bears. The extended road trip provided George Calhoun, who was serving as the team's publicity machine, with the perfect opportunity to showcase Green Bay on a national level. "In those days when professional football attracted little attention in prestigious papers like the *New York Times* or *Herald-Tribune,*" former executive committee member John Torinus commented in *The Packer Legend,* "Cal got more ink for the Packers than any other team in the league could muster," especially after their 7–0 victory over the defending NFL champion New York Giants at the Polo Grounds.

The excitement surrounding the Packers' early season potential led to disappointment in December. The team's late-season stumble left the boys in blue and gold to finish a distant fourth with a 6–4–3 record. Despite falling short of a championship, the Packers received a joyous reception when their train rolled into Green Bay at season's end. At that moment Curly Lambeau, who navigated his way through the sea of dedicated fans on hand, could already be seen looking ahead to next season. Sportswriter Arch Ward remarked about Lambeau's desire to win a championship, "Always a perfectionist, [he] said that the addition of at least three more players in key positions would make them *that* kind of team."

> "[George Calhoun] got more ink for the Packers than any other team in the league could muster."
> —PACKERS EXECUTIVE COMMITTEE MEMBER JOHN TORINUS

• • •

By 1929 Green Bay had become the NFL's longest-tenured community to field a single franchise without winning a title. The Packers would become NFL champions only if civic pride coexisted with civic boosterism—a distinction not lost on an enthusiastic Curly Lambeau. "I know the whole town is behind us in spirit," he told the team's executive committee and board of directors after returning from the league's annual meeting that summer. "We've shown other clubs that we are not a weak sister. Let's show them that we don't talk this game here, but come out to see it."

The Packers' newly elected team president and original Hungry Five cofounder W. Webber Kelly initiated an aggressive 1929 season-ticket campaign. His head of ticket sales, Spike Spachman, coordinated the efforts of three dozen ticket agents who enticed loyal businesses around Green Bay, many of which had supported the Packers since the hat-passing days, into purchasing more season tickets. To generate additional ticket sales outside of Green Bay, Hungry Five cofounder Gerald Clifford served as the team's primary ambassador, meeting with prominent business owners and fans throughout northeastern Wisconsin and Michigan's Upper Peninsula. When the advance ticket sale goal of $15,000 was almost reached, the Packers could afford to sign the talent necessary to capture Green Bay's first NFL championship.

Curly Lambeau had a reputation throughout the league for being able to identify gifted athletes and recruit them to play in the NFL's smallest city. It was a necessary skill in the days before the NFL sanctioned a player draft and when the reserve clause kept a player beholden to his previous season's team. "He had an unmatched talent for discovering inexpensive players and converting them into great stars and national names," Ray Evrard, who had just stepped down as the Packers' second president in 1928, said of Lambeau.

Prior to the start of the 1929 season, Lambeau's reputation served the Packers well. He traded for Giants' lineman Cal Hubbard, who wasn't too fond of the bright lights of New York City and had demanded, "Either trade me to Green Bay or I quit playing football." When the New York Yankees folded after the 1928 season, Lambeau convinced fullback Mike Michalske to sign with the Packers and converted him into an offensive lineman to maximize his diverse combination of speed, agility, and power. With the team's offensive line solidified, Lambeau went about finding the Packers a distinct scoring threat.

Of the available players Lambeau considered signing before the 1929 season began, none was more notorious than Johnny "Blood" McNally, who was joining his fourth team in five years. By the time the "Vagabond Halfback" arrived in Green Bay, the free spirit had a league-wide reputation for breaking team rules, ignoring curfews, missing trains, eluding teammates assigned to watch him, and having a taste for booze without much success in handling it. "Over the years, Lambeau would deal with both sides of the Johnny Blood coin," McNally biographer Denis Gullickson remarked. "While Lambeau, the coach, might not have appreciated Johnny Blood's penchant for the party life, Lambeau, the manager, knew that the off-field antics and on-field heroics combined to bring paying spectators to the game. The resulting cash flow kept the football machine moving. In turn, the cash flow for Johnny Blood kept his party train moving."

When Curly Lambeau signed Johnny "Blood" McNally (left) and Robert "Cal" Hubbard (right), along with Mike Michalske, before the start of the 1929 season, the Packers acquired the missing pieces they needed to win their first NFL championship. (BOTH PHOTOS COURTESY OF TOM PIGEON COLLECTION)

When McNally first joined the Packers, he asked for a salary of $100 a game. After Lambeau countered with an offer of $110 with the stipulation that he couldn't drink past Tuesday of each week, "I countered with an offer to take the $100 I had proposed and drink through Wednesday," McNally recalled. "Curly agreed."

When the Packers held their first practice of the season on September 8, almost 2,000 fans were in attendance. Those clamoring to get their first glimpses of Michalske, Hubbard, and McNally practicing with established fan favorites Red Dunn and Lavvie Dilweg noticed who was spending more time with a whistle hanging out of his mouth instead of a football in hand. "For all purposes, Lambeau was through as a player himself, but he was coming into his own as a coach and organizer," sportswriter Chuck Johnson remarked.

During the practice, Spachman and his men hustled through the crowd, offering season box seats at City Stadium for anywhere from $12 to $25. The arrival of Hubbard, Michalske, and McNally prompted ticket sales to soar, including bringing out a crowd of 5,000—the largest in team history to date—for an exhibition game between the Packers and the Portsmouth Spartans a week before the start of the regular season.

After the Packers shut out the Dayton Triangles in the season opener, Green Bay prepared for the arrival of the Bears the following weekend. In anticipation, local merchants ran ads in the pages of the *Press-Gazette* supporting the Packers. Players had no problem selling extra blocks of tickets to their friends and neighbors. Projected attendance for the game prompted the team to turn to the Manitowoc and Seymour Fair Associations and Green Bay's East and West High Schools to contribute whatever portable seats they owned. Not one seat was left empty as a record crowd of 13,000 patrons packed into City Stadium, augmented by dozens of youngsters and adults clinging to branches in the surrounding trees overlooking the field. All in attendance, paid and unpaid, witnessed the Packers' 23–0 annihilation of their Windy City rivals that afternoon.

The Packers went on to win their first five games, all at home, by a combined score of 79–4. Their domination continued as they went on the road for the eight remaining games on their schedule, never allowing more than 6 points in a game all season. When the undefeated Packers headed east for the anticipated showdown against the undefeated New York Giants at the Polo Grounds, it was "the first time that I really got the feeling that I was in the big leagues," McNally recalled. "It was really something to get out there in front of all those people."

In a steady rain, the Packers and Giants battled in the gridiron slop for all sixty minutes of regulation. During this "Iron Man" era of professional football, sixty-minute performers were the rule rather than the exception. Regulars who played offense also played defense. Substitutions were limited to when injury or exhaustion could no longer be covered by pride. "In those days a team carried only sixteen or seventeen players," halfback Verne Lewellen recalled. "We were down to the bare minimum. We had to pace ourselves to go the distance and still have something left at the finish."

That afternoon, Green Bay used only eleven men for the first fifty-nine minutes of play before Lambeau switched out an injured Jim Bowdoin with Paul Minick at right guard. "Oh, how we hated to see the substitute come in," lineman Jug

> "It was really something to get out there in front of all those people."
>
> —HALFBACK JOHNNY "BLOOD" MCNALLY

Earp remarked. "We had wanted to go all the way without help. We told Curly, 'We don't need him. Jim'll be all right. He just got a little bump.' But Curly sent Paul in, anyway."

Lambeau wasn't about to risk losing the game. The winner would be in the best position to finish the season as NFL champion. The heightened stakes of the game required that Lambeau take an aggressive approach to defeating the big-city rivals. The strategy of defending against an opposing line by stringing out eleven players in front of each other, creating a horizontal tug-of-war, was becoming outdated. Offenses specializing in the forward pass forced defenses to create a corresponding "secondary," set up in the form of a string of defensive men farther back to thwart aerial attacks. "That left an open area in the defense, and slowly the idea of the line-backer evolved," future Packers coach Phil Bengtson said of the innovative strategy used that afternoon. "Lambeau created a sensation by pulling one of his linemen a step back of the line and giving him 'roving duty.' The tactic resulted in a 20–6 victory over the Giants and foretold of things to come."

Four days after clinching their ninth consecutive victory, in New York, the Packers found themselves facing the Frankford Yellow Jackets. "The result was that the bout ended in a scoreless draw, although Calhoun and several Packer veterans of the team contend that the officials fired the gun too soon, exploding it just when the Packers were on the Frankford nine," sportswriter Arch Ward recalled in *The Green Bay Packers: The Story of Professional Football*. "The Packers only a few minutes before had been told that seven minutes remained to play."

Although Green Bay's dreams of an undefeated season were dashed, the squad rebounded three days later to flatten the Providence Steam Roller, 25–0, during the Packers' third contest in eight days. Before returning to Green Bay, they stopped in Chicago long enough to shut out the Bears for the third time that season while securing their twelfth victory of the season against no losses and a lone tie. It was the first time since the 1923 Canton Bulldogs completed their regular schedule with a perfect percentage of 1.000 that the NFL celebrated an undefeated team among its ranks.

The town team that Curly Lambeau and George Calhoun had organized almost a decade earlier had captured its first National Football League championship, and in an impressive fashion. The 1929 Packers dominated their opponents, scoring 198 points while giving up only three touchdowns and a total of 22 points in their thirteen regular-season games. When word of the Packers' success spread across northeastern Wisconsin, "Green Bay residents threw a civic celebration that was unmatched anywhere for a pro football team until the late 1950s," according to author Craig Coenen. Green Bay would host a homecoming for the Packers the likes of which hadn't been seen since the end of World War I.

The party started the minute word reached Green Bay by telegram that the Packers had shut out the Bears in the season finale. The next day, when the team's train approached Green Bay, police had to escort it into town. For nearly five miles, thousands of boosters ignored the freezing cold and lined the rails with red flares in hand to light the tracks into town. A crowd of 20,000 fans carrying gold and blue banners and signs proclaiming WELCOME, PACKERS and HAIL CHAMPIONS! rushed the train as it pulled into the station. Screeching sirens, bellowing locomotive whistles, and blaring car horns greeted the players and coaches as they paraded through town in automobiles.

> **"Green Bay may be the 241st city in size in the United States, but it is the first city in football."**
>
> —MAYOR JOHN DIENER

The festivities continued into the next day and evening. Fans organized a victory banquet for the team at the Beaumont Hotel, where four hundred folks squeezed into the dining room. Thousands more listened at home on the radio. During the dinner, each Packer was awarded a Hamilton watch and a check for $220 tucked into a new leather wallet. The unprecedented bonus checks were from boosters who had raised more than $5,000 through individual and corporate donations. Despite their new championship status, individual Packers were within the league's average salary range of $100 to $200 per game, which maintained itself throughout the 1920s and early 1930s. Johnny "Blood" McNally thanked the fans and Packers ownership at the banquet, acknowledging, "I am especially grateful for the check."

When lineman Jug Earp, the Packers' most senior player, took to the podium, he was reflective: "Some of the early years were lean ones as Mr. Turnbull told you earlier in the evening. On those rainy days when they asked us to go for 'half fare' things looked dark, but we would look at one another and decide that we could 'stall' the landlady for another week or two."

Although several players and team officials spoke that evening, nobody summed up the Packers' civic value better than Mayor John Diener, who exclaimed, "Green Bay may be the 241st city in size in the United States, but it is the first city in football."

The Green Bay community understood that its NFL franchise had become an important civic asset, one that needed to be supported at all costs if the team was to survive into the next decade. During the course of the Roaring Twenties, forty-nine teams competed in the NFL at various times, with franchises in small towns like Duluth, Toledo, Muncie, and Racine all succumbing to the league's growing financial burdens as larger cities such as New York, Detroit, St. Louis, and Cleveland were encouraged to take their places.

In a similar fashion to Green Bay, the residents of small-town teams in Rock Island, Illinois; Pottsville, Pennsylvania; and Portsmouth, Ohio, treated their professional football teams as valued assets. The four communities were somewhat alike: they were isolated from large metropolitan areas, they didn't compete with any other major college or professional sports nearby, and they experienced considerable economic growth during the Great Depression with stable industries. Although each franchise received a high level of interest from its community and hometown fan base, only the Packers avoided chronic financial problems. The other three franchises lost considerable amounts of money since none of them was owned by wealthy individuals or a large business willing to assume the ongoing debts. "The Portsmouth Spartans lost more than $43,000 in their first two seasons," author Craig Coenen recounted in *From Sandlots to the Super Bowl*. "During their first season, the [Rock Island] Independents jeopardized further gridiron success by only being able to pay players two-thirds the average league salary—about sixty-six dollars per player per game."

Regardless of whether its teams were from Duluth or Detroit, the NFL struggled to keep all of them solvent during its first decade. Between 1920 and 1925, small-city teams dropped out of pro football at a rate of 26 percent per season, while large-city clubs folded at a rate of over 31 percent. After 1925, when Red Grange debuted with the Bears, the annual rate of failure for small-city teams rose to 30 percent, while large-city franchises failed at the even greater rate of 45 percent between 1926 and 1931. Nevertheless, the NFL continued to shift away from its dependence on small-town teams while lobbying to secure new franchises in larger cities. "Pro football's carnival like atmosphere began to wane as the league entered its second decade in 1930," author Joe Ziemba chronicled in *When Football Was Football: The Chicago Cardinals and the Birth of the NFL*. "Rules were tightened, schedules finalized, and the organization began to approach big-league status."

∎ ∎ ∎

As the 1930 season approached, Green Bay found that being the NFL's defending champions created an increased sense of pride throughout northeastern Wisconsin. "There were a lot of good times in Green Bay, it was a swell town in those days," Johnny "Blood" McNally recalled of the team enjoying a surge in popularity. "We were kind of riding on top of the world."

While the Packers' 1929 championship banner waved atop a blue flagpole at the west end of City Stadium, Curly Lambeau was being celebrated by his hometown as the handsome and charismatic husband and father whose dedication had put Green Bay on the professional football map. Behind closed doors, he was leveraging his growing influence by forcing the Packers to elect their fourth team president in four years. Lambeau was engaged in personality conflicts with several members of the executive committee and board of directors—in particular, with whoever was president. Back when Andrew Turnbull was president of the board, Lambeau had often gotten his own way while being kept on a very short financial leash. Before Dr. W. Webber Kelly was elected president as Ray Evrard's successor, he and Lambeau had gotten along well. However, once the doctor became team president, he began clashing with Lambeau over issues that often stemmed from Lambeau's attempts to take advantage of Kelly's new status. When Kelly refused the demands, Lambeau became increasingly belligerent and uncooperative. The Packers' success on the field seemed to only fuel the tension and dissension between Lambeau and Kelly. After serving only a year as team president, Kelly stepped down and Lee Joannes was elected by the team's board of directors to fill the vacancy.

As the pressure to repeat as NFL champions mounted, Curly Lambeau and his Hungry Five associates understood that regardless of a community's size, successful franchises shared two threads of continuity: stable team management and the ability to retain a nucleus of players from one season to the next. That meant the Packers' title as defending NFL champions was meaningless if the team didn't have increased financial resources to re-sign players like McNally, Michalske, Hubbard, Dunn, and Dilweg. It also meant the Packers would have to double their efforts not only to compete in the upcoming 1930 season but also to avoid a fate similar to one of their small-town rivals, the Pottsville Maroons, who folded at the end of the 1928 season.

Lambeau was able to secure the services of eighteen of the Packers' twenty-eight players from the 1929 championship squad, with Eddie Kotal being the biggest-name departure. Of the newcomers to fill the roster vacancies, the most

Curly Lambeau (with hand on football) coached the Packers to their third consecutive NFL championship in 1931 with contributions from (left to right) Arnie Herber, Mike Michalske, Red Smith, Milt Gantenbein, and Hank Bruder. (COURTESY OF TOM PIGEON COLLECTION)

noted addition was Green Bay native Arnie Herber, who became the Packers' latest potent passer, joining previous air aces Red Dunn, Verne Lewellen, and Curly Lambeau.

The Packers shut out the Cardinals in the season opener and followed up the next week by blanking the Bears. But as the season progressed, Green Bay's defense wasn't as dominant. Their offense kept them undefeated through the season's first eight games before they dropped three of their last six contests of the year. After tying the Portsmouth Spartans in their regular-season finale, the Packers had earned a 10–3–1 regular-season record, good for a .769 winning percentage. With the Giants' 13–4–0 falling just short at .765, Green Bay was crowned NFL champion by .004 of a percentage point. Although New York's owner, Tim Mara, was upset his Giants didn't win their second championship, he later described the benefit of having played the popular Packers twice that season: "I agreed to go to Green Bay for $4,000 and the Packers signed to come to New York for $5,000. We cleared $60,000 on the two games."

The NFL's first repeat champions since the Canton Bulldogs won it all in 1922 and 1923, the Packers earned the heartiest of congratulations from NFL president Joe Carr: "When the smallest city in the league can win the championship two years in a row, it's something to be proud of, and I'm as proud of the Green Bay Packers as any of their fans up there in Wisconsin."

For Packers fans, the *Green Bay Press-Gazette*, *Milwaukee Journal*, and *Milwaukee Sentinel* continued providing excellent newspaper coverage and in-depth analysis on the team. Meanwhile, radio was emerging as an invaluable medium for promoting the Packers throughout Wisconsin. During a time when baseball and other sports avoided the airwaves, fearing attendance would suffer if their product was given away for free, Green Bay and most of the NFL's other franchises welcomed radio's ability to reach larger audiences. By the late 1920s Green Bay's WHBY made games part of its regular programming, with Harold Shannon and Hal Lansing calling the action. Milwaukee's WTMJ began broadcasting games with announcer Russ Winnie providing play-by-play re-creations based on tickertape results. On December 7, 1929, the first Packers road game was broadcast from Chicago with Winnie bringing the play-by-play action against the Bears into Wisconsin living rooms as it happened.

Radio was introducing new fans to the game, which resulted in larger crowds packing into the expanded City Stadium. Total attendance for the Packers' first three games of the 1930 season surpassed the team's season totals for 1921 and 1922 combined. When 8,000 ticket holders poured into City Stadium for the team's fourth home game, against the Frankford Yellow Jackets, the season's attendance surpassed 37,000 patrons. The new medium continued to generate capacity crowds for the Packers at City Stadium and increase advertising sales for the radio stations that carried the games, but it failed to provide any significant compensation to the team for the broadcast rights.

■ ■ ■

In the midst of a growing worldwide economic depression, in 1930 the Packers and the rest of the NFL's teams were far from financially secure, dependent on filling every seat in their respective stadiums on game days. During the offseason, the league readjusted its franchise lineup for the eleventh straight year after the Minneapolis Red Jackets and Newark Tornadoes ceased operations. When Cleveland reentered the league for the fourth time, the NFL was left with ten teams to start the 1931 season. Every franchise questioned whether it could survive the season with the national economy in such terrible shape. Even the Packers weren't safe, despite being back-to-back champions. They were aware of the fate that befell the league's last repeat champions, the Canton Bulldogs, who had followed their 1922 and 1923 championship seasons by folding prior to the start of the 1924 season and selling several star players to a franchise in Cleveland.

Another harsh reminder that the Packers organization was far from being financially stable occurred in the summer months of 1931 when the team was fined $1,000—along with the Bears and the Portsmouth Spartans—for using college players. In Green Bay's case, quarterback Arnie Herber had dropped out of Regis College before joining the team, but that was still considered a violation of the league rule, which stated a player couldn't sign an NFL contract until his class had graduated. The fine was absorbed after another successful preseason ticket drive provided the Packers with enough capital to remain competitive in their quest for a third consecutive championship.

After opening the season with a shutout win against the Cleveland Indians in Green Bay, the Packers faced their most formidable foe since entering the league in 1921. While the Packers clobbered the Brooklyn Dodgers in the season's second game at City Stadium, spectator Willard J. Bent was injured after falling from some temporary grandstands, which had been inspected and declared safe by city inspectors just the week before. The franchise carried liability insurance to protect itself against these sorts of accidents, but the issuing insurance company, Southern Surety, folded soon after the incident occurred. Because the Green Bay Packers Football Corporation had an active stake in the bankrupt mutual insurance company, the court assessed the football corporation $2,500 to help pay the insurer's debts and further obligated the team to settle directly with the fan. The mess soon escalated when Bent sued the Packers for $20,000, prompting team attorney Gerald

Clifford to argue that the plaintiff had been drinking, with his inebriated condition the cause of the fall. Over the next few years, the case would make its way through Wisconsin's legal system, leaving the Packers' financial fate in the hands of a judge.

On the field, the Packers strung together nine straight victories to start the 1931 season. With a roster filled with time-tested veterans—whose nicknames were as colorful as their exploits on the field—Green Bay's Jim Bowdoin, Hank Bruder, Bernard "Boob" Darling, LaVern "Lavvie" Dilweg, Joseph "Red" Dunn, Francis "Jug" Earp, Milt Gantenbein, Arnie Herber, Robert "Cal" Hubbard, Verne Lewellen, Johnny "Blood" McNally, Mike Michalske, John "Bo" Molenda, and Tom Nash relied on their coach's proven formula for success. "Ever since he had taken over the town team back in 1919, Lambeau had used the same basic offensive alignments and plays," author Larry Names recounted, "and season after season, he shoved this offense down the throats of Green Bay's opposition."

Lambeau's strategic use of offensive single-wing and T formations was a large reason the Packers were in a two-team race for the NFL crown against the league's other surviving small-town team, the Portsmouth Spartans. In 1931 the two teams weren't scheduled to face each other but had talked about the possibility of sched-uling a playoff game at the end of the regular season to determine an undisputed champion. When Green Bay finished with a 12–2 record, the second-place Spartans, at 11–3, insisted on the playoff game. Portsmouth's management even complained to league officials in an attempt to hold Packers president Lee Joannes accountable to a verbal agreement that the two teams would play on the Sunday following the regular-season finale. The controversy wasn't extinguished until league president Joe Carr dismissed the Spartans' claim, determining that the proposed playoff game had been nothing more than tentative.

Carr's executive decision resulted in Green Bay claiming its third consecu-tive NFL championship. Without the extra game, the Spartans found themselves $16,000 in debt by season's end. The franchise called out to the community for help in a similar fashion to the Packers' efforts nearly a decade earlier. By December 1931 a vigorous "Save the Spartans" campaign had raised $23,500 in pledges, with 1,429 Portsmouth boosters purchasing stock at $10 per share. It was enough to keep the franchise alive for another season, but many wondered if the team, or any small-town NFL franchise, could continue resisting the growing challenges brought about by the nation's worsening economic malaise.

■ ■ ■

By 1932 the Great Depression had engulfed the entire country, as a quarter of the nation's workers were unemployed and home foreclosures reached epidemic proportions. At the same time, the NFL proclaimed almost every team had set attendance records, with its Bears and Giants franchises averaging more than 20,000 fans per game. What wasn't mentioned was that Frankford, Cleveland, and Providence were folding; Portsmouth, Brooklyn, and Staten Island were deep in debt; and the Chicago Cardinals were far from being financially stable. If a team showed a profit, it was oftentimes in the hundreds of dollars, while deficits ran into the tens of thousands.

Before the start of the season, NFL membership fell to eight teams, featuring three teams in New York, two in Chicago, and one in Boston. The smallest franchise roster in league history supported president Joe Carr's vision of a National Football League anchored by big-city franchises. Small-town teams, which had won six of the league's first twelve titles, had become an endangered species. Only Portsmouth and Green Bay remained as Carr's premeditated tactics to absolve the NFL of its small-town franchises became public. "No other small city will be admitted to the National League," he vowed before the start of the 1932 season. "We have too many big cities knocking at our door."

Carr's mandate came after league officials entertained several offers to place teams throughout the country, including a second franchise in Wisconsin. "In 1930 and 1931, D. C. Haderer, owner of Milwaukee's independent pro football team, applied for NFL membership, but the league took no action because officials expected Green Bay's franchise to be the eventual occupant of that market," author Craig Coenen revealed in *From Sandlots to the Super Bowl*. "They urged the Packers to move or at least play a portion of their home schedule there. Doing so would help cultivate a fan base, thereby making a complete transfer easier. Because of their deep financial crisis, Packer management relented to league pressure and agreed to play one of six home games in Milwaukee starting in 1933."

Curly Lambeau (left, alongside Wuert Engelmann, Hank Bruder, John "Bo" Molenda, and Tom Nash) opened training camp in 1932 with hopes of securing a fourth straight NFL title. (MILWAUKEE JOURNAL SENTINEL)

After the Packers generated only a modest profit as a result of winning their third consecutive championship, team president Lee Joannes understood how the growing economic conditions brought about by the Great Depression would further impact Green Bay's ability to support the team. Because revenue generated by fans being in the stands was the team's primary source of income, he announced the team would decrease season-ticket prices from $15 to $12, with box seats being cut from $25 to $20 and bleacher seats and standing-room-only seats set at fifty cents each.

Featuring the cheapest tickets in the league, City Stadium continued hosting large crowds as the Packers started the 1932 season with nine wins and one tie in their first ten games. Despite finishing the season with an impressive 10–3–1 record, Green Bay fell short of winning its fourth consecutive NFL championship. The Packers won more games than the Bears that season, but ties weren't counted then. Chicago's 7–1–6 record calculated into a winning percentage of .875, which trumped Green Bay's .769. Despite the Bears' inability to score any points in their first four games, including three scoreless ties, they were crowned NFL champions.

The Bears' championship season almost collapsed before it began. "I had gone into the 1932 season surrounded with IOU's. I kept afloat by giving more notes," Chicago's George Halas recalled in his autobiography *Halas by Halas*. When only 3,000 spectators braved the elements to attend the Bears' 9–0 victory against the Packers in the season finale at Wrigley Field, "I couldn't pay Green Bay its guarantee of $2,500," Halas said. "I told Lee Joannes, the Packers' president, 'Lee, I'm out of chalk.'"

If anyone could sympathize with the plight of the Bears' owner, it was Joannes, who agreed to accept $1,000 in cash from Halas and a note for $1,500 promised to be paid within six months. "The next year when the Bears played in Green Bay, Halas said I should take the $1,500 out of the guarantee. I marked the note paid, but Halas will never get it back," Joannes recalled of his generosity in keeping the Packers' rival financially solvent.

By the close of 1932, the Packers' continued and unprecedented success had propelled Curly Lambeau into the national spotlight. He was becoming the most celebrated coach in either the pros or college football. Newspaper articles across the country heralded his coaching genius. Even appearing on magazine covers as pro football's best-dressed coach, he found his celebrity status transcending football as he became *the* person Hollywood stars wanted to socialize with. Lambeau in turn began finding more excuses to entertain his interests by spending more time on the West Coast. "Between Calhoun's publicity and his Packers' own accomplishments," author David Zimmerman remarked, "Lambeau was being elevated to intoxicatingly lofty heights that enabled him to see far beyond Green Bay."

LAMBEAU'S LEAP

At end of the 1932 season, the Green Bay Packers enjoyed nationwide recognition as the darlings of professional football. Despite ending the year mere percentage points away from securing its fourth consecutive NFL championship, the franchise was broke and in need of a quick influx of cash. As the holidays approached, team president Lee Joannes announced that the Packers had accepted an invitation to play a pair of exhibition games in Hawaii—on Christmas Day and New Year's Day—and another pair of exhibitions in San Francisco and Los Angeles, with all travel expenses to be reimbursed and the team receiving a portion of each game's gate receipts. "The trip to Hawaii and California was seemingly meant to bail out the corporation," Larry Names recounted in *The History of the Green Bay Packers: The Lambeau Years, Part Two*, "but all it did was add to the problem because the organizers of the contests failed to make good on the guarantees they had promised the players and the corporation for sending the team on the trip," forcing the team to exhaust its cash reserves to compensate the players.

Upon their return to Green Bay, the Packers were now $12,300 in debt. Their financial problems continued after spectator Willard J. Bent was finally awarded a $5,200 judgment for his doctor bills, lost wages, and personal pain and suffering after having fallen from the City Stadium bleachers in 1931. The Packers were in no position to absorb the financial setback—regardless of whether it was for only a portion of the original $20,000 Bent sought—and they immediately appealed the verdict to the Wisconsin Supreme Court. Unable to afford the customary bond and on the verge of bankruptcy, the Green Bay Football Corporation was vulnerable to Bent's attorneys, who could examine the corporation's records and subject the team to collection action, placing a levy on the corporation's assets and income

Throughout the 1930s and 1940s, crowds continued to file into Green Bay's City Stadium (seen here in 1947), regardless if the Packers were competing for an NFL championship. (COURTESY OF GREEN BAY PRESS-GAZETTE FROM TOM PIGEON COLLECTION)

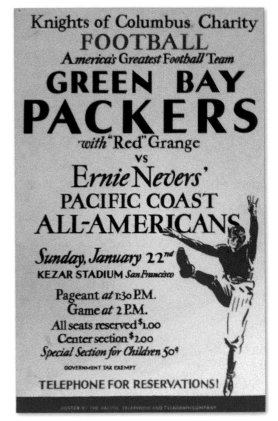

In January 1933 Curly Lambeau (left, seated next to movie star Myrna Kennedy) employed the Chicago Bears' Harold "Red" Grange to play with the Packers in a series of exhibition games during a West Coast barnstorming tour (right). (LEFT: MILWAUKEE JOURNAL SENTINEL; RIGHT: COURTESY OF CHRIS NERAT)

from ticket sales, gate receipts, and other sources of revenue—meddling that could disrupt and potentially destroy the franchise.

To avoid this nightmare scenario, the Hungry Five of Andrew Turnbull, Dr. W. Webber Kelly, Gerald Clifford, Lee Joannes, and Lambeau went about defusing any actions by Bent's legal team. They began on August 15, 1933, by filing for bankruptcy and petitioning the circuit court to appoint a receiver for the corporation. "Joannes then loaned the corporation $6,000 in cash that it needed to pay off bills, making him a creditor of the corporation, and a bigger one than Bent, effectively allowing him to call the shots on behalf of all the creditors," Names said.

Overseeing the appointment was Joannes's good friend and circuit court judge Henry Graass, who assigned the Packers a friendly receiver, Green Bay accountant Frank Jonet. After the receivership was announced, the organization went about reinforcing how important the team was to Green Bay and the surrounding area by publishing supportive articles in the *Green Bay Press-Gazette* and sending team officials to meetings around town, including the Kiwanis, Lions, and Rotary clubs. With the nation in the grips of the Great Depression, Green Bay needed to keep as many of its citizens employed as possible. The Packers meant jobs at City Stadium and throughout the community. Six or seven times a year, thousands of folks ventured to Green Bay to attend games. It was estimated those visitors infused between

$1 and $5 per person, per visit, into Green Bay beyond what they spent at the City Stadium concession stands, buying meals, renting hotel rooms, filling their cars with gas, and purchasing souvenirs. It was an influx of revenue the region couldn't afford to lose if the Packers went away.

Before the start of the 1933 season, the Staten Island Stapletons became the latest NFL franchise to succumb to the economy's downward spiral. Also burdened was George Marshall, the owner of the Boston Braves—soon to be renamed the Redskins—who had amassed more than $46,000 in debt after just one season in the NFL. At the league's annual meeting, Marshall proposed dividing the league into East and West Divisions, with a playoff game to determine a league champion. After Marshall suggested that fans would be more supportive of a third-place team in a five-team division than a sixth-place team in a ten-team league, his plan was adopted. The economic potential of having more teams play more meaningful games later into the season and in front of larger crowds wasn't lost on NFL team owners. Plus, the additional revenue generated by the marquee matchup of division champions at season's end would benefit all ten teams in the league—including new franchises in Pittsburgh, Cincinnati, and Philadelphia, each of which paid $2,500 to join the league.

That summer the NFL addressed the growing epidemic of low-scoring games and ties by adopting rules that encouraged forward passing and field goals to help inflate scoring. (Between 1920 and 1932, an astounding 64 percent of all NFL games finished in a shutout for one team, while 6 percent of contests ended in a 0–0 tie, and the league didn't want a reputation for grudge matches that lacked the drama that came with a team pulling out a last-second victory.) Team owners also approved the funding of the NFL's first centralized publicity department with hopes of further improving professional football's public image beyond a small but dedicated fan base. The publicity department set up offices in Chicago and New York to be close to the major press outlets, while the league headquarters remained in Columbus, Ohio. That first year, the NFL allotted meager sums to publicity, but the public relations fund grew as the sport's popularity increased. For the Packers, it was money well spent when they made a change to their upcoming home schedule.

As the 1933 season approached, Charles "Buckets" Goldenberg, Lavvie Dilweg, and Joe Kurth (left to right) prepped their equipment to dig up the turf in hopes of the Packers capturing their fourth title in five years.
(MILWAUKEE JOURNAL SENTINEL)

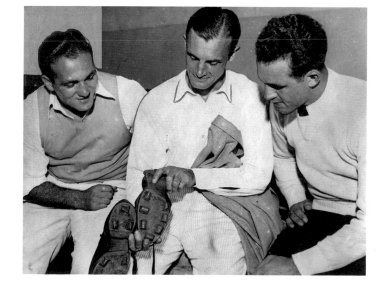

In September the Packers announced they would play their upcoming October 1 home game against the New York Giants at Milwaukee's Borchert Field, fueling rumors the team would move there if the game enjoyed a large turnout. In reality, the Packers were desperate for the revenue a large Milwaukee crowd would generate. Playing in Milwaukee would also appease the league, which was mounting pressure to move the Packers to a larger market. The antiquated wooden stadium, which was home to the minor-league Milwaukee Brewers, attracted an impressive 12,467 fans, strengthening the league's argument that the franchise should move to Milwaukee on a permanent basis. By midseason, stories about the Packers' potential relocation ran rampant as a confident *Chicago Tribune* reported that "the Green Bay Packers will move to Milwaukee next fall and if the change is not made then it certainly will be made in 1935."

In Green Bay, the Packers publicly admitted that tapping into Wisconsin's largest market was intended to generate additional revenue for the team and expand its fan base—but said moving there on a permanent basis was never considered. The executive committee was also strategizing that playing a limited number of games on an annual basis just one hundred miles south of Green Bay would further thwart NFL aspirations to establish a professional team in Milwaukee.

On the field, the Packers struggled to stay competitive, a direct result of the team's unstable financial situation. By season's end, the team's twenty-five-man roster had only fourteen men under contract. The economizing of talent resulted in the franchise's first losing season, with only five wins, seven losses, and one tie, placing them third in the Western Division. But despite suffering through another season of financial hardship, the Packers were still solvent. Portsmouth, the NFL's other small-town team, found itself bankrupt after the 1933 season, having succumbed to the growing challenges of the Great Depression. When the Portsmouth Spartans were sold to G. A. "Dick" Richards, the team moved to Detroit and became the Lions. The Packers were now the league's lone remaining small-town franchise, "in spite of Joe Carr's many efforts to rid the league of every small-town team," Names recalled. "Carr had the power to finish off the Packers once and forever, but the Packers refused to die. It made no sense to Carr, to Halas, and to many others from large cities. What these men couldn't comprehend was the spirit of the people of a small town."

■ ■ ■

Before the 1934 season got under way, NFL president Joe Carr attempted to further strip the Packers of their small-town status, requiring them to play a portion of their home schedule in Milwaukee. The team accommodated the decision by arranging for two of the team's six home games to be played at State Fair Park, on the city's western outskirts. Although the Packers had expanded City Stadium's capacity over the years to 22,370, the Milwaukee venue was still larger, with room for 32,000 spectators. Fans in northeastern Wisconsin condemned the decision at first, but eventually "Green Bay residents accepted the fact that they had to share the Packers in order to keep them," Craig Coenen remarked in *From Sandlots to the Super Bowl*.

On the field, the Packers finished 1934 with a mediocre 7–6 record, bearing faint resemblance to the championship squad earlier in the decade. Meanwhile, Curly Lambeau was basking in his growing national celebrity status, and in Green Bay his image was beginning to deteriorate. His marital infidelity, well known in football circles, went public after he divorced his high school sweetheart, Marguerite, to be with Miss California beauty pageant contestant Susan Johnson. Even his strongest supporters felt his actions were a form of betrayal, not only of his former wife but of the entire community of Green Bay. "I guess Curly was a human guy after all," halfback Johnny "Blood" McNally recalled. "He was not perfect, not an angel. But there weren't many angels in the pro league back then."

With the Packers still more than $19,000 in debt with less than $6,000 in cash reserves, the franchise was at risk of being ordered by the courts to sell its assets. The only tangible asset the Green Bay Football Corporation owned, however, was a National Football League franchise. The NFL was also growing impatient with the Packers' foundering financial situation. "League officials gave the city one last chance," author Craig Coenen noted. "If the franchise could not get out of receivership in 1935, it would fold or move to Milwaukee."

The growing threat that Green Bay could lose its franchise prompted Lee Joannes and Andrew Turnbull to invite two dozen of the area's top merchants and bankers to an exclusive meeting at Joannes's wholesale grocery office in January. They proposed a plan to reorganize the franchise before it was too late. The guests in attendance guaranteed sizable personal contributions in support of the plan, before commencing on a citywide campaign to solicit $10,000 in stock sales by the end of the month. "Word of their meeting went round the town, and grocer Joannes soon found himself devoting all of his time to accepting voluntary contributions from daily visitors in his office," sportswriter Arch Ward said in *The Green Bay Packers: The Story of Professional Football*. "Policemen, firemen, bootblacks, housewives, bricklayers, and high school students besieged him with donations, some as low as fifty cents."

At a time when the national economy had never been worse, fans pledged almost $5,000 by the end of the campaign's first week. Unlike the rest of the country, Green Bay's economy was stable thanks to a thriving paper industry that employed more than half of all blue-collar workers in the area. Between 1929 and 1935,

The Packers reorganized in 1935 and sold three hundred shares of outstanding stock. (COURTESY OF THE GREEN BAY PACKERS)

Hoberg Paper, Northern Paper Mills, and other local paper mills saw statewide employment in their industry grow by nearly 25 percent. With the area's largest paper mill (owned and operated by Kimberly-Clark) increasing the size of its workforce by more than 40 percent, Coenen concluded that "during the Depression, toilet paper and paper towels saved the Packers in Green Bay."

By ten days into the stock campaign, Turnbull and Joannes had received enough pledges to dissolve the Green Bay Football Corporation. Once again, the Packers were a football phoenix, rising from the ashes of financial ruin with another affirmation that retained the basic principles of the franchise: the business reorganized as Green Bay Packers, Inc., a nonprofit corporation that would donate any profits to the Sullivan Post of the American Legion. By early February more than 154 boosters, including Green Bay mayor Dominic Olejniczak, had pledged more than $13,029 toward the team's financial reorganization. "Before we had the Packers, you couldn't get any civic cooperation worth mentioning," W. Webber Kelly remarked of the intangibles the team brought to the community. "Now things are different. I think Green Bay can thank the Packers for the spirit."

■ ■ ■

In the shadow of the Great Depression, professional football continued to grow. Overall league attendance and revenue were on the rise. As the decade progressed, fewer job opportunities in the public and private business sectors meant more graduating college athletes chose pro football as a career. The influx of well-educated athletes into the NFL helped legitimize the sport and improve its public image. Teams benefiting from the arrival of better players motivated coaches to find the next competitive advantage.

Before the 1935 season opened, Curly Lambeau felt his players needed more conditioning and study time, and he arranged for the team's first official training camp at the Pinewood Lodge on Lake Thompson, outside of Rhinelander. In years past, players wandered into Green Bay about a week before the season's first game to participate in workouts and strategy sessions, but it was far from formal. Lambeau felt the camp, located more than 150 miles northwest of Green Bay, was an environment with few distractions. Camp opened on August 24, three weeks before the start of the regular season, with each day's schedule consisting of players being bused four miles into town twice a day to practice at the Rhinelander High School football field.

In attendance was the Packers' next rookie sensation, Don Hutson. His journey to Wisconsin had begun after he was discovered by Lambeau's keen eye for talent during a scouting trip in 1935. "Curly Lambeau once told me that he had been out to California and watched our Alabama team practice for the Rose Bowl," Hutson recalled years later. "And he said that it was the first time he'd ever seen fakes run at sharp angles. He was very enthused. He thought it was great."

For Lambeau, getting Hutson to play in professional football's smallest community would test his tenacity when the receiver agreed to contracts with both the Packers and the upstart Brooklyn Dodgers football squad. With both teams staking a claim to Hutson, NFL president Joe Carr intervened, agreeing to honor whichever contract arrived at his office with the earliest postmark. When Green Bay's letter arrived with a time stamp of 8:30 a.m., seventeen minutes before Brooklyn's pact, Lambeau joked, "It's lucky I sent my letter special delivery."

As a result of the bidding war with Brooklyn, "When I got to Green Bay, Curly told me he didn't want the other players or anybody else for that matter to know how much I was earning," Hutson recalled of his $300-per-game salary—more than any other veteran player on the roster. "Well, there were two banks in Green Bay in those years and the Packers had an account in each. So, to keep it a secret, I got two checks after each game, one hundred and fifty each, and each was drawn on a different bank."

With Hutson, the Packers now possessed a viable threat in their pass-happy offense. "Curly Lambeau may not have been the greatest coach, but he seemed to

> "Curly Lambeau may not have been the greatest coach, but he seemed to be a step ahead of the times."
>
> —LINEMAN MIKE MICHALSKE

be a step ahead of the times," lineman Mike Michalske recalled. "It was Lambeau's idea to move Don Hutson out on the flank. This was the first time any team had used or seen a flanker."

After the Packers dropped their 1935 opener to the Cardinals, Hutson's reputation as a vital weapon in Green Bay's offensive arsenal began to spread across professional football's gridirons. The next week against the Bears, quarterback Arnie Herber showcased his new receiver's potential when the two connected for the game-winning touchdown. "The best way I can describe Hutson is if you could picture a gazelle, running through a defensive secondary in the National Football League. He had a deceptive stride, and he did the hundred in something like 9.7," fullback Clarke Hinkle recalled. "And what great moves he had. One day I saw him fake Beattie Feathers of the Bears out of his shoes, literally fake him out of his shoes. They had to call time out so he could put them back on."

As the 1935 season progressed, Don Hutson's abilities elevated the Packers to a championship-caliber team. With an 8–4 record, Green Bay finished behind the eventual NFL champion Detroit Lions and their 7–3–2 record. Three defeats at the hands of the Cardinals—by a total of 6 points—kept the Packers from winning their first Western Division crown. The Packers' turnaround was a testament to the man responsible for stockpiling Green Bay's roster with unparalleled talent over the past fifteen years. "With a cunning eye for talent, Lambeau somehow always found young players who responded to his motivational techniques and played with a determination and desire that is so important in football," biographer David Zimmerman testified in *Lambeau: The Man Behind the Mystique*. "However, his ability to sign anyone from anywhere would change in 1936."

• • •

In an effort to equalize talent and achieve parity among all its franchises, the NFL instituted its first players' draft on February 8, 1936. Between 1929 and 1935, the NFL championship and division titles had been captured every season except one by one of "the Big Four": the Packers, Bears, Giants, and Redskins. Those four franchises also

The Packers' rivalry with the Chicago Bears—as old as the franchises themselves—is captured in this editorial cartoon from the *Green Bay Press-Gazette*'s Harold Barrie. (FROM THE GREEN BAY PRESS-GAZETTE ARCHIVES, REPRINTED BY PERMISSION)

READY TO GO HUNTING FOR ANOTHER BEAR SKIN

When Don Hutson (14) joined the Packers in 1935, quarterback Arnie Herber (38) further established himself as one of the NFL's most potent and accurate quarterbacks. (COURTESY OF ALL-AMERICAN SPORTS, LLC)

shared extensive financial benefits generated by division rivalries and postseason gate receipts. The disparity left the remaining six NFL clubs with less money to sign quality players, forcing them to field bad teams, which resulted in them drawing poorly at the gate and obligated them to sell their best players in order to cover their financial losses. "This league would never survive unless we had some system whereby each team had an even chance to bid for talent against each other," future NFL commissioner Bert Bell said. Cooperation among teams would benefit everyone, according to Bell, because "the league is no stronger than its weakest link."

The NFL's draft would have teams choose players in the reverse order of their place in the standings the previous season. Not only would the draft foster competition among the stronger and weaker teams, but it would also hold down salaries as players were forced to negotiate with only the team that chose them. In the inaugural draft, eighty-one players were picked—nine per team—with fewer than half signing contracts, opting instead for careers other than professional football. The first two players drafted opted for careers that appeared more lucrative at the time, leaving the day's third selection—Riley Smith, chosen by the Boston Redskins—to be the first to sign, contracting for $250 a game and a small bonus. Following the draft, the NFL took further steps to equalize competition, instituting the waiver rule whereby teams with the poorest records would have the first opportunity to sign players that other teams released.

In Green Bay, Curly Lambeau went about re-signing many of his trusted veterans. When it came to negotiating contracts, he was as tough as he was shrewd, playing no favorites. It seemed every Packer came out on the short end of his bargaining tactics, including Charles "Buckets" Goldenberg, who explained, "Contract negotiations with Curly were like a three act play. You started out full of hope. Then Curly started to talk down your demands. At the end, you felt like a bad guy trying to rob the Packers."

Johnny "Blood" McNally began the 1936 season holding out for more money— a bold move considering his already contentious relationship with Lambeau. "I was getting $150 a game, and Hutson was getting $175," McNally recalled. "I figured I deserved to get paid as much as he did. Curly didn't see it that way, at first, but he came around after I missed the first three games." The Packers' first-ever contract holdout went over Lambeau's head to get his raise, approaching the Packers' board

Before the creation of the NFL draft, Curly Lambeau stopped at nothing to recruit the most talented college players from across the country, including an offensive lineman from the University of Michigan named Gerald Ford. Ford declined Lambeau's invitation, instead opting for law school at Yale before starting a career in politics that would culminate with his becoming the thirty-eighth president of the United States. (COURTESY OF GERALD R. FORD PRESIDENTIAL LIBRARY)

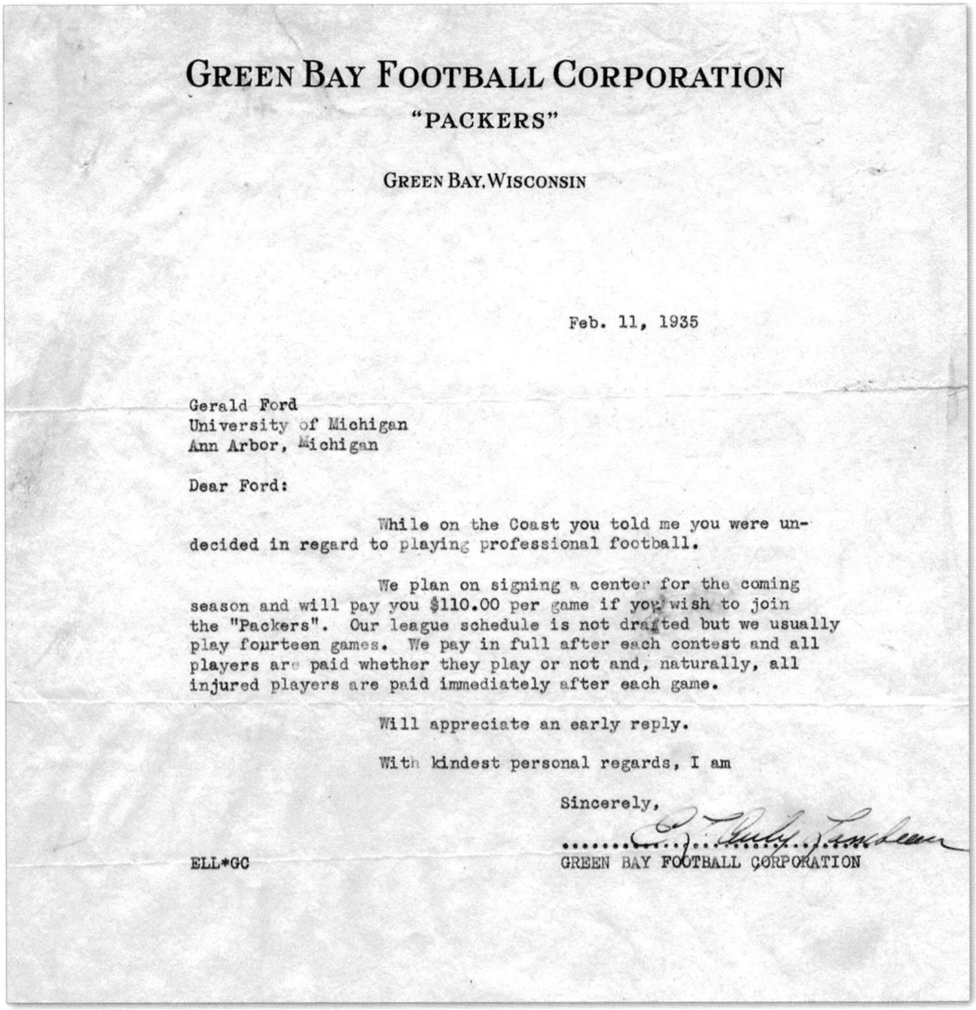

GREEN BAY FOOTBALL CORPORATION

"PACKERS"

GREEN BAY, WISCONSIN

Feb. 11, 1935

Gerald Ford
University of Michigan
Ann Arbor, Michigan

Dear Ford:

While on the Coast you told me you were undecided in regard to playing professional football.

We plan on signing a center for the coming season and will pay you $110.00 per game if you wish to join the "Packers". Our league schedule is not drafted but we usually play fourteen games. We pay in full after each contest and all players are paid whether they play or not and, naturally, all injured players are paid immediately after each game.

Will appreciate an early reply.

With kindest personal regards, I am

Sincerely,

GREEN BAY FOOTBALL CORPORATION

ELL*GC

of directors with the suggestion: "I made All-Pro last year and I'm underpaid here." When they agreed, Lambeau was given his orders, which was no doubt a factor in McNally's release at the end of the season.

With a roster filled with accomplished veterans, the Packers went on to dominate their regular-season opponents, finishing ahead of the Bears to capture their first Western Division crown. Five holdovers from the 1931 championship squad—McNally, Arnie Herber, Hank Bruder, Milt Gantenbein, and Chester "Swede" Johnston—helped Green Bay to its 10–1–1 record. Possessing the most potent passing game in the league, "with Hutson and myself as receivers and Arnie Herber throwing, we were a real scoring threat," McNally recalled of the Packers outscoring their opponents 248–118 during the regular season.

Since the championship game site alternated yearly, the Eastern Division champions were scheduled to host the Packers. However, before the game Redskins owner George Marshall announced he was relocating his franchise to Washington, D.C., as soon as the game was over, citing an overall lack of support from Boston fans and local newspapers as the reason. He had no interest in hosting the championship game at Fenway Park and was successful in convincing the NFL to move it to New York.

Although New York's Polo Grounds were considered a neutral site, the Packers soon felt at home. Less than three minutes into the game, they scored on a 48-yard touchdown pass from Herber to Hutson. The Redskins countered with a touchdown but failed to convert the extra point. In the second quarter, Green Bay's Milt Gantenbein extended the Packers' lead to 14–6 on an 8-yard pass from Herber. After Clarke Hinkle recovered a fourth-quarter fumble, Bob Monnett plunged into the end zone to complete the game's scoring and secure the Packers' fourth NFL championship with a 21–6 victory. Although 29,545 fans were in attendance at the Polo Grounds that afternoon, generating a gross income of $33,471, each Packer received a winner's share of only $224 after it was determined that 5,000 children, at forty cents admission apiece, were included in the crowd figure.

When the NFL champions' train returned home the next day, "hell, the whole town was there to greet us. There was a lot of celebrating, a parade, a banquet. The town was football-crazy," Don Hutson recalled of the ecstatic hometown boosters honoring their champion Packers. "Of course, it was a big thing for the city of Green Bay. After all, they were just a little town of about 25,000 people then and they won it over teams that came from all the big cities, like New York and Chicago."

Within a week of the team's victory banquet at the Columbus Community Club, the champion Packers headed west for several exhibition games. The barnstorming tour not only filled the team's coffers and the players' billfolds but also fed into

> "Hell, the whole town was there to greet us. . . . The town was football-crazy."
> —END DON HUTSON

More than a thousand cheering fans crowded into Green Bay's Columbus Community Club to pay tribute to the 1936 NFL champion Packers. (MILWAUKEE JOURNAL SENTINEL)

Lambeau's growing Hollywood ambitions. He arranged to make the *Pigskin Champions* movie short with MGM Studios featuring his championship squad, earning each of them an additional $650 besides their barnstorming tour earnings. When adding the revenue collected from the West Coast exhibition games, the Packers' championship season turned into a profitable one. But the franchise wouldn't be deemed financially solvent until the circuit court overseeing the receivership accepted the franchise's reorganization plan in 1937, releasing it from the terms of its bankruptcy.

In Green Bay, the same players who were reveling in the perks of being a Packer found they were being held to an even higher standard of player conduct as defending champions. After the Packers began their 1937 season with consecutive losses to the Bears and Cardinals at home, it was hard to hide in Green Bay. If Curly Lambeau wasn't policing his players directly, he had the local citizens looking out for the team's best interests at all times. Oftentimes, he would levy a fine on a player based on the eyewitness account. "The fans told the truth, too," halfback Clarke Hinkle admitted. "They were interested enough that if a guy was drinking on Wednesday or Thursday, why, they felt it was their duty to report it."

The Packers won seven consecutive games before bookending the season with consecutive losses against the Giants and Redskins. Stumbling to a 7–4 finish, they tied the Lions for second place in the Western Division behind the Bears. It was a trying season for the Packers, who were competing not just against the NFL's nine other franchises but also against a handful of upstart rival leagues.

■　■　■

Even as the country was immersed in its greatest financial crisis ever, professional football was an enticing investment. Between 1936 and 1941, three professional football leagues were in direct competition with the more established National Football League. The South Atlantic Football League—later renamed the Dixie League—competed for talent when it was organized in 1936 before folding in 1947. A second incarnation of the American Football League had big-league aspirations when it was organized in 1936, placing teams in New York, Boston, and Pittsburgh. But after its inaugural season, the rival league lost its most successful franchise, the Cleveland Rams, when that team defected to the NFL. The AFL replaced them with the Los Angeles Bulldogs, who finished with a 9–0 record, further exposing a lack of competitive balance that would lead to the league's demise after only two seasons. In 1940 a third version of the American Football League arose after organizers successfully lured the original Cincinnati Bengals, the Columbus Bullies, and the Milwaukee Chiefs away from the minor-league American Professional Football

Dedicated listeners to Packers' radio broadcasts during the 1930s and 1940s tuned in to WTMJ's Russ Winnie, who in 1938 received assistance from his wife, Evie, in spotting players while he provided his colorful play-by-play.
(MILWAUKEE JOURNAL SENTINEL)

Association to join three new franchises in Boston, Buffalo, and New York City. Although that league lasted only two years as well, its impact was felt for years after its open policy of poaching NFL rosters for talent escalated player salaries.

In Green Bay, the Packers entered the 1938 season in the black. As a result, the Packers expanded City Stadium again, increasing the capacity to 25,000. Curly Lambeau's father, Marcel Lambeau, supervised the construction, which included the installation of restrooms. The Packers' locker room was also expanded, but Green Bay kept its home field advantage by continuing to make visiting teams dress at a downtown hotel or in the East High School locker room, next to the stadium. To fill the new seats at City Stadium, the Packers placed ticket outlets in three hundred communities throughout Wisconsin, Minnesota, and Michigan's Upper Peninsula. The team's growing popularity across the region was a direct result of the work of publicist George Calhoun, who continued to keep the Packers in the news. On a year-round basis, his weekly one-page sheets entitled *Green Bay Packer News* were carried in seventy-five newspapers throughout the area.

Calhoun had lots to write about during the 1938 season as the Packers finished with an 8–3 record, securing their second Western Division crown in three years and earning a trip to New York to face the Giants for the NFL championship. Newspapers across the country hyped the game as Green Bay's David versus New York's Goliath. On Sunday, December 11, 48,120 fans—the largest crowd ever to see a championship game up to that time—witnessed a bruising battle that was without the healthy services of the Packers' most proficient offensive weapon. "That was the only game I can remember when an injury really affected me," Don Hutson recalled. "I had a pulled ligament in my leg, which I'd gotten a week or two earlier in a game against the Detroit Lions."

Even without the league's premier pass catcher in the game, the Giants couldn't contain Green Bay's offense. But in a contest that belonged statistically to the visitors, the only numbers that counted were the final score, where the Packers found themselves on the short end of a 23–17 outcome. "I felt we were a better team than they were," Hutson remarked. "We should have won the game. We even played better than them that day, but we lost it on a couple of kicks they blocked and were able to take advantage of."

Despite the outcome from the Packers' perspective, the game was a resounding success overall. It generated $68,332 in gross income, the most lucrative gate in NFL history to date, and the players' shares increased to $504.45 for each Giant and $368.84 per Packer. The game provided further evidence that NFL president Joe Carr's vision of a league embraced by the nation's largest metropolises was coming to fruition, as demonstrated by the glowing account of the game published afterward in the *New York Times*: "The play for the full sixty vibrant minutes was absolutely ferocious. No such blocking and tackling by two football teams ever had been seen at the Polo Grounds. Tempers were so frayed and tattered that stray punches were tossed around all afternoon. This was the gridiron sport at its primitive best."

The league was enjoying unprecedented popularity and financial prosperity, which resulted in the owners awarding Joe Carr with a new ten-year contract to continue serving as NFL president at the league's annual meeting in February 1939. When Carr suffered a fatal heart attack three months later, the NFL was left without one of its most influential voices. "With the possible single exception of George Halas, no man to that time could even come close to having done more to give the pro game major sport status than Carr," author Larry Names declared. "Although some of his methods might have been suspect, he always acted with the singular thought of doing what was best for the National Football League."

To fill the void, Carr's responsibilities as president were assumed by league vice president Carl Storck, who promptly moved the organization's headquarters from Columbus to his hometown of Dayton, Ohio. At the time neither he nor the most optimistic NFL team owner could predict how television would impact the game's future. During the 1939 season, professional football began experimenting with the new medium despite fears it would create fans at the expense of overexposure. Owners were willing to risk introducing the game to a larger audience in hopes that those viewers would pay to attend future games in lieu of watching them in the comfort of their own homes for free. After successfully broadcasting a Major League Baseball game in August, NBC-TV approached the NFL's Brooklyn Dodgers, offering $1,100 to televise their October 22 contest against the Philadelphia Eagles.

That afternoon the Ebbets Field crowd of 13,051 outnumbered those viewers at home. New York City had only about a thousand television set owners at the time, and those who tuned in enjoyed a 23–14 Brooklyn win until the two iconoscope cameras fell victim to the encroaching dusk. "When the sun crept behind the stadium there wasn't enough light for the cameras. The picture got darker and darker and eventually it

During the Great Depression the Packers became dependent on the revenue generated by hosting games in Milwaukee, while also enjoying the promotional effects of becoming Wisconsin's NFL franchise. (WHI IMAGE ID 87508)

went completely blank and we reverted to a radio broadcast," the game's announcer, Allen Walz, recalled.

In Green Bay, the defending Western Division champion Packers finished the 1939 regular season with a 9–2 record, but they had won only three of their games by more than 7 points. Repeating as division champs, the Packers would host the upcoming championship game against the Giants. The jubilant fans who filed into the Green Bay streets ceased their celebration when team management announced the game would be played in Milwaukee with the following statement: "Green Bay fans overlook the great debt owed to Milwaukee. Without the support we receive from our Milwaukee games annually, we would be unable to maintain a National League franchise in Green Bay."

From a financial standpoint, the executive committee's decision to host the contest in Milwaukee was a wise one. From 1933 to 1939, twelve of the Packers' forty-three home games had been held in Milwaukee, with the larger State Fair Park venue generating an additional $15,000 to $45,000 in revenue per year. Ignoring national rumors of the team's imminent move south, almost 11,000 Green Bay boosters—nearly a third of the entire city—traveled on chartered trains, buses, and automobiles to support the team at the championship game in Milwaukee. Upon their arrival, they found Packers management cashing in on hosting its first NFL championship contest. During an era when minimum wage was forty cents an

Under Curly Lambeau, the Packers always traveled first class, staying in nice hotels, eating the finest food, and even carrying their own dining car on the best Pullmans. Lambeau felt the team should project a professional image to the public—which included everyone wearing matching blazers. Seen here in 1939 (left to right): Buford "Baby" Ray, Tom Greenfield, Red Smith, Dick Weisgerber, Carl Mulleneaux, Paul Kell, Clarke Hinkle, Harry Jacunski, Larry Craig, and Curly Lambeau. Those in the train door are unidentified. (MILWAUKEE JOURNAL SENTINEL)

hour, seats at State Fair Park cost up to $4.40 each. The price was considered exorbitant even by Giants officials, who had charged only half that for the previous year's championship game in New York. The unprecedented ticket prices didn't matter. The game sold out in two days.

State Fair Park was far from an ideal venue to watch football, especially a championship game. Its permanent seats were located on only one side of the field, with bleachers on the opposite side and six thousand temporary seats placed on the automobile racetrack encompassing the field, which caused the blustering, thirty-five-mile-per-hour gusts that afternoon to whistle right across the field. "It was very windy that day, I remember, and passing was difficult," Don Hutson recalled.

In the first half the game was close, with an Arnie Herber touchdown pass to Milt Gantenbein being the game's only score. The second half saw Green Bay suffocate the Giants' offense as Charley Brock's two interceptions and his tackle of Alphonse "Tuffy" Leemans preserved the 27–0 shutout for the Packers. "We broke their hearts in the third period this afternoon when we scored ten points against the wind," Hutson told reporters after the game.

When the champion Packers returned to Green Bay, more than 10,000 fans greeted them at the train station. Thousands more lined their parade route to City Hall. Two days later, in what was becoming a Green Bay tradition, the champions were honored at a banquet where more than 1,500 civic leaders and boosters crammed into the Columbus Community Club, some with signs proclaiming WELCOME HOME, WORLD'S CHAMPIONS, ALL IS FORGIVEN.

Meanwhile, State Fair Park's capacity crowd of 32,279 brought in record revenue of $83,510, generating a winner's share of $703 for each Packer and $455 for each Giant. The outstanding tally at the gate reignited the argument from league officials and team owners that the Packers should relocate to Milwaukee, prompting the franchise's greatest on-field rival to become Green Bay's strongest ally. Everybody in Wisconsin knew that George Halas despised the Packers for two Sundays every football season. What was less publicized was the respect he held for his rivals to the north the other 363 days of the year. Even before the Packers had extended him a $1,500 loan in 1932 to keep his Bears solvent, Halas had defended their efforts to stay in Green Bay. Going back to the NFL's infancy, his unheralded support for Green Bay went beyond the rivalry's take at the gate. Whenever his fellow NFL owners challenged the Packers' ability to survive in Green Bay, one of pro football's most respected statesmen cited the intangibles of how both franchises and the league benefited from their rivalry. "Green Bay will retain its franchise," Halas stated after the championship game, "as long as I have anything to say about it."

• • •

While the Great Depression suffocated the American economy, the Packers and the National Football League enjoyed a steady growth in popularity. Game attendance throughout the league averaged more than 20,000 fans, with millions more listening at home on the radio. Before 1940 only local markets broadcast regular-season and postseason contests. When twelve radio stations, all in NFL host cities, broadcast the 1939 NFL championship game, the ratings were so good that the Mutual Broadcast Company paid the league $2,500 to broadcast the 1940 NFL championship game from coast to coast on 128 stations. The game was going national, and the late Joe Carr's vision had come to fruition: by 1940 seven of the league's eight teams were in cities among America's ten largest, with Green Bay—its population of 46,235 ranking that city a distant 240th—the only exception.

In Green Bay, the Packers' executive committee rewarded Curly Lambeau, who had won five NFL championships in eleven years, with a new five-year contract. It called for an annual $10,000 salary, an additional $1,000 a year for office expenses, and a hefty percentage of the net proceeds earned from exhibition and playoff games. "In a good year, with all incentives paid off, his annual salary could have reached $20,000, an exceptionally high income during the 1940s when the average was under $3,000," author David Zimmerman wrote in *Lambeau: The Man behind the Mystique*. "He was probably the highest paid NFL coach at the time, with the exception of George Halas, who owned the Bears and took out the club's profit for himself."

Further acknowledging Lambeau's success, the Packers' board of directors created a second vice presidency position exclusively for him. He was now the team's

As far back as 1922, Curly Lambeau instituted daily practices, and years later he was a pioneer of establishing training camps before the team's exhibition season began. In 1940 his backfield combination of Eddie Jankowski (7), Joe Laws (24), Cecil Isbell (17), and Larry Craig (54) were kept busy with a series of drills. (MILWAUKEE JOURNAL SENTINEL)

head coach and general manager and an executive on the board of directors with almost complete control of the organization. "As the team grew more successful and his image developed into a larger-than-life character," Zimmerman noted, "[the] continued success also inflated his ego, which in turn had a tendency to give him a distorted view of his own importance."

Despite high expectations surrounding the start the 1940 season, Curly Lambeau soon found his dreams of repeating as an NFL champion coach vanquished by his longtime rival, George Halas. At City Stadium in week two, the Packers were handed the worst defeat in franchise history, a 41–10 shellacking by Chicago. The rematch at Wrigley Field resulted in a 14–7 Bears victory in front of 45,434 fans, the largest crowd ever to see a regular-season game. The two losses cost the Packers the Western Division crown as their 6–4–1 regular-season record was good enough only for second place behind Chicago's 8–3 finish. Halas had gotten the best of Lambeau that year, but their rivalry—nearly two decades old—went deeper than wins and losses. Just tallying profits at the gate proved how dependent they were on each other to succeed. But on game days, vanity and pride prevented either of them from acknowledging the other in a positive light, if at all. "Shake hands! That would have been a lie," Lambeau commented on how the bitter rivals refused to speak to one another before or after games. "If I lost, I wanted to punch Halas in the nose. If he lost, Halas wanted to punch me."

As the 1941 season approached, NFL owners replaced interim president Carl Storck with Elmer Layden. Upon taking office, pro football's new commissioner focused on enhancing the game's aura of respectability as high-class entertainment. First, he moved the league offices to Chicago; then he forbade players and coaches from endorsing liquor or cigarettes; he no longer allowed commercials to be read over stadium public address systems during games; and he prohibited players from wearing dirty, tattered, or misfit uniforms for publicity pictures.

The Packers reported a profit after the 1940 season at the annual stockholders' meeting in Green Bay, a result of the extra revenue generated by hosting games in Milwaukee—which in turn made it hard to entice opponents to travel to City Stadium. Other team owners noted that Milwaukee attracted larger crowds and said the expenses associated with traveling the additional one hundred miles north cut into their visitor's share. As Charles Bidwell, owner of the cash-strapped Cardinals, complained, "I lose money every time I play at Green Bay and I make money every time I play the Packers at Milwaukee." The Packers' five Eastern Division foes—the New York Giants, Philadelphia Eagles, Washington Redskins, Pittsburgh Steelers, and Brooklyn Dodgers—avoided playing in Green Bay at all costs.

The Packers had faced that same complaint twenty years earlier but defused it by fielding winners year after year, which also made them a good draw on the road.

> "If I lost, I wanted to punch Halas in the nose. If he lost, Halas wanted to punch me."
> —CURLY LAMBEAU

But those were the days when 15,000 patrons through the Polo Grounds or Wrigley Field turnstiles was considered a great draw. Now those same teams expected crowds of more than 40,000 fans per home game. At the same time, the Packers averaged 20,000 fans at City Stadium and 25,000 in Milwaukee. But in 1941, the club's drawing power at State Fair Park dropped to fewer than 15,000 a game, a direct result of the surging Milwaukee Chiefs. The rival AFL club had captured the imaginations both of fans thirsting for pro football and of local Milwaukee business owners who understood the sport's influence as a great marketing tool. In an effort to stonewall the upstart Chiefs' growing popularity, Packers officials added another game to the team's Milwaukee schedule. But that wasn't the only financial burden the team dealt with that year.

When training camp opened in mid-August, several veteran Packers were holding out for new contracts. The team's favorable financial balance announced earlier that summer left Curly Lambeau showing little interest in sharing the wealth with his players. For the past decade, his customary player contract averaged $125 a game, or about $1,700 a season. Clarke Hinkle, who had been a loyal Packer since 1932, held out before receiving a contract that would pay him $10,000 for the 1941 season—a Green Bay record at the time. "In his early days he was just as tough and mean as anybody else," Hinkle said later of Lambeau's tightfisted negotiating style. "You think Lombardi's tough? Lambeau was tougher."

After years of dedicated service to his hometown Packers, veteran holdout Arnie Herber sought a sizable raise, but Lambeau wanted a thinner Herber. Negotiating what is believed to be the first contractual weight clause, Lambeau stipulated that his quarterback would weigh in on the Saturday before each game and would forfeit $50 of his salary whenever he tipped the scales over two hundred pounds. The clause was never enforced, since Herber was cut after the second preseason contest of 1941.

With their contract disputes settled, the Packers found themselves battling the defending NFL champions for first place in the Western Division all season. The 1941 division crown would go through Chicago since the Bears found little opposition against their successful execution of one of football's oldest plays, the T formation. "To combat it, Lambeau went to the library one day in Green Bay to look for a defense in one of the old books on early football history," Clarke Hinkle remembered. "Lambeau found one that was used back about 1890, a seven-spear defense, I think they called it." The newfound strategy contained the Bears' explosive offense that afternoon. "Our linemen followed the ball and they had a field day," Hinkle recalled of the Packers' 16–14 victory. "I played 58 minutes of that game and had the pleasure of kicking the winning field goal in the fourth quarter."

Hinkle would have played all sixty minutes, but the Bears' powerful fullback Bill Osmanski cut him on the leg with his cleats. "It put about a four-inch gash along

RIGHT: Tony Canadeo (3) played offense and de-fense, ran with the ball, threw passes, caught passes, returned punts and kickoffs, punted, and intercepted passes during his eleven years with the Packers. (COURTESY OF ALL-AMERICAN SPORTS, LLC)

BELOW, LEFT: In ten years with the Packers, Clarke Hinkle (30) was known for a pile-driving running style and versatility as a pass catcher out of the backfield that made him one of the most prominent iron men of his era. (COURTESY OF ALL-AMERICAN SPORTS, LLC)

BELOW, RIGHT: Don Hutson (14) was not only an in-novative receiver but also a feared defender. During his career he intercepted thirty-nine passes, second in league history to Johnny "Blood" McNally's forty. (COURTESY OF ALL-AMERICAN SPORTS, LLC)

The Packers' rivalry with the Bears reached epic proportions in 1941 when the two teams were scheduled to face each other in their first postseason matchup, with the winner going to the NFL championship game. The week before, Curly Lambeau (left with binoculars, alongside Buford "Baby" Ray and Joe Laws) scouted his rivals when they faced the Chicago Cardinals at Comiskey Park. (COURTESY OF CHRIS NERAT)

my shin and it went clear down to the bone," Hinkle recalled. Still he wanted to go back into the game, earning him a reputation as one of the toughest men to play football in the Iron Man era. "Lambeau gave me hell for it when I came to the sideline. I said I wanted to put a pad over it, that I didn't like to look at the bone."

Behind Hinkle's bruising exploits on the field, the Packers marched to a 10–1 regular-season record after beating the Redskins in the season finale. With Green Bay a half-game up in the standings, the Bears had to defeat the Cardinals the following week if they wanted a share of the division crown. Just before that game's kickoff on December 7, the first bombs fell at Pearl Harbor. Only when announcements were made throughout the stadium for all soldiers, sailors, and marines to report to their bases immediately did fans learn of the attacks.

The Bears won that game 34–24. Exactly one week later the Packers and Bears, with identical 10–1 regular-season records, faced off in a divisional playoff game at Wrigley Field. With the winner earning the right to face the Giants in the NFL championship game, the two teams combined for eight fumbles, seven interceptions, and fifteen penalties. When Green Bay came up short in the game's 33–14 outcome, sportswriter Arch Ward exclaimed, "Any football fan will agree that it isn't easy to go through eleven games with only a single defeat, then lose a playoff game to the same team."

Despite the loss, the Packers organization invested $10,000 of the profits the team earned from the contest in wartime Liberty Bonds. The executive committee wanted the team to accumulate sufficient financial reserves in the event of unforeseen emergencies. The uncertainty of war had cast a shadow of doubt over the entire nation.

● ● ●

Within weeks of the Pearl Harbor attack, the Packers lost their first player, defensive end Bob Adkins, to the war effort. In a matter of months, almost one-third of the men who had played the previous season on the NFL's ten rosters had received draft notices and were active in the armed forces. The Packers were hit hardest, with sixteen veterans and eighteen of twenty college draftees never reporting to the team's 1942 training camp in August. "It is possible our club won't be as strong as it was

To help support the war effort in 1942, Don Hutson (left), Curly Lambeau (right), and many fellow Packers players donated blood at the Red Cross plasma center after having defeated the Steelers in Milwaukee the day before. (MILWAUKEE JOURNAL SENTINEL)

last season," Curly Lambeau told the *Los Angeles Times* of the military playing no favorites when recruiting NFL players to serve abroad. "But the other teams were hit, too, and I think you will find the losses pretty evenly distributed. The caliber of play may not be quite as high throughout the league, but it still will be worth seeing."

As the war machine intensified, even the NFL's most stable franchises saw their profit margins disappear. Teams from the Eastern Division used financial strife as an excuse to avoid traveling to Green Bay, pleading for the Packers to schedule home games in Buffalo and Toledo. Other teams tried persuading the franchise to relocate to Milwaukee, St. Louis, or Cincinnati. At the league meetings that summer, Lambeau held his ground, insisting the Packers host six games in Wisconsin—four in Green Bay and two in Milwaukee. But the league continued to apply pressure and eventually forced a compromise, with three games scheduled in Green Bay, two in Milwaukee, and six on the road. For Lambeau, it was a minor concession since the Milwaukee Chiefs and the entire AFL had folded after just two seasons, reestablishing the Packers as Wisconsin's only pro football team.

Back in Green Bay, Lambeau used the NFL's continued threats to relocate the Packers as motivation to improve attendance at City Stadium. With the assistance of the Green Bay Association of Commerce, the team launched a one-day season-ticket sales drive. The community responded by purchasing an additional 1,437 season tickets, raising the year's total to nearly 4,000 tickets.

Going into the 1942 season, Lambeau wasn't sure how his patched-together roster would fare against the defending champion Bears, who were favored to repeat. Refusing to sulk over the loss of Clarke Hinkle and other veterans to the war effort, he focused on the team's remaining strengths, creating the record-breaking tandem of receiver Don Hutson and quarterback Cecil Isbell. The Packers passed on nearly 50 percent of their plays that season as Isbell became the first quarterback in NFL history to throw for 2,000 yards in a season and to throw twenty-four touchdown passes. Hutson shattered many of his own records, catching seventy-four passes for 1,211 yards and seventeen touchdowns. The season-long aerial assault secured an 8–2–1 record and second place in the Western Division for the Packers, but the undefeated 11–0 Bears lost their perfect season to the Redskins, 14–6, in the championship game.

■ ■ ■

As the country's involvement in World War II entered its second year, the Packers and the NFL had to make a critical decision that offseason—play the 1943 season with the available players, or suspend operations until the war ended. President Franklin Roosevelt urged that football, like baseball, continue, a sentiment echoed by Curly Lambeau: "Sports' main obligation to the nation now is to carry on beyond all normal duty toward an all-out war effort with what athletes are left." Yet Lambeau also warned, "This is no time for sports to look for profit!"

Deciding to forge ahead, the NFL reduced team rosters from thirty-three to twenty five men, a cost-cutting measure in response to the recent college drafts, which had garnered less than stellar results. Prior to the war, 40 to 50 percent of NFL draft picks signed with teams, but that number dropped to 29 percent by 1942 and well below 10 percent in 1943 and 1944. Limitations created by the reduced roster size prompted the league to permit unlimited substitutions. Before 1943, a player could enter a game only once each quarter, except in the fourth quarter, when two players from each team could be brought in twice. Easing these restrictions on substitutions was considered a temporary fix, but it paled in comparison to the league's bigger problem of franchise instability.

Although nine of the NFL's ten teams were owned by millionaires, the league was besieged by rumors it would be reduced from ten to eight or even six teams by the start of the season. "Primary among the teams that were being mentioned for elimination from the loop for the duration of the war was Green Bay," author Larry Names recounted. "The eastern owners wanted to drop the Packers from the NFL rolls, and once again George Halas came to Green Bay's rescue. He let his fellow owners know that he wanted the Packers to remain in the league at all costs."

The Cleveland Rams withdrew from the league for the upcoming season due to a lack of manpower. The Philadelphia Eagles and Pittsburgh Steelers combined their remaining rosters and divided their home games between their two cities. Between the incarnation of the "Steagles" and the loss of the Rams, the NFL was left with eight teams, four in each division, balancing the schedule to ten games per franchise.

The Packers were confident they could absorb the projected financial losses and survive the war, despite estimates the team would lose $25,000 to $30,000 during the 1943 season. In addition to receiving $7,500 from its first radio broadcast agreement with WTMJ in Milwaukee, the franchise benefited from the executive committee's diligence in building up the team's cash reserves.

Those cash reserves would come in handy a few years later when Curly Lambeau convinced the Packers to purchase Rockwood Lodge before the 1946 season—a forty-room, fifty-three-acre estate north of Green Bay. "Curly's idea was to house the team there during the training season," executive committee member John

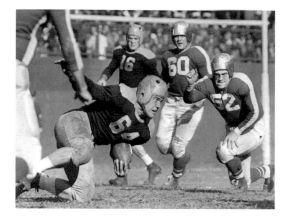

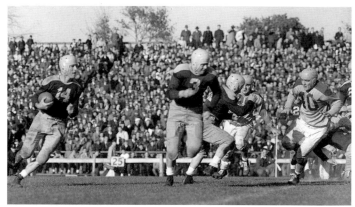

LEFT: World War II had ravaged NFL rosters by 1943, as many players were called on to serve their country. On December 5 the depleted Packers beat the merged Philadelphia and Pittsburgh franchises, nicknamed the Steagles, 38-28, behind the efforts of Ted Fritsch (64) and Lou Brock (16). (COURTESY OF CHRIS NERAT)

RIGHT: Throughout the war the Packers continued to succeed in the NFL thanks to Don Hutson (14) and Tony Canadeo (3). (COURTESY OF GREEN BAY PRESS-GAZETTE FROM TOM PIGEON COLLECTION)

Torinus explained. "Rockwood Lodge had been built by the Catholic Diocese as a recreation center but had not achieved the success that had been hoped, so the Packers were able to buy it for $32,000. They put another $8,000 into refitting the facilities and also bought six pre-fabricated houses."

From the moment the Packers purchased it, Rockwood Lodge was a source of controversy. "Lambeau's stated intention may have been to provide housing for his ballplayers, but it was his underlying hope that Rockwood would allow him to exert more control over his team," author Don Gulbrandsen claimed in *Green Bay Packers: The Complete Illustrated History*. "It was also probable he was trying to physically distance himself from the prying eyes of both the executive committee and the citizens of Green Bay."

At the time, Lambeau was considered a visionary for creating football's first self-contained training complex, complete with a practice field marked out on the spacious lawn in front of the lodge that housed his team. But Rockwood Lodge wasn't an ideal location for holding practice. Lambeau's players soon began suffering shin splints, sore feet, and other nagging injuries. When it was discovered only a shallow layer of topsoil covered the practice field atop a hard limestone bluff, the players were bused the seventeen miles from the lodge to their old training field in Green Bay. The purchase of the lodge and subsequent daily bus trips into town were a major distraction for the Packers players and executive committee members. But the growing controversy didn't receive any attention in George Calhoun's weekly *Packer Football News*, which enjoyed nationwide distribution to sportswriters, radio announcers, and servicemen abroad as the prime source for news regarding the team.

One major story that couldn't be ignored was Cecil Isbell's announced retirement before the 1943 season to take a job as backfield coach at his alma mater, Purdue. Having lost half of his record-breaking passing tandem, Lambeau received

The fifty-three-acre complex known as Rockwood Lodge (seen here in background) served as the Packers' training facility from 1946 to 1949 and is believed to have been the first self-contained team training facility in pro football history. (COURTESY OF TOM PIGEON COLLECTION)

another scare when Don Hutson also announced that he was retiring from football to go into business. But when the Packers coach offered Hutson a contract that would make him the highest-paid player in the league, the receiver found himself in the Packers' lineup on opening day. He wasn't happy for long and by midseason announced his retirement again, effective at the end of the season. Despite the constant distractions from Hutson's threatened retirement announcements, the Packers ended 1943 with a 7–2–1 record, but they were unable to overcome the Bears. Green Bay finished in second place behind Chicago for a fourth straight season, leaving Lambeau to vow the Packers would finish second to no one in 1944.

• • •

As the United States entered its third year at war, professional football continued growing in popularity. Its stature as a major-league sport only benefited from the downsizing of college programs and semipro teams folding under similar financial constraints, which left many football-starved fans to turn their loyalties toward the professional game. The NFL was now in an enviable position. Team moguls, who only a few years earlier considered disbanding the league altogether in the face of World War II, were now considering offers to place new teams into Baltimore, Miami, Los Angeles, and San Francisco. Of those applications, the most viable one came from a group led by actor Don Ameche, who wanted to put a team in Buffalo with the condition the franchise could relocate to Los Angeles after the war ended. Pub-

The Packers' City Stadium adorns the letter R on this 1944 postcard sending "Greetings from Green Bay." By the 1940s the entire community of Green Bay understood the intangible benefits of being a big-league community, supporting the team as both civic treasure and tourist attraction. (WHI IMAGE ID 86617)

licly, NFL team owners claimed Ameche's franchise would have been accepted if it had agreed to stay in Buffalo, but when the actor refused, his application was denied. NFL owners admitted the Boston Yanks into the league instead, further protecting Charles Bidwell's interest in moving the Cardinals to Los Angeles after the war.

Following the "Steagles" divorce after just one season, with the Eagles returning to their former identity in Philadelphia, the Pittsburgh Steelers were forced to merge with the struggling Chicago Cardinals to survive the 1944 season. The formation of the Card-Pitts (pronounced "Carpets"), along with the return of the Cleveland Rams after a one-year absence, restored the NFL to a ten-team league, which allowed owners to table all other expansion applications until after the war ended.

In Green Bay, Tony Canadeo was the most prominent player to exchange his blue and gold uniform for military green fatigues, bringing the number of Packers serving overseas to twenty-seven. The armed services also continued affecting NFL draftees, as only 12 of the 330 players selected in the 1944 NFL draft played for their respective teams. Many coaches spent the majority of the offseason coaxing veterans out of retirement—including Curly Lambeau, who didn't get Don Hutson to sign a contract until two weeks before the season's first game.

The league's unusual 1944 schedule gave the Packers their first five games at home—three in Green Bay and two in Milwaukee—followed by five consecutive games on the road. Starting their season with a six-game winning streak, Green Bay finished with an 8–2 record as Western Division champions.

Facing the Giants in the NFL championship game at New York's Polo Grounds on December 17, Lambeau used Hutson as a decoy, focusing on the Packers' rushing attack. The strategy worked as Joe Laws led Green Bay to victory with 72 yards on the ground while intercepting three passes. Ted Fritsch scored both Packers touchdowns in the second quarter, and "for the first time this year, the ball club operated at full efficiency," Lambeau told reporters after the game.

At New York's Polo Grounds, the Packers won the 1944 championship through a team effort, allowing the Giants to cross midfield only three times. The passing combination of quarterback Irv Comp and end Don Hutson (14) helped set up two touchdowns from Ted Fritsch, and Joe Laws intercepted a playoff-record three passes. (BOTH PHOTOS COURTESY OF TOM PIGEON COLLECTION)

The Packers' 14–7 victory over the Giants attracted a crowd of 46,016 fans to New York's Polo Grounds, establishing record gate receipts of $146,205.15 and a winner's share of $1,449 per player. After capturing their sixth title, the Packers were now tied with the Bears for the most championships in NFL history. Following the game, Don Hutson made another one of his annual retirement statements, proclaiming, "If I ever play on this field again, I'll jump off the Empire State Building—and I mean it."

■ ■ ■

When the war ended in August 1945, teams replenished their rosters with the players returning from the battlefield. Throughout the duration of World War II, 638 active NFL players served in the armed forces, with 69 of them decorated. The war also claimed the lives of at least twenty NFL men—eighteen active and former players, a former head coach, and a front-office worker.

Although 1945 marked the end of World War II and peace for the Western world, it was just the start of the pro football war. The NFL, enjoying unprecedented popularity, reopened the discussion of expanding the league and heard from several interested cities. However, several team owners felt expanding beyond the NFL's current slate of ten teams could be disastrous, citing fears that overexpansion would dilute demand. "They believed professional football was a closed club presided over by the NFL," author Larry Names explained. "The expansion of pro football was okay and even desirable—*but only on their terms.*"

For years, NFL owners had justified their pattern of dismissing prospective franchise owners and ignoring rival leagues, citing how the league had survived the launch of three separate American Football Leagues. The NFL had been debating expansion since 1940, when team owners raised the entrance fee from $10,000 to $50,000 in hopes of eliminating all but the most sincere—and wealthiest— franchise seekers. Even when a prospective owner met all the NFL's requirements, league owners were quite particular about whom they allowed into their league and where franchises would be placed. As a result, NFL owners decided to play the 1945 season with just ten teams after rejecting "five franchise applications, four of which were accompanied by $50,000 nonrefundable deposits," according to Craig Coenen in *From Sandlots to the Super Bowl.*

Back in Green Bay, Curly Lambeau was certain he could will *his* team to another championship. By 1945 the attention he had received from colleagues and sportswriters running story after story about the genius coaching in Green Bay had only expanded his ego. "He was beginning to believe all his press clippings," Names remarked. "Lambeau had built a fantasy world around himself where he saw himself

Green Bay's service clubs—the Kiwanis, Rotary, and Lions—hosted a dinner at the Beaumont Hotel on August 9, 1945, to mark the Packers' twenty-fifth anniversary. Those sitting at the head table included Curly Lambeau, Lee Joannes, W. Webber Kelly, Andrew Turnbull, and George Calhoun. (FROM THE GREEN BAY PRESS-GAZETTE ARCHIVES, REPRINTED BY PERMISSION)

as God's gift to professional football. He had come to believe that he hadn't just founded the Green Bay Packers but that he did it all by himself."

After Lambeau was awarded a new contract that ran through the 1949 season, "he was never the same," fullback Clarke Hinkle recalled. "He was not beating the bushes, and I think the reason was because he had attained financial success and didn't have the desire anymore."

At the time, Lambeau addressed rumors that the team would relocate as part of the NFL's talk of postwar expansion, guaranteeing, "I was born in and have lived in Green Bay all my life and I have no intentions of moving. My home is here and will always be here."

A sense of jubilation and relief swept through Green Bay as the 1945 season began. On opening day, the Packers' Lumberjack Band, under the direction of Wilner Burke, launched the season with a triumphant rendition of the team's fight song, "Go! You Packers Go!" while raising their newest championship banner atop City Stadium. Following a 31–21 defeat of the Bears to start the season, the Packers engaged with the Lions in what Ed Press of the *Chicago Tribune* considered "the most devastating quarter in the history of professional football."

In less than fifteen minutes, both teams piled up a combined 41 points, firing six touchdowns on nine plays, all of them through the air. By the time the madness ceased, the Packers had trounced the Lions 57–21 in what would become the last

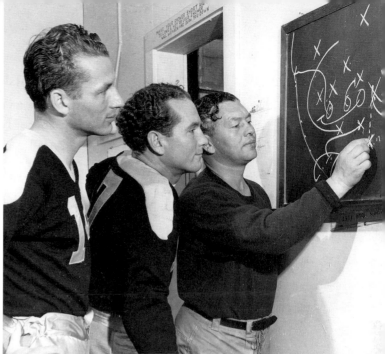

Curly Lambeau never missed an opportunity to coach football. On a flight to New York in 1940 (above, left), he gave a blackboard drill talk to Cecil Isbell, Arnie Herber, and Don Hutson. In 1941 (above, right) he outlined a play for Don Hutson and Cecil Isbell. And in 1945 (left) he used a tablecloth to discuss a play with Don Hutson, Nolan Luhn, Clyde Goodnight, Ken Keuper, and Bruce Smith. (TOP LEFT: COURTESY OF CHRIS NERAT; TOP RIGHT: COURTESY OF TOM PIGEON COLLECTION; BOTTOM: COURTESY OF CHRIS NERAT)

shining moment in Don Hutson's storied career. He caught four touchdown passes and kicked five extra points in the second quarter alone to set an NFL record. "It was damn near impossible for me to quit football in Green Bay," Hutson said years later of walking away at the end of that season from an annual $15,000 salary. "You know what the Packers meant to the town and I'd been having some good years. I got the feeling they wanted me to play forever."

The Packers' heady start to the season soon sobered. Stumbling through the second half of their schedule, Green Bay finished at 6–4 and in third place behind the Rams and Lions. It was the first time Lambeau's boys had failed to finish in first or second place in the Western Division since 1934. Their late-season collapse and inability to repeat as champions brought about increased criticism from fans and executive board members, much of which was directed toward their coach. The Packers' slight dip in the standings and the Cleveland Rams' seizing of the Western Division title in 1945 indicated the NFL's postwar landscape was in transition. The Rams were the first team other than the Packers or Bears to win the division since the 1935 Detroit Lions. The Rams also broke the exclusive stranglehold the Big Four had on NFL championships after they defeated the Redskins 15–14 for the 1945 crown. In the nine years dating back to 1936, the Bears and Packers had each won three titles, the Redskins two, and the Giants one. The increased parity among the NFL's ten teams fueled its increased popularity as attendance reached 1,918,631 in 1945 after fewer than 900,000 fans attended games in 1942. Within the thriving postwar economic boom, NFL owners expected even greater popularity and greater profits for all ten of the league's franchises in the years ahead.

Meanwhile, a group of rejected millionaires, including Don Ameche, sought to challenge the league's supremacy. Arch Ward, the *Chicago Tribune* sports editor who organized the College All-Star Game and baseball's All-Star Game, chaired a meeting on June 4, 1944, that included representatives from Buffalo, Chicago, Cleveland, Los Angeles, New York, and San Francisco. By the end of that day, the foundation had been laid for a new league: the All-America Football Conference.

In public NFL officials welcomed their newest competitors, but they had no intention of cooperating with them. They didn't have to. For years assorted rival leagues had announced their grand intentions only to collapse in financial ruin, much to the satisfaction of NFL owners. As recently as spring 1944, a United States Football League had claimed its ten-team league in cities throughout the Northeast and Midwest and Honolulu would compete with the established NFL, but it never got off the ground. Before the AAFC even played a game, two of its owners—the Chicago Rockets' Jack Keeshin and the Cleveland Browns' Paul Brown—met with NFL commissioner Elmer Layden with hopes of arranging interleague cooperation regarding amateur drafts, salary ceilings, anti-raiding policies, interleague games,

> "I got the feeling they wanted me to play forever."
> —END DON HUTSON

and mutually advantageous schedules. Afterward, the NFL announced that "there is nothing for the National Football League to talk about as far as new leagues are concerned until someone gets a football and plays a game."

From that moment the war was on, as neither league chose to recognize the other's players under contract—which resulted in the immediate escalation of salaries. The AAFC lured almost one hundred men who had played in the NFL the previous season, secured contracts with forty-four of the sixty players on the 1946 College All-Star team, and encouraged African Americans, who had often been shut out by the NFL, to join the upstart league.

The war's first casualty was NFL commissioner Elmer Layden, who became the scapegoat for the drastic ballooning of players' salaries. Ousted before the AAFC had played its first game, he was replaced by Bert Bell in January 1946. As a team owner, Bell had kept the Philadelphia Eagles operating through the Great Depression and later as owner of the Pittsburgh Steelers during World War II. Now he had inherited a ten-team league, with its champion Cleveland Rams franchise about to relocate to Los Angeles after posting $40,000 in losses. "Teams say their payrolls have increased from fifty to one hundred percent," sportswriter Arch Ward reported of Bell's financial forecasting. "At the April 1946 meeting of the National [Football] League, Commissioner Bert Bell anticipated the situation with the apt remark, 'Our last year's maximum is this year's minimum.'"

With the Rams announcing their move to Los Angeles and the Cardinals deciding to stay in Chicago, the NFL sought to place a team in San Francisco to amortize traveling costs for teams over two games and to compete with the AAFC's 49ers. It was well known around football circles that Bell wanted an established team to relocate instead of granting an expansion franchise to an inexperienced owner. His aspirations of landing a second franchise on the West Coast soon leaked to reputable newspapers, including the *San Francisco News*, which reported, "The national league will bring a team to our town this year. It will be one of three already established concerns in the old loop; namely the Green Bay Packers, Chicago Cardinals or the Boston Yanks."

One of professional football's most respected pioneers, Curly Lambeau (far left) is seen here holding the rapt attention of (left to right) future NFL commissioner Bert Bell, current commissioner Elmer Layden, and Detroit Lions owner Fred Mandel during a meeting in 1945. (COURTESY OF CHRIS NERAT)

Bell's first choice was the Packers. NFL officials and team owners pressured Packers president Lee Joannes to relocate the franchise west, but Green Bay executives refused, citing that team stockholders would reject the offer. Joannes threatened to wage a legal battle if the league tried to force the team to move, which kept the Packers in Green Bay for the 1946 season. But the pro football war would continue to escalate, with serious ramifications for the franchise.

■ ■ ■

In 1946 Lambeau failed to sign any of his draft picks as they opted for the rival league. Even his first-round pick and sixth overall—Milwaukee native and Marquette graduate John Strzykalski—chose to play for the 49ers instead of the Packers. With the promise of lucrative contracts, the AAFC also made strong, but failed, overtures to Green Bay veterans Irv Comp, Ted Fritsch, and Tony Canadeo. When the Packers opened training camp at Rockwood Lodge in August, the team was in disarray, suffering from a lack of young talent and loss of several key veterans. Yet, even the retirement of Don Hutson, the league's most dominating player for the past decade, didn't prompt the Packers coach to change his decades-old strategies. "Lambeau stubbornly stuck to his single-wing, or Notre Dame box formation, while most of the other NFL teams had converted to the much more effective T-formation," author David Zimmerman explained.

By the time Don Hutson (seen here in 1941 with fullback Frank Balazs) finally followed through on his threats and retired after the 1945 season, he held eighteen NFL records, including 488 career receptions and 99 touchdown catches. (COURTESY OF THE NEVILLE PUBLIC MUSEUM OF BROWN COUNTY)

Without Hutson, the Packers' antiquated offensive attack was exposed. They scored only 148 points in eleven games. Quarterback Irv Comp completed only 29 percent of his passes as the team threw for an anemic 841 yards all season. Hutson's replacements, ends Clyde Goodnight and Nolan Luhn, led the team with just sixteen receptions each. The Packers managed to finish third in the Western Division with a 6–5 record. Green Bay had survived its first season immersed in the pro football war but found its organization swimming in red ink. By the end of 1946, only the Giants, Bears, and Redskins in the NFL and the AAFC's Browns reported profits, while operating budgets for teams jumped to around $500,000 each.

The Packers' financial woes paled in comparison to the growing turmoil among its executive committee members. When the first real rifts in the relationship between Curly Lambeau and the other members of the Hungry Five developed, or over what and why, nobody other than those within

On November 24, 1946, W. Webber Kelly—the Packers' longtime team physician and former team president—introduced members of the Packers "All Time" team during the homecoming celebration at halftime of a game against the Chicago Cardinals. The relationship between Kelly and Lambeau had already deteriorated to the point that Kelly refused to mention Lambeau by name during the festivities. (FROM THE GREEN BAY PRESS-GAZETTE ARCHIVES, REPRINTED BY PERMISSION)

"We took all the grief and criticism when things were going tough, and Lambeau took credit for things when the going was good."

–PACKERS PRESIDENT LEE JOANNES

the executive committee seemed to know. But after Lambeau terminated W. Webber Kelly as the team's physician and replaced him with Dr. Henry Atkinson, the rift became public. An infuriated Kelly, who had been the team physician since 1921, no longer hid his resentment, becoming one of Lambeau's most outspoken detractors.

Lambeau's decision to change team doctors without consulting the executive committee was seen as a crass move, but that paled in comparison to his firing of George Calhoun as team publicist. On March 24, 1947, "Cal's long and intimate association with the Packers came to a tragic end," executive committee member John Torinus recounted in *The Packer Legend*. "One morning as he was reading through the sports news which came over the Associated Press teletype machine, he read a story from Chicago to the effect that 'General Manager Curly Lambeau of the Green Bay Packers announced today that George Strickler, former sports editor of the *Chicago Tribune*, has been named publicity director for the Packers in Green Bay. He will replace George W. Calhoun, who has retired.' That was the way Cal learned that his old pal Curly Lambeau had dumped him."

From that day forward, Calhoun joined three of the original Hungry Five—Kelly, Lee Joannes, and attorney Gerald Clifford—to become Lambeau's biggest critics, saying that his increasingly boorish behavior was no longer in the best interest of the team. In July Joannes stepped down as team president. After providing the Packers with sound leadership through the Great Depression and World War II, he was tired of the constant feuding with Lambeau. "We took all the grief and criticism when things were going tough," Joannes said upon resigning, "and Lambeau took credit for things when the going was good."

Lambeau further alienated himself from his once loyal supporters by spending his winters on the West Coast. His second marriage had failed, but "he married another woman from California who took over the decorating of the cottage at the [Rockwood] lodge," Torinus said of Lambeau's growing intoxication with fame, fortune, and beautiful women. "At one meeting of the Executive Committee, the financial committee threatened to resign over the bills which were being presented

Curly Lambeau used his emerging nationwide fame and the game's growing popularity to help recruit players like Babe Weber (seen here with his wife in 1944) by bragging about his numerous appearances in magazines and newspaper articles. (MILWAUKEE JOURNAL SENTINEL)

by Lambeau for decorating the cottage that he and his wife were occupying. It was about this time that the Monday morning quarterbacks in Green Bay began to remark that Lambeau had 'gone Hollywood.'"

The executive committee, concerned about its mounting power struggle with Lambeau, elected as Joannes's successor local businessman Emil R. Fischer, who had been on the board of directors since 1936. Since he wasn't considered one of Lambeau's allies, Fischer had a tumultuous relationship with Lambeau from the onset of his presidency. He reduced Lambeau's all-inclusive control of the Packers as its coach by increasing the board of directors from twenty-two to twenty-five members and expanding the executive committee from nine to twelve members. "In an attempt to regain control," sportswriter Chuck Johnson explained in *The Green Bay Packers: Pro Football's Pioneer Team*, "[Lambeau] sought election as president of the Packers' corporation. In this he was defeated and Lambeau's personal fortunes, along with those of the Packers, continued their steady decline."

Although he made no derogatory remarks in public, Lambeau seethed in private over the changes. His resentment toward those who stripped him of his sole oversight of all team matters soon intensified. The emasculation of Lambeau continued while he was out of town when "Jerry Clifford called an executive board meeting and, with a quorum of eight members, pushed through the organization of subcommittees on finances, grounds, contracts, publicity, league representation and the draft," Johnson recounted. "When Lambeau returned to Green Bay, he tried unsuccessfully to disband the subcommittees."

Desperate, Lambeau attempted to use the *Green Bay Press-Gazette* as a public forum to regain his front-office responsibilities. "I believe these men, all good businessmen, acted for what they thought were the best interests of the Packers, but the plan just won't work," he argued. "You can't run a football team if you have to go to this committee for that and that committee for this."

Even when Andrew Turnbull, the last of Lambeau's allies from the original Hungry Five, tried to broker peace between the coach and the executive committee, "this proved impossible," Johnson said. "Besides variance of opinion on matters of policy, Lambeau and his antagonists had personal differences." The Packers' front office was fractured, and with the war between the NFL and AAFC intensifying during the offseason, Green Bay's pro football franchise was as vulnerable as ever.

■ ■ ■

Nobody outside of Wisconsin thought the Packers would survive the pro football war in Green Bay. Those outside the franchise viewed the team as the NFL's weakest link. Football insiders thought it was only a matter of time before the team folded or relocated, insinuating that the Packers would become the pawn that would sway the outcome of the war. Rumors persisted even after the *Chicago Tribune* published NFL commissioner Bert Bell's claim that "Green Bay's Packers, rumors to the contrary, which have popped up more persistently than ever in the last two years, aren't going to pack up and find a new home. I would say that the Green Bay Packers, after twenty-six years in the league, are here to stay."

In 1947 the NFL was losing ground to the AAFC. The high-stakes competition for talent had owners from both pro circuits pushed to the threshold of bankruptcy as skyrocketing salaries caused even the most successful team's coffers to be overdrawn. Back in 1941 only a few star players received salaries over $10,000, with most rookies receiving about $2,000 to $3,000 per season and total team payrolls ranging between $45,000 and $84,000. In 1946 alone, the Los Angeles Rams' team payroll escalated to $170,000, and the Eagles' payroll had almost doubled in less than a year to $190,000. By 1948 most NFL payrolls were exceeding $200,000, with further increases expected since the average football player salary had jumped to almost $8,000 per season, approaching that of a Major League Baseball player. The NFL also saw its fan base defecting to the new league. After two years the AAFC enjoyed a 33 percent increase in league-wide attendance, more than 33,000 a game, while challenging NFL teams in three cities—New York, Chicago, and Los Angeles—for support. At the same time, the NFL suffered a 6 percent slip, averaging fewer than 31,000 fans per game.

Needing to expand its popularity, the NFL turned to the medium of television. Nationwide, the number of homes with television sets had risen from 12,500 in 1946 to more than 100,000 the following year, and by 1950, 8 million households would have a set, reaching at least 20 million Americans. Regardless of those figures, the league considered television nothing more than a marketing tool, allowing individual owners to do whatever they wanted in hopes of encouraging more fans to attend games. Several franchises contracted with local television stations to broadcast some or all of their contests. In 1946 four teams—the Los Angeles Rams, New York Giants, Chicago Bears, and Philadelphia Eagles—had experimented with the broadcasting of games, but only the Giants televised all their home contests. The individual deals generated little revenue for stations or team owners, and many stations in NFL cities declined to carry games altogether.

In Green Bay, nobody understood the potential revenue television could generate better than Curly Lambeau. He knew the Packers would soon fall behind the rest of the league if television's revenue stream was structured in a similar fashion to that of radio, where larger markets commanded higher rates for advertising. Because teams negotiated their own individual broadcast agreements, Green Bay's smaller population and advertising limitations would only expand the financial disparity between the Packers and the rest of the league. The circumstances left Lambeau to conclude that the Packers would have to relocate to one of the available larger television markets, such as Dallas, Cincinnati, St. Louis, or San Francisco. In hopes the franchise could be wrestled away from its stockholders, several NFL owners who were aware of Lambeau's unhappiness in Green Bay made offers to help save the league. "If Curly was successful and he could move his team to San Francisco," Names remarked, "the NFL could keep up its fight with the upstart loop for one more year and probably win the war."

While conspiring behind closed doors, Lambeau was also preparing for the 1947 season. During the team's training camp at Rockwood Lodge in July, he informed his players that the Packers were switching from the single-wing, or Notre Dame box formation, to the T formation. Behind Lambeau's new offensive strategy, the Packers were competitive during the NFL's new twelve-game season but lost four games by 4 or fewer points. Those losses cost the Packers the Western Division crown as their 6–5–1 record found them finishing third behind the Bears and the first-place Cardinals. "The game kind of passed Curly by," lineman Dick Wildung recalled of rising doubts Lambeau could keep the Packers competitive. "It was inevitable where pro football was going."

> ## "The game kind of passed Curly by."
> —LINEMAN
> DICK WILDUNG

■ ■ ■

The optimism surrounding the Packers' ability to challenge for the Western Division title in 1948 ignored the fact that only six players remained from Lambeau's 1944 championship squad. Furthermore, the college draft had done little to replenish the loss of veterans Don Hutson, Buckets Goldenberg, and Charley Brock. Only two draft choices from 1946 and 1947 remained with the club in 1948. The AAFC had lured away Packers draft choices with more lucrative contracts, but one draft choice Lambeau did sign in 1948 came at an intangible cost. After Green Bay outbid the AAFC's New York Yankees with a $10,000 contract for the services of Marinette native Earl "Jug" Girard, "the fact that Lambeau paid that kind of money to an unproven, undisciplined rookie did not sit well with many of the veterans who were making considerably less," author David Zimmerman wrote in *In Search of a Hero*.

Team morale dissolved even further after a 17–7 loss to the Chicago Cardinals in front of nearly 35,000 fans at Milwaukee's State Fair Park. Despite the Packers' 2–2 record, which had them still in contention for the division title, Lambeau fined the entire team after the game. "He claimed we hadn't been trying, so he docked us a week's salary, which was a big chunk to all of us," running back Tony Canadeo recalled. "Everybody was really ticked off. But we thought we'd get the money if we played well the next week against the Rams. Well, we did, shut them out 16–0, but we didn't get the money from Curly. After that we all were twice as mad and everything went downhill from there."

The Packers didn't win another game all year, losing seven straight and finishing with a 3–9 record, next to last in the division. Only after the season ended did Lambeau return the docked money, but by then the damage had been done. "The team was pretty much done," Jug Girard recalled in Jerry Poling's *Downfield*. "Nobody said anything about it, but that was the general feeling."

The Packers' first losing season in Green Bay since 1933 was reflected in the team's profit-and-loss statement. Home games at City Stadium and State

In 1948 the Packers were on their way to a 3-9 record when an irate Curly Lambeau lashed out at his players following a 17-7 loss to the Cardinals. His antics generated criticism from players, fans, and *Milwaukee Sentinel* editorial cartoonist Frank Marasco. (TOP: COURTESY OF GREEN BAY PRESS-GAZETTE FROM TOM PIGEON COLLECTION; RIGHT: MARQUETTE UNIVERSITY/ MILWAUKEE JOURNAL SENTINEL)

Fair Park were no longer guaranteed sellouts. When the executive committee met in December to review the financial situation, the Packers' bottom line looked to be the team's most formidable foe in 1949. If the feud between the NFL and AAFC continued, the Packers were prepared to fold.

• • •

By the end of the 1948 season, sixteen NFL and AAFC clubs, including the Packers, were hemorrhaging financial losses totaling almost $2 million. The Bears and Redskins were the only two NFL clubs claiming a profit, and in the AAFC only the Cleveland Browns and San Francisco 49ers were considered solid franchises. Rumors of the AAFC's impending collapse only fueled speculation that a merger between the two leagues would result in the NFL eliminating one or two of its weakest franchises, which now included the Packers. Without the fiscal resources to bid on top players, Green Bay was settling for second-rate talent and no longer competing for division titles, much less championship crowns. The Packers' inability to field winning teams didn't diminish the average crowds of 24,000 per game in Green Bay, but Milwaukee's crowds had declined from 30,000 per game earlier in the decade to 12,000 per game by 1949. Even after team management made their financial problems public, pleading with Milwaukeeans to buy tickets, the State Fair Park crowds continued to shrink, averaging fewer than 6,000 in late 1949. Incurring estimated

NFL commissioner Bert Bell (second from right) visited with Packers officials (left to right) Andrew Turnbull, Curly Lambeau, team president Emil Fischer, and Gerald Clifford at Rockwood Lodge during the summer of 1948. (FROM THE GREEN BAY PRESS-GAZETTE ARCHIVES, REPRINTED BY PERMISSION)

total losses of $155,000, the team had more than eliminated the financial reserves it had accumulated during the first half of the decade. Once again, the Packers were on the verge of bankruptcy.

In the months leading up to the 1949 season, persistent rumors that the NFL could scrap the Packers at its discretion prompted NFL commissioner Bert Bell to admit publicly that he suggested the team relocate to a larger city. But he also confirmed that he was powerless to move or revoke the team's franchise unless it failed to meet its financial obligations. Meanwhile, Curly Lambeau found himself at constant odds with the team's executive committee over finances and responsibilities. The power struggle intensified in August when Lambeau lobbied for the election of his close friend Victor McCormick to replace the retiring Andrew Turnbull on the executive committee and as the board's director. "In the inglorious years following World War II when the Packer teams descended from mediocre to lousy, Lambeau's personality evolved into the unsavory figure of a fallen champion," author David Zimmerman remarked. "He had become visibly more vain, often displaying extreme pride when dealing with his team and the Packer board of directors."

On the eve of the season opener, Lambeau was confident his 1949 club would compete for the Western Division crown, despite having failed to address the team's shortcomings from the previous season. The Packers' lack of depth and experience was exposed from the onset of their 17–0 opening-day loss to the Bears as they failed to complete even one pass for the first time in franchise history. After the game Lambeau addressed his players in the team's dressing room beneath the City Stadium stands: "This is only one game," he told them in a calm demeanor, his words of encouragement seeming a bit hollow. "And there are eleven more to go. Your effort out there today was all right and if you keep it up, you're going to win a lot of ball games."

The following Friday, Lambeau made the startling announcement that he was relinquishing his coaching responsibilities to his trio of assistants: line coach Tom Stidham, backfield coach Bob Snyder, and defensive coach Charley Brock. He would continue to serve in an "advisory capacity" but would focus his efforts on rebuilding the roster through his responsibilities as the Packers' vice president and general manager. The executive committee perceived his decision as an ambush on their authority, and although they publicly supported Lambeau's coaching change, they were upset that he had made his latest decision without their knowledge.

Because Lambeau failed to empower any of the three assistants to act as the head coach, two days later the lack of leadership resulted in an embarrassing 48–7 loss to the Los Angeles Rams. As the defeats mounted, team morale sank to new depths. "Everybody was thinking 'let's just get this season over,'" end Nolan Luhn recalled.

> "Everybody was thinking 'let's just get this season over.'"
> —END NOLAN LUHN

By November, with the team's debts mounting, "the financial situation became critical," executive committee member John Torinus recalled. "At a special directors meeting, Lambeau was ordered to drop a number of players from the roster and renegotiate the salaries of all the other players."

The Packers were desperate for cash if they wanted to finish the 1949 schedule. Without any cash reserves and few assets to liquidate, they looked to sell Rockwood Lodge. It had become a liability, proving too expensive to maintain. Although it was the club's most valuable asset, selling the property would take time—time that the organization didn't have. After team president Emil Fischer disclosed the team's bleak financial outlook during a breakfast meeting at Green Bay's Northland Hotel, the audience of one hundred Packer Backers rallied to organize an intrasquad exhibition at City Stadium on Thanksgiving Day.

Curly Lambeau (center) with his trusted assistant coaches in 1949 (left to right): Charley Brock, Don Hutson, Bob Snyder, and Tom Stidham (MILWAUKEE JOURNAL SENTINEL)

Lambeau's abandonment of his head coaching responsibilities in 1949 left the Packers (seen here playing the Rams that October) fumbling for answers and wins. They finished with the NFL's second-worst record, 2–10, ahead of the hapless 1–10–1 New York Bulldogs, who folded at season's end. (COURTESY OF GREEN BAY PRESS-GAZETTE FROM TOM PIGEON COLLECTION)

Green Bay Press-Gazette cartoonist Harold Elder depicted the Packers' need for statewide support for their upcoming Thanksgiving Day exhibition in 1949. (FROM THE GREEN BAY PRESS-GAZETTE ARCHIVES, REPRINTED BY PERMISSION)

Nearly 15,000 fans ignored the snow and cold to see their favorite players from the past and present sport the blue and gold jerseys for charity. "That's the only game we ever played where nobody hit the ground! We faked the hell out of that game. It wasn't even as rough as a touch ball game or tag game," halfback Tony Canadeo recalled of Jug Girard's Blues beating Stan Heath's Golds 35–31, while more than two thousand prizes were raffled, including a chance to become a "barbershop quarterback" and sit on the bench to help coach the teams. "But the fans really came out. I'm proud that we raised a lot of money from the game!"

The exhibition raised nearly $50,000, enough for the Packers to finish the season, but the fate of the franchise was still uncertain. NFL commissioner Bert Bell remained tight-lipped about the league's future and whether the Packers deserved their NFL status beyond the 1949 season. "Green Bay's troubles today are many," *Milwaukee Journal* sportswriter Oliver Kuechle wrote at the time. "They run the gamut from real club problems to differences on the executive committee due to strong personal jealousies and they add up to a mess which could well cost the city its franchise in the National league."

The executive committee determined the only way to rescue the franchise from its financial bind was by conducting another sale of stock. Chairing the stock drive was the team's newest board member, Victor McCormick. When Lambeau informed the executive committee that he knew of four investors willing to put up $50,000 for stock if the Packers converted into a for-profit rather than nonprofit corporation, "it was easily surmised that McCormick was one of the four," executive committee member John Torinus said later. "He had inherited a great deal of wealth from an uncle some years before."

Disgusted by the offer, the executive committee rejected it, declaring the Green Bay Packers organization would remain as first conceived by the Hungry Five: a community-owned, nonprofit corporation. Their public declaration proved that Lambeau had lost favor with the organization. He was now perceived as a liability, a theory supported by his delegation of head coaching responsibilities to his three assistants. The Packers' 2–10 record in 1949 saw the team losing by an average of 23 points per game and scoring 7 or fewer points in seven contests. "The Packers had now hit rock bottom," author David Zimmerman noted. "They were in total disarray both on and off the field. The once-proud Packers were now a pitiful professional football team."

ABOVE: The Packers' inaugural 1919 squad reunited on Thanksgiving Day, 1949, during an exhibition to raise money to keep the Packers solvent through the end of the season. Left to right: Herman Martell, Herb Nichols, Martin Zoll, Al Petcka, Sammy Powers, Gus Rosenow, John Des Jardins, Andy Muldoon, Wally Ladrow, George Calhoun, and Carl Zoll. Not pictured were Jimmy Coffeen, H. J. "Tubby" Bero, Art Schmaehl, and the only deceased member of the original team, Nate Abrams. (COURTESY OF GREEN BAY PRESS-GAZETTE FROM TOM PIGEON COLLECTION)

LEFT: Packers greats from the past reunited to help save the franchise by raising $50,000 to keep the team solvent. Standing, left to right: Fee Klaus, Herb Nichols, Curly Lambeau, Jug Earp, Lavvie Dilweg, Vern Lewellen, and Johnny "Blood" McNally. Kneeling, left to right: Charley Brock, Don Hutson, Arnie Herber, and Joe Laws. (COURTESY OF GREEN BAY PRESS-GAZETTE FROM TOM PIGEON COLLECTION)

RIGHT: A crowd of almost 15,000 patrons watched the Veteran Blues, quarterbacked by Jug Girard, defeat the Newcomer Golds 35–31 in the exhibition. (COURTESY OF GREEN BAY PRESS-GAZETTE FROM TOM PIGEON COLLECTION)

Curly Lambeau (wearing dark suit, hat, and glasses) exited the Brown County Courthouse on November 30, 1949, after his contract was renewed for two years—but not before his future with the franchise was heatedly debated behind closed doors. (FROM THE GREEN BAY PRESS-GAZETTE ARCHIVES, REPRINTED BY PERMISSION)

When the Packers' board of directors convened at the Brown County Courthouse on November 30, their five-hour meeting turned into a series of heated exchanges between warring factions. Before the meeting, Lambeau demanded his enemies be eradicated from the board and that he be given total control over the corporation. Former team president W. Webber Kelly resigned from the board as a result of the power struggle, but two of Lambeau's biggest detractors, team attorney Gerald Clifford and former publicist George Calhoun, refused to step down and continued leading the anti-Lambeau faction among the board members. The debate to extend Lambeau's expiring contract for two more years became so rancorous that observers standing outside the courthouse could hear the directors shouting at one another behind closed doors.

Ultimately the group reached a compromise, and team president Emil Fischer confirmed to reporters that Lambeau's contract as head coach and general manager had been verbally renewed for another two years. "The Packers have successfully passed another crisis and are back on a sound footing. As far as Green Bay is concerned, this can be the start of a new era," Fischer announced. "But we are operating with an obsolete organization, geared to professional football fifteen years ago, an organization that is too inflexible to meet the many new and complex problems that have grown out of the game's rapid and tremendous progress in recent seasons."

During the meeting the board of directors also approved scheduling another stock sale to raise capital, ensuring the Packers would remain a publicly owned franchise. The organization felt it had strengthened its position as a legitimate professional football franchise during the ongoing war between the NFL and the AAFC, but on December 9, 1949—two days before the Packers' season finale against the Lions—the feuding leagues reached a merger agreement. "When Curly failed [to steal the Packers from the stockholders], Halas and the boys were left with no other choice except to settle matters with the AAFC," author Larry Names proclaimed of the Packers' pivotal role in the subversive negotiations taking place between leagues.

The merger called for the AAFC to dissolve, with its Cleveland Browns, San Francisco 49ers, and Baltimore Colts franchises being admitted into the NFL for the 1950 season. Its four other clubs—the New York Yankees, Buffalo Bills, Chicago Hornets, and Los Angeles Dons—were to fold, and those teams' players would be placed into a special NFL draft pool. The expanded league, which called itself the National-American Football League for a brief time before returning to the name National Football League, would host thirteen franchises in 1950.

Although the Packers were included as part of the original merger, their future still hinged on raising enough money to meet their financial obligations in time for the NFL owners' meeting in June. There was already talk that league officials wanted to reduce the franchise roster to twelve teams, maximizing pro football's popularity as a result of the pro football war. "While local patronage and civic support remained the base of pro football's economic survival," author Craig Coenen remarked, "it started to lose ground as the desire to capitalize on a national market now seemed to be within owners' grasp."

By late January Curly Lambeau had yet to receive a copy of his new two-year deal from the Packers. Regardless of whether the contract was never presented to him or he received it only to reject it, he showed no interest in resolving his philosophical differences with the executive committee. During a press conference, which he organized, Lambeau claimed that the handling of the club's affairs by the executive committee had become "obsolete and unworkable" during a time when the team's future depended on good management. "No group of twelve men can get together once a week during the football season, for an hour and a half, including lunch, and run a professional football team. That can't be done," Lambeau said of his situation. "I can't possibly bring the corporation up to date in such a short time. I am not a brilliant man, but I certainly feel qualified to run our organization."

As the infighting continued and Lambeau waited in limbo, his beloved Rockwood Lodge burned to the ground on January 24, despite several fire departments responding to the call. An investigation into the fire's cause showed no wrongdoing, blaming faulty wiring in the attic. The Packers received a $50,000 insurance settlement, which

When Curly Lambeau (seen here with his future wife, Grace, at the Northernaire Resort in Three Lakes, Wisconsin) and the Packers divorced in January 1950, he had amassed a career coaching record of 212-106-21, which included a 3-2 postseason record and six NFL championships. (MILWAUKEE JOURNAL SENTINEL)

went to addressing several of the team's financial shortcomings. The club's inability to sell the Rockwood Lodge property for months had left many frustrated Green Bay residents unsympathetic about its demise, including Tony Canadeo, who admitted, "I didn't set the Rockwood Lodge fire, but I was sure fanning it."

Less than a week after the last burning embers were extinguished at Rockwood Lodge, Curly Lambeau resigned as head coach and general manager of the Packers. On January 31, 1950, word of his sudden departure swept through Green Bay, but "it was no surprise to members of the Packer Board and Executive Committee, who knew that the real disagreement between Lambeau and the Packers had come over the ownership issue rather than his team's performance on the field," Torinus said.

The next day, when the Chicago Cardinals announced Lambeau had agreed to become their next head coach and vice president, Packers executive committee and Hungry Five member Gerald Clifford boasted, "We've had two good breaks in Green Bay in the last two weeks. We lost Rockwood Lodge and we lost Lambeau. If Lambeau had stayed for two more years, we would have gone completely busted."

On that cold February afternoon, the six championship flags hanging limp atop City Stadium served as a symbolic end to an era in Green Bay. After thirty-one years, Earl "Curly" Lambeau was no longer a Green Bay Packer, leaving former guard Buckets Goldenberg to exclaim, "I don't see how the Packers can last without him. He *was* the Packers."

TARNISHED GOLD

When the merger of the National Football League and All-America Football Conference was announced in December 1949, league officials and team owners viewed Green Bay as a growing burden in the league's revenue-sharing structure. The Packers played in the smallest stadium with the cheapest tickets. Following the 1949 season, the NFL hierarchy placed an unofficial stipulation on the franchise: guarantee other teams will make money by drawing well in Wisconsin, or get thrown out of the league. The Packers had to raise $120,000, which was the total amount of guarantees for their six home games in 1950, before the league's next meeting in June. To raise the capital necessary to cover the guarantee, the executive committee had to be quick and decisive with a solution. Further burdening their circumstances was a substantial debt totaling $75,000, still on the books after Curly Lambeau's hasty exit from Green Bay.

Within hours of Lambeau's departure, speculation flooded Green Bay watering holes and newsrooms across the football landscape about his potential successor. Rising above the conjecture was Gene Ronzani, who had strong credentials as a successful assistant coach and former quarterback with the Chicago Bears. He also possessed an intangible qualification none of the others had: strong ties to the region as a native of Iron Mountain, Michigan, and graduate of Milwaukee's Marquette University. Although Ronzani had never been a head coach, the Packers considered him to be a well-known attraction who would generate fan interest throughout northeastern Wisconsin and Michigan's Upper Peninsula as well as Milwaukee. At a special stockholders' meeting, team president Emil Fischer introduced Gene Ronzani as the Packers' new head coach. After Ronzani signed a three-year contract with the Packers, former team president Lee Joannes explained, "We're

Workers put the finishing touches on a tote board erected on the Brown County Courthouse lawn in downtown Green Bay to track the 1950 stock sale's progress, with a ball carrier—wearing Don Hutson's number 14—racing toward a $200,000 goal. (FROM THE GREEN BAY PRESS-GAZETTE ARCHIVES, REPRINTED BY PERMISSION)

New Packers head coach Gene Ronzani (center) looked over his contract with team president Emil Fischer (left) and secretary-treasurer Frank Jonet (right) in February 1950. (FROM THE GREEN BAY PRESS-GAZETTE ARCHIVES, REPRINTED BY PERMISSION)

> **"It is impossible to place a monetary figure on the value of the Packers to Green Bay and to all of Packerland."**
>
> *—GREEN BAY PRESS-GAZETTE EDITORIAL*

not taking a chance on Ronzani, he's taking a chance on us. Hell, he doesn't even know if he is going to get paid."

Since the announcement of Ronzani's hiring occurred just six days after Lambeau resigned, "some thought the whole thing had been arranged in advance," *Milwaukee Journal* sportswriter Chuck Johnson remarked. "A faction of the executive committee and many of the fans never accepted Ronzani."

Following Ronzani's introduction, the executive committee initiated the second stock drive since 1923. Under the same terms and conditions that had existed in previous stock sales, the Packers organization made 9,500 new shares available for sale at $25 each, with hopes of raising at least $200,000. Because the number of authorized stock shares in the corporation increased from 500 to 10,000, the executives further amended the articles of incorporation, to forbid the sale of more than 200 shares of stock to any one person or group, thus preventing anyone from gaining control of the organization.

The push to sell the new stock began in March as advertisements for the campaign went up all around town. The Packers launched the stock drive on April 12 during a pep rally at Green Bay's Central Catholic High School, with more than 1,500 boosters in attendance and thousands more listening on the radio. That night more than one thousand shares were sold, bringing in more than $25,000. For the next month, more than four hundred volunteers, including future team president Judge Robert J. Parins, solicited prospective buyers by going door to door and making phone calls. "There were shares, for example, bought by, like, Irene's Restaurant," Parins recalled. "A couple of guys would get together, throw in a couple of bucks and buy a share of stock."

To track the stock sale's progress, a scoreboard proclaiming the slogan "Back the Drive with Twenty-Five" was erected on the lawn of the Brown County Courthouse with an image of a halfback racing toward the $200,000 goal. "A lot of people didn't think we'd raise that kind of money," recalled Max Murphy, a Green Bay insurance man who helped spearhead the drive.

The stock sale got the support of the *Green Bay Press-Gazette*, which made sure to remind residents of the team's significance: "It is impossible to place a monetary figure on the value of the Packers to Green Bay and to all of Packerland. There is no method of computing the worth to a community, its people and its institutions of a great athletic institution like the Packers," the editorial explained. "We feel certain

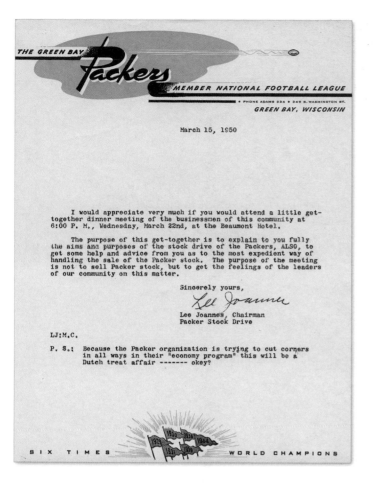

THE GREEN BAY *Packers*

MEMBER NATIONAL FOOTBALL LEAGUE

• PHONE ADAMS 334 • 349 S. WASHINGTON ST.

GREEN BAY, WISCONSIN

March 15, 1950

I would appreciate very much if you would attend a little get-together dinner meeting of the businessmen of this community at 6:00 P. M., Wednesday, March 22nd, at the Beaumont Hotel.

The purpose of this get-together is to explain to you fully the aims and purposes of the stock drive of the Packers, ALSO, to get some help and advice from you as to the most expedient way of handling the sale of the Packer stock. The purpose of the meeting is not to sell Packer stock, but to get the feelings of the leaders of our community on this matter.

Sincerely yours,

Lee Joannes

Lee Joannes, Chairman
Packer Stock Drive

LJ:M.C.

P. S.: Because the Packer organization is trying to cut corners in all ways in their "economy program" this will be a Dutch treat affair ------- okey?

SIX TIMES   WORLD CHAMPIONS

Stock drive chairman Lee Joannes sent letters to prospective business leaders and team boosters in the spring of 1950 to help support the Packers' upcoming stock drive. The team's financial situation was so grave that Joannes asked invitees to pay for their own meals at this "Dutch treat affair." (WHI IMAGE ID 81786)

that the public will never let the fighting Packers down."

To broaden the stock sale's prospective audience, team president Emil Fischer reiterated how important statewide support was to the team's long-term survival: "We want Milwaukee and we need Milwaukee as well as other communities in the state." In an effort to spike any loose talk that the Packers would play all their future home games in Green Bay, Fischer added, "There will be two league games at State Fair Park next fall, and we will continue to play there or at the new stadium when it is completed. We're certainly hoping Milwaukee wants us."

The executives lowered the drive's initial goal of $200,000 to $100,000 when sales began to plateau. "When we were at about $80,000, I went down to Milwaukee and talked to Fred Miller," Murphy recalled of speaking to the brewery magnate. "He said, 'Don't worry, we'll take care of it for you.' He got a lot of the big industries to put it over. I think they gave us about $30,000. That was a lot of money in those days."

The surge of support was inspiring. In one eleven-day period alone, the team raised roughly $50,000, and in three weeks the stock offering surpassed its revised goal, bringing in $105,825. When it was over, nearly 1,700 individuals and businesses had donated almost $125,000 and more than 10,000 season tickets were purchased. "All those rumors that Green Bay was going to be dropped out of the league ought to be laid to rest now," Fischer proclaimed. "It shows that the small town still is an important cog in this new machine."

But the franchise's ultimate fate still had to be determined at the NFL's league meeting in June. Only after NFL commissioner Bert Bell proclaimed the Packers "out of the financial woods" was Green Bay guaranteed a place in the thirteen-team league's realigned, seven-team National Conference for the 1950 season.

Now that professional football was enjoying peace for the first time in almost five years, team owners focused on experimenting further with America's newest leisure activity: television. The medium was proving to be a great tool in generating

A stock certificate issued as part of the Packers' 1950 stock drive (COURTESY OF THE GREEN BAY PACKERS)

No. 1138   (1) Shares

GREEN BAY **PACKERS** INCORPORATED

INCORPORATED UNDER THE LAWS OF THE STATE OF WISCONSIN

This Certifies that _____ is the owner of

One _____ Shares of the No Par Value Capital Stock of

THE GREEN BAY PACKERS, INC.

transferable on the books of the Corporation in person or by duly authorized Attorney upon surrender of this certificate properly endorsed, but only to persons permitted to hold stock according to the regulations of the Corporation.

The Holder hereof understands and agrees:

That no dividend shall ever be paid on said stock, nor is the stock assessable;

That if the Corporation is dissolved all the assets shall go to Sullivan-Wallen Post No. 11 of the American Legion for the purpose of creating a soldiers' memorial.

In Witness Whereof, the said Corporation has caused this Certificate to be signed by its duly authorized officers and sealed with the Seal of the Corporation this 24th day of _____ May _____, 1950.

_____ SECRETARY   _____ PRESIDENT

THE GREEN BAY PACKERS, INC.

SHARES

ISSUED TO

_____

For Value Received, subject however, to his eligibility to hold stock according to the regulations of the corporation, I hereby sell, assign and transfer unto

post-office address

_____ shares of the Capital Stock represented by the within certificate and do hereby irrevocably constitute and appoint

_____ attorney to transfer said stock on the books of the within named Corporation with full power of substitution in the premises.

Dated _____ 19___

In presence of _____

NOTICE: THE SIGNATURE OF THIS ASSIGNMENT MUST CORRESPOND WITH THE NAME AS WRITTEN UPON THE FACE OF THE CERTIFICATE, IN EVERY PARTICULAR, WITHOUT ALTERATION OR ENLARGEMENT, OR ANY CHANGE WHATEVER.

interest and national exposure for the game. Commissioner Bell continued allowing individual teams to negotiate their own contracts with television broadcasters and to structure their regional network agreements in similar fashion to their radio contracts, which paralleled how Major League Baseball handled the new medium. By 1949 total NFL television rights were worth about $75,000.

Fear of diminished gate receipts didn't deter Bears owner George Halas from televising all six of Chicago's home games in 1947 for a fee of $4,500. Over the next few years, he prospered at the gate as the growing fan base from the team's television audience began attending games. Halas was so eager to keep his team on the air, he assumed the liability for all unsold commercial time and arranged for the Bears to appear live on eleven Midwest stations. Despite losing money from the network arrangement, he boasted, "More people have seen the Bears play this year than the first thirty years of our existence put together."

In 1950 the Los Angeles Rams became the first team to televise all of its games, home and away. The experiment backfired, as ticket sales at the Los Angeles Coliseum declined almost 50 percent. As a response, Bell implemented the league-wide policy that any home games not sold out in advance would be blacked out in their respective television markets. He reasoned, "You can't give a game to the public for free on television and expect them to pay to go to the ballpark for the same game."

At the start of the decade, televising football games in Green Bay had yet to emerge as a legitimate revenue generator. Radio was still king, and when the Packers signed a new agreement with Milwaukee radio station WTMJ, Miller Brewing Company sponsored all twelve broadcast games throughout Wisconsin and Michigan's Upper Peninsula. The brewery's president, Fred Miller, was one of the Packers' biggest boosters, and he understood the marketing influence of professional sports and its ability to reach young male consumers. Miller would play a pivotal role in the arrival of baseball's Milwaukee Braves and basketball's Milwaukee Hawks later in the decade. In 1950 his commitment to the Packers provided the franchise with much-needed advertising revenue and the benefit of being associated with one of the state's most influential companies.

Prior to the start of the 1950 season, Ronzani, feeling it was only appropriate for a team from Green Bay to have green in its color scheme, retired the traditional blue and gold uniforms the Packers had worn for all but two years under Curly Lambeau. When the team was introduced on opening day, the gold numbers on the front and back of their kelly green uniforms were the only way the City Stadium crowd could identify the players. "Gene Ronzani had little respect for the roster built by Curly Lambeau, and he gutted it as the 1950 season approached," author Don Gulbrandsen recounted in *Green Bay Packers: The Complete Illustrated History*. "His aggressive rebuilding wasn't a surprise: Curly had not left much talent behind."

> "Ronzani knew a helluva lot about football."
> —HALFBACK TONY CANADEO

Tony Canadeo (3) was one of the only superstars left from Lambeau's last championship squad. Although in 1949 he had become only the third player to rush for more than 1,000 yards in a season, Canadeo could do little to revive the Packers' championship hopes in 1950. (COURTESY OF GREEN BAY PRESS-GAZETTE FROM TOM PIGEON COLLECTION)

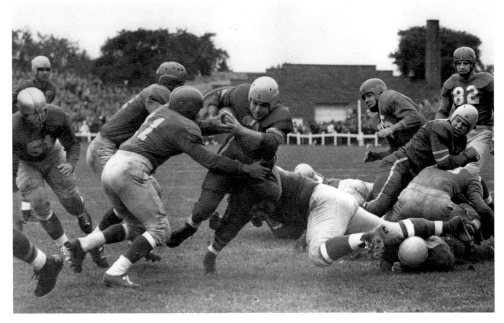

Even though the Packers' 1950 season had most players—including Paul Christman (28) and Jug Girard (36)—feeling dejected, quarterback Tobin Rote (38) couldn't help but be optimistic about the team's prospects for the future. (COURTESY OF TOM PIGEON COLLECTION)

Ronzani started the season with just ten holdovers, about a third of the players from the previous season. "He was trying desperately to rebuild the football team and that was a pretty tough job," halfback Tony Canadeo recalled. "Ronzani knew a helluva lot about football."

Recognizing he needed help replenishing the roster with talent, Ronzani hired twenty-three-year-old Jack Vainisi before the start of the season. For the next decade, Vainisi would oversee the Packers' college drafts as the team's scouting director, personnel director, and chief contract negotiator, having "one of the most exceptional and underappreciated careers in professional football," according to Lombardi biographer David Maraniss.

But in 1950 Vainisi couldn't put points on the scoreboard, and the Packers' porous defense allowed nearly 34 points per game. Still, when Green Bay finished in fifth place with a 3–9 record, the organization viewed the season as a success. On top of winning one more game than in 1949, the team would "not only pay all expenses out of this year's gate receipts, but we'll have a little left over," executive committee member John Torinus told the Associated Press. "We have more than $100,000 in cash from our fund drive last year still not touched."

The team's $12,990 profit had Packers president Emil Fischer exclaiming, "They don't have to worry about us when they start talking about trimming off the thirteenth member of the NFL," as the organization continued combating rumors it was about to surrender its franchise. The gossip intensified when the Baltimore Colts announced they had lost $83,078 during their inaugural NFL campaign. Football pundits were quick to predict the demise of both clubs, with franchises ready to replace them in Buffalo and Houston. Not until the Colts folded that offseason and the NFL confirmed it would play the 1951 season with just twelve teams, six in each division, did the Packers survive another public scare.

■ ■ ■

Back in Green Bay, Gene Ronzani announced the Packers would host their upcoming training camp in Grand Rapids, Minnesota, boasting that the move west would generate an estimated $20,000 in added revenue for the team. His offseason was made busier by his continued efforts to replenish the franchise's roster, which was further hindered by the escalating Korean War. Although the war's impact on professional football rosters wasn't as significant as World War II, the Packers did lose five veterans to Uncle Sam and tried to avoid drafting college players who were thought to be heading overseas. Burdened with a weak crop of rookies and aging veterans, Ronzani built his offense around Tobin Rote, a quarterback he thought could revitalize the team's ailing passing game. But it turned out one of the Packers' brightest stars in 1951 was a late-season pickup off 1950's waiver wire.

Although the Packers signed African Americans Jim Thomas and Jim Clark during the 1950 preseason, both were released before the start of the season. In an era where teams were slow to sign black players, Green Bay became the NFL's fifth team to integrate its roster when Ronzani picked up receiver Bob Mann after the Lions released him late in the 1950 season. Upon his arrival in Green Bay, Mann infused some speed and agility into the team's anemic passing game. By 1951 he was Tobin Rote's primary passing target, catching fifty passes for 696 yards, including eight for touchdowns.

The improved aerial attack, however, couldn't overcome a series of injuries and disappointments that mired the Packers' season. Green Bay closed out its 1951 schedule on a seven-game losing streak while suffering through its second consecutive 3–9 record and posting an $18,000 loss. To eliminate some of the team's growing debt, the Packers announced that Milwaukee would host a third home game in 1952. "This move was taken solely with the best interest of the future of

LEFT: As the 1951 season approached, the Packers' Don Hutson (far left) and Lee Joannes (standing) conducted a ticket drive in Milwaukee with the cooperation of Max Murphy (right), the drive's director, and Harold Taylor. (MILWAUKEE JOURNAL SENTINEL)

BELOW, LEFT: With their aggressive 1951 season-ticket campaign, the Packers hoped to attract more female fans to City Stadium. (FROM THE GREEN BAY PRESS-GAZETTE ARCHIVES, REPRINTED BY PERMISSION)

BELOW, RIGHT: A Packer Buck from the 1951 ticket drive (WHI IMAGE ID 81774)

the Packers in mind," chairman of the board Lee Joannes stated as a response to the public outcry in Green Bay. "We are not moving the Packers to Milwaukee. The Packers can survive only as a Green Bay team, but we are asking all of Wisconsin and particularly Milwaukee to help us support the Packers so that Green Bay will always be in the National Football League."

The Packers' decision was also based on the additional seating available inside the state-of-the-art Milwaukee County Stadium, which was scheduled to be completed in time for their 1952 season. But when a construction strike in May delayed the stadium's completion, the Packers were forced to relocate their Milwaukee games to Marquette University. The venue change did little to detract from ticket sales as former Packer Buckets Goldenberg, now a goodwill ambassador for the team, led a spirited campaign to surpass last season's ticket sales even before the start of training camp.

Bowing to overwhelming pressure from the NFL's eleven other teams, the Packers continued dividing their home game schedule between Green Bay and Milwaukee in an effort to keep the team financially solvent and prevent another franchise from moving into the fertile region. (WHI IMAGE ID 87361)

· · ·

That offseason, the Packers received another infusion of revenue from radio after taking bids for their broadcast rights. When the Wisconsin Network, an affiliation of state stations that broadcast University of Wisconsin football games, matched WTMJ's $20,000 offer, the Packers sold it the rights. For the next five years, announcer Earl Gillespie would be the voice of the Packers on radio, creating a loyal following with his hometown perspective from flagship station WJPG, which was owned by the *Green Bay Press-Gazette*. His colorful play-by-play that first season benefited from the Packers' crop of young stars Vito "Babe" Parilli, Billy Howton, Bobby Dillon, and Dave Hanner.

However, Green Bay's offense often sputtered due to a lackluster running attack and weak offensive line. As a result, Ronzani decided to place his quarterback, Tobin Rote, 5 to 7 yards behind the line of scrimmage to give him a few extra seconds to locate an open receiver or run the ball himself. "During the 1952 season," executive committee member John Torinus recalled of Ronzani's innovative quarterback placement, "he was the inventor of what is now known as the shotgun formation."

Implementing the shotgun helped the Packers to an impressive 6–3 record by the second half of the season.

In playoff contention, they went on the road for their final three games. They soon squandered away their postseason hopes with consecutive losses against the Lions, Rams, and 49ers. The late-season collapse dropped the Packers to a 6–6 record and a fourth-place finish. Still, it was their best season since 1947, when the club had finished 6–5–1, and that prompted the executive committee to hand Gene Ronzani a new three-year contract. The Packers could afford the expense. With the $100,000 nest egg from the 1950 stock sale still untouched, the team posted an $11,960 profit for 1952. "If Coach Gene Ronzani comes up with another contender," Lloyd Larson wrote in the *Milwaukee Sentinel*, "the 1953 business prospects are bright."

The New York Yanks weren't as fortunate. Back in 1951 the franchise had conceded losing its popularity battle to the crosstown Giants. The Yanks were sold and relocated to Dallas. Rebranded as the Texans, they became the Lone Star State's first pro football franchise, but due to sparse crowds they soon found themselves playing as a full-time road team headquartered out of Hershey, Pennsylvania. Following the 1952 season, the franchise folded, marking the last time an NFL team went out of business. With an uneven slate of eleven teams in the league, commissioner Bert Bell approved an expansion franchise in Baltimore, reincarnating the Colts for the start of the 1953 season.

The Packers' potent passing game was enhanced by pass catchers Bob Mann (left) and Billy Howton (right), who caught a combined 83 passes and scored 19 touchdowns in 1953. (LEFT: COURTESY OF GREEN BAY PRESS-GAZETTE FROM TOM PIGEON COLLECTION; RIGHT: COURTESY OF TOM PIGEON COLLECTION)

• • •

During the summer of 1953, the Packers lost one of their strongest leaders when Emil Fischer retired after a six-year tenure. "When he stepped down as president, the Packers were in better shape than when he was given the leadership reigns," author Larry Names remarked in *The History of the Green Bay Packers: The Shameful Years, Part Four*. "Fischer had directed the fortunes of the Green Bay Packers, Inc., according to the sound business principles that had worked so well for him."

Replacing Fischer as team president was Russell W. Bogda, who had been a dedicated board member since 1947. As the head of the Bogda Motor Company, the new Packers president was quick to infuse his business sense into the franchise. "He treated the Packers like a car dealership," Names wrote. "The terms of steady growth and continuity were foreign to him; he was accustomed to getting results today no matter what it took."

Under new leadership, the Packers launched a season-ticket drive in June to fill the brand-new 37,000-seat Milwaukee County Stadium. Although the Packers lost their 1953 debut there to the Cleveland Browns, the modern facility was considered a vast improvement over the team's previous Milwaukee confines at Marquette Stadium and State Fair Park. County Stadium, which was built to lure a major-league baseball franchise to Milwaukee, was the nation's first major-league baseball stadium built completely with civic funding. That meant accommodating the dimensions of a football field was an afterthought. The field was wedged between the first- and third-base foul lines, forcing fans to watch the action play out across the gridiron at odd angles. The stadium wasn't much more accommodating to teams, as both benches were located on the same side of the field between left and center field. Players could enter and

New team president Russ Bogda was quick to mention the Packers' upcoming contest against Curly Lambeau's Redskins in his letter to season-ticket holders as incentive to renew their seats in 1953. (WHI IMAGE ID 81789)

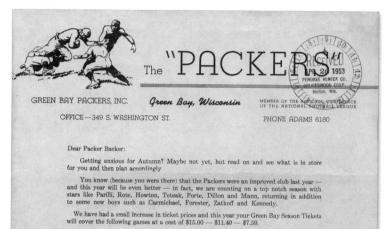

exit the field only from the first- and third-base dugouts. And when the baseball and football seasons overlapped in September, the stadium's infield dirt ran across one corner of the football field and through the end zones, creating unpredictable footing for even the most agile athletes. Yet those were concessions the NFL, the Packers, and their Milwaukee boosters were willing to make to keep the Packers in Wisconsin. "All of us want to see the Packers stay in Green Bay," Miller Brewing president Fred Miller explained. "The Packers wouldn't be the Packers if they weren't in Green Bay. And the way to keep the Packers in Green Bay is for Milwaukee to support the Packers in Milwaukee."

The Packers began their 1953 season stumbling to a 2–6–1 record, with both wins over the resurrected Baltimore Colts franchise. With the team destined to suffer through another losing season, Gene Ronzani found himself spending more time strategizing against local disdain than opposing teams, claiming, "Situations in the past have forced the Packers to go to the public for aid. And now everybody in town feels he has a voice in the club."

"Every Tuesday in Green Bay after practice, the whole team would have lunch with the executive committee at the YMCA," defensive back Bob Forte recalled. "The committee members would question the coaches carefully. When lunch was over, each of the thirteen men on the committee would corner two or three or four of the players and try to find out what was wrong with the coaches, the other players and the team."

It was an environment that bred second-guessing by even the most football-knowledgeable board members. "Bogda took a well-oiled ship and tinkered with it until it began springing leaks," author Larry Names remarked, "and the first thing he did was exactly what all sales managers do when sales fall off: he pointed the finger of blame and started firing people."

On Thanksgiving Day Green Bay gave up 27 unanswered points while blowing a 15–7 lead on national television to the Lions. After the game, the Packers fired their head coach. "The fall of Gene Ronzani started the day after Russell W. Bogda was elected to the presidency of the corporation," Names claimed. "It was a well-known fact within the inner circle of the organization that Bogda had been opposed to Ronzani being hired in the first place."

Ronzani's abrupt departure with two games remaining in the season was triggered by his contract. If he wasn't dismissed before December 1, 1953, the Packers would have had to honor his full 1954 salary of $12,500. Instead, the Packers paid him

> "The Packers wouldn't be the Packers if they weren't in Green Bay."
>
> —MILLER BREWING PRESIDENT FRED MILLER

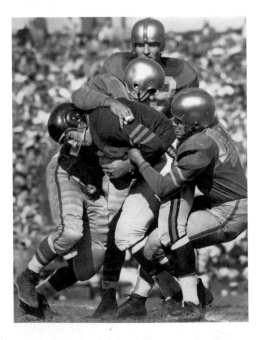

The 1953 Packers could beat only the hapless Baltimore Colts—back after a two-year hiatus—despite a hard-hitting defense that included Bob Forte (left), Bill Forester (top center), and Ben Aldridge (right), seen here playing the Bears in a 17–13 loss. (MILWAUKEE JOURNAL SENTINEL)

The Packers began splitting their home game schedule between Green Bay and Milwaukee in 1933, with games played at Borchert Field in 1933; Wisconsin State Fair Park (above, left) between 1934 and 1951; Marquette Stadium (above, right) in 1952; and Milwaukee County Stadium (below) from 1953 to 1994.
(ALL PHOTOS COURTESY OF TOM PIGEON COLLECTION)

Gene Ronzani (right) had few answers for radio announcer Earl Gillespie (left) when he was no longer the Packers' head coach with two games remaining in the 1953 season. In less than four seasons Ronzani had coached the team to a 14-31-1 record. (FROM THE GREEN BAY PRESS-GAZETTE ARCHIVES, REPRINTED BY PERMISSION)

the $7,500 provided in the dismissal clause. Following his departure from Green Bay, Ronzani prophesied about the team's future, telling the *Milwaukee Journal*'s Ollie Kuechle, "The situation has grown so serious that unless the 'powers that be' take the bull by the horns, the same thing will happen to the next coach, and maybe the ball team. If I was the cause of our failure, they can now prove it. I'm glad to be out of it."

To fill the Packers' head coaching vacancy, the executive committee assigned a trio of assistant coaches—Chuck Drulis, Hugh Devore, and Ray "Scooter" McLean—for the season's final two games. Three days later, the team announced that Drulis was departing the Packers to tend to his seriously ill father, leaving Devore and McLean to co-coach the last two games in California against the 49ers and the Rams. The demoralized Packers suffered consecutive blowout losses and finished the season in the Western Division cellar with a 2–9–1 record.

Despite the tumultuous season, the team reported a profit of $29,267 in 1953—more than doubling that of 1952—as it benefited from the NFL's first national

With two games remaining in the 1953 season and Gene Ronzani no longer the Packers' head coach, team president Russ Bogda (center) assigned two of his assistants, Hugh Devore (left) and Ray "Scooter" McLean (right), the duties. (FROM THE GREEN BAY PRESS-GAZETTE ARCHIVES, REPRINTED BY PERMISSION)

television contract. Westinghouse Electric Company, the American Broadcasting Company, and the DuMont Broadcasting Network agreed to pay the NFL $1.3 million for its broadcast rights, televising nineteen games on Saturday nights. The broadcast revenue equated to as little as 3 percent of a team's total revenue, but it was fast becoming an essential source of income. In 1953 the Packers received $12,000 from their Thanksgiving Day date with Detroit and $20,000 from the league's overall deal.

Television could no longer ignore the public's growing appetite for professional football. During the first half of the decade, network giants NBC and CBS showed no interest in pro football, dismissing the sport in favor of baseball. That allowed the DuMont Broadcasting Network to secure the exclusive broadcast rights for the 1951 title game between the Los Angeles Rams and Cleveland Browns for $75,000. That same year, DuMont also televised five regular-season games, a number that would grow to twelve by 1954. Being the first network to comprehend the popularity of football on a national level, DuMont paid $95,000 for the rights to the title game each subsequent year until the network began to fold in 1954. In 1955 NBC assumed the television rights to the title game, paying the league $100,000 for broadcast rights. In 1956 CBS began broadcasting some regular-season games to selected television markets across the nation at a fee of $1.8 million per year, but only teams featured in games received a portion of the rights fees. Since the Packers had become an NFL doormat, their exposure on national television was rare, creating a disparity between them and the more successful franchises in larger, more lucrative television markets. "The first year I was doing the Packer games, in 1956, I think the Packers got just $35,000 for their television rights from CBS," television announcer Ray Scott recalled. It was a financial rift that would continue to expand throughout the decade and would once again jeopardize the future of the franchise in Green Bay.

> "If I was the cause of our failure, they can now prove it. I'm glad to be out of it."
> —HEAD COACH GENE RONZANI

■　■　■

In the four years since Curly Lambeau's departure from Green Bay, the Packers had operated without someone serving in the official role as general manager. Gene Ronzani and Jack Vainisi handled many of the position's trivial responsibilities, but the team's executive committee fulfilled the position as a whole, vowing that after Lambeau's reign they would never allow one single person to have that much authority over the team—ever again. Although the executive committee acted in what it thought was the Packers' best interests, it was apparent the team couldn't succeed with a group of part-time volunteers handling the full-time administrative responsibilities of a professional football organization. Only after months of debate in 1954 did the Packers' executive committee decide to separate business management from the head coaching duties by creating its first stand-alone business manager position, responsible for signing players and managing business affairs.

To fill the position, the executive committee turned to a familiar face, Brown County District Attorney Verne Lewellen, who had played for the Packers during their 1929–1931 championship run. His first assignment was to find a permanent successor to Ronzani. When Hugh Devore declined to return as the team's sole head coach in 1954, Lewellen suggested the executive committee consider a very successful high school coach from Wisconsin. "The Executive Committee wanted to avoid hiring a coach with strong ties to another pro team," author Don Gulbrandsen wrote. "Gene Ronzani's long history with the Bears had actually undermined his relationship with veteran Packers who had little respect for their Chicago rivals."

Lisle "Liz" Blackbourn was a lifelong Wisconsinite, born in Beetown and a high school sports star at nearby Lancaster. At Lawrence College he had been a prominent football tackle and baseball catcher. Before accepting the head coaching position at Marquette University in 1950, he had earned a reputation as one of the state's most successful football coaches while at Washington High School in Milwaukee.

Wisconsin native Lisle Blackbourn was expected to turn around the Packers' fortunes as the team's third head coach. (COURTESY OF TOM PIGEON COLLECTION)

On January 7, 1954, Blackbourn was hired as the Packers' permanent successor to Gene Ronzani, receiving a three-year contract and an annual salary just under $20,000 with no escape clause. But according to sportswriter Chuck Johnson, several of those within the organization were opposed to hiring a coach from the collegiate ranks. "The 13-man executive committee had been split over the hiring of Blackbourn, but soon even those who had opposed him swung over to his side, publicly and privately," he wrote. "The subcommittees were disbanded and Blackbourn was allowed to coach without interference."

After Blackbourn relocated the team's training camp to Stevens Point State Teachers College in late July 1954, the Packers struggled through a lackluster preseason. To start the season, the Packers lost their first three games after blowing fourth-quarter leads against the Steelers, Bears, and 49ers. "Nobody realizes any more than I do we've lost our three league games by a total of fourteen points," Blackbourn told reporters. "It drains you, and it was the same thing during the exhibition season. That's slicing 'em about as thin as you can slice 'em."

The Packers' fortunes soon turned around after upsetting the Rams in Milwaukee, the Colts in Baltimore, and the Eagles in a nationally televised Saturday night contest in Philadelphia. When returning to Green Bay, the team was greeted at the airport by nearly

Miller Brewing president Fred Miller (center) understood the appeal of athletes in promoting his product, and he employed several of them during the offseason as spokesmen, including (left to right) 49ers quarterback Y. A. Tittle, Giants defensive back Emlen Tunnell, Packers fullback Fred Cone, Bears halfback Don Kindt, Packers linebacker Clayton Tonnemaker, Packers quarterback Tobin Rote, Milwaukee Braves pitcher Lou Burdette, Braves equipment manager Joe Taylor, Braves outfielder Andy Pafko, former Packers halfback Bob Forte, and Braves outfielder Billy Bruton. (MILWAUKEE JOURNAL SENTINEL)

10,000 fans and the Lumberjack Band for an impromptu pep rally. For the majority of the season, the Packers found themselves in contention for the division crown. They were no longer getting blown out of games early; seven of the Packers' eight losses in 1954 were by 8 points or fewer. Although the team finished with a 4–8 record, Blackbourn finished just one vote shy of being named Coach of the Year by the United Press. The Packers rewarded him with a raise and a two-year contract extension.

Despite their losing record for 1954, the Packers enjoyed the largest profit in the corporation's history: $69,594. The NFL's television agreement with the DuMont Network constituted a large portion of the team's $114,350 generated from radio and television rights fees.

With the franchise on secure financial footing, its home venue, City Stadium, became a topic of growing controversy throughout the league. When the facility opened in 1925, it had been the envy of the league. Three decades later, it was more of a liability than a legacy. The stadium's decrepit wooden bleachers, inadequate toilets, and unacceptable locker room facilities no longer met modern standards. "The locker room was horrendous," defensive lineman John Martinkovic recalled of its location underneath the stands. "There were concrete floors. It was from the medieval ages."

The stadium's location was also becoming a victim of America's obsession with automobiles and suburbanization. Fans were now willing to drive in from

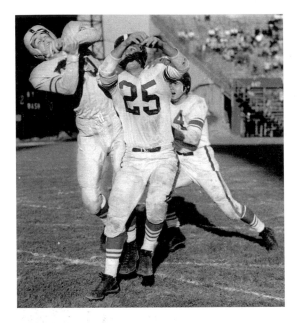

Max McGee (far left) and the Packers couldn't hold on to victories, as seven of the team's eight losses in 1954 were by 8 points or fewer. (COURTESY OF TOM PIGEON COLLECTION)

surrounding communities to attend games, creating a need for parking facilities, which City Stadium lacked. When Milwaukee County Stadium opened in 1953, NFL team owners offered Green Bay's stadium shortcomings as a new excuse to schedule their games in Wisconsin's largest city. Since the Packers were playing as many home games in Milwaukee as in Green Bay between 1952 and 1957, "Green Bay boosters had to fend off an effort by Milwaukeeans to rename the franchise the Wisconsin Packers," author Craig Coenen wrote in *From Sandlots to the Super Bowl*. "As Milwaukee gate receipts once again began to outpace those in Green Bay by the mid-1950s, it seemed only a matter of time until the franchise relocated."

The fate of City Stadium was addressed in the *Green Bay Press-Gazette* before the 1955 season. In a letter published by the newspaper, the Sullivan-Wallen American Legion Post recommended a new stadium be built to keep the Packers in Green Bay. It was a sentiment shared by local boosters who understood how the Packers represented the entire state of Wisconsin and Upper Michigan. The team's executive committee, led by president Russ Bogda, opposed the construction of a new stadium, arguing it was in the team's best interest to renovate. Even when

A teacher at heart, head coach Lisle Blackbourn is seen here at the Packers' 1955 training camp, directing the next play from scrimmage to center Ray Paxton, quarterback Charlie Brackins, and guard Gene Snipes. (MILWAUKEE JOURNAL SENTINEL)

cost-prohibitive building estimates projected that nearly two-thirds of the stadium had to be replaced, Bogda and the executive committee claimed the club didn't have the capital available to build a new stadium. "Their good intentions were totally misguided as they suffered from that small town myopia, which has always been the major cause of stagnation and eventually the erosion and death of the very thing that such well-meaning people seek to protect with their obsolete attitude," author Larry Names remarked of the Packers' survival being left, once again, to the actions of the franchise's loyal boosters.

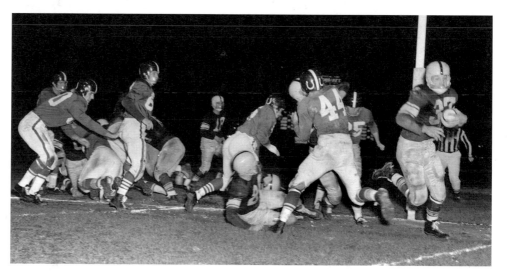

The Packers had few bright moments during the 1955 season while finishing with a 6–6 record. ABOVE: End Gary Knafelc (84) was carried off the City Stadium gridiron by fans after a 20–17 season-opening victory over the Lions. RIGHT: Two weeks later, a spirited effort by Howie Ferguson (37) under the Milwaukee County Stadium lights at night wasn't enough as the Packers lost 24–20 to the Colts. (BOTH PHOTOS COURTESY OF GREEN BAY PRESS-GAZETTE FROM TOM PIGEON COLLECTION)

No American community valued its "big-league" status more than Green Bay, Wisconsin. So it was no surprise that local leaders hatched their own plan to save the Packers. If the team agreed to pay half the cost of building a new stadium, the city would float a $960,000 bond to cover its construction. It was an unprecedented offer. Milwaukee had built the first civically funded stadium for a baseball team, but never before had a modern sports facility been built exclusively for a pro football team, paid for in part by a city government. The Packers agreed, and the cooperation between the franchise and its community became the key selling point to voters who would have to approve the bond the following year.

Enthusiasm surrounding the proposed stadium seemed to spill onto the field as the Packers won three of their first four games to start the 1955 season. Even during a 24–20 loss to the rejuvenated Baltimore Colts, they were within inches of a victory under the Milwaukee County Stadium lights when Tobin Rote's pass missed Billy Howton's outstretched fingertips as time expired. The Packers stayed in the middle of the Western Division race following a three-game losing streak and two-game winning streak. But when they lost their Thanksgiving Day contest to the Lions and split their West Coast games, they fell to third place. Yet their 6–6 record was reason to speculate that Lisle Blackbourn was building a winner in Green Bay.

■ ■ ■

Blackbourn's modest success on the field equated to the Packers' posting $88,578 in revenue in 1955, the result of increased ticket sales that generated more than $51,000 in Green Bay and $32,000 in Milwaukee. Although the team's fortunes were riding high, the Packers were still dependent on the voters approving the stadium bond. In the weeks preceding the April 3, 1956, referendum on the new stadium, the entire professional football world was focused on Green Bay. "Old friends like Gene Ronzani and George Halas of the Chicago Bears came to the Packers' support," executive committee member John Torinus recalled of their unbiased lobbying efforts. "In a mammoth pep rally at the Columbus Club on the weekend before the vote, Halas came to Green Bay and bluntly told Packers fans that the only way they could continue to compete in the National Football League was to build the new facility."

Would the citizens of Green Bay be willing to finance a new stadium for a team that hadn't enjoyed a winning record in nearly a decade? "If the question doesn't win voter approval, the Packers will pull up stakes within the next few years and move elsewhere," *Associated Press* writer Chuck Capaldo speculated. "Possible future sites of the club include Milwaukee, Buffalo, Miami and Minneapolis."

The Packers' first "Golden Girl," Mary Jane Sorgel, helped promote the 1956 season during training camp in Stevens Point. (COURTESY OF TOM PIGEON COLLECTION)

On the eve of Election Day, business manager Verne Lewellen addressed the local Kiwanis Club luncheon, making the bold prediction that the Packers' "golden era is going to be in the 1960's."

When the votes were tallied, Green Bay residents proved once again that they understood what it took to be a big-league community. The project's funding was approved by a margin of two to one—11,575 to 4,893. All of the league's eleven other clubs played in venues designed to host other sports, be it a park for baseball or even an Olympic track-and-field stadium such as the Los Angeles Coliseum. The Packers would become the NFL's first franchise to play in a stadium built solely for professional football.

Following the vote that spring, the city purchased and annexed forty-eight acres of farmland on the southwest edge of town from Victor and Florence Vannieuwenhoven for $73,305. Adjacent to Highway 41, the future site of New City Stadium would provide fans easy access to drive in from all over the state and have ample space for parking. By year's end, the stadium plans submitted by local architect John Somerville were approved. "The stadium contract originally called for a 32,000 seating capacity," Somerville said of his design to allow for gradual expansion. "But when we did the geometry, we figured in for 56,000-plus."

> "When I first came here [in 1956], this team hadn't won in a long time."
>
> —OFFENSIVE TACKLE FORREST GREGG

The new stadium's initial increase in seating capacity and its potential to accommodate growth intimidated even the most optimistic of Packers supporters, including executive committee member John Torinus: "I well remember getting a telegram from Andy Turnbull in California in which he warned me that erecting a stadium of 32,500 seats would mean the bankruptcy of the Packers because we would never be able to sell out that many seats on a season ticket basis." Despite the concerns, the executive committee moved forward, anticipating the new stadium's additional seats would be filled with female fans willing to attend games, since the new stadium would offer plenty of adequate restroom facilities.

The Packers enjoyed an undefeated exhibition season and looked to start the 1956 season strong. When the regular season began with two straight losses, however, fans grew frustrated with the team's inability to win on a consistent basis. "When I first came here [in 1956], this team hadn't won in a long time," offensive tackle Forrest Gregg recalled. "All we ever heard about was Curly Lambeau and Don

The Packers entered the 1956 preseason with high expectations, due in large part to coach Lisle Blackbourn's latest college draft class that included Forrest Gregg, Bob Skoronski, Hank Gremminger, and an unheralded quarterback chosen in the seventeenth round, Bart Starr.
(LEFT: WHI IMAGE ID 87362; RIGHT: WHI IMAGE ID 87429)

BART STARR
No. 16 — Quarterback

Hutson and Mike Michalske and Clarke Hinkle and Arnie Herber. The fans would just go down that list of ex-Packers greats because those were the fond memories."

As a result, the executive committee, already grumbling about Blackbourn's tendency to tinker and make roster decisions without their approval, resumed the weekly lunch meetings with him. "I actually felt sorry for the members of the committee, the way they got crucified," Blackbourn said of how fans would pressure them whenever the team struggled. "They used to show up for the luncheons all tied up tight like fiddle strings."

The executive committee's meddling did little to rectify the team's fortunes on the field. The Packers' erratic play continued, winning two in a row, losing four in a row, and knocking off the division-leading Lions and Cardinals in successive weeks only to finish the season with consecutive losses on the West Coast to the 49ers and the Rams. The Packers lost all their home games at City Stadium while finishing the season at 4–8 and tied for last place in the Western Division.

Despite their poor performance in the standings, the Packers still reported a profit of $28,683 in 1956, compared to the previous year's $47,124, which was a direct result of the drop in ticket sales. The Packers had a $142,993 cash reserve to compensate for the smaller profit, but that wouldn't sustain the team for long. Rising team payrolls, which were nourished by television revenue, were widening the competitive disparity among NFL clubs. While the Browns' $368,031 and the

The 1956 Packers, including defensive end Nate Borden (87) and running back Al Carmichael (48), couldn't block out the competition during a 4–8 campaign. (COURTESY OF GREEN BAY PRESS-GAZETTE FROM TOM PIGEON COLLECTION)

The Packers and Cardinals found themselves battling for the NFL's worst record throughout the 1950s. Despite Green Bay's 24-21 victory on December 2, 1956, both teams found themselves eligible for the first pick in the upcoming draft. (WHI IMAGE ID 86564)

Rams' $352,958 led the league, the Packers' $277,642 in player contracts was the tenth highest of twelve team payrolls in 1956. Only the Steelers and Redskins spent a few thousand dollars less.

Even with television revenue bolstering team coffers, only a handful of superstar players cashed in with lucrative contracts. Average player salaries experienced only a slight increase during the decade. Following the end of the pro football war, NFL player salaries rose just 5 percent, from $8,000 per player in 1949 to around $8,400 by 1956. As a result, a group of disgruntled players from throughout the league organized the National Football League Players Association in hopes of changing the culture that had dominated pro football for decades—owners paying players poorly, offering no benefits, and refusing to guarantee contracts or job security. "In those days any time you wanted to change the personnel on your team, you could do it in a matter of a day," center Jim Ringo recounted. "If you picked up your check and there was a pink slip in the envelope, you were gone. No contracts, no injury clauses, none of that."

The NFLPA went to the owners in 1956 to demand that clubs provide players a league-wide minimum salary, per diem pay, and continued payment of salaries while injured; they were turned away without ever receiving a meeting. Publicly, owners never responded to any of the association's proposals, but in the next few years they did incorporate several of their demands, including a basic salary structure, minimal insurance policies, and a pension plan.

The revenue generated by television also forced the NFL to consider expanding into broadcast-friendly markets like Dallas and Buffalo. Enlarging the league from twelve to fourteen teams would provide easier logistics when scheduling games and further justify lengthening the season by two more games—both scenarios adding revenue for owners through ticket sales and television revenue. NFL commissioner Bert Bell disagreed, claiming that new franchises would become doormats for the rest of the league, hurting the overall integrity of the game. While Bell was attempting to keep the NFL self-contained, television was ritualizing professional football into the game that millions of Americans watched on a weekly basis. Not only was football's popularity eclipsing that of baseball, its cultural influence was expanding into the mainstream. Although sports magazines covered the game during the 1940s, more than a half-dozen pro football annuals were devoted to forecasting the sport by 1956 while popular weekly periodicals such as *Sports Illustrated* and *Sport*, along with the more mainstream *Saturday Evening Post*, *Look*, *Life*, *Time*, and *Newsweek*, took greater notice of the NFL.

Professional football's growing popularity was a direct result of the agreement CBS had struck with selected NFL clubs earlier that year to broadcast several games in selected parts of the country. While teams like the Giants, Bears, and Rams secured lucrative six-figure contracts for televising their games in their large metropolitan markets, the Packers received a lesser rate of $75,000 for each of the next three years. While helping to negotiate the Packers' deal with CBS, Commissioner Bell realized the league would be stronger if its broadcast rights were sold as a package, with proceeds divided equally among all the clubs. "Bell was adamant, pointing out that if this disparity in revenues was not corrected, competition within the league would gradually shrink, to be dominated by a few wealthy clubs," executive committee member John Torinus recalled. "And teams like Green Bay were bound to disappear."

When Bell first approached the networks to bid on a league-wide package, he was stonewalled. The U.S. Supreme Court decided that professional football, unlike professional baseball, was subject to federal antitrust laws. Since 1922 baseball had enjoyed immunity from antitrust prosecution after the Supreme Court ruled that baseball was merely for amusement and was not a commercial enterprise. No other professional sport in America enjoyed such an exemption. The legislation Bell sought from Congress to exempt professional football from the Sherman and Clayton antitrust laws would take time—time that the Packers could not afford.

■　■　■

Following the 1956 season, the Packers and Chicago Cardinals were the last two teams eligible for the NFL's bonus pick, a process instituted in 1947 whereby one

When Green Bay selected Paul Hornung (center) with the NFL's bonus pick, team officials, including (left to right) Jack Vainisi, Bernard Darling, W. Webber Kelly, unknown, team president Russ Bogda, and Lee Joannes, expected the Packers to become immediate championship contenders. (COURTESY OF THE HENRY LEFEBVRE COLLECTION OF THE NEVILLE PUBLIC MUSEUM OF BROWN COUNTY)

team would receive the first draft pick via lottery and be eligible for the pick only once. When the coin flip landed in Green Bay's favor, college football's most sought-after talent, Notre Dame's Heisman Trophy winner Paul Hornung, headed to Green Bay. He signed his three-year, $16,000-per-season contract with the Packers despite receiving a tempting offer from the Canadian Football League. From the beginning, Blackbourn was full of praise for his top pick ("He is a natural athlete, a tremendous competitor, has great speed and can take the punishment dealt in the National Football League"), but he failed to explain how he'd utilize Hornung in the Packers offense. "We can use him at quarterback, halfback or fullback."

On the afternoon of September 29, 1957, Hornung made his Green Bay debut as the Packers introduced New City Stadium to the rest of professional football in an event filled with pomp and pageantry. Highlighting the afternoon's guest list were Vice President Richard Nixon, Miss America Marilyn Van Derbur, NFL commissioner Bert Bell, and TV star James Arness. The energy inside the stadium bowl was electric as the Packers took to the field to face their rivals from Chicago. "I went to the University of Michigan where we had 100,000 seats," rookie tight end Ron Kramer recalled. "[In Green Bay] there were 32,500 people there, and you would have thought we were playing for the world championship."

When Gary Knafelc caught quarterback Babe Parilli's pass for the winning touchdown in the fourth quarter, it almost seemed ordained. "It just wouldn't have been appropriate if we hadn't won," receiver Billy Howton said of Green Bay's surprise 21–17 victory over the Bears.

The town was buzzing after the opening-day victory, which only heightened expectations for the season. When Blackbourn arrived at the executive committee luncheon the next day, the thirteen men in the room gave him a standing ovation. The coach did all he could to defuse the committee's enthusiasm. Blackbourn warned them that the players had received too much praise for just one victory and they wouldn't be focused in time for next week's contest. As he predicted, the Packers fell flat against the Lions and began limping through what would become a miserable season.

As the losses mounted, the executive committee interrogated Blackbourn as to why he wasn't playing the team's high-priced rookie, Paul Hornung, more often.

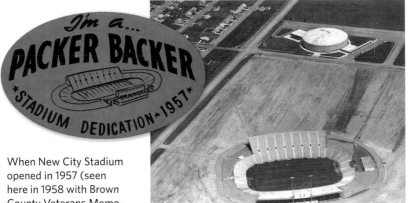

When New City Stadium opened in 1957 (seen here in 1958 with Brown County Veterans Memorial Arena), it marked the first time the team played a home game in Green Bay west of the Fox River. (LEFT: WHI IMAGE ID 81760; RIGHT: COURTESY OF THE HENRY LEFEBVRE COLLECTION OF THE NEVILLE PUBLIC MUSEUM OF BROWN COUNTY)

By 1957 the Packers often found themselves struggling against more talented teams, including the Baltimore Colts and their legendary quarterback Johnny Unitas (19) and running back Alan Ameche (35). (COURTESY OF TOM PIGEON COLLECTION)

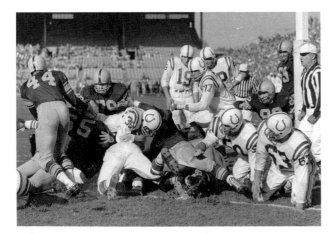

Although it was committee policy not to interfere in the coaching of the football team, "when the team was losing, [the executive committee] became the object of ridicule—everything was their fault," Blackbourn explained. "They couldn't fight the whole world. They had to take it out on the man fixed in front of them—the coach. And they did."

Despite enjoying a profit for the fourth straight season, the entire organization was frustrated. When Blackbourn started lashing back at the committee, telling them it was none of their business how he coached the team, their relationship deteriorated. "He was a very good coach who didn't get along with the executive committee," end Gary Knafelc said. "I think he would have won if they would have allowed him to go along."

In 1957 the Packers didn't win often, finishing their season at 3–9 and stuck in last place for the second consecutive year. A few days after the team lost its season finale in San Francisco, the executive committee received the resignation of team president Russ Bogda, who was dying of cancer. The board refused to accept his resignation. Instead, they created an executive vice president position and elected former Green Bay mayor Dominic Olejniczak to serve in that capacity. Olejniczak, a Green Bay native, had been one of the Packers' original backers as a member of their knothole gang as a kid. He was now acting as the corporation's president in Bogda's absence. Meanwhile, rumors swirled that Blackbourn was about to be replaced, despite a year still remaining on his contract. Before departing on a scouting trip following the 1957 season finale, a suspicious Blackbourn told the committee, "If anything is coming up concerning me, I want to be here to defend myself."

Just as Blackbourn arrived in Alabama to attend college football's Senior Bowl, he received a phone call from the executive committee. When he refused to resign over the phone, the executive committee responded by firing him. "Blackbourn wasn't run out of town for the same reasons that

Ronzani had been, but his dismissal was handled just as poorly," author Larry Names wrote. "The executive committee lied to him, then acted cowardly by not letting him have the chance to defend himself."

"A board certainly can fire a losing coach," *Milwaukee Journal* sportswriter Oliver Kuechle commented, referring to Blackbourn's 17–31 record as the Packers' head coach. "What it won't show, though, will be the behind the scenes maneuvering directed principally by Lee Joannes and his pawn, Dominic Olejniczak. Or the bitterness between Joannes and Blackbourn almost from the beginning. (Joannes never wanted Blackbourn as coach in the first place.) Or the insults Joannes hurled at Blackbourn from the stands at games right here in Milwaukee as an example of his feelings. Or the interference from the ruling soviet during the season which included calling in the assistants and certain players for reports."

Second-year quarterback Bart Starr (15) was offered little protection at Wrigley Field in a 21-14 loss to the Bears, as the Packers stumbled to a 3-9 record in 1957. (MILWAUKEE JOURNAL SENTINEL)

The wolves depicted in Al Rainovic's *Milwaukee Journal* editorial cartoon could no longer be silenced after the 1957 season. Lisle Blackbourn was fired after compiling a 17–31 record over four seasons as the Packers' head coach. (UWM LIBRARIES, ARCHIVES DEPARTMENT RAINOVIC COLLECTION IMAGE 350)

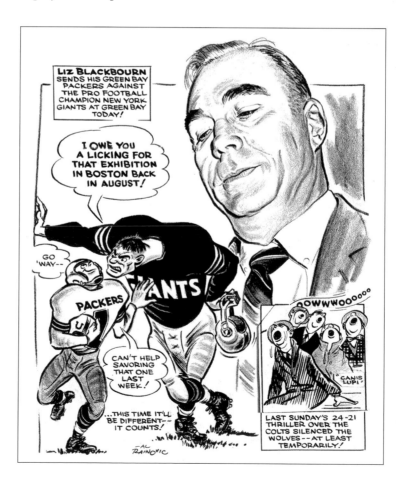

In hindsight, Blackbourn proved to be a good judge of football talent. During the five drafts he oversaw with Jack Vainisi, the Packers selected five future NFL Hall-of-Famers. His 1958 draft class, including center/linebacker Dan Currie in the first round, fullback Jim Taylor in the second, and offensive guard Jerry Kramer in the fourth, would be instrumental in laying the foundation for future Packers teams. Furthermore, he decided his third pick, a fullback from Illinois, was "also a possibility as a defensive end." That player was Ray Nitschke.

■ ■ ■

The failures of Gene Ronzani and Lisle Blackbourn found the 1958 Green Bay Packers a full decade removed from their last winning record. Since Curly Lambeau coached the team to a 6–5–1 mark in 1947, Green Bay had won a total of thirty-six games against eighty-three losses and a lone tie. "But coaching good or bad is not the thing that has been disturbing the Packers for the last ten or fifteen years," sportswriter Oliver Kuechle ranted in the *Milwaukee Journal*. "This thing is a lot deeper than that. It's the confounded meddling by a lot of men with ladles in the soup and the ability of a few of them to control all of the ladles. . . . The Packers today need not a board of directors of forty-five, not an executive committee of thirteen, not a bunch of committees—they need a general manager with absolute authority to run the club."

The executive committee instead chose to retain continuity throughout the organization in its "almost unanimous" decision to elevate popular assistant coach Ray "Scooter" McLean as Blackbourn's successor. An unnamed spokesperson for the team told the *Milwaukee Journal* it was "advisable to hire McLean instead of a coach from the college ranks because McLean is familiar with the Packer personnel." The only other candidate the executives considered for the position was former Los Angeles Rams coach Hampton Pool, who was coaching at Toronto in the Canadian Football League.

At first the decision to promote the mild-mannered, soft-spoken northeasterner was considered a popular one, not only with the fans but also with the players. That sentiment was shared by one executive committee member who proclaimed: "The people of Green Bay demanded that we give Scooter a chance. He's such a nice guy."

McLean, who had been an assistant coach with the Packers since Gene Ronzani's tenure, received only a one-year contract from the executive committee. "Blackbourn's firing and Scooter's hiring were probably knee-jerk reactions to the pressures being put on the executive committee by the board of directors who were getting the same pressures from the stockholders and fans," author Larry Names recounted in *The History of the Green Bay Packers: The Shameful Years, Part Four*.

"We're shooting for the moon. We're going for the title."

—HEAD COACH RAY "SCOOTER" MCLEAN

The Packers replaced Lisle Blackbourn with fan favorite Ray "Scooter" McLean (right), who was also an appealing figure for broadcast sponsors including (left to right) W. R. Jepson of Humphrey Chevrolet, Fred Miller of Rahr Green Bay Brewing Company, and Glenn Holznecht, commercial manager of WJPG. (COURTESY OF THE PRESS-GAZETTE COLLECTION OF THE NEVILLE PUBLIC MUSEUM OF BROWN COUNTY)

Following the death of Russ Bogda, Dominic Olejniczak was elected to succeed him as team president in April. Olejniczak inherited a team that had just announced a $50,130 profit in 1957 with another $170,426 in reserves. When business manager Verne Lewellen warned of the team's increasing operating budget, the Packers decided to offset the added costs by returning one of their Milwaukee games to Green Bay, where they could reap parking and concession revenues. The announcement raised the ire of stockholders and fans who were loyal to County Stadium. "Milwaukee is a good football town, and if the Packers don't want anything to do with Milwaukee, you can bet there will be some negotiating for a pro franchise," Buckets Goldenberg threatened, further implying that the Chicago Cardinals, who were shopping for a new home, might move north. But by April tempers had simmered, and the Packers moved forward with their plan to host just two games in Milwaukee that season.

As the 1958 regular season approached, hopes were high in Green Bay that the Packers would return to their winning ways. Scooter McLean tried creating a positive energy in the locker room by exclaiming to the press, "We're shooting for the moon. We're going for the title." He even returned the team's training camp to Green Bay, housing his players at St. Norbert College and claiming, "It will do wonders for building the morale of the team and that morale is a good 80 percent of winning."

At first McLean's style was considered refreshing. He believed that "the players will be on their honor. They've set up a committee and will have their own system of fines for discipline." But McLean had inherited a roster filled with undisciplined malcontents who wasted no time taking advantage of his good-natured, easygoing personality. "Scooter would play poker with the players the night before the game," Knafelc recalled. "And what was worse is he wasn't even good at it. [Max] McGee would just take him to the cleaners."

With devoted followings firmly established in both Green Bay and Milwaukee, the Packers sought to build further fan loyalty as "Wisconsin's Team." (WHI IMAGE ID 81762)

According to defensive end Jim Temp, "The players just didn't have any respect for him," because he didn't exercise any authority when it came to enforcing team-mandated dress codes, curfews, or repercussions for players who missed meetings.

From the beginning of McLean's tenure as coach, his players appeared to be confused and distracted. "If they had spent as much time concentrating on their play on the field as they did practicing their moves with the ladies, the Packers under McLean might have enjoyed a reasonable amount of success," executive committee member John Torinus suggested. Unfortunately, McLean was not the disciplinarian the team needed.

But the problems didn't end with the players' behavior off the field. During an era when other NFL coaches began specializing players in particular positions, McLean turned back the clock by having many of his players perform on both offense and defense. He claimed his strategy was intended to strengthen his bench, but it succeeded only in depleting the team's precious practice time and creating more injuries as players overextended themselves with their extracurricular positions. "Those days were just miserable," linebacker Tom Bettis recalled.

From the start of their 34–20 opening-day loss to the Bears, Green Bay was the league's doormat in 1958. As the season progressed, the team squandered several large first-half leads when McLean failed to make proper halftime adjustments. Despite several club officials questioning McLean's coaching credentials, "the executive committee didn't want to admit that they had made a mistake while they still had time to correct their error," author Larry Names suggested. "Instead, they let poor Scooter make a fool of himself through the 1958 season."

After the Packers were clobbered by the Colts, 56–0, for the worst defeat in team history, "the hurt was made worse when one sportswriter labeled them the 'Conga Team,'" future coach Phil Bengtson recalled in his autobiography *Packer Dynasty*, "because all year they had done little more than go 1-2-3-kick, 1-2-3-kick."

With the Packers in last place at 1–5–1 just seven weeks into the season, morale in Green Bay was at an all-time low. For an upcoming contest against the Rams, just 28,051 tickets were sold, signifying the only time New City Stadium ever hosted fewer than 30,000 paid fans. In downtown Green Bay, disgruntled fans hung new team president Dominic Olejniczak in effigy. When Hugh Strange, a member of the team's forty-five-man board of directors, resigned in disgust, he called for a complete housecleaning of how the team was being managed. "Why a board of directors of forty-five? Why an executive committee of thirteen that has to have its fingers in the pie every week?" he questioned. He further suggested that "there shouldn't be all of the hocus pocus that has been going on. This is a business and a big business. It should be run like a business. And there should be a general manager with absolute authority, responsible only to the executive committee."

By the time Green Bay's nightmare season ended, Scooter McLean had coached the Packers to their worst record in team history, 1–10–1, prompting New York

> "The Packers overwhelmed one opponent, underwhelmed ten and whelmed one."
> —SPORTSWRITER RED SMITH

When Ray "Scooter" McLean (above) amassed a 1-10-1 record in his one year as the Packers' head coach, fans held team president Dominic Olejniczak responsible, hanging him in effigy (right) outside the team's ticket office at 349 South Washington Street in downtown Green Bay just five days before the 1958 season finale. (ABOVE: MILWAUKEE JOURNAL SENTINEL; RIGHT: FROM THE GREEN BAY PRESS-GAZETTE ARCHIVES, REPRINTED BY PERMISSION)

sportswriter Red Smith, a Green Bay native, to pen, "The Packers overwhelmed one opponent, underwhelmed ten and whelmed one."

McLean saved the executive committee the trouble of firing him, resigning as head coach of the Packers on December 17, 1958, and taking a job as backfield coach for the Detroit Lions the same day. Suffering through eleven straight seasons, Green Bay had become "the Siberia of pro football," according to halfback Paul Hornung. "Any player who did something wrong was threatened to be sent to Green Bay."

It was understandable if Green Bay's players and fans developed an inferiority complex. Over the past eleven seasons, they had survived on a diet of just 3.3 wins per season against 8.4 losses. No other NFL team had ever endured failing over such a long period of time. The once-proud Packers had hit rock bottom. Defeatism reigned. Backup quarterback Bart Starr was on the verge of joining the coaching staff at Marquette University. Paul Hornung contemplated quitting football outright. "The situation was pretty hopeless," he later commented, "and I was fed up. After the '58 season I was hoping they would trade me."

The team was in shambles, a sentiment Iowa coach Forest Evashevski, who was the Packers' first choice to replace McLean, expressed when he refused their offer. "As 1959 began, the Green Bay Packers were in total confusion. They couldn't find a coach, and no one was sure where to look for one," writer Larry Names said of how no established head coach would consider Green Bay—it had been too bad for too long. "Then a miracle happened, as it always seems to with the Packers."

VINCE LOMBARDI
and His Amazing
Technicolor Trenchcoat

On Wednesday, January 28, 1959, Vince Lombardi was named head coach and general manager of the Green Bay Packers, giving him full control of the team's football operations. "What we lacked was leadership and Coach Lombardi provided that the day he walked in the door," quarterback Bart Starr said. "In my opinion, the greatest form of leadership is through example."

The bespectacled, gap-toothed Lombardi was now responsible for making all the decisions, everything from hirings and firings to the purchasing of toilet paper and "how many stripes of what width and color he wanted on the jerseys," his assistant coach Phil Bengtson said in *Packer Dynasty*. According to Bengtson, Lombardi "gave instructions to make the nameplate on his door read 'Mr. Lombardi,' not 'Coach Lombardi.' If it smacked of dictatorship, that's what was needed."

Before Green Bay approached Lombardi, the organization's executive committee considered a vast number of candidates for both positions. However, the men the team was interested in weren't interested in the job. The men who wanted the job weren't of interest to the Packers, either: "One of the notable applicants for the general manager job was none other than Curly Lambeau," executive committee member John Torinus revealed in *The Packer Legend*. Team president Dominic Olejniczak wasn't interested, and "when the board of directors met, Lambeau's name wasn't even brought up," according to Lambeau biographer David Zimmerman.

On the suggestion of Jack Vainisi, Olejniczak focused his search on forty-five-year-old Lombardi, who at the time was an assistant coach with the New York Giants. After the Packers received impeccable recommendations from Giants owner Wellington Mara, the Bears' George Halas, the Browns' Paul Brown, and NFL commissioner Bert Bell, Lombardi emerged as the top candidate. "You had to like him

Green Bay rechristened itself Titletown USA in the 1960s, when local residents and businesses were swept up in a pride rivaled only by the most dedicated college boosters. (COURTESY OF THE HENRY LEFEBVRE COLLECTION OF THE NEVILLE PUBLIC MUSEUM OF BROWN COUNTY)

Packers team president
Dominic Olejniczak wel-
comed Vince Lombardi and
his wife, Marie, to Green
Bay upon their arrival in
1959. (COURTESY OF THE
PRESS-GAZETTE COLLECTION
OF THE NEVILLE PUBLIC MU-
SEUM OF BROWN COUNTY)

The Packers' executive
committee that oversaw
much of the Lombardi
dynasty in Green Bay
included (back row, left
to right) Tony Canadeo,
Bernard Darling, Jerry
Atkinson, Carl Mraz, Fred
Leicht, Les Kelley, Heraly
MacDonald; (front row,
left to right) Richard Bour-
guignon, Charlie Mathys,
Dominic Olejniczak, Lee
Joannes, John Torinus,
Fred Trowbridge. (COUR-
TESY OF THE HENRY LEFEBVRE
COLLECTION OF THE NEVILLE
PUBLIC MUSEUM OF BROWN
COUNTY)

because he knew where the hell he was going," commented former halfback Tony Canadeo, who had
become a member of the Packers' board of directors. "He came to Green Bay and the board liked
him right away."

When Lombardi accepted the Packers' salary
offer of $36,000 for the dual roles of coach and gen-
eral manager—the first person to hold both roles
in the organization since Lambeau—he joked at a
farewell party in New York, "All I have to do is win
two games and Green Bay will have improved one
hundred percent."

Upon his arrival in Green Bay, Lombardi felt he
had inherited a roster filled with malcontents who
were in his opinion "a disease" that infected the entire squad—an attitude he would
eradicate during his first team meeting. "My number one job in Green Bay is doing
away with the defeatist attitude I know is here," he told his new players. "Defeatists
won't be with the club very long."

Since the club grossed only $836,000 and published a net profit of $37,300 in
1958, Lombardi had few resources available to help improve his roster. Yet he was
determined. "There's no room for sentiment. My job is to build the best team I can,"
Lombardi said. "I'll trade anybody on the team anytime if I think it will help us."

"And he wasn't kidding," assistant coach Phil Bengtson said of Lombardi's
constant effort to acquire better players, offering Paul Hornung, Bart Starr, Jim
Taylor, Jerry Kramer, Ray Nitschke, Dave Hanner, Forrest Gregg, Max McGee, and
Dan Currie as trade bait throughout most the 1959 season. Bengtson noted, "The
Packer telephone bill kept
mounting. The charges
for the month of March
equaled the team's entire
phone budget for the pre-
vious year."

Lombardi's absolute
authority to reshape the
franchise left many med-
dling members of the
team's executive commit-
tee and board of directors
restless. "Where many

From the moment Vince Lombardi arrived in Green Bay, he changed the atmosphere of the franchise, from the field to the front office. Seen here (with back to camera) on July 22, 1959, he addressed last-minute instructions to his staff (left to right): Tom Miller (dark shirt), Earl Falck (glasses), Verne Lewellen (tie), Jack Vainisi (leaning on counter), Merrill Knowlton, Ruth McKloskey, Norb Hecker, John "Red" Cochran, (Jan Marvil is obscurred by Lombardi), and Phil Bengtson. (COURTESY OF THE PRESS-GAZETTE COLLECTION OF THE NEVILLE PUBLIC MUSEUM OF BROWN COUNTY)

> **"I'll trade anybody on the team anytime if I think it will help us."**
> –HEAD COACH VINCE LOMBARDI

ladles once stirred the broth, and helped spoil it, one ladle is now stirring it and is getting somewhere," sportswriter Oliver Kuechle wrote in his *Time Out for Talk* column. "A few of the old ladles were poised and eager to dip into the broth again and gently he has had to remind them *he's the boss.*"

During training camp, Lombardi had new players arriving and departing on a daily basis. No player was safe from his wrath as he weeded out potential playboys, shirkers, and troublemakers. When Green Bay's leading pass receiver Billy Howton threatened to quit if he didn't get more money, Lombardi retorted with, "Go ahead and quit." Although Howton didn't quit, he soon found himself traded to Cleveland, joining a growing list of once familiar faces not found on Green Bay's opening-day roster. "Billy was probably one of the best pass receivers to ever play the game," end Gary Knafelc recalled. "All of us knew then, if he's getting rid of our best player, boy, this guy is serious."

On a misty and murky afternoon, the Packers opened the 1959 season against the Bears. In dramatic fashion, fullback Jim Taylor scored on a 5-yard run to give the Packers a 7–6 lead with 7:15 remaining in the game. Defensive tackle Dave Hanner then sacked Bears quarterback Ed Brown in the end zone for a safety to clinch the Packers' 9–6 victory. As the clock ticked away the final minute of regulation, the 32,150 fans crammed into New City Stadium had no idea they'd be witnessing the birth of a dynasty. When the gun went off, players hoisted their coach onto their shoulders for the first of many rides off the field. "Everybody involved was so inexperienced at it that Lombardi almost tumbled backward before grabbing [Lew] Carpenter's helmet for support," Bengtson recalled.

The Packers were the NFL's only undefeated team after three weeks, but they were unable to maintain the momentum, losing their next five contests. "Had our fast start been only an illusion?" Hornung recalled of how the promising season was disintegrating. "Was the old Pack back? These were the questions being asked in the newspapers."

Despite the losing streak, the Packers were coming of age. They finished the season with four straight wins—including a 21–0 victory over the Redskins, Green Bay's first shutout in ten years. The Packers' 7–5 record brought joy to the fans and several honors to the team, including Coach of the Year for Vince Lombardi and Rookie of the Year for receiver Boyd Dowler. "It did indeed seem like a magical transformation," Bengtson recalled, referring to the Packers winning seven games in a season for the first time since 1944. "If, that is, you were not around to see the toil and labors of July that made possible the glass slipper of December."

The success on the field in 1959 had a big impact on the team's coffers, as the Packers became a million-dollar operation for the first time. During his annual report to stockholders, Lombardi announced the franchise had made a net profit of $75,208 on total income of $1,006,914—compared with $37,905 in 1958 on a

As depicted in a 1959 Al Rainovic cartoon in the *Milwaukee Journal,* the Packers were part of a professional sports industry that was expanding into new frontiers as a result of increasing television revenues. (UWM LIBRARIES, ARCHIVES DEPARTMENT RAINOVIC COLLECTION IMAGE 457)

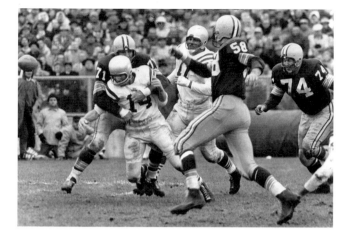

total income of $835,967. The cost for Green Bay to field a team in 1959 increased $92,503 to $875,030. The sale of radio and television rights brought in $108,000. Lombardi also told the stockholders that 22,227 season tickets had been sold in Green Bay. "I think Vince took care of the Packer money better than he took care of his own money," Canadeo said in *The Vince Lombardi Scrapbook*. "He was a real watchdog for the Packer Corporation."

■ ■ ■

The Packers played aggressive football in 1959, as illustrated by linebacker Bill Forester (71) sacking 49ers quarterback Y. A. Tittle. Dan Currie (58) and Henry Jordan (74) almost recovered the resulting fumble during the 21-20 victory. (MILWAUKEE JOURNAL SENTINEL)

The National Football League was stronger than ever as the 1950s came to a close. The league's most profitable decade to date not only benefited from seven consecutive seasons in which none of its franchises folded or relocated, but also enjoyed increased attendance eight years in a row. Across the country, the game had become great theater for the millions of television viewers who made watching football a Sunday afternoon ritual. Almost three-quarters of all American families owned a television set by the mid-fifties, and the marriage of pro football and television was witnessed by an estimated 10.8 million homes. Performed in the cathedral-like surroundings of Yankee Stadium, the NFL's 1958 championship game between the Baltimore Colts and the New York Giants was dubbed "the greatest game ever played" after Baltimore's Johnny Unitas handed the ball off to Alan Ameche for the winning touchdown in sudden-death overtime.

The championship game thriller prompted millionaires from seven cities to apply for new franchises before the start of the 1959 season in hopes of gaining acceptance in the exclusive club of NFL ownership. Rather than accept their bids, the current NFL owners urged the applicants to purchase existing teams, fearing their product would be diluted if the league expanded beyond twelve teams. They cited how boxing, pro wrestling, and roller derby had suffered serious declines in popularity after being overexposed on television. Meanwhile, no NFL team was entertaining offers. Even the Chicago Cardinals turned down six bids, including one from Texas oil tycoon Lamar Hunt, who offered to buy the perennial last-place team for $1.5 million—two and a half times the sale price of the league champion Cleveland Browns just four years earlier. "The NFL's refusal to expand left many boosters and franchise seekers discontented and ready to look elsewhere for a way to break into pro football," author Craig Coenen explained in *From Sandlots to the Super Bowl*. "The television era had elevated pro football to a meaningful national

As depicted in this illustration by *Milwaukee Journal* cartoonist Al Rainovic (left), the Packers had a renewed sense of hope entering the 1960 season. Fans were hopeful too; in July Packers ticket-office attendant Karen Marie Kaiser (right) held the last available season tickets in Green Bay before they were sold out on a permanent basis later that season. (LEFT: UWM LIBRARIES, ARCHIVES DEPARTMENT RAINOVIC COLLECTION IMAGE 366; RIGHT: COURTESY OF THE PRESS-GAZETTE COLLECTION OF THE NEVILLE PUBLIC MUSEUM OF BROWN COUNTY)

sport with seemingly unlimited potential. [NFL owners] failed to fully capitalize on pro football's rapidly expanding national market. They were soon awakened."

Of the NFL's twelve franchises, most were concentrated in the Midwest and Northeast, with the Redskins the southernmost franchise and the Rams and 49ers the only two teams west of the Mississippi River. With cities like Denver, Buffalo, and Boston void of professional football, Lamar Hunt and a group of businessmen who had been refused admittance into the autocratic NFL ownership circle chose to form their own league that would begin play in the autumn of 1960. The American Football League became their opportunity to end years of frustration by establishing an entrance fee of $100,000 per franchise and requiring only a modest $25,000 down payment.

Achieving its first objective toward survival, in June 1960 the AFL signed a broadcast agreement with ABC to televise its games in exchange for $8.5 million over five years. By packaging all of the league's games for sale to one network, each AFL team would earn more television money in its first season than any individual NFL franchise. In its inaugural season, the league drew less than $1 million in paid attendance—averaging only 16,538 fans for each of its fifty-six games—and was

swimming in a scalding bath of red ink estimated in the $4 million range. Yet it was still in a lucrative position. The AFL's innovative approach toward sharing the revenue equally among all its franchises meant it would remain a threat to the elder league the longer it survived.

NFL owners continued to ignore the prospects generated by the new league's revolutionary television contract, choosing to abide by their antiquated, individual-team television contracts of years past. But when their commissioner, Bert Bell, died from a sudden heart attack in October 1959, the league was forced to reexamine its future. After extensive deliberation, team owners named Pete Rozelle Bell's successor. From the first day he assumed the role, "Rozelle was the genius who knew how to marry the NFL to Madison Avenue and the television networks," Hornung said, describing how the new commissioner put into action his simple philosophy that the league came first.

Now any and all decisions would be made with the best interests of the entire league in mind. Rozelle was overseeing a twelve-team league with combined revenues totaling less than $20 million. He felt that if the league was to thrive, every team would need the same economic tools to create an equal opportunity—if managed properly—to compete for a championship. If the NFL was going to command the sort of television dollars awarded to the AFL, Rozelle would have to begin petitioning broadcast networks on the idea of selling his league's broadcast rights as a whole. "His background as a PR man taught him how to handle the media, which was one of his greatest assets as commissioner," Hornung said.

Still, it would be a challenge, since at the time of Bell's death professional football's television marketplace was cluttered and fragmented. The NFL had just sold the broadcast rights to its 1959 championship game for only $200,000. The clubs' individual television deals ranged from $75,000 for Green Bay to $175,000 for the New York Giants. The Browns had their own independent network. NBC owned the broadcast rights to both the Steelers and the Colts but would televise only one game per week. And CBS, which had contracts with nine teams, was threatening to stop televising some of the smaller-market teams altogether, including the Packers.

Although NFL officials claimed that the AFL's actions didn't affect them, they announced the addition of a team in Dallas for the 1960 season and a team in Minneapolis–St. Paul the following year. In addition, the Cardinals would relocate from Chicago to St. Louis in 1960. Within eighteen months, the NFL would expand into three new cities, all of which NFL owners had ignored for nearly a decade before the AFL arrived.

In Green Bay, the Packers began their second season under Lombardi with little turnover on their roster; just one veteran had retired and three others were poached in the 1960 expansion draft by Dallas. To help fans keep track of their

> "Rozelle was the genius who knew how to marry the NFL to Madison Avenue and the television networks."
>
> –HALFBACK
> PAUL HORNUNG

ABOVE: All eyes—including CBS television cameras—were on Green Bay when the 1960 season opened as America became captivated by Vince Lombardi's ability to mold the Packers into winners. (COURTESY OF TOM PIGEON COLLECTION)

ABOVE, RIGHT: The anchor of Vince Lombardi's gridiron attack was the Packers' offensive line, featuring (left to right) tackle Norm Masters, guard Jerry Kramer, center Jim Ringo, tackle Forrest Gregg, guard Fred "Fuzzy" Thurston, and tackle Bob Skoronski. (MILWAUKEE JOURNAL SENTINEL)

favorite players for the upcoming season, *Green Bay Press-Gazette* sportswriter Art Daley published the Packers' first team yearbook. His idea of doing an annual encyclopedia of pictures, player biographies, and statistics surfaced in the mid-fifties but didn't come to fruition until Lombardi gave his blessing. Lombardi hoped it would spark season-ticket sales—which it did, according to *Milwaukee Journal* sportswriter Chuck Johnson, who reported: "For the four league games played in Green Bay in 1960, City Stadium was sold out for its 32,150 seating capacity almost two months before the season opened."

The frenzy over tickets didn't diminish despite Green Bay's regular-season opening-day loss to the Bears. Lombardi's men reversed the slide with four straight wins, but after losing three of their next four games, the Packers were tied for first place with a modest 5–4 record and their three final games scheduled on the road. As the Packers were about to head to Chicago, they were forced to prepare for the Bears with heavy hearts. The organization had lost personnel director Jack Vainisi, who died the Sunday after Thanksgiving of a heart attack at the age of thirty-three. "[Vainisi] had suffered through nine losing seasons and then died before he could witness the wonder of a team that he, almost as much as the famed Lombardi, had built," author David Maraniss noted in *When Pride Still Mattered*.

The Packers responded by humiliating the Bears, shutting down the 49ers in San Francisco, and trouncing the Rams in Los Angeles to finish the regular season with an 8–4 record. Upon the team's return from the West Coast, a crowd of more than 10,000 ecstatic fans and the Lumberjack Band greeted the players at Green Bay's Austin Straubel Airport. The Packers had edged out the 49ers and Lions for the Western Conference crown, and Green Bay was returning to the NFL championship game for the first time in fifteen years. The upstart Packers would go nose to nose against a grizzled group from Philadelphia. "Their squad was an honorable assemblage of veterans," Bengtson said of the 10–2 Eagles team.

ABOVE: The Packers' ability to execute Lombardi's Power Sweep allowed halfback Paul Hornung (5) to take the handoff from quarterback Bart Starr (15) and run up the alley created by Jerry Kramer (64), Jim Taylor (31), Fred "Fuzzy" Thurston (63), and Forrest Gregg (75). (COURTESY OF GREEN BAY PRESS-GAZETTE FROM TOM PIGEON COLLECTION)

ABOVE, RIGHT: Fullback Jim Taylor (31) was stopped short of the goal line, preventing the Packers from securing their first NFL title since 1944 in a 17-13 loss to the Philadelphia Eagles. (COURTESY OF TOM PIGEON COLLECTION)

Philadelphia's Franklin Field hosted the NFL's twenty-eighth championship game, and the 67,325 fans who paid $8 and $10 a ticket witnessed a gridiron classic. Early on, the Eagles overcame deficits of 6–0 and 13–10 before taking a late 17–13 lead into the game's final seconds. "With time for only one play, [quarterback Bart] Starr found [fullback Jim] Taylor open to his left and connected," Bengtson recalled. "Jimmy lowered his head and charged. But at the nine, tireless old pro Chuck Bednarik hit him with a standing bear-hug tackle—two titans slamming together on the muddy field and wrestling until they fell."

As Bednarik squatted on Taylor, the game clock expired. The Packers had fallen 8 yards short of winning their first NFL championship under Lombardi. Despite the final score, Green Bay had whipped the Eagles from a statistical standpoint—401 yards to Philadelphia's 296, a 22–13 edge in first downs, and a three-to-one advantage in takeaways. Defensive back Jesse Whittenton recalled, "[Lombardi] told us we hadn't been beaten; we had just run out of time."

The Packers found little comfort in the record loser's share of $3,105.14 each of them would receive after the championship game generated a gross gate of $747,876 in receipts. "We were in the dressing room after the game with tears in our eyes," center Jim Ringo said afterward. "Before Vince let the press in, he said, '*This* is the last time anything like this will happen to us. After today we will be world champions.'"

• • •

With success comes attention. Following the 1960 championship game, Green Bay, Wisconsin, became the focus of the football world once again. The offseason was filled with speculation Lombardi would return to New York as the Giants' new head coach. "Vince wanted to take the Giant job," team president Dominic Olejniczak later told reporter Tom Dowling of *The Washingtonian*. "The executive committee turned him down, and he stayed on."

The Packers rewarded Lombardi with a new five-year contract and a raise. Afterward, he told the executive committee, "I've got news for you," regarding the 1961 NFL championship game. "If I win this thing this year, I want it in Green Bay."

Further exerting his influence over the franchise, Lombardi decided the Packers needed to update their look. The team had utilized a few different official logos, but none of them generated the recognition he felt they would achieve with an updated, sleek symbol of excellence. Lombardi approached Green Bay's equipment manager, Gerald "Dad" Braisher, to oversee the design of the team's new logo, and soon after the "G" was placed on the Packers' yellow helmets. It was the first and only monogram to appear on the team's headgear and would become one of the most recognizable symbols in professional football.

Helmet logos were just the latest innovation football teams were using to distinguish themselves on television. Back in 1957 the NFL had instituted the rule that visiting teams would always wear white uniforms to differentiate from home teams. Television's growing influence over the sport was obvious, and it was motivated by the potential of nearly infinite profits still to be achieved. NFL commissioner Pete Rozelle, using the AFL's successful business model that all of a league's teams would be stronger if the television revenue were shared among them equally, looked to persuade his league's major-market owners—the Mara family in New York, George Halas in Chicago, and Dan Reeves in Los Angeles—that their individual teams' short-term sacrifices would pay long-term dividends. Only if all of the NFL's owners agreed to share their television revenue would the league enjoy parity and financial stability. After much deliberation, the owners allowed Rozelle to negotiate the broadcast deals on behalf of all the NFL teams in January 1961. The commissioner first brokered a two-year contract with NBC for radio and television rights to the championship game for $1,230,000—$615,000 annually. Later that year, Rozelle hustled to get federal legislation passed allowing all sports leagues—professional

During training camp in 1961, Vince Lombardi was as determined as ever to direct the Packers to a championship, here providing clear instructions to tight end Ron Kramer (88). (MILWAUKEE JOURNAL SENTINEL)

and collegiate—to negotiate collectively on broadcast contracts, and on September 30, 1961, President John F. Kennedy signed Public Law 87-331, the Sports Broadcasting bill, into the books. "The single network contract legislation meant that teams couldn't negotiate independently; it was the perfect blend of socialism and capitalism and it ensured their mutual interest," according to author Phil Schaaf in *Sports, Inc.* "Simply put, this meant that broadcast income would rise dramatically as leagues negotiated national, not regional, deals."

> "If there was any danger of our being cocky, I think the Eagles took care of that."
>
> —HEAD COACH
> VINCE LOMBARDI

The NFL's league-first negotiating philosophy paid immediate dividends. "The whole thing was equalizing the competition on the field," Rozelle said of the NFL's exemption from antitrust statutes that created the financial structure for a team from Green Bay to compete with the New York Giants. "The sharing of income gave everyone the tools, and the money, to compete equally."

On January 10, 1962, CBS, already holding broadcast-rights contracts with several individual teams, paid $4.65 million per year—almost $360,000 per team—for the right to broadcast all of the NFL's 1962 and 1963 regular-season games—more than double what the AFL earned from ABC. Then in 1964 CBS added two more years to its deal at $14.1 million per season and an additional $1.8 million for each championship game. In just three years each NFL club had nearly tripled its television income from about $360,000 to more than $1 million. No team would benefit more from the NFL's revenue-sharing policy and television contract extravaganza than the Packers. In fact, Lombardi claimed years later, "The TV package deal probably saved Green Bay."

But back in the autumn of 1961, television was the furthest thing from Vince Lombardi's mind. He was determined to let nothing prevent the Packers from winning the NFL championship that season. "If there was any danger of our being cocky, I think the Eagles took care of that," he told reporters before Green Bay stumbled in its opening-game upset at the hands of the Detroit Lions.

The Packers bounced right back, posting six straight victories despite having to reshuffle their lineup on a weekly basis because of injuries and military obligations. "First-stringers [Paul] Hornung, [Boyd] Dowler, and [Ray] Nitschke were marching down the field for us one week and for the U.S. Army the next," Bengtson remembered. "Vince, meanwhile, managed to keep a semblance of cohesion as we went out to do battle every Sunday."

Finishing with an 11–3 record, Green Bay clinched the Western Division title and was about to host its first NFL championship game. The entire community rallied behind the team, and by the time the Eastern Division champion New York Giants arrived, the city was plastered with signs on storefront windows, billboards, hotel lobbies, car bumpers, and telephone poles proclaiming Green Bay as "Title-town USA."

After claiming their second straight Western Division title with a 20–17 victory over the New York Giants, the Packers lifted Vince Lombardi onto their shoulders and carried him off the Milwaukee County Stadium field. (MILWAUKEE JOURNAL SENTINEL)

In anticipation of the Packers hosting the 1961 NFL championship game, euphoric Green Bay residents decorated the entire town in a green and gold Titletown USA frenzy. (WHI IMAGE ID 81761)

On December 31 temperatures hovered around twenty-one degrees at kickoff as a brisk ten-mile-per-hour wind raced through the record crowd of 39,029 patrons jammed into Green Bay's New City Stadium. "It was a cold day," defensive end Willie Davis remembered. "I think that the whole team was focused. Nothing was going to stand in the way of our beating the New York Giants on that day—the weather, an injury, or anything."

The team's focus was a product of Lombardi's unbridled zeal leading up to kick-off. "He built it up so the thing was you were defending the pride of Green Bay as much as you were the pride of the Packers," Davis said of the coach's David-versus-Goliath motivational technique. "It was big ol' New York against li'l ol' Green Bay. And we all knew how much it meant to him personally."

After a scoreless first quarter, the Packers buried the Giants under 24 unanswered second-quarter points. Paul Hornung, whose 6-yard run started the scoring, wasn't even supposed to be in uniform that day—at least not in a Packers' green and gold one. The circumstances had prompted Lombardi to request a favor. Packers' trainer Domenic Gentile remembered being in the room when Lombardi made the call to President Kennedy's private White House line: "I listened as Lombardi

The Packers' convincing 37–0 victory over the Giants in Green Bay showcased a defense that allowed only six first downs all afternoon and triggered interceptions by Herb Adderley, Hank Gremminger, and Ray Nitschke (66). (COURTESY OF GREEN BAY PRESS-GAZETTE FROM TOM PIGEON COLLECTION)

explained to the president of the United States that he needed Private Paul Hornung's services for the NFL championship game."

When President Kennedy told Lombardi that "Paul Hornung isn't going to win the war on Sunday, but the football fans of this country deserve the two best teams on the field that day," the Packers halfback was on a plane back to Green Bay even before the colonel could deliver the furlough pass.

While on leave that afternoon, Hornung tied a playoff record with 19 points. The Packers battered New York into submission with a beautiful exhibition of Lombardi-style football, amassing four touchdowns and three field goals against the NFL's top defensive team in a 37–0 victory. The Green Bay defense, led by Willie Davis and Ray Nitschke, intercepted four passes, recovered one fumble, and held New York to six first downs and 130 total yards, including just 31 on the ground. On offense, the Packers finished with 345 total yards while dominating the line of scrimmage. "Our offensive line was devastating," Davis recalled. "The whole five of [Forrest] Gregg, [Jerry] Kramer, [Jim] Ringo, Fuzzy [Thurston], and Bob Skoronski, they were just sensational. And they blocked the New York Giants probably unlike they'd ever blocked them before."

The small-town team that started on a hunch and a handout forty-two years earlier was now an NFL champion again after their epic defeat of the metropolitan Giants. Lombardi had won his first NFL championship as a head coach with the same core group of men that he had addressed at his first Packers team meeting. "Nine of the guys on our offensive starting team in the championship game also started when we lost our tenth game in 1958," center Jim Ringo recounted. "Vince made a lot of boys into men."

> "Vince made a lot of boys into men."
> —CENTER JIM RINGO

After the game, Lombardi climbed onto a locker room bench and raised his arms for attention. Dozens of reporters crowded around him alongside the players and coaches as the Packers coach addressed his team with a sense of pride he rarely shared: "You're the greatest team in the National Football League today. And I *mean* it."

Meanwhile, the New City Stadium crowd outside refused to go home, even as the afternoon temperatures plunged. Chants of "Titletown USA" echoed through the bowl as fans began straddling the crossbars. They swayed back and forth until the uprights of the goalposts bent, sagged, and tore off ten feet above the ground. "It was a two-thousand-dollar expenditure that would become an annual budget item," Bengtson remarked.

Sacrificing the goalposts was a small price to pay in light of the Packers' victory, especially when factoring in that the 1961 NFL championship game was the first to earn a million-dollar gate with gross receipts, which included radio and television rights, totaling $1,013,792. With an estimated 55 million fans watching the game at home on television, the record audience proved the exclusive $9.3 million two-year contract CBS signed with the NFL earlier that year, which placed more than $664,000 into each team's coffer, was a wise investment.

At the team stockholders' meeting the following spring, Lombardi reported that the club cleared a net profit of $175,075 in 1961—the largest in team history and more than 50 percent above 1960—despite the team's operating income rising to $1.5 million. When the net profits were added to the club's accumulated surplus, the NFL champion Packers now had $573,141 in the bank. "Lombardi probably did not have too much experience in running an organization before he came to Green Bay," team assistant Tom Miller said in *The Vince Lombardi Scrapbook*. "But he had a natural organizational ability. After a while, we had the best run organization in all of sports."

● ● ●

Although pro football was generating millions of dollars in profits for its owners, the players had yet to reap any of the financial benefits. The majority of stars and journeymen who were grappling on the NFL gridirons still played football for the love of the sport, supplementing their modest salaries with offseason jobs to pay the rest of their bills. Before the days of high-profile agents securing staggering signing bonuses and long-term deals, most players were left to hammer out their own deals with their respective teams. For those on the Packers' roster, they had to negotiate with the team's coach and general manager. "There was no way I could talk contract with Lombardi," center Jim Ringo remarked. "Hell, I'd go in looking

> "[Lombardi] had a natural organizational ability. After a while, we had the best run organization in all of sports."
>
> —TEAM ASSISTANT TOM MILLER

for a thousand-dollar raise, and by the time he got done talking to me, even though I went to the Pro Bowl, even though we were a championship team, I felt as if I should pay him for the privilege of playing at Green Bay."

In 1962 the Packers conquered their first ten opponents leading up to their annual Thanksgiving contest against the Lions. They had dominated their opponents, outscoring them 309–74, but "were tired, strained, and in need of rest," Bengtson recalled. "Some of our players were ten or fifteen pounds under playing weight."

From the game's opening kickoff, the Packers found themselves under assault by a hostile Detroit squad that sacked quarterback Bart Starr eleven times as one Green Bay player after another limped off the field dazed and bloodied. They fought back from their 23–0 halftime deficit, but it wasn't enough. "The momentary lapse, while embarrassing, was another step in our character-building," Bengtson said of the 26–14 loss that would become Green Bay's only blemish on an otherwise near perfect 13–1 season.

Although the Lions were the superior team that afternoon, "the character of our team surfaced," quarterback Bart Starr said. The Packers had outscored Detroit 14–0 in the fourth quarter. "As we walked off the field, I *knew* we would destroy our next opponent."

The following week, the Packers walloped the Rams, 41–10, en route to repeating as Western Division champions. The NFL's title game would be a rematch against the Giants in New York. "It seemed that both teams played through the season just to get it over with and get back at one another again," linebacker Ray Nitschke said of the team's growing rivalry. "We were defending champions, and this was a sort of homecoming for coach Lombardi."

The Packers' coach had brought his football juggernaut into his hometown to defend Green Bay's NFL championship against a team with a definite chip on its shoulder. "The Giants were playing angry. They were on a mission," sportswriter Bud Lea wrote in *Magnificent Seven*. "They wanted to show their fans and the world that what happened to them a year ago in Green Bay had been a 37–0 fluke. For the two weeks before the championship game, there was a sign hanging prominently in the Giants' locker room. It had no words, just a number: 37. The numerals were two feet high."

While the Giants focused on revenge, the rest of the country was fixated on the football dynasty materializing in Green Bay. Winning games with more than might and mastery on the field, the Packers players were a cast of colorful characters that brought romance to the game. Bart Starr, Jim Taylor, Paul Hornung, Ray Nitschke, Herb Adderley, Willie Davis, Forrest Gregg, Jerry Kramer, Fuzzy Thurston, Boyd Dowler, Henry Jordan, and Willie Wood all became household names as hundreds of thousands of rabbit-eared black-and-white televisions tuned in to see Lombardi's

By 1962 the Packers' success was creating an onslaught of media and endorsement requests for players and coaches alike. As the NFL's 1961 Most Valuable Player, Paul Hornung (right) was interviewed alongside Chicago Bears tight end and NFL Rookie of the Year Mike Ditka at Green Bay television station WBAY. (COURTESY OF THE HENRY LEFEBVRE COLLECTION OF THE NEVILLE PUBLIC MUSEUM OF BROWN COUNTY)

At the height of the Cold War, Bart Starr, Jim Taylor, and Max McGee volunteered to help move twenty-seven tons of emergency civil defense supplies into community fallout shelters in nine downtown Green Bay buildings. (COURTESY OF THE PRESS-GAZETTE COLLECTION OF THE NEVILLE PUBLIC MUSEUM OF BROWN COUNTY)

Vince Lombardi was all smiles while participating alongside his cohost, Don Hutson, during the thirteen-week run of *The Vince Lombardi Show,* which featured analytical previews and postscripts of the previous week's games. The new series, sponsored by Old Milwaukee Beer of the Joseph Schlitz Brewing Company, was carried throughout the state of Wisconsin and in parts of Iowa and Minnesota. (MILWAUKEE JOURNAL SENTINEL)

In 1962 even baseball's Milwaukee Braves got caught up in the excitement of the Packers, sponsoring a billboard in Green Bay and another two dozen all over Wisconsin. (FROM THE GREEN BAY PRESS-GAZETTE ARCHIVES, REPRINTED BY PERMISSION)

men chase perfection. But it would be their coach whose influence transcended professional football. "You have to remember that our teams of that time came along just as television was bringing pro football into the limelight," Starr recalled. "That helped make him the legend he became, but it also worked the other way. His mystique and the Packers' great success helped build the game's image, as well."

After Lombardi appeared on the cover of *Time* magazine in December, his cultural currency rose above the gridirons of Green Bay. He was no longer just a successful coach known around the National Football League for his fiery oratory. He had become a national symbol for those who believed traditional America was under assault from a growing counterculture, fueled by civil rights and antiwar protestors.

During an era of confusion and growing discontent in America, the Packers were striving toward an easily understood goal with a clear result: either victory or defeat. For the millions of Americans crouched around their magic tubes on Sunday afternoons, Lombardi symbolized such traditional qualities as teamwork, the need to rise above adversity, and a sense of purpose. Lombardi biographer Robert W. Wells remarked, "One commentator in a highbrow journal called him the legitimate folk hero of the quiet mass movement—a movement that 'tells us much about our sense of what we have lost and our sense of what we need.'"

Lombardi had built his Packers into winners. "When the writers and commentators began making [the team's reputation] the main topic of their stories and pregame shows," Bengtson recalled, it "became almost a psychological weapon."

The Packers' swagger, described by CBS telecaster Ray Scott as "Here we are; try to stop us," couldn't have been more evident when they took the field in front of 64,892 dedicated New Yorkers for the 1962 NFL championship game. As the thermometer stood at a mere seventeen degrees above zero, a swirling storm of newspapers and trash whipped across the field at forty miles per hour. "The wind was so ferocious in Yankee Stadium that I remember they had those old wooden benches on the sidelines that looked like something from a high school locker room," offensive guard Jerry Kramer remembered. "The wind was blowing so hard that it actually blew the benches over at halftime and onto the field."

The bitter weather conditions made it tough for either team to move the ball on offense. The field had frozen over by the end of the first quarter, handcuffing the aerial acrobatics of Giants quarterback Y. A. Tittle, who had set a league record that year for throwing thirty-three touchdown passes. The Packers led 10–0 at halftime on fullback Jim Taylor's touchdown run and a Jerry Kramer field goal. "Our philosophy was move the chains, first down, first down, and they can't score when we got the ball," Taylor said of the Packers' grind-it-out running attack.

When the Giants blocked a punt in the end zone and recovered it for a touchdown, it was the only score the Packers allowed all day. Kramer added two more

> "Nobody ever called us 'Bushville, USA' anymore. From then on it was 'Titletown USA.'"
> —LINEBACKER RAY NITSCHKE

The 1962 Packers repeated as NFL champions after defeating the Giants 16–7 at Yankee Stadium behind Jim Taylor's (31) brutal running and offensive lineman Bob Skoronski's (76) blocking. (COURTESY OF TOM PIGEON COLLECTION)

field goals, with the last one late in the fourth quarter. "Probably the biggest moment in my career," he said of sealing the 16–7 victory. "All the guys were jumping on me. For an offensive guard, that doesn't happen."

"It's got to give you a little extra kick for the smallest town in major league sports to knock off the biggest city in the nation," said the game's Most Valuable Player, Ray Nitschke, of how the entire community of Green Bay benefited from the Packers' second consecutive NFL championship. "Nobody ever called us 'Bushville, USA' anymore. From then on it was 'Titletown USA.'"

After it was announced that the game's total gross receipts reached $1,243,110 and each Packer would receive a record winner's share of $5,888.57, defensive tackle Henry Jordan summed up his teammates' priorities: "We can hold our heads high, and our wives can go shopping."

Even as the champagne flowed on the turbulent plane ride back to Green Bay, "there remained, however, a juicy plum we wanted to pick: the first NFL triple crown," Bengtson recalled. Not since the '29–'31 Packers had an NFL team won three championships in a row, and, more importantly, nobody had accomplished it in the modern history of the league. "Without invoking the 'no-hitter jinx' of talking about it, we all began thinking ahead," Bengtson admitted. "Unfortunately, the jinx was already on the third crown; a few shocks awaited the Green Bay Packers."

That number 15 jersey was a familiar sight for fans attending the Wisconsin Badgers/Minnesota Gophers college basketball game at Milwaukee Arena on Sunday, February 10, 1963, as Bart Starr lined up behind center for some tomfoolery while playing an exhibition hoops game against the Detroit Lions. (MILWAUKEE JOURNAL SENTINEL)

• • •

Before the 1963 season kicked off, the Packers—despite shattering season-ticket sales and posting an all-time net profit to date of $255,501 the previous year—were under siege from forces that they couldn't have predicted. After a two-year investigation, NFL commissioner Pete Rozelle announced that halfback Paul Hornung, along with the Lions' Alex Karras, would be suspended from the league after it was determined the two had placed bets, ranging from $50 to $200, on a number of NFL games. But even without his star halfback, Lombardi was confident Green Bay could win a third consecutive championship. "Most teams would have been somewhat discouraged over the prospect of playing an entire season without one of their most valuable assets," quarterback Bart Starr said. "We weren't like most teams."

From the moment training camp started, Lombardi challenged his players to overcome Hornung's absence, drilling his players while driving himself and his staff even harder. The Packers coaches worked every night except Thursday as putting in fifteen-hour workdays became routine. "Someone once figured out, on an hourly basis during the season, a Green Bay coach earns less than a Green Bay garbage man," offensive guard Jerry Kramer joked.

After dropping a 10–3 decision to the Bears on opening day, Green Bay went on to dominate its next eight opponents, despite Starr being injured for almost half the season. When the 8–1 Packers faced the 8–1 Bears in Chicago, Green Bay was once again shut down, losing 26–7. After demolishing the 49ers, the Packers looked to make up ground in the standings against Detroit. Dating back to 1951, the Lions annually hosted the Packers on Thanksgiving. The tradition began because Detroit wanted to play a team they could beat, which would draw well on television. The Lions won seven of the first eight holiday contests before Lombardi arrived. But after the Packers' debacle in 1962, Lombardi lobbied NFL commissioner Pete Rozelle to schedule other teams against Detroit for the Turkey Day game. Although the league decided that all of its teams would rotate through Detroit on Thanksgiving, with the Packers not returning to Detroit on Thanksgiving until 1984, that didn't help the 1963 squad. They battled to a 13–13 stalemate with the Lions, further jeopardizing any chance of repeating as NFL champs.

> ## "Someone once figured out . . . a Green Bay coach earns less than a Green Bay garbage man."
> –OFFENSIVE GUARD JERRY KRAMER

The Packers, including (left to right) Jesse Whittenton, Hank Gremminger, Herb Adderley, and Willie Wood, were all smiles heading into the 1963 season. (COURTESY OF TOM PIGEON COLLECTION)

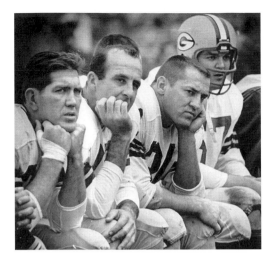

The Packers finished the season with road wins against the Rams and 49ers, but as impressive as their 11–2–1 record was, their two losses against the loathed Bears, who finished 11–1–2, left them a half-game short of the Western Division crown. "The frustration of finishing second to the Bears in 1963, despite their sterling record, lingered for months with many of the players and our coaches," quarterback Bart Starr revealed.

Despite falling short of their third straight championship, the Packers continued posting a profit on the corporate ledger. At the team's annual stockholders' meeting the following May, Lombardi announced the 1963 Packers had generated less revenue, spent more, and made less than in 1962. He disclosed a profit of $149,045, with income of $1,792,497 and expenses of $1,643,452 and compared those figures with 1962's, which were $255,501 profit, $1,831,195 income, and $1,575,658 expenses. With its publicly released profit-and-loss statements, Green Bay was proving how lucrative pro franchises had become, which Lombardi downplayed: "With television income up for 1964, and with competition from the American Football League, it is becoming an increasing problem in talking [contracts] with players."

The mood on the bench during a 26–7 loss to the Bears at Wrigley Field summed up the team's 1963 season, leaving (left to right) Lew Carpenter, Max McGee, Jim Taylor, and Dan Grimm little to cheer about. (MILWAUKEE JOURNAL SENTINEL)

Vince Lombardi had little to say to his players, including Jim Ringo (51), Herb Adderley (26), Dave Robinson (89), Dan Grimm (67), and Bill Forester (71), after the Packers failed to make the NFL championship game despite posting an impressive 11–2–1 record in 1963. (MILWAUKEE JOURNAL SENTINEL)

Since the team's expenses nearly doubled from 1959 through 1963, Lombardi was quick to manage the crowd's expectations: "At the moment we have a solid picture," he told them. "But things can fluctuate. If we aren't contenders we could be down financially." Lombardi knew that the cost of recapturing the NFL championship was about to get a lot more expensive.

■   ■   ■

By 1964 the prosperous business of professional football had gained the attention of Wall Street, while teams' annual payrolls continued to rise, reaching around $1,115,000 per team. Every banker, broker, and self-made millionaire wanted to buy into the NFL, especially after a *Fortune* magazine article noted that the NFL's fourteen franchises had grossed a collective $18 million at the gate and an additional $16 million from television in the past year alone. While ticket prices hovered around $4.50 per game, the $75,000 per minute the NFL's broadcasters demanded from advertisers earned pro football the highest advertising rates in daytime television. It was a price companies were willing to pay to reach the ever-expanding pro football audience. Football's unprecedented growth and popularity were a result of NFL commissioner Pete Rozelle's creative marketing of the game, which included the eventual formation of NFL Films to produce a weekly highlight program and NFL Properties to ensure all fourteen teams had high-quality hats, shirts, and other team memorabilia available. "Today we take for granted the fans that proudly wear their favorite team's logo and colors," author Don Gulbrandsen remarked in *Green Bay Packers: The Complete Illustrated History*. "But it's easy to appreciate Rozelle's genius when you think of those people as millions of walking billboards for the NFL and its franchises."

When the NFL began entertaining offers on its new television contract in 1964, all three networks were willing to do whatever it took to secure the league's lucrative broadcast rights. "I remember I sat down at the table and there were three envelopes in front of me, each holding a bid from the networks," NFL commissioner

During the 1960s the NFL capitalized on its growing popularity by developing a creative marketing and merchandizing bonanza that included licensing players' likenesses on numerous products, including soda bottle caps. (WHI IMAGE ID 87352, 87357, 87356)

TOP: Vince Lombardi was known for being ruthless with drills during the Packers' annual training camp, often explaining firsthand the proper techniques. During 1964's camp, he prepared to level a forearm at aide Tom Fears (second from left) while assistants Norb Hecker (left) and John "Red" Cochran watched as Bob Skoronski (76, far right) listened. Twelfth-round draft pick Dwaine Bean (48) did not make the squad. (MILWAUKEE JOURNAL SENTINEL)

CENTER: A busload of Packers headed back to St. Norbert College after an intense afternoon scrimmage at Green Bay. In the foreground is Jerry Norton; Forrest Gregg and Henry Jordan are seated at the left; and Dave Hanner occupies the other side. Not shown is the driver: tackle Willie Davis. (MILWAUKEE JOURNAL SENTINEL)

BOTTOM: It wasn't all work and sweat at the Packers' training camp. Engaged in a cribbage game were (seated, left to right) Paul Hornung, Ron Kramer, Max McGee, and Jerry Kramer, while Fred "Fuzzy" Thurston (standing at left) and Jerry Norton (in print shirt) watched. (MILWAUKEE JOURNAL SENTINEL)

Pete Rozelle told *Sport* magazine in 1964. "I shuffled them, then opened the top one, which was from NBC. I called the bid out aloud; it was around $10.8 million per year, which was six million above the old contract. The next envelope was ABC's. When I called out their bid, approximately $13 million for a year, I figured that's it, they're the winners. Then I opened the CBS envelope, and there it was—$28.2 million for two years. What a feeling!"

The CBS bid had more than tripled what the network had been paying for the rights to the previous two seasons. When Rozelle accepted the offer, the new regular-season contract ensured no team would lose money. Each franchise was estimated to earn almost $1 million a year from the deal, a significant increase from the annual $365,000 the clubs had each been earning and more than ten times more lucrative than what any team had earned in television revenue under Bert Bell just five years earlier. Three months later, CBS secured the broadcast rights to the 1964 and 1965 NFL championship games for $1.8 million per game, more than double what NBC had paid to broadcast the 1963 championship game.

When NBC lost the broadcast rights to the NFL's championship game, the network agreed to televise the AFL, paying the league $36 million over five years, beginning with the 1965 season. Each of the eight teams would earn an approximate $900,000 per year in television revenue, a substantial increase from the $261,000 each had earned from ABC on an annual basis. In the space of seven days in late January 1964, television had committed more than $64 million to the game of professional football.

Long lines formed outside Milwaukee County Stadium when the Packers put a limited number of league-game tickets on sale in August 1964. Within hours, the tickets were sold out. (MILWAUKEE JOURNAL SENTINEL)

A 1964 Harris Poll supported what the television networks had invested in. Professional football had vaulted over baseball as the favorite sport among American sports fans. With its ever-expanding audience reaching an estimated 21 million viewers every week, the Sunday afternoon football game became a fixture in households nationwide.

In Green Bay, Vince Lombardi was focused and uncompromising in his quest for a third NFL championship in four years. The Packers won their season opener against the Bears 23–12 on two Bart Starr touchdown passes and three Paul Hornung field goals. But soon the toll of Hornung's yearlong suspension from the game would be exposed, as Green Bay lost three of their first six games by a total of 5 points. Their 24–23 loss to the Vikings was a result of Hornung missing a crucial extra point, the difference between a tie and a defeat. In the season's second game, the Packers lost 21–20 to the Colts, and they also fell short in the rematch, 24–21, after Hornung missed five field goal attempts. Assistant coach Phil Bengtson explained, "A different outcome in those two games would have given us a record equal to theirs, and our big-game mentality would have carried us the rest of the way."

The Packers' disappointing 3–4 start "gave you the sense of reality that you're not invincible, that you're not unbeatable," fullback Jim Taylor explained. Although the Packers rallied late in the season to finish second in the Western Division with an 8–5–1 record, the 1964 Green Bay squad failed to execute when it counted—including Paul Hornung, who despite scoring 107 points converted only twelve of

Former president Dwight Eisenhower visited with Vince Lombardi and members of the Green Bay Packers after attending a September 1964 dedication ceremony at Green Bay's National Railroad Museum for the locomotive that pulled his train in England during World War II (COURTESY OF DWIGHT D. EISENHOWER PRESIDENTIAL LIBRARY)

thirty-eight field goal attempts that year. "We didn't make the big play at the big moment," Bengtson recalled. "We didn't score on twenty-two occasions when we were inside the thirty-five-yard line, sometimes going two or three drives without scoring a point."

As soon as the season ended, Lombardi knew what it would take to reclaim the NFL championship: "The difference [between a good coach and an average coach] is knowing what you want, and knowing what the end is supposed to look like. If a coach doesn't know what the end is supposed to look like, he won't know it when he sees it."

• • •

As the 1965 season approached, one of Green Bay's most polarizing figures was finding his place in history. "It seemed the more successful Lombardi and the Packers became, [Curly] Lambeau became just another fan and seemingly no longer the subject of resentment," Lambeau biographer David Zimmerman wrote. "Even the oldest of Packer fans now saw the elderly Lambeau as the patriarch of the Packers. The venerable representative of a bygone era."

When Lambeau died of a heart attack in Sturgeon Bay at the age of sixty-seven on June 1, 1965, he was recognized with fondness as one of the NFL's true pioneers. "The city of Green Bay and the state of Wisconsin will have to be eternally grateful to Curly, because we would not have professional football were it not for his untiring efforts and personal sacrifices," team president Dominic Olejniczak expressed to reporters.

On the day after Lambeau's death, the Pro Football Hall of Fame in Canton, Ohio, hung its NFL flag at half-staff in his honor as gridirons across the country celebrated his legacy. In Green Bay, the city and team rechristened New City Stadium as Lambeau Field a week before the 1965 season started. *Milwaukee Journal* sportswriter Oliver Kuechle noted, "Few men anywhere have ever done as much for their hometown as Lambeau for his."

The Packers entered the 1965 season healthier than ever, having posted a net profit of $404,730 in 1964, the largest in team history and more than double the previous season's profits of $149,045. When the team assembled at St. Norbert College for training camp in August, quarterback Bart Starr recalled, "After two winning but less-than-stellar campaigns in 1963 and 1964, coach Lombardi returned more energized than ever."

During their season opener in Pittsburgh, the Packers found themselves behind, 9–7, at halftime. With their lone score coming from defensive back Herb Adderley's touchdown on a 34-yard interception return, Lombardi was disgusted with his

Afraid spies for other teams might be watching, Vince Lombardi made it a common practice for his players, regardless of stature, to wear different uniform numbers during practice—including Ray Nitschke (71), Willie Wood (40), and Ron Kostelnik (63), seen here during calisthenics. (MILWAUKEE JOURNAL SENTINEL)

squad's slow start: "So far this season the defense is doing a fine job—they've even scored six of our seven points. It's about time the offense returned the favor." The insult worked, as Hornung, Taylor, and the rest of the backfield rushed for 134 yards and the Packers scored 34 unanswered second-half points in the 41–9 victory.

Green Bay went on to win six consecutive victories to start the season. Meanwhile, Lombardi tried extinguishing rumors he was leaving to coach the new Atlanta Falcons expansion franchise at the end of the season. "I'm very happy to stay in Green Bay," he told the prying press, stating that his contract had been extended through 1973. "This is our home. This is where our friends are and this is where my job is."

After the Packers dropped consecutive losses to the Bears and Lions, they finished strong, and their 10–3–1 record placed them in a tie with Baltimore for the Western Division crown. To determine who would face the Cleveland Browns for the NFL championship, the Packers and Colts met in a playoff game on December 26 in Green Bay. "The reporters were asking us how difficult it was going to be to beat the Colts three times in one year," linebacker Dave Robinson recalled. "Lombardi said, 'If you're better than they are, you can beat them ten times in one year.' We thought, 'He's right. Let's beat them and get out of here.'"

Lombardi made sure the offense always wore dark jerseys and the defense wore white. Seen here at training camp are Herb Adderley (45), Dennis Claridge (8 on sleeve), Lionel Aldridge (78), Lee Roy Caffey (66), Bob Jeter (9 on white jersey), Paul Hornung (6 on dark jersey), Steve Wright (58), Dan Grimm (4 on dark jersey), and Lloyd Voss (51). (MILWAUKEE JOURNAL SENTINEL)

The 1965 Packers defense was anchored by Lionel Aldridge (82), Henry Jordan (74), Ron Kostelnik (77), and Willie Davis (87), along with Ray Nitschke (66), Tom Brown (40), and Herb Adderley (26, behind Davis). (MILWAUKEE JOURNAL SENTINEL)

The Colts were without their injured star quarterback, Johnny Unitas. Green Bay lost its field general, Bart Starr, to a rib injury only twenty-one seconds into the game, which forced reliable backup Zeke Bratkowski to lead the Packers. Baltimore held a 10–0 lead at halftime, but Paul Hornung scored on a one-yard run in the third quarter to cut the deficit. With time running out in regulation, Packers placekicker Don Chandler kicked a 22-yard field goal, which the Colts disputed, saying it had veered wide right, high above the upright. As Chandler shook his head in desperation, the referee underneath the goalpost raised his arms high and without hesitation as the ball crossed overhead, confirming that the Packers had tied the score at 10. "The Colts can say what they want," end Bob Long exclaimed. "The ref was standing right underneath the goal post when the ball went over."

To start the sudden-death overtime period, the Colts won the toss, but they soon found their drive stalled by the Packers' smothering defense. On Green Bay's next possession, Chandler drilled a 25-yard field goal to win the game, sending the Packers back to the NFL championship game. But the controversy surrounding his earlier kick still loomed. Although it didn't change the outcome of the game for the Colts, the NFL decided to lengthen the uprights to twenty feet above the crossbar the next season to avoid future indecision.

The following Sunday, 50,777 hearty fans packed into Lambeau Field for the Packers' 1965 NFL championship contest against the defending league champion Cleveland Browns. The Browns had steamrolled through their regular season with an 11–3 record, punishing opponents with one of the greatest running backs of all time, Jim Brown. "In the exhibition season that year," Packers defensive back Bob Jeter recalled, "Brown busted four of my ribs and they carried me off the field."

The sky above Lambeau Field was gloomy and gray that morning. The temperature hovered around twenty-six degrees and a moderate wind blew through the stadium bowl, hampering the efforts of the grounds crew. As they tried to remove more than three inches of snow, their efforts became futile as the field began disintegrating into a muddy quagmire. The Browns, who had spent the night before in Appleton, found the weather preventing them from getting to Lambeau Field. "The Browns bus eventually arrived," offensive tackle Forrest Gregg recalled. "But they were so late the Cleveland players had to hustle to get dressed in time for kickoff."

On the game's opening drive, Green Bay passed on all but two plays, culminating in a 47-yard scoring strike from Starr to receiver Carroll Dale. The Browns answered with a touchdown but failed to convert the extra point. After the teams exchanged a pair of field goals, Green Bay held a slight 13–12 lead at halftime. In the second half, the Packers began to establish their superiority over the Browns as the weather worsened, bringing more snow, fog, and mud. The surging Green Bay offensive line was winning its war in the trenches as the bulldozing blocks of Forrest Gregg, Fuzzy Thurston, Bob Skoronski, Ken Bowman, and Jerry Kramer cleared running lanes for Jim Taylor and Paul Hornung, who finished the day with a combined total of 201 rushing yards. When Hornung scored on a 13-yard run late in the third quarter, the Packers took a dominating 20–12 lead. Green Bay's defenders— Henry Jordan, Willie Davis, Ron Kostelnik, Lionel Aldridge, Ray Nitschke, Lee Roy Caffey, and Dave Robinson—held Jim Brown to just 50 yards rushing that afternoon. "They were all over him," Hornung said of the Packers' swarming, gang-tackling defense. "If you really look at the film from that game, Cleveland's offensive linemen didn't score too well with their blocking assignments. I don't care who you are—even Jimmy Brown—you need somebody to block. You can't do it all yourself."

Don Chandler's fourth-quarter field goal cemented the Packers' 23–12 victory, and Lombardi met with reporters in the locker room after the game. "The snow and mud were our allies," he exclaimed. "When you have conditions like these, it's best to be basic, not fancy. And we're the most basic offensive team there is."

The Packers dominated the 1965 championship game to secure their third NFL title in five years, running sixty-nine plays to Cleveland's thirty-nine in the sodden grime that Lambeau Field became. (MILWAUKEE JOURNAL SENTINEL)

While Green Bay claimed its third NFL championship under Lombardi, the war between the NFL and the AFL was about to claim its participants if peace wasn't reached soon. Team owners from both leagues continued offering extravagant contracts to prospective college players in hopes of luring them away from the rival league. When quarterback Joe Namath spurned the NFL's St. Louis Cardinals to sign with the AFL's New York Jets for $427,000—an unheard-of sum for a pro football player at the time—not even lucrative television revenue from the NFL's recent two-year, $37.6 million contract with CBS would cover player salaries for much longer.

By the autumn of 1965, the AFL-NFL rivalry had created a cutthroat urban arms race between municipalities looking to land a professional football franchise. At the beginning of the decade, the NFL granted Dallas and Minneapolis–St. Paul franchises for $600,000 each to keep them from hosting AFL teams. The NFL now had a team in each of the country's top ten television markets, which helped secure their $75.2 million agreement with CBS to continue broadcasting games through the 1969 season. As a result, the NFL began focusing on growing metropolitan areas to place future franchises. In June 1965 the NFL recruited Atlanta to host the league's fifteenth team, the Falcons, at an expansion fee of $8.5 million. Two months later the AFL responded by securing its first expansion team in Miami, the Dolphins, for an entrance fee of $7.5 million. Professional football had become an invaluable big business, providing cities immeasurable benefits and recognition well beyond the economic benefits of hosting a team, evidenced by Vince Lombardi's comment earlier in the decade: "As general manager I like to play some games in Milwaukee, but as coach I'd rather play them all in Green Bay."

Fueling the fear that Wisconsin's largest metropolis could lose the Packers was the fact that Milwaukee, the eleventh largest city in the United States, had lost its Major League Baseball Braves to Atlanta in a bitter, public divorce. Still wanting to be considered a "big-league" sports town, Milwaukee struggled with how to rebrand itself. When the AFL showed interest in placing one of its expansion franchises in Milwaukee, controversy erupted. Many public officials, fans, and those in the local press were at odds over the possible encroachment on what many considered Packers territory. Even outspoken *Milwaukee Journal* sports editor Oliver Kuechle "struggled with the thorny problem of wanting to support big time sports for Milwaukee and at the same time support the Packers on all fronts," according to Milwaukee businessman Marv Fishman.

Fishman lobbied for the AFL to place an expansion franchise in Milwaukee; he felt Wisconsin could support a second professional football team because "the Packers were so strong that there was a waiting list of 15,000 for season tickets. They could sell out four games in Green Bay and three in Milwaukee with the potential to sell probably twice as many tickets." Fishman further argued, "There was room for

ABOVE: The Packers were becoming household names across the country thanks to their winning ways. Herb Adderley (26) and Willie Wood spoke with television broadcaster Ray Scott following the Packers' 23–12 victory over the Browns in the 1965 NFL championship game. (FROM THE GREEN BAY PRESS-GAZETTE ARCHIVES, REPRINTED BY PERMISSION)

ABOVE, RIGHT: Quarterback Bart Starr helped promote Milwaukee's public cleanup campaign by placing trash in a can, drawing the approval of Auntie Litter. (MILWAUKEE JOURNAL SENTINEL)

RIGHT: Offensive guard Jerry Kramer, here attending a car dealership promotion in 1966, became a sought-after author when he wrote *Instant Replay* a few years later. (COURTESY OF ALL-AMERICAN SPORTS, LLC)

another football team that would play seven games in Milwaukee. And if the leagues ever did get together, what would be a greater rivalry than between a Milwaukee team and the Packers?"

During the summer of 1965, Fishman found his aspirations to place an AFL team in Milwaukee squashed. "Challenging Lombardi in Wisconsin was like challenging God," Fishman admitted in his book *Bucking the Odds*. "We might have overcome the hold that the magic of Lombardi had on public opinion, but we could not overcome the hold Lombardi had over public officials."

When Fishman tried hosting an AFL exhibition game between the New York Jets and Miami Dolphins at County Stadium on August 20, 1966, the request became trapped in a labyrinth of bureaucratic red tape protecting the best interests of the Packers. "I wouldn't do anything that would hurt the Packers down here," Eugene Grobschmidt, Milwaukee County board chairman and the chairman of the board's special sports committee, told the *Milwaukee Sentinel*. "Unless Vince Lombardi okays it, I won't go along with it."

The Packers, who had exclusive rights in their contract with Milwaukee County Stadium, formally denied the request, prompting the AFL to abandon its expansion plans in Milwaukee. "If I couldn't get the stadium for an exhibition game, I certainly would not be able to get a contract for seven regular season games," Fishman recalled. "As upset as I was at the time, I never did hold it against Lombardi. He was protecting Green Bay's interest, which was his job."

> ## "Challenging Lombardi in Wisconsin was like challenging God."
>
> —MILWAUKEE BUSINESSMAN MARV FISHMAN

With the threat of Marvin Fishman placing an AFL franchise in Milwaukee, Vince Lombardi signed a contract in September 1966 guaranteeing his team's exclusive rights to County Stadium through the 1975 season, as county officials looked on. From left: Bill Anderson, Paul Pullen, Joseph Greco, John Doyne, Eugene Grobschmidt, Marty Larsen, and Larry Last. (MILWAUKEE JOURNAL SENTINEL)

• • •

As the AFL and NFL continued their public feud during the early months of 1966, a secret meeting took place underneath a Texas Ranger statue in the Dallas airport between Lamar Hunt of the AFL's Kansas City Chiefs and Tex Schramm of the NFL's Dallas Cowboys. It was one of many covert rendezvous league leaders would organize in the coming months to discuss the two bastions of professional football merging into one league. Combining into a single league had become a business necessity after six years of the two leagues' overspending, poaching players, and exhausting their financial resources in a futile effort to discredit one another in the court of public opinion. After the two leagues agreed on the terms, NFL commissioner Pete Rozelle announced on June 8, 1966, they would merge into a single, expanded National Football League. The two leagues would transition into a single schedule beginning in 1970 and would hold a common draft starting in January 1967. In the meantime, the two leagues would end each season with a championship game, the first of which would be played at the Los Angeles Coliseum following the 1966 regular season.

Almost from its inception, the NFL-AFL championship game was known as the Super Bowl, a nickname originated by AFL founder and Kansas City Chiefs owner Lamar Hunt: "My kids have this ball; maybe you've seen it advertised on television. It's about the size of a handball, but it bounces ten times higher than a normal ball. They call it a Super Ball. My kids kept talking about it so much that the name stuck in my mind. It just popped out—Super Bowl—when we started meetings to arrange the championship game."

Professional football was about to become a Goliath, not only in the world of sports, but in business as well. The merger required the federal government's approval since the combining of leagues was considered interstate commerce. The NFL was operating on a coast-to-coast basis, so U.S. antitrust laws had to be observed. Because football, unlike baseball, did not enjoy an antitrust exemption, the league was dependent on Capitol Hill politics to finalize the merger. After Louisiana Senator Russell Long and Congressman Hale Boggs pushed through the immunity amendment on October 21, essentially legalizing the AFL-NFL merger, a humble Rozelle said, "Congressman Boggs, I don't know how I can thank you enough for this." Boggs, a veteran politician, replied, "What do you mean you don't know how to thank me? New Orleans gets an immediate franchise in the NFL." Just eleven days after the congressional maneuver finalized the AFL-NFL merger on November 1, New Orleans was awarded its expansion franchise: the Saints.

In Green Bay, "we were determined to start 1966 where we left off," assistant coach Phil Bengtson declared. "We had all the old players back plus a million dollar

During the Packers' 1966 training camp, Ray Nitschke still wore his Milwaukee Braves cap, despite that team having departed for Atlanta earlier in the year, leaving the Packers as the only major professional sports team in Wisconsin. (MILWAUKEE JOURNAL SENTINEL)

list of potential superstars headed by Donny Anderson and Jim Grabowski, the 'Gold Dust Twins' who would be groomed to fill the shoes of Hornung and Taylor."

Before the merger was announced, each league tried luring away as many marquee draft picks as possible, spending more than a combined $7 million on rookie signings in 1966. The estimated cost for the Packers to keep their two prized draft picks from signing with AFL clubs—$600,000 for Anderson not to defect to the Houston Oilers and $400,000 to keep Grabowski from joining the Jets—infuriated Lombardi. Yet, Green Bay's annual income had climbed to around the $5 million mark, and the team was willing to spend it. "The next year one of our players was speaking at an offseason banquet in Milwaukee when he turned to Vince and said, jokingly, 'How does it feel to be the third-highest-paid member of the Green Bay Packers?'" trainer Domenic Gentile recalled. "Everyone in the room laughed except Vince, who stared straight ahead. He was not amused."

The $1 million Green Bay contracted between the two rookies was more than the club had grossed before Lombardi arrived in 1959. It was also larger than any contract offered to one of the Packers' plethora of veteran players that season. Teams' continued offerings of exorbitant salaries to unproven rookies and refusal to give established players comparable contracts created several conflicts between team owners and veteran players. Although players considered themselves underprivileged for years, their salaries were lucrative compared to the average American's working wage: In 1946 an average annual player salary was $4,000 with the national salary average less than $3,000. By 1949, after three years of competition with the AAFC, the average had risen to $8,000. By the mid-1960s the average hovered around $15,000 due to the AFL-NFL war, while average annual Americans' salaries had yet to exceed $5,000.

Fueling the players' resentment was the multitude of ways teams tried controlling their salaries. Fearing free agency would alienate the league's competitive balance and financial stability, owners operated under a reserve system that ensured every player was bound to play for the team with which he had signed a contract, for the full term of the contract plus one additional year at the option of the club. If a player chose to play out the option year of his contract, he was subject to a 10 percent salary reduction that season. The potential pay cut often enticed a player to agree to a contract extension with his current team before entering the option year. Only after a player fulfilled the option year of his contract was he allowed to become a free agent. "If there was one small spot of tarnish [during that 1966 season], it was Jim Taylor's decision to 'play out his option,'" Phil Bengtson recalled of the frustrated Packers veteran reacting to Lombardi's signing of the "Gold Dust Twins" and becoming a free agent at season's end.

Lombardi was very aware that his veterans were reaching the twilight of their careers, and he often opted to replenish the team's roster with younger talent. At training camp the newcomers were quickly interspersed among the team's reputed living legends and championship aura. "Standing in the Packer locker room," rookie center Bill Curry recalled, "gave you the strong feeling that everyone in there could push over a wall."

To start the 1966 season, the Packers overpowered the formidable Browns, Rams, and Lions en route to a dominating 12–2 record, with their only blemishes being a 21–20 loss to San Francisco and a 20–17 upset loss to the Vikings. Although Green Bay's offense wasn't as explosive as in years past, their defense was smothering, allowing 16 points or fewer in ten of the team's fourteen games and holding six of its foes to single digits. Upon securing their second consecutive Western Division crown, the Packers traveled to Dallas to face the 10–3–1 Cowboys for the NFL championship.

When they met at the Cotton Bowl on New Year's Day, both teams were rolling—Green Bay with a five-game winning streak and Dallas having won five of its last six. The game, matching onetime colleagues and assistant coaches with the New York Giants in Lombardi and the Cowboys' Tom Landry, "was one of the most exciting sixty minutes in the history of football," Bengtson recalled, "but to this day most people remember only the first four minutes and the last four."

Green Bay burst out to an early 14–0 lead on a touchdown pass from Starr to Elijah Pitts and, on the ensuing kickoff, a Jim Grabowski fumble recovery returned for a touchdown. The undaunted Cowboys tied the game at 14 before Starr connected for long touchdown passes to receivers Carroll Dale and Boyd Dowler. With four minutes left in the game, the Packers led 34–20. It should have been a more comfortable 35–20 lead, but Don Chandler's fifth extra-point attempt was blocked, and that gaffe loomed more and more important as the game reached its conclusion.

The Cowboys cut the deficit to 34–27 late in the game. They were driving deep into Packers' territory with only seconds remaining and "there was nothing we could do but pray," Max McGee remarked. "We hadn't stopped the Cowboys all afternoon and we knew they were going to score, and when that happened, we'd all be dead. Dallas had the momentum and we were emotionally exhausted."

Quarterback Don Meredith drove the Cowboys all the way to the Green Bay 2-yard line, just six feet away from forcing the second overtime championship game in NFL history. Facing fourth and goal, Meredith rolled out with the Packers' Dave Robinson encroaching. As receivers and defenders crisscrossed the field with their arms waving

> "We hadn't stopped the Cowboys all afternoon and we knew they were going to score, and when that happened, we'd all be dead."
>
> —RECEIVER MAX MCGEE

Defensive back Tom Brown (40) intercepted Don Meredith's fourth-down pass in the end zone to preserve the Packers' 34–21 victory in Dallas. (COURTESY OF TOM PIGEON COLLECTION)

in the air, "I had his [Meredith's] left arm completely paralyzed and I had his right arm at the elbow," Robinson recalled. "So he just flipped it with his wrist. I thought it was a good move on his part." Meredith's weak pass lofted toward the end zone into the sea of madness. For what seemed like an eternity, the pass arced toward the Cowboys' Bob Hayes, but it fell short and into the hands of the Packers' Tom Brown. As the defensive back pulled it down, he essentially was hugging the NFL championship against his chest.

The victory in Dallas earned Green Bay its second consecutive NFL championship and fourth in six years. But with one more game yet to play, the Packers had some work to do. "The toughest coaching job we faced in the entire nine years of the Lombardi regime was preparing to meet the Kansas City Chiefs in the first NFL-AFL World Championship game," Bengtson admitted. "How do you convince men who have beaten the Colts, the Rams, and the Cowboys over the past three weeks that they'll have to be prepared to make the same supreme effort to top the representative of a young, new league with no reputation and allegedly no strength to match your own?"

The week before the game, the magnitude of the upcoming championship contest took on a life of its own. While the Packers practiced in Santa Barbara, Lombardi was inundated with passionate letters and telegrams from all of the NFL's franchise owners. Even George Halas asked his rival to save the league from an enormous embarrassment. "We *had* to win," Bengtson said. "If we got complacent and let the Chiefs pull an upset, we'd go down in history on the same page with Goliath and the Spanish Armada."

It was a sentiment shared by the entire Packers squad. "Here you had new guys challenging the old establishment," defensive end Willie Davis said of an ingrained sense of honor among his teammates. "We had a job to do and my attitude was, 'What better team to do it than the Packers?'"

In past championship games, the Packers prided themselves on preparing for their opponents, understanding the task at hand, and knowing who stood across from them on the line of scrimmage. But "we didn't know a thing in the world about Kansas City," offensive tackle Forrest Gregg recounted years later. "We had never seen them play except on TV."

On the night before the game, the Packers focused on their experience when

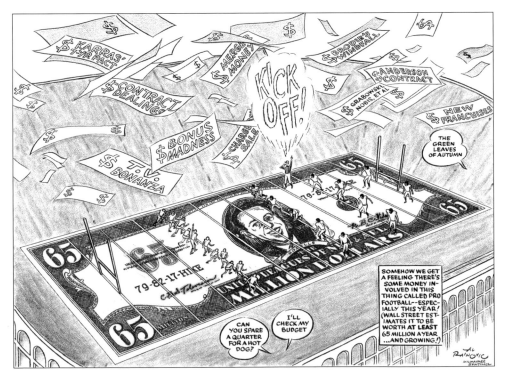

Milwaukee Journal editorial cartoonist Al Rainovic offered these symbolic depictions of how NFL commissioner Pete Rozelle transformed professional football into a multimillion-dollar business. (UWM LIBRARIES, ARCHIVES DEPARTMENT RAINOVIC COLLECTION IMAGES 386 AND 378)

While the team was practicing in Santa Barbara, California, an uptight Vince Lombardi took no chances, making sure his backfield stars Elijah Pitts (37), Bart Starr (47), and Jim Taylor (39) were misidentified during workouts. (COURTESY OF CHRIS NERAT)

coaxed by the inquiring media. "Pressure? You think the pressure [is] on us?" defensive tackle Henry Jordan retorted. "Take a look around you. How many bald heads do you see in here? How many grey heads? They've been there before."

It was true. The Packers' roster included twenty-eight players who had participated in at least two NFL championship games, with nine starters playing in all five of Lombardi's championship games, all of which left offensive guard Fuzzy Thurston to boast, "We will win this game because we have the greatest football mind in the world on our side."

On January 15, 1967, sunny skies and a delightful seventy-two-degree day provided the perfect backdrop for the first NFL-AFL championship game. The inaugural contest received so little interest from the national media that the Los Angeles Coliseum was able to accommodate all the credentialed print media along with NFL and AFL staff members, several coaches from other teams, politicians, and assorted celebrities. Despite tickets priced at $6, $10, and $12, the stands were a third empty at kickoff. With only 61,946 fans in attendance, both CBS and NBC, who had agreed to pay $1 million each to share the broadcast rights, were forced to black out the game in Los Angeles. "Fortunately, those were the last empty seats we have had for a Super Bowl," NFL commissioner Pete Rozelle remarked. "We worked hard—we had tried everything—to sell seats. It was difficult to explain."

Following the modest pageantry of the teams being announced on the field, broadcaster Frank Gifford approached his former Giants colleague for an impromptu interview before kickoff. Only then did he realize how much pressure Lombardi was struggling to contain. "We talked for almost five minutes," Gifford recalled, "and all that time he gripped my arm and shook like a leaf."

"It was the only time I ever saw Lombardi that tense and uptight," linebacker Ray Nitschke recalled. "He was so tense and nervous about everything, he made us tense and it carried over into the game—which is something he *never* did. I really believe Lombardi's mentality before that Super Bowl affected us so much that we played poorly in the first half."

Announcer Ray Scott, who was the play-by-play announcer for CBS during the first Super Bowl, chatted with Bart Starr on the field of the Los Angeles Coliseum prior to kickoff. (MILWAUKEE JOURNAL SENTINEL)

Looking to protect the NFL's reputation against the upstart AFL and its Kansas City Chiefs, a confident Packers squad was led onto the field by Max McGee (85), Ken Bowman (57), Donny Anderson (44), Bob Long (80), Lionel Aldridge (82), and Ron Kostelnik (77). (COURTESY OF GREEN BAY PRESS-GAZETTE FROM TOM PIGEON COLLECTION)

On the Packers' first series of downs, receiver Boyd Dowler left the game with an injury. Lombardi, forced to alter his well-strategized game plan, turned to one of his trusted veterans, Max McGee, as Dowler's replacement. McGee went on to catch a 37-yard pass from Bart Starr for the first touchdown in Super Bowl history. It was one of the few exciting plays Green Bay executed during the first half as they took a slim 14–10 lead by halftime. "The Packers played probably unlike they had ever played before," defensive end Willie Davis recalled. "We played kind of protecting something rather than being all-out aggressive, the way we typically had played over the years leading into that first Super Bowl."

At halftime Lombardi gave one of his motivational speeches. "He said, 'Okay, what happened?'" Davis remembered. "'You played thirty minutes adjusting to the Kansas City Chiefs. Now what I ask you to do is to go out and play thirty minutes of Green Bay Packer football and let the Chiefs adjust to you.'"

After the second-half kickoff had to be rekicked because NBC wasn't back from its commercial break, the Packers broke the game open in the third quarter. Defensive back Willie Wood intercepted a Len Dawson pass and ran it back to the Chiefs' 5. Then half-back Elijah Pitts scored on a 5-yard run followed by another Max McGee touchdown to give Green Bay a commanding 28–10 lead. "That, for all

After a lackluster first half, Jim Taylor (31) and the Packers dominated the Chiefs in a 35–10 victory during the only Super Bowl that wasn't sold out. (COURTESY OF GREEN BAY PRESS-GAZETTE FROM TOM PIGEON COLLECTION)

purposes, was the end of the game," Bengtson remarked.

En route to a 35–10 victory, Green Bay relied on power football, executing a minimum number of plays with maximum effort. "It was almost as if we had played a cruel trick on the young AFL hopefuls, threatening them with Taylor, the ailing-but-ready Hornung, and a host of other players in their prime, then sending out an 'old man' to humiliate them," Bengtson said of McGee's performance of catching seven passes for 138 yards and two touchdowns.

For winning their two games in January, the Packers players each received checks for $24,813.63, which included $15,000 for the Super Bowl victory. Professional football had come a long way since its first title game held at Wrigley Field in Chicago back in 1933, when each winning Bears player received $210.34. The unprecedented payoff was a result of the NFL championship game's gross gate exceeding $2 million for the third straight year, with its game at the Cotton Bowl generating a total of $2,773,861.20, including $2 million for the television, radio, and movie rights. Gate receipts still accounted for between 70 and 90 percent of total income for NFL teams in the 1960s, so the continued surge in revenue coincided with the overall rise in attendance at all league games. In 1966 the NFL reported a new regular-season attendance record of 5,337,038 customers, representing stadiums at almost 87 percent of capacity and selling out 63 times in 105 games. Regardless of team record or location—from its last-place Giants in New York to the world champion Packers in Green Bay—the NFL's financial windfall was being enjoyed by all the league's franchises, prompting Lombardi to exclaim, "It just goes to show how far professional football has gone."

With Wisconsin Governor Warren Knowles at left, Vince Lombardi couldn't help but smile as he held the championship trophy that would one day bear his name. (COURTESY OF GREEN BAY PRESS-GAZETTE FROM TOM PIGEON COLLECTION)

The following spring Lombardi was proud to announce, "When I finished my first year at Green Bay as general manager and coach, we showed a net profit of $75,203. The next year, it had risen to $115,128, and each year, I have received a vote of thanks. For 1966, we showed a net profit of $827,439."

The Packers' record profit also accounted for the team's gross operating income of $3,384,923, which was enhanced by the fact that the 1966 draft was held in 1965 and that the 1967 draft wouldn't be held until 1967. Thus, the rookie bonuses of 1967 wouldn't impact the team's ledger until the following year.

Green Bay's Stadium Commission, which operated Lambeau Field, also announced a record profit in 1966 of $58,059. The commission's income—including $44,000 for the Packers to rent the stadium, $33,378 from concessions, and $22,967 for parking—totaled more than $110,000. The plethora of prosperity was tangible proof the Packers were one of the marquee organizations in professional sports—for excellence achieved both on and off the field.

■   ■   ■

Throughout the 1960s professional football enjoyed a golden age of profits and popularity. With the addition of the New Orleans Saints in 1967, the NFL had swelled to sixteen teams, forcing officials to restructure the divisional alignment and playoff format. Since 1933 the NFL had comprised two divisions, Eastern and Western, with its postseason consisting of a one-game playoff between division champions. To avoid a pair of bloated divisions containing eight teams each, the NFL streamlined itself into four divisions of four teams each. Traditional rivalries were maintained under the realignment, with the Packers assigned to the Central Division alongside the Bears, Lions, and Vikings.

Prior to the start of the 1967 season at a speaking engagement in Minnesota, Cowboys coach Tom Landry told the group, "Within two years, some team will displace the Packers. They are approaching an age problem and other teams are improving."

The bold statement fueled Lombardi's resolve to overcome speculation the Packers were getting too old. Yes, the Packers were the oldest team in the NFL, featuring ten players in at least their tenth season and several others close behind. But during the past eight seasons, Lombardi's need to prove something had made him the face of professional football's pop-culture revolution in America, and the 1967 season would be no different. He had built a pigskin dynasty that had captured the imaginations of millions of television viewers across the nation. The team's uniforms—forest green jerseys with yellow and white piping on the sleeves and bright yellow pants with green and white trim on the sides—were now heralded as

**"That $15,000 you
all made at the
end of last year for
winning the Super
Bowl made you
all fatheaded."**

**–HEAD COACH
VINCE LOMBARDI**

a national symbol of excellence, much like New York Yankee pinstripes and Boston Celtic green. Expectations had been raised in Green Bay; indeed, "all fans could talk about was whether this Packer team could match Curly Lambeau's 1931 squad and deliver a third straight championship," author Don Gulbrandsen said, noting that no team had won three consecutive championships since the NFL's playoff system started in 1933. "Having fallen short of this goal in 1963, Lombardi put extra pressure on himself to match this accomplishment—especially important now that he coached home games in a stadium named for Lambeau."

From the first day of training camp, anyone not dedicated to the cause was considered beneath contempt in Lombardi's eyes. "Some of you people are fat," he scolded his veterans after their first scrimmage. "You're fat in the head and fat in the body. That $15,000 you all made at the end of last year for winning the Super Bowl made you all fatheaded."

Lombardi knew there wasn't a team on their schedule that wasn't going to be ready for the Packers. "This is the price of winning," he said. "This is the price of the last two championships. You're paying for it now because everybody in the league wants to beat you. They're giving it their maximum supreme effort. There's no loafing, no halfway, against the Green Bay Packers."

A tough preseason schedule exposed Green Bay's depleted running game. Following the offseason departures of Jim Taylor and Paul Hornung, the Packers "were

Vince Lombardi emphasized conditioning at the Packers' training camp, cracking his verbal whip on the squad during two-a-day drills that began with calisthenics and ended with his infamous grass drills. (MILWAUKEE JOURNAL SENTINEL)

down to bare bones for running backs after Elijah Pitts and Jim Grabowski were lost for the season [due to injuries]," sportswriter Bud Lea recounted in *Magnificent Seven*. "They brought in two yard-sale fullbacks, Chuck Mercein and Ben Wilson, to fill the holes."

"We weren't quite the ballclub we were in '62," offensive guard Jerry Kramer later admitted. "We had to rely much more on heart and desire and pride and all of those intangibles that Lombardi had talked about."

As the season progressed, Bart Starr led a prominent list of veterans nursing numerous injuries, which kept the team's starting lineup in a state of flux each week. "They were a dominant team in '66, but in '67, they had a fight on their hands," *Green Bay Press-Gazette* sports editor Art Daley commented years later. "The 1967 season was Lombardi's best coaching job."

As injuries depleted his roster, Lombardi relied on his veteran defense to carry the Packers through the 1967 season as they limped to a less-than-spectacular 9–4–1 record. But because of the NFL's realigned divisions, this was good enough to secure them the Central Division title and an invitation to the postseason. "Few teams in NFL history have achieved success with that kind of attrition," Bengtson remarked.

In the first round of the NFL's expanded playoff format, Green Bay faced the Rams, who boasted to reporters that they had broken the Packers' mystique after beating them two Sundays earlier in Los Angeles. The odds-makers agreed, picking the visitors as favorites in the rematch at Milwaukee County Stadium. What they didn't factor into the equation was that the Packers had already clinched their division, and the Rams were in desperate need of the victory to keep pace with the then-undefeated Baltimore Colts. By beating the Colts in their last game of the season, Los Angeles swiped the Coastal Division crown from Baltimore on a tiebreaker, since both teams had identical 11–1–2 records.

The Rams, behind quarterback Roman Gabriel, jumped out to an early first-quarter lead with a 29-yard touchdown pass to Bernie Casey. In the second quarter Green Bay rookie halfback Travis Williams responded with a 46-yard touchdown run. Those would be the Packers' first 7 of 28 unanswered points scored against the Rams' famed "Fearsome Foursome" defense that afternoon. Meanwhile, Lombardi's defense extinguished any hope George Allen's meticulously strategized offense had of reaching the end zone. "Everybody's been saying we were dead," Lombardi remarked after the 28–7 victory, "that we'd won in a patsy division, that we weren't the Packers we once were. We had something to prove."

The following Sunday morning, on December 31, 1967, Lambeau Field resembled the surface of a glacier. Overnight, a mass of arctic air had settled over the region and temperatures were holding steady at minus-thirteen degrees Fahrenheit.

Fifteen-mile-per-hour winds dropped the wind-chill factor to thirty-eight below, leaving *Los Angeles Times* sportswriter Jim Murray to ponder in his column, "I don't know why they scheduled this game here. I guess because the top of Mt. Everest was booked."

Throughout the afternoon, television cameras panned across the sellout crowd of 50,861 to find even the most dedicated of Packers fans struggling to cope with the arctic winds during the game that would soon be nicknamed the Ice Bowl. Lambeau Field's press box provided no refuge from the cold, either. When CBS color analyst Frank Gifford reached for his cup of coffee, it had frozen solid as a popsicle in a matter of moments, prompting him to joke, "I think I'll have another bite of my coffee."

As the players stepped onto the field, their feet crackled atop grass blanketed in chipped ice. Hoping to avoid just this situation, the Packers had installed fourteen miles of heating cable six and a half inches below the surface to prevent the field from freezing; the system's thermostat was supposed to turn on the power for the 780,000-watt system whenever air and turf temperatures dipped below 45 degrees. But the night before the game, the weather conditions had deteriorated so fast that the $80,000 electrical heating system failed to handle the intense cold. After the kickoff, the referee's whistles also became a casualty of the cold. They didn't have rubber mouthpieces, forcing the officials to abandon the instruments and simply holler when plays were to start or stop. The predicted weather and heating system had received so much publicity before the game that a confident Lombardi boasted to reporters, "Weather won't beat the team that loses this game."

The game itself looked as if it would be decided early after Starr threw a pair of touchdown passes to receiver Boyd Dowler. "Then the 'breaks,' which is a handy catch-all label for the other side's defensive moments and our uncharacteristic lapses, all went their way," Bengtson recalled.

The Cowboys scored their first touchdown of the day on a recovered fumble generated by a quarterback sack of Bart Starr and then kicked a short field goal to cut the deficit to 14–10 just before halftime. Following a scoreless third quarter, Dallas took its first lead of the day when Dan Reeves connected on a surprise halfback option pass to Lance Rentzel. With the Packers now trailing 17–14, the numbing cold was making it downright improbable either team would score again. When the Packers retained the ball on their 32-yard line with 4:50 left on the scoreboard clock, "we got our last chance at the triple crown, the Super Bowl, immortality, and a renewal of our pride and confidence in ourselves," Bengtson remarked.

The moment quarterback Bart Starr stepped into the huddle and looked into the eyes of his teammates, "I knew instantly that nothing needed to be said regarding the importance of that opportunity. Everyone knew exactly what was at stake and what would be required."

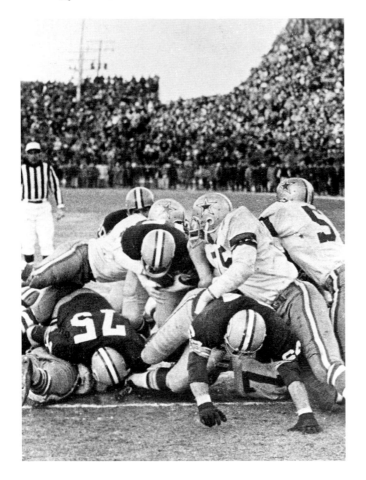

One of the most iconic images in professional football history, known simply as "the Sneak" (FROM THE GREEN BAY PRESS-GAZETTE ARCHIVES, REPRINTED BY PERMISSION)

The Packers' offense would have to navigate across 68 yards of ice-slicked turf while avoiding further punishment at the hands of Dallas' "Doomsday" defense. "That was the point," Starr said, "where our mental conditioning took over."

In eleven plays, Green Bay's offensive unit found themselves at third down and goal on the Dallas one-yard line. With just sixteen seconds remaining, the Packers were down to their final play. After using the team's last timeout, Starr conferred with Lombardi on the sideline. They discussed several options, including kicking a field goal to send the game into sudden-death overtime. Nobody would have criticized the coach for making that decision, but the players knew "it would have meant he didn't have confidence in our ability to take that last step," linebacker Ray Nitschke said, "to rise to the limits of our ability when all the chips had been shoved to the center of the table."

The sun descended behind Lambeau Field's scoreboard as long shadows draped Starr and his Packers teammates. After breaking the huddle, they approached the line of scrimmage to execute *the play*—Brown Right, 31-Wedge. Taking the snap on a quick count, Starr tucked the ball into his stomach, lowered his helmet, and dove forward to his right. Offensive guard Jerry Kramer and center Ken Bowman created a momentary gap in the Dallas defensive line, allowing Starr to lunge into the end zone. When the field judge signaled touchdown, an exhausted Kramer looked back at his quarterback hunched over the goal line. "It was," Kramer would later say, "the most beautiful sight in the world."

After Don Chandler's extra point made it 21–17, the gun sounded. The euphoric Lambeau Field crowd erupted. Fans, no longer feeling the effects of the subzero temperatures, stormed the field to tear down the goalposts. In the locker room, the team's jubilation was comparatively subdued. They had been there before. "This was it. This was our greatest one," Lombardi declared. "This is what the Green Bay Packers are all about. They don't do it for individual glory. They do it because they love one another."

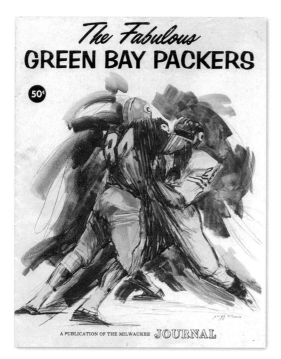

The Fabulous
GREEN BAY PACKERS
50¢

A PUBLICATION OF THE MILWAUKEE JOURNAL

With the Packers at the height of the Lombardi dynasty in 1967, businesses and publications across the state celebrated the team's unprecedented success. (WHI IMAGE ID 87285)

The Packers had two weeks to thaw out before representing the NFL against the AFL champion Oakland Raiders in Miami, but "after the emotional peaks of the last two weeks in December—in fact, after the whole mountain range of emotional peaks over the past three years—it was difficult to get the players up for the second Super Bowl," according to Bengtson.

"I've never been around a flatter football team than we were preparing for that Super Bowl," Starr recalled. "I don't think we even started to come around until the Thursday before that game."

Followers of the game expressed little doubt over the outcome, leading the media and gossipers to focus their attention on the growing rumor that Lombardi would retire at season's end. It was an all-too-common scenario that Packers players dismissed in the past, but this time something was different. The year before, Lombardi had been short with newsmen in California but uncharacteristically mellow in Miami. He also broke a long-standing rule, allowing the players' wives to accompany the team to Florida. Several former players, including Paul Hornung, visited the team during practice. On the Thursday before the game, Lombardi spoke to his team. With his voice cracking, he confessed, "I've never been so proud of you." Although he soon collected himself, the players now knew the truth: their next game would be the last one Vince Lombardi coached as a Green Bay Packer.

On January 14, 1968, Miami's Orange Bowl was packed to capacity as a crowd of 75,546 witnessed the Packers take control of the game from the moment linebacker Ray Nitschke blew up an Oakland sweep on the game's first play from scrimmage. Following two early field goals, Starr connected with Dowler for a 62-yard touchdown strike. When Don Chandler added his third field goal conversion, Green Bay took a 16–7 lead into halftime. In the Packers locker room, the group of ten veterans who had been with Lombardi from the start—Forrest Gregg, Henry

Media coverage intensified for Super Bowl II, including Green Bay's WLUK-TV's sports director Jim Irwin (right)—who would later broadcast Packers games on the radio—making sure he got good highlights in an already overcrowded press box. (COURTESY OF THE PRESS-GAZETTE COLLECTION OF THE NEVILLE PUBLIC MUSEUM OF BROWN COUNTY)

An uncharacteristically relaxed Vince Lombardi stood with defensive back Doug Hart (43), backup quarterback Don Horn (13), and assistant coach Phil Bengtson (with hands in the air) as the Packers dominated the Oakland Raiders in Super Bowl II. (COURTESY OF GREEN BAY PRESS-GAZETTE FROM TOM PIGEON COLLECTION)

The Packers overwhelmed the Oakland Raiders from the beginning of Super Bowl II, thanks to an aggressive offensive attack led by quarterback Bart Starr (15) and running back Donny Anderson (44) and precision blocking from Gale Gillingham (68) and Bob Skoronski (76). (COURTESY OF GREEN BAY PRESS-GAZETTE FROM TOM PIGEON COLLECTION)

Herb Adderley's (26) interception return for a touchdown early in the fourth quarter put the game out of reach for the Raiders, securing the Packers' second consecutive Super Bowl championship. (COURTESY OF GREEN BAY PRESS-GAZETTE FROM TOM PIGEON COLLECTION)

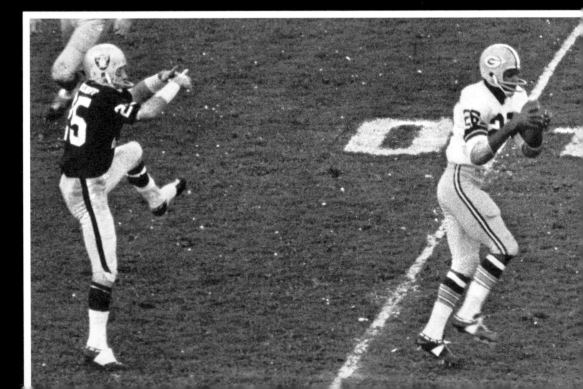

Jordan, Ray Nitschke, Willie Davis, Bart Starr, Boyd Dowler, Jerry Kramer, Bob Skoronski, Fuzzy Thurston, and Max McGee—gravitated toward each other and vowed to "play the last thirty minutes for the Old Man."

For the next thirty minutes the Packers played cool, calculated football. Holding onto the ball for all but two and a half minutes of the third quarter, they scored a touchdown on a 2-yard run from halfback Donny Anderson and another field goal from Chandler. Early in the fourth quarter, defensive back Herb Adderley returned an interception 60 yards for a touchdown. The Packers' defense held the Raiders to minimal yardage and an inconsequential late score to secure the 33–14 victory. When the gun went off to signal the end of the game, Lombardi was lifted onto the shoulders of his offensive linemen Jerry Kramer and Forrest Gregg. "One more time, Coach," Kramer requested as Lombardi grinned, admitting, "This is the best way to leave a football field."

A somber Vince Lombardi (center) accepted the championship trophy from NFL commissioner Pete Rozelle (right) as CBS commentator Frank Gifford interviewed the two. Super Bowl II would be Lombardi's last game as head coach of the Packers. (COURTESY OF GREEN BAY PRESS-GAZETTE FROM TOM PIGEON COLLECTION)

CHASING LEGENDARY SHADOWS

Just two weeks after grasping his second NFL-AFL championship trophy, Vince Lombardi announced his retirement as head coach of the Green Bay Packers, while retaining the position of general manager, explaining, "Because of the nature and growth of the business and the corporate structure of the Packers, I believe it is impossible for me to try to do both jobs." He noted, "When I came here, our total income was $600,000. Last year it was nearly $5,500,000."

If anyone understood that the NFL had grown into a financial juggernaut over the past decade, it was Lombardi. He had always been intrigued with the business aspects of football, commissioning a survey through a Washington research firm to showcase the direct and indirect economic stimuli generated by the Packers. Published under the heading "An Official Statement of the Green Bay Packers' Contribution to the Communities of Green Bay and Milwaukee and the State of Wisconsin during the 1967 Season," the survey calculated that the Packers had brought more than $8.5 million in measurable income to the state of Wisconsin during the past year. More than $2 million of that was spent directly by the Packers, visiting teams, and the press, and another $5 million was spent by fans. The report expressed in great detail pro football's less tangible influence on the city's business, entertainment, and culture. Because of the Packers, Green Bay was considered the best-known city of its size in the United States. The city's association with a major-league sports attraction now went far beyond the team's green and gold combination enhancing delivery trucks, signboards, and restaurant menus throughout town. Green Bay was now synonymous with excellence—a "prestige factor" that all of Wisconsin benefited from because "the image of success conveyed an image of teamwork, efficiency, and precision."

The Packers, much like kick returner Steve Odom (84) in 1974, found themselves fumbling away opportunities to return to the playoffs after Vince Lombardi left Green Bay. (WISCONSIN STATE JOURNAL)

Thanks to their unprecedented success on the field, the Packers were the focus of numerous articles and reports by those fascinated with their unique business model as a publicly owned franchise. A *Fortune* magazine article entitled "The Profitable Nonprofit in Green Bay" heralded the team's success as "an extreme example of the separation of ownership and control," which writer Harold B. Meyers indicated allowed the franchise to thrive because "most professional football teams gratify the egos of a few rich owners. The Packers gratify the collective ego of a community."

Despite all his success, Lombardi still aspired to own a piece of an NFL franchise. He approached the Packers executive committee about letting him purchase part of the team, but unwilling to tamper with Green Bay's publicly owned status, the committee declined. "He's always told us that he'd be interested if he could ever obtain an ownership in another club," vice president and executive committee member Richard Bourguignon explained of holding Lombardi to his contract. "But we've always said we wouldn't let him coach for another club."

At the press conference announcing his intention to step down as head coach, an emotional Lombardi cited his poor health as the main reason, but he had confided in friends, "You know, the pressures of losing are bad. But the pressures of winning are worse, infinitely worse, because they keep on torturing you and torturing you."

To his critics, the move smacked of a man bailing out on a team in decline, but according to halfback Donny Anderson, "Anybody who had been around Lombardi knew he made the only move he could possibly have made at the time."

"He was physically whipped, mentally exhausted and perhaps struck by the notion that, having won three straight championships, there were no more mountains to climb," author Steve Cameron speculated in his book *The Packers! Seventy-five Seasons of Memories and Mystique in Green Bay.*

"Let's face it. Lombardi was a realist," executive committee member John Torinus said of the aging Packers, who were in need of an aggressive roster overhaul to stay competitive. "He also knew that as the league had expanded it had become more difficult to acquire new talent through the draft or by trade."

Since Lombardi was staying in Green Bay as the Packers' general manager, he handpicked his successor. Phil Bengtson, who played a major role in the Packers' five NFL titles as the architect of the team's dominating defense, would succeed the coaching legend in Green Bay. As soon as Bengtson took over the team's head coaching duties, Lombardi began regretting the decision. "He made a real mistake in judgment in leaving coaching in the first place," running back Chuck Mercein recalled. "I think about two or three weeks into training camp . . . he realized it."

Lombardi, who was a man of discipline, followed through on his promise to not interfere or second-guess how his longtime lieutenant coached the team. Instead, "he

"Once the season started, [Lombardi] looked tragic, no other word for it. Just tragic."
–RUNNING BACK CHUCK MERCEIN

Phil Bengtson (foreground) inherited the team's head coaching position in 1968, but he couldn't escape the shadow his predecessor Vince Lombardi (background) cast over the franchise. (COURTESY OF THE PRESS-GAZETTE COLLECTION OF THE NEVILLE PUBLIC MUSEUM OF BROWN COUNTY)

was sort of lurking about, peeking around corners, seeing what was happening, and very reserved about it, wouldn't show himself too much," Mercein remembered. "And once the season started, he looked tragic, no other word for it. Just tragic."

While Lombardi tried distancing himself from his old job, Bengtson became embroiled in his first crisis as the Packers' head coach. At the team's training camp, "I was starting with a mixed bag of thirty-nine rookies and free agents, because the NFL players' association had called a strike of all veterans," Bengtson recounted in his autobiography *Packer Dynasty*. "So, in effect, I was a coach without players."

The dispute was far more complicated than ordinary labor-management problems. It was a direct result of the profits NFL teams enjoyed from huge television contracts. With television paying the Packers $1,424,000 in 1967, the team enjoyed financial figures similar to those of the previous year, which included posting a $1,514,000 profit. As in years past, profits not used for capital improvements went into the club's surplus fund—a fund whose value the Packers would not reveal but that *Fortune* writer Harold B. Meyers speculated was "probably approaching $2 million." The Packers and other teams began using their cash reserves to sign unproven rookies to bloated contracts, causing veterans to demand similar treatment. When negotiations between the National Football League Players Association and the owners broke off in late May, the players went on strike, and teams countered with a lockout. "I'm very unhappy about this," Lombardi told the press. "I didn't put thirty years in this business to come to this. . . . I've never seen the owners so united. They made a very generous offer to the players."

The striking players demanded three things: an increase of $100,000 per club in contributions to the pension fund, a minimum salary of $15,000, and $500 pay for each participant in a preseason game. Under the existing system, players were given a flat $10-a-day compensation while in training camp, and exhibition games were considered part of practice. "Fortunately, a compromise settlement was reached after a week, with the clubs satisfying all the players' demands in part," Bengtson recalled.

Once the strike ended, the Packers resumed training camp with Bengtson directing his full complement of veterans, rookies, and journeymen. Lombardi, still struggling with his reduced role as just the team's general manager, had a sound-proof cubicle installed at Lambeau Field to prevent anyone from hearing him yell advice or insults during games. "He felt lost up in the press box. He was the type of general who couldn't fight a war from his desk," Packers legend and executive committee member Tony Canadeo said years later. "He had to be down on the field with us, with his people, yelling, 'What the hell is going on out there?'"

Not only did Bengtson have to follow in the coaching footsteps of a living legend, but he also had to live with the realization that Lombardi would be staring down at him every Sunday. "The evening of our first exhibition, he took his new season seat high in the press box," Bengtson recalled. "After the game he drew me aside and demanded: 'Who were all those people on the sidelines? There was a whole crowd of people standing around the bench.' 'It was the same people as always,' I replied. 'Bud Jorgensen, Dad Braisher, Dave Hanner, Vern Biever taking pictures, Brian (my youngest son) helping with the equipment, Dr. [James] Nellen—' Vince shook his head. 'Yeah, yeah. I guess I just never noticed. It looks different from up there.'"

The Phil Bengtson era began in Green Bay with a 30–13 opening-day victory over the Philadelphia Eagles. However, injuries quickly began to sideline key contributors, including quarterback Bart Starr, who missed at least part of eight games. As a result, the Packers struggled near the .500 mark all season, unable to win in consecutive weeks, except once. The offense lacked consistency, and the retirement of placekicking specialist Don Chandler hampered the team's ability to pull out close games: the Packers lost five games by a total of 22 points and tied another. After they dropped two of their last three contests, they finished third in the Central Division with a disappointing 6–7–1 record. Green Bay had endured its first losing campaign since 1958, and although "Lombardi never interfered with Bengtson," *Milwaukee Sentinel* sportswriter Bud Lea remarked, "he could not let everything go unnoticed."

"Vince that one year as general manager was like a cat on a hot tin roof. He didn't know what to do with himself," Canadeo recalled. "He said it was the hardest thing in the world to sit there and watch them and not be part of the decision."

Some felt Lombardi could have taken back his coaching job since "nobody, probably not even Phil, would have objected," trainer Domenic Gentile remarked. "But Lombardi would never even consider such an act of disloyalty to a friend."

Phil Bengtson (at right, next to quarterback Zeke Bratkowski, 12) found the 1968 season to be a frustrating one as the Packers went from defending Super Bowl champions to third-place finishers in the NFC Central Division. (WISCONSIN STATE JOURNAL)

On August 6, 1968, the usually stoic Vince Lombardi (left) was visibly moved throughout the day of celebration in his honor, which included the renaming of Green Bay's Highland Avenue as Lombardi Avenue and "An Evening with Vince Lombardi" (above) that included retired Packers stars (left to right) Fred "Fuzzy" Thurston, Paul Hornung, and Max McGee singing a "Run to Daylight" song. (LEFT: COURTESY OF THE PRESS-GAZETTE COLLECTION OF THE NEVILLE PUBLIC MUSEUM OF BROWN COUNTY; ABOVE: MILWAUKEE JOURNAL SENTINEL)

"A Green Bay Salute To Vince Lombardi"

AN EVENING WITH VINCE
PICNIC SUPPER
6:30 P.M. WEDNESDAY, AUG. 7, 1968
BROWN COUNTY VETERANS MEMORIAL ARENA
ARENA — — — $2.50
NO REFUND

SEC. 2 ROW M SEAT 13
BROWN COUNTY ARENA
Good Only
WEDNESDAY EVE. AUG. 7
AMERICAN TICKET CORP. MILW.-CHICAGO-KAN.C. 77

"A Green Bay Salute To Vince Lombardi"

AN EVENING WITH VINCE
PICNIC SUPPER
6:30 P.M. WEDNESDAY, AUG. 7, 1968
BROWN COUNTY VETERANS MEMORIAL ARENA
ARENA — — — $2.50
NO REFUND

SEC. 2 ROW M SEAT 14
BROWN COUNTY ARENA
Good Only
WEDNESDAY EVE. AUG. 7
AMERICAN TICKET CORP. MILW.-CHICAGO-KAN.C. 77

(WHI IMAGE ID 81772)

Earlier that year, "it was obvious he wasn't happy," receiver Boyd Dowler admitted after reports surfaced that Lombardi was part of a group that failed to buy the San Francisco 49ers in the spring. "I never believed he would stay long in Green Bay as just general manager."

When the Packers went to Washington, D.C., in late November, Lombardi traveled with the team. There he met with Redskins team owner Edward Bennett Williams to discuss his possible return to coaching. Although he was under contract with the Packers for another five years, he never bothered to inform the team he was engaged in talks with Williams. He later claimed that when the Redskins asked the Packers for permission to talk with Coach Lombardi about the position, "Vince Lombardi asked General Manager Vince Lombardi."

On Monday, February 3, 1969, the inevitable occurred: Vince Lombardi requested that the Packers release him from the last five years of his contract so he could become the top executive officer, head coach, and part owner of the Washington Redskins. Throughout Green Bay and the entire state of Wisconsin, "the reaction among Packers fans was swift and angry—most turned on their once-beloved coach, accusing him of being greedy and lacking loyalty," author Don Gulbrandsen wrote in *Green Bay Packers: The Complete Illustrated History*. "Their reaction was unfair, especially considering how business-orientated the NFL had become, and Lombardi was making a brilliant business decision, but the move was unimaginable for many Packer fans, so deep was their devotion to their city and their football team."

Under considerable pressure, the Packers' executive committee allowed him to leave—but if they had insisted, Vince said later, he would have stayed. "They could have condemned me, but they didn't," Lombardi said afterward. "They released me from my contract when I asked. They probably understood me better than I did myself."

Without hesitation, the Packers' executive committee assigned the general manager duties to head coach Phil Bengtson. The transition of power appeared seamless. When team president Dominic Olejniczak told reporters, "Phil is being given a free rein," he left no doubt that the Packers' executive committee expected Bengtson to continue Green Bay's success after inheriting all the responsibilities that were "the same as those which were given to Mr. Lombardi."

In the weeks leading up to Lombardi's departure, Bengtson assumed many of the team's general manager responsibilities. Even on the day of the NFL draft, he was tasked with choosing Green Bay's draft picks after Lombardi decided at the last moment not to participate, instead choosing to sit in his office alone. For those searching hard for a silver lining, "some of the Green Bay citizens in that February of 1969 saw Vince's departure as a good omen for the team," Lombardi biographer

> **"I never believed he would stay long in Green Bay as just general manager."**
> —RECEIVER
> BOYD DOWLER

When Vince Lombardi left the Packers for the Washington Redskins, he had amassed an overall 98–30–4 record that included an unprecedented 9-1 record in the postseason. In nine years as Green Bay's head coach, his nine postseason wins included five NFL championships and two Super Bowl victories. (COURTESY OF THE PRESS-GAZETTE COLLECTION OF THE NEVILLE PUBLIC MUSEUM OF BROWN COUNTY)

The Packers celebrated the 1969 season as their fiftieth year in professional football. (WHI IMAGE ID 87286)

Robert W. Wells wrote in *Vince Lombardi: His Life and Times*. "Phil Bengtson would no longer have to coach in the shadow of the master."

For Bengtson, that would still prove difficult. Even when he traveled to and from work every day, he had to drive along the newly named Lombardi Avenue to get to Lambeau Field. "It was an impossible situation for him," *Green Bay Press-Gazette* sportswriter Lee Remmel recalled. "It would have been an impossible situation for anyone."

• • •

In spring 1969 the Packers posted a net profit of $580,706 for 1968, a decrease from the previous season due in large part to the team's absence in the postseason. Bengtson was optimistic the team would return to the playoffs, but many of Green Bay's stars were retiring or moving on to other teams. Those who remained were quickly becoming relics in their own museum. "At that point, Phil probably should have cleaned house and started over," trainer Domenic Gentile surmised. "But he felt a tremendous loyalty to players such as Ray Nitschke, Elijah Pitts, Dave Robinson, Bart Starr and Travis Williams. These were guys who won championships. What was he supposed to do—trade them to the Bears?"

Retired Packers defensive tackle Henry Jordan (left) served as toastmaster at the second annual dinner of the Wisconsin chapter of Professional Football Writers of America. The evening honored Green Bay's Travis Williams, Dave Hampton, and Dave Robinson, here standing alongside team president Dominic Olejniczak at right. (MILWAUKEE JOURNAL SENTINEL)

The Packers started the 1969 season strong, shutting out the Bears in the opener en route to an early 5–2 record. But injuries and consecutive losses to the Colts, Vikings, and Lions derailed their playoff aspirations. Behind quarterback Don Horn, who had replaced an injured Bart Starr, the Packers finished a respectable 8–6 after winning three of their last four games. But Green Bay's second consecutive third-place finish in the Central Division prompted some of the team's executive committee members to reach out to a potential coaching replacement, regardless of whether Bengtson still had a year left on his contract. "There was some interest and contact there. I wanted out in Baltimore, and the thought of coaching the Packers interested me," coaching legend Don Shula admitted years later, "but the Packers decided not to fire their coach, and Joe Robbie and the Dolphins came up with an offer, and I've been with Miami ever since." Packerland may have been frustrated, but its optimism had

Despite Phil Bengtson's best efforts in 1969, the Packers found themselves being outrun by the Bears' Gale Sayers (40) and the rest of the NFL, stumbling into third place in the Central Division. (COURTESY OF GREEN BAY PRESS-GAZETTE FROM TOM PIGEON COLLECTION)

yet to be tarnished, as green and gold bumper stickers continued to blare the messages "The Pack Will Be Back" and "We'll Win with Bengtson" during the offseason.

■ ■ ■

By 1970 pro football had become ingrained in American culture. Beyond surpassing baseball in popularity, the game had captured the imaginations of fans, communities, and television executives across the country. In four short years the Super Bowl had become the nation's biggest sporting event. When the New York Jets pulled off their historic upset of the Baltimore Colts in Super Bowl III, a record television audience estimated at more than 40 million viewers watched. The next year, when the Kansas City Chiefs upended the Minnesota Vikings in Super Bowl IV, a new record was set as the television audience increased by more than 10 percent and the game generated gross receipts of $3.98 million, the largest for any previous sporting event. When ABC began broadcasting Monday Night Football in 1970, the spectacle's bright lights, creative camera angles, and compelling story lines were an instant television-ratings bonanza. Attendance at stadiums had enjoyed a steady rise throughout the sixties, averaging 54,430 per game by 1969, and broadcasting pro football in prime time only fueled the game's popularity. Even the president of the United States recognized football's prominent place in the country; while addressing Green Bay residents at a civic rally honoring Bart Starr in 1970, President Richard Nixon proclaimed: "The 1960s will be remembered as the decade in which football became America's number one sport."

However, before professional football could enjoy the spoils of the upcoming decade, owners of the AFL and NFL had to finalize their realignment as outlined in the original merger agreement of 1966. When two meetings resolved nothing, NFL commissioner Pete Rozelle oversaw a third, drop-dead realignment meeting that lasted almost thirty-six hours where owners argued, lobbied, and debated before reaching a compromise. The new postmerger NFL found itself reaching out to almost every corner of the lower forty-eight states. Teams

By 1970 television coverage of NFL games had evolved into a multi-camera extravaganza that expanded beyond Sunday afternoons into Monday night prime-time viewing. (COURTESY OF TOM PIGEON COLLECTION)

In 1970 the Packers paid tribute to their legendary quarterback Bart Starr with a day in his honor that included celebrities and dignitaries such as President Richard Nixon. (COURTESY OF THE PRESS-GAZETTE COLLECTION OF THE NEVILLE PUBLIC MUSEUM OF BROWN COUNTY)

would now be divided between the National and American Football Conferences, with three former NFL teams—the Steelers, Colts, and Browns—accepting $3 million apiece to switch to the AFC, giving each conference thirteen teams. The merger agreement further outlined that each of the three division winners in each conference—East, Central, and West—would earn a playoff spot with a fourth "wild card" team—the division runner-up with the best overall record—qualifying for the playoffs. Although the Packers found themselves sustaining their rivalries against the Bears, Lions, and Vikings in the NFC Central Division, "sadly, even with more slots available to make the playoffs," author Don Gulbrandsen noted, "Green Bay would take relatively little advantage of the opportunities in the decade ahead."

Once the merger was finalized, the NFL secured a four-year, $185 million television agreement, with CBS broadcasting all NFC games and NBC receiving the AFC games. In early July 1970, the National Football League Players Association, which had been recognized as the exclusive bargaining representative for all NFL players two years earlier, asked its players not to report to training camp. The strike, organized by John Mackey of the Baltimore Colts, Packers player representative Ken Bowman, and several other prominent players, was an attempt to get improved pension benefits, disability insurance, and working conditions for players. For three weeks, players and owners bickered. With no resolution in sight and the preseason in jeopardy, NFL commissioner Pete Rozelle intervened, and, "in a marathon twenty-two hour session with the NFLPA and representatives from each team, he accomplished what federal mediators had been unable to do: reach an agreement, in this case, a four-year pact," author Eric Goska explained in *Green Bay Packers: A Measure of Greatness*.

When a settlement was announced on August 3, few felt the players had gained any concessions over the owners, prompting the head of baseball's player union, Marvin Miller, to sneer, "It wasn't a strike, it was a student demonstration. The students marched around campus and then went back to class."

Even Mackey, who served as the NFLPA's president during the negotiations, was bitter about the outcome: "They gave us what they wanted to give us, made us smile and say 'thank you.' But from that day forward, we decided to build a legitimate union."

As the labor dispute dragged on that summer, Vince Lombardi was in and out of a Georgetown hospital. For months he had been complaining of stomach problems.

His condition soon deteriorated and on September 3, he succumbed to colon cancer. His funeral was held over Labor Day weekend at St. Patrick's Cathedral in New York. Thousands of spectators stood behind police barricades to pay their last respects in person, marking the end of a truly memorable era for professional football. "The power of Vince Lombardi's personality swept the world of sports," President Richard Nixon said as he led the nation in mourning. "Vince Lombardi believed in the strength of a nation, through its playing fields."

In the harshest of terms, Lombardi's death signified that the Packers' most recent run of success was over. "Few people knew then that Vince was not happy in Washington," trainer Domenic Gentile revealed of how the coach felt his arrangement with the Redskins did not live up to his expectations. "He and Marie wanted to return to Green Bay, and Vince had had discussions with some members of the Executive Committee to that effect. But a triumphant return to Titletown was not meant to be."

Back in Green Bay, the Lombardi era was still benefiting the corporation's overall financial health. At the annual stockholders' meeting, Bengtson announced that the Packers had netted an overall profit of $653,109 in 1969. The modest $70,000 profit increase from the previous season was after expenses of $2,945,972 were deducted from the team's income of $3,619,189. Despite keeping the franchise in the black, Bengtson was beginning to buckle under mounting pressure to return the Packers to prominence. "Bengtson went into the hospital that spring with a bleeding ulcer," executive committee member John Torinus recalled. "Phil couldn't take the pressures of the dual responsibilities like Lombardi did," he continued, further declaring, "Bengtson really didn't want to be general manager."

On opening day, a sellout Lambeau Field crowd of 56,263 witnessed the Lions thrash the Packers, 40–0. During the shutout—the first at home since 1949— "I encountered a new experience," quarterback Bart Starr recalled of the fans, accustomed to winning, expressing their displeasure. "I was booed while returning to the sidelines after throwing an incomplete pass on third down."

Once again the Packers were plagued by injuries. Many of their veterans played hurt for most of the season, including Starr, whose arm was so numb that he threw the ball without any feeling for most of the season. "After our last Super Bowl, I was going to quit," Starr confessed in *Sport* magazine. "But then when Coach Lombardi stepped down, I didn't feel I could run out on Coach Phil [Bengtson]. Now we don't enjoy the stature we did then, and that makes it more difficult to quit."

When the Packers limped to a disappointing 6–8 record, "That wasn't good enough for the Executive Committee, which still had the Lombardi golden decade firmly in mind," Torinus explained. "Phil is one of the finest gentlemen I have ever known, and he was a damn good football coach. He was just in the wrong place at the wrong time."

> **"Phil couldn't take the pressures of the dual responsibilities like Lombardi did."**
> —EXECUTIVE COMMITTEE MEMBER JOHN TORINUS

Following three disappointing seasons as Lombardi's handpicked successor, Phil Bengtson resigned from the Packers after posting a 20–21–1 record as head coach. (MILWAUKEE JOURNAL SENTINEL)

Two days after the Packers were shut out in their season finale, Bengtson announced, "Because of a very disappointing season in 1970, and hoping that a change will improve the win-loss record of the Packers in 1971, I hereby tender my resignation to become effective February 1, 1971."

What a difference a decade had made in Green Bay. The 1960s had begun with considerable optimism surrounding Lombardi's Packers—with the results exceeding even the most optimistic fan's expectations. The 1970s started on a much more somber note. Bengtson's resignation was thought to be the end of a frustrating three-year stretch in which "the whole social mood of the city is centered around the success or failure of the Packers," as public relations director Chuck Lane described in *The Vince Lombardi Scrapbook*. "That's one of the things that made losing in Green Bay so unbearable."

Even after the Packers posted a 6–8 record in 1970—the team's worst since it went 1–10–1 in 1958—many fans, team officials, and players were in denial that the Packers were a team in decline. "We got the veterans here who still know how to win," defensive back Bob Jeter said of his feelings that the Packers dynasty didn't need to be rebuilt, just resurrected. "Sure, there was a letdown after Lombardi left, but most of the veterans were still ready, and barring injuries we had the team to go all the way."

The Packers' executive committee was tasked with bringing in another Lombardi protégé or looking outside the organization for the team's seventh head coach in club history. In hopes of finding another gifted candidate, team president Dominic Olejniczak asked the board to consider what they had done right when deciding on Lombardi. The executive committee members, after concluding they had chosen an ambitious, focused, and disciplined man from the ranks of coaching obscurity in Lombardi, contradicted themselves by deciding to seek out an established, big-name coach to replace Bengtson. Their first choice was believed to be George Allen, who had just been fired by the Rams.

When Allen was promptly hired by the Redskins, the Packers turned to the college ranks, interviewing Frank Kush of Arizona State, a ranter in the Lombardi mold; Joe Paterno of Penn State, a high-spirited extrovert; and Dan Devine of the University of Missouri, a soft-spoken man of extraordinary reserve and tact. When Paterno and Devine emerged as the frontrunners, a strong difference of opinion divided the executive committee. "We never really knew whether Paterno would have taken the job if it had been offered to him," Torinus remarked. "He had been wooed by other NFL clubs before and had turned them down."

After much debate, "the executive committee's route to hiring Devine on the heels of Bengtson and Lombardi was eerily similar to the events of two decades earlier," author Don Gulbrandsen explained, "when college coaching veteran Lisle Blackbourn replaced a long-time NFL assistant [Gene Ronzani] who failed to fill the shoes of a coaching legend [Curly Lambeau]." The Packers hoped Devine's college success would ascend to the pros.

Devine had already amassed overwhelming credentials as a college coach—a 27–3–1 record at Arizona State University and a 93–37–7 record at the University of Missouri—before impressing the Packers' executive committee with his candor during their interview. "I can answer your questions like Vince Lombardi would have, if you are looking for another Lombardi," he told them. "But I'm going to answer them the way I would answer them. If you are looking for another Lombardi, you don't want me."

When introduced as head coach and general manager of the Packers, Devine made it clear he was the man in charge, since "I was the only man in the room with a five-year contract." At the age of forty-six, not only was Devine as old as Lombardi was when he took charge of the Packers twelve years earlier, but he also was burdened with the same expectations to win championships in Green Bay. When speaking with reporters, Devine was blunt in outlining how he would improve a club that had finished last in total offense and total defense—both by a large margin—in the Central Division the previous year: "Green Bay is a good organization with good players. My job is to put it all together. But I am not going on any crash program. I'll always keep an eye on the future. Frankly, I intend to be in Green Bay for the rest of my career, fifteen or twenty years."

Rather than wait until July to evaluate the players he inherited in person, Devine organized a special training camp in April. His spring camp turned into a shakedown where he made it clear that there would be no sacred cows in his locker room. "There are certain guys on the team who are not willing to buy me—some pretty good players," Devine remarked, adding with tongue ever so slightly in cheek that "I'll help them get another job."

The Packers' new head coach, Dan Devine (bottom center), posed with (left to right) Mike McCoy, Bart Starr, Donny Anderson, and Willie Wood at the 1971 Wisconsin Pro Football Writers' Awards dinner. (MILWAUKEE JOURNAL SENTINEL)

Almost half of the 1971 Packers were disciples of Lombardi—Willie Wood, Lionel Aldridge, Ken Bowman, Donny Anderson, Carroll Dale, Gale Gillingham, Bob Jeter, Jim Grabowski, Ray Nitschke, Dave Robinson, Zeke Bratkowski, and Bart Starr—who found their new coach's dismissive attitude toward them and their prior accomplishments frustrating. "He'd tell us that the Green Bay sweep was really his play and Vince Lombardi got it from him," Wood recalled. "That's the kind of things he'd say."

Even Perry Moss, who was an assistant coach with the Packers at the time, noticed that "there was all sorts of turmoil and division within that team. It was a really divided ship with some Lombardi guys left and then Devine's guys."

Publicly and in the locker room, Devine didn't hesitate to compare his current Packers players with those he had coached in college. During his first meeting with his new team, he opted to run highlight footage from his University of Missouri games. "That didn't go over real big," defensive tackle Mike McCoy remarked. To the press, Devine commented, "We don't have as good a football team as I thought. . . . I had much more speed, for example, when I was at Missouri than I have here."

Despite what he had inherited in Green Bay, Devine was confident his coaching experience would revitalize the Packers' winning ways. "People say it's a difficult transition from the colleges to the pros," he claimed in an interview with *Sport* magazine. "But just look at the films of [Missouri's] Notre Dame game last year. From the defensive spacings we used you would have thought we were pros. In some ways the college game is getting like the pros and the pros are getting like college."

What Devine now had in Green Bay that hadn't been available to him at the University of Missouri were the unprecedented financial resources to rebuild his aging roster. At the annual stockholders' meeting in May, the Packers reported their largest profit in history—$1,139,379 for 1970—despite experiencing their poorest season on the field in more than a decade. The substantial gain compared to 1969's reported profit of $653,109 was due to Lambeau Field increasing its seating capacity from 50,861 to 56,161, as well as increased ticket prices in both Green Bay and Milwaukee. In 1970, 61 percent of all income came from ticket sales, which amounted to $2,957,803 as the Packers drew a total of 1,022,103 fans in twenty games—home and away, regular-season and exhibition games. More than 26 percent of income came from television and radio agreements, totaling $1,354,858. The team also listed current investments of $3,100,656 and total capital and retained earnings at $5,782,946.

For those 115 stockholders present at the meeting, the Packers' corporate ledger further outlined that team profits and the subsequent cost of doing business in the NFL had skyrocketed since Lombardi arrived in Green Bay twelve years earlier. Income from ticket sales went from $888,222 in 1959 to nearly $3 million in 1970.

Radio and television revenue leaped from $118,692 to $1,391,950 during that same time frame. Meanwhile, the team's operating expenses jumped from $875,030 in 1959 to slightly over $3 million by 1970. Season expenses, which included mostly player salaries, shot up from $512,760 in 1959 to $2,151,452 in 1970.

The growing business of pro football meant Devine needed someone to oversee the administrative end of the Packers. "I couldn't do all of the administrative front-office work and still put in the time I thought was necessary to function as the coach of the Packers, preparing game plans and getting the players ready to play. There physically were not enough hours in the day for one person to do all of the work that needed to be done," he admitted in his autobiography, *Simply Devine*. Devine hired Bob Harlan—a public relations director from the front office of baseball's St. Louis Cardinals—to be his assistant general manager in Green Bay. "[Harlan] had no experience in football," according to Devine, "but he met every other qualification and came with high recommendations."

When Harlan arrived, "the first reporter I talked to in Green Bay after I took the job was Lee Remmel, who was working for the *Green Bay Press-Gazette*," he recalled, "and his first question to me was, 'What does a baseball guy know about football?' I told him, 'We'll find out.'"

As the 1971 season approached, profound optimism circulated throughout Packerland. New yellow and green stickers proclaiming "The Pack Is Devine" on the bumpers of Green Bay automobiles implied that the Packers would become a team of destiny. "There was something prophetic about the first game Dan Devine coached in the National Football League," executive committee member John Torinus confessed, describing the sideline pileup of players that brought an early end

When Dan Devine needed an assistant general manager in Green Bay, he hired Bob Harlan, who had ties to Wisconsin as a graduate of Milwaukee's Marquette University. (COURTESY OF THE PRESS-GAZETTE COLLECTION OF THE NEVILLE PUBLIC MUSEUM OF BROWN COUNTY)

More than 50,000 bumper stickers declaring "The Pack Is Devine" were distributed in advance of Dan Devine's arrival in Green Bay as the team's new head coach and general manager. (WHI IMAGE ID 81768)

Dan Devine left his first game as the Packers head coach on a stretcher (right) after breaking his leg, prompting him to coach his second game from the press box and third game on the sidelines on crutches (below). (BOTH PHOTOS MILWAUKEE JOURNAL SENTINEL)

to Devine's Lambeau Field debut. "The Packer head coach was carried from the field on a stretcher with a broken leg."

Devine was forced to listen to the rest of the Packers' 42–40 opening-day loss to the Giants from St. Vincent Hospital. He returned to coach the Packers to a victory the next week against the Broncos from the Milwaukee County Stadium press box. By the season's third week, he was back on the sidelines, coaching on crutches as Green Bay beat the Bengals. Starting at 2–1, the Packers became a team in transition, enduring two separate three-game losing streaks over the course of the season. Many of the key contributors from years past saw their playing time reduced due to injuries, including Starr, who missed the season's first ten games only to return as a shadow of his former self. Devine also insisted on inserting his younger players into the lineup, which found linebacker Ray Nitschke backing up Jim Carter in all but two games that year. The Packers' offense, led by quarterback Scott Hunter, was respectable behind rookie halfback John Brockington, who ran for 1,105 yards. But the team's once-dominant defense could no longer keep opponents out of the end zone as Green Bay finished 4–8–2 and in the NFC Central Division cellar for the second year in a row.

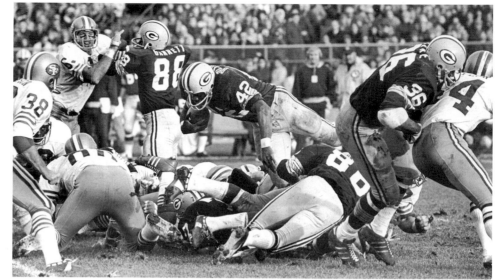

Under Devine, the Packers found their rushing attack rejuvenated by John Brockington (42), who became the first NFL player to rush for 1,000 or more yards in each of his first three seasons. (WISCONSIN STATE JOURNAL)

• • •

During a busy offseason, Devine looked to accelerate his roster reconstruction plan for the Packers. During the NFL draft, he chose defensive back Willie Buchanon with the seventh overall selection in the draft. With the team's second first-round pick, he selected former Green Bay prep star and Nebraska quarterback Jerry Tagge. From the moment his name was announced, Tagge was considered to be the Packers' quarterback of the future. He would replace the now retired icon Bart Starr, who was staying on as an assistant coach. In the second round, Devine not only made the stunning decision to draft a placekicker, but he chose Chester Marcol, a complete unknown from a school few could find on a map: Hillsdale College. The Packers had suffered through nine kickers, who combined to convert only 45 percent of their field goals between 1968 and 1971 following Don Chandler's retirement after Super Bowl II. Marcol rejuvenated Green Bay's kicking game, leading the league in scoring during his rookie campaign, hitting thirty-three of forty-eight field goals, including three game winners.

For those positions not addressed in the draft, Devine orchestrated several savvy trades, sending Donny Anderson to the Cardinals for fullback MacArthur Lane and defensive end Lionel Aldridge to San Diego for safety Jim Hill. Remaining Lombardi holdovers—Zeke Bratkowski, Elijah Pitts, Willie Wood, and Doug Hart—announced their retirements, prompting veteran linebacker Dave Robinson to claim, "Devine never could learn to deal with the ghost of Lombardi, and that's why he purged the roster of Vince's guys."

> **"Devine never could learn to deal with the ghost of Lombardi, and that's why he purged the roster of Vince's guys."**
>
> —LINEBACKER DAVE ROBINSON

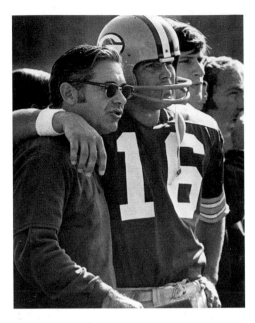

By 1972 Dan Devine (in sunglasses) entrusted the Packers' quarterback duties to Scott Hunter (16). (MILWAUKEE JOURNAL SENTINEL)

Further indication that the Packers' glory years had ended was evident in the team's financial statement for 1971. During the annual stockholders' meeting, team president Dominic Olejniczak gave no explanation to the 97 stockholders in attendance why profits had dropped almost 33 percent from a year earlier. The $766,361 profit for 1971, down $373,018 from 1970's total of $1,139,379, did include a slight raise in radio and television revenues, which climbed from $1,354,858 to $1,437,296. However, Green Bay's total operating expenses in 1971 of $3,771,480 were $690,336 higher than in 1970. Furthermore, team expenses had also increased $358,556, and administration costs jumped from $770,280 in 1970 to $1,024,276 in 1971. Despite all the added expenses, the Packers' $766,361 profit was still the fourth best in team history compared to earnings of $653,109 in 1969; $580,706 in 1968; $805,823 in 1967; and $827,439 in 1966.

The Packers opened the 1972 season with a victory in Cleveland, followed by a loss at home to Oakland. In week three they received a huge dose of confidence after beating the defending Super Bowl champion Dallas Cowboys in Milwaukee. "It was a team that played over its head," Devine said of how his replenished roster of youngsters wanted to write their own history. "There were good players at every position. There weren't any bad weaknesses."

Green Bay's rigid defense, led by Associated Press NFL Rookie of the Year Willie Buchanon, helped the Packers win several close games and enjoy a 4–3 record at midseason. Devine's disciples finished the season strong, putting together two three-game winning streaks sandwiched around a loss to the Redskins, en route to a 10–4 record. The Packers had secured their first NFC Central Division title since 1967, averaging just 253 yards a game on offense, of which 162 came on the ground. "We flat-out ran over everybody," center Ken Bowman recalled of the combination of John Brockington and MacArthur Lane, who ran for 1,027 yards and 821 yards, respectively, that season. "Once you got those two in the backfield, it really didn't matter who you handed the ball to. We could move the ball on anybody."

Green Bay's reliance on the ground game was a direct result of Devine's lack of confidence in his quarterback, Scott Hunter, who completed just 43 percent of his passes and threw for only six touchdowns all season. "I remember we'd be leading late in a game and I'd call time out and bring Scott over to the sidelines," Devine later admitted. "I'd tell him to take off his helmet and look me straight in the eye. Then I'd tell him, 'Scott, the only way we can lose this game is if you screw up.' Then I'd send him back to the huddle."

Despite the Packers' winning record in 1972, dissension grew between the younger players Devine had brought into Green Bay—like Scott Hunter (16) and Rich McGeorge (81)—and those who had played for Lombardi, such as Carroll Dale (84). (WISCONSIN STATE JOURNAL)

It was classic Devine, a psychology major in college who never feared saying or doing whatever it took to get the results he wanted. In the two short years he had been in Green Bay, he had earned a reputation for being an eccentric enigma, often creating paradoxes between his droll, folksy persona off the field and his crisp, strident, authoritarian style on the gridiron. "He was different," center Larry Mc-Carren recalled. "We'd be in team meetings and then he'd flip off the projector after a mistake and there'd be a pregnant pause. That's when we knew someone was going to get it."

But in 1972, his coaching style produced results. "I was named the NFC coach of the year by the Football Writers of America," Devine proclaimed. "And to be included with a group of people that included George Halas, who was like a hero to me, was a tremendous thrill."

Preparing for the postseason, the Packers awaited a rematch with their week-eleven foes, the Washington Redskins, whose 11–3 record was the NFC's best. In the divisional playoff game, "Washington coach George Allen came up with a defensive alignment the Packers had never seen before, stationing one of his biggest defensive [linemen] on the Packer center's nose," John Torinus recalled of the five-man defensive front used to stop the Packers' dominating running game.

During the 1972 playoffs, there was a philosophical—and visible—disconnect between head coach Dan Devine and assistant coach Bart Starr, which contributed to the Packers' 16–3 loss to the Redskins. (MILWAUKEE JOURNAL SENTINEL)

"Bart and Devine were fifty feet apart. They weren't talking."
—QUARTERBACK SCOTT HUNTER

With assistant coach Bart Starr calling the plays, Green Bay captured the game's first lead on Chester Marcol's 17-yard field goal in the second quarter. "I thought, 'If they stay in this [five-man front] we'll kill them,'" quarterback Scott Hunter recalled, noting how effective Starr's playcalling was. "They only had two linebackers. We knew we could hit the back coming out of the backfield."

However, on the next series the Packers ran three straight running plays, resulting in an immediate punt. The next time Hunter was in the huddle, two separate plays were sent to him by two different players. "Devine tried to take over and start calling the plays during the game," cornerback Ken Ellis recalled. "Bart had prepared Scott for the five-man front. Bart would call a play and Devine would change it."

"Bart and Devine were fifty feet apart," Hunter remarked, describing the head coach's determination to overrule his assistant coach. "They weren't talking."

"By the third quarter, Bart was totally disattached from the game: he was down at the thirty-yard line. It was Devine's play; he got outcoached and it was not a pretty sight," running back John Brockington added.

For the rest of the afternoon, the Packers couldn't move the ball on the ground. "We'd run into that five-man front two weeks earlier and Bart Starr said if they do that again, run two backs out of the backfield and throw it," Brockington recalled. "But Dan never did because he decided he wanted to coach that day. Nobody could believe we let that happen. I ran into [Redskins linebacker] Chris Hanburger a few weeks later and he said, 'Why didn't you guys throw the ball? We didn't expect to stay in that defense all day.'"

A stubborn Devine refused to throw the ball, determined he could run it against the Redskins' defensive scheme. But the maneuver completely halted the Green Bay running game. Brockington managed just 9 yards on thirteen carries, and the Packers were held to their lowest rushing output of the season—78 yards—in the 16–3 loss to Washington. In the game's aftermath, "the story came out that Starr had recommended some changes in the game plan to counter the unique Allen defense, but Devine did not take Starr's advice," Torinus noted. "Many fans credited the Packers' success that year to Starr's offensive strategy. At any rate, Starr did not return to the staff after that season."

• • •

Despite making their first postseason appearance in five years, the Packers failed to transfer that success to their corporate ledger. For the second consecutive year, team profits dipped; their 1972 profit of $480,203 was down $286,157 from 1971. Regardless of the profit margin, expectations in Green Bay were raised to a fever pitch the likes of which hadn't been experienced since the days of Lombardi. "With the nucleus we had, we thought we could add on to the roster and get better," kicker Chester Marcol remarked. "But I don't know what the heck happened."

During the offseason Devine did little to address the needs of the Packers roster, insisting he had put together a talented team. Soon whispers began circulating around Lambeau Field questioning whether he was capable of managing a professional football franchise.

When Bart Starr didn't return as the team's quarterbacks coach, the position lacked direction. Devine's solution was to rotate among journeyman Scott Hunter, the recently acquired Jim Del Gaizo from Miami, and the team's quarterback of the future, Jerry Tagge. The scenario wreaked havoc with the Packers' ability to gain yards and score points. "I think one of Devine's biggest mistakes was changing quarterbacks early in the season," trainer Domenic Gentile said of the decision to bench Hunter in favor of Del Gaizo. "That destroyed Hunter and fragmented the team."

To open the season, the Packers shut down Joe Namath and the Jets in Milwaukee; the team had every reason to believe they were playoff contenders with a 2–1–1 record after the season's first four weeks. "We had managed to overcome some injuries in 1972 to still enjoy a terrific season," Devine recalled, "but we weren't so fortunate in 1973."

Starting in week six, the offense was held to fewer than 100 yards for three straight games—all losses. The season seemed to unravel from there. "I could have coached better, and we could have played better, and our final record of 5–7–2 was a big letdown from the playoff high of the previous year," Devine remarked.

The lone bright spot for a team that scored an average of just 14 points per game was that John Brockington became the first man in NFL history to rush for more than 1,000 yards in each of his first three seasons. Although the Packers' 21–0 shutout of the Bears kept them out of the NFC Central Division cellar, Devine's relationship with the press had deteriorated. He began to lose favor in Green Bay. He even claimed that his family dog had been shot, "presumably by an irate fan," John Torinus recalled. The story appeared in the October 9, 1974, issue of *Time* magazine, in an article entitled "Haunted in Green Bay" in which, according to Torinus, Devine "was quoted extensively with some rather derogatory remarks about the people in Green Bay"—which "didn't help his relations with members of the Executive Committee."

■ ■ ■

Over the course of the 1973 season, the NFL succeeded in negotiating significant raises into its television contracts with ABC, CBS, and NBC. The overall four-year agreement—which totaled $269 million and increased the annual income each team would receive from $1.8 million to $2.6 million through 1977—only reinforced the perception that pro football was a lucrative business for the league, its team owners, and the host cities, thus creating a natural reaction. Now more than ever, wealthy investors wanted to become team owners, and cities lobbied to host a franchise. Because the NFL, which was still adjusting to its recent merger with the AFL, had no immediate plans for expansion, a rival league emerged out of the demand for more football.

The World Football League was formed in 1973 by attorney Gary Davidson, who had already cofounded two successful "rogue" leagues, the American Basketball Association and the World Hockey Association. The WFL assembled twelve teams— including franchises in several non-NFL cities like Memphis, Portland, Birmingham, and Honolulu—to begin playing a twenty-game season in the summer of 1974. The new league's original goal was to expand in five years to twelve other cities through-out the world, creating a twenty-four-team league with two twelve-team divisions of American and international teams. But the WFL would endure a tumultuous in-augural season. Franchises in Detroit and Jacksonville folded after fourteen games. Teams originating in New York and Houston relocated to Charlotte and Shreveport, respectively, at midseason. Over two years, the epidemic of franchise turnover and financial instability resulted in five teams being sold three times, one team sold twice, and four other teams sold once. The WFL's inability to develop popular teams in New York, Los Angeles, and Chicago eliminated national television as a revenue source. In 1975, just fourteen weeks into its sophomore season, the league folded after having lost an estimated $30 million.

Although its existence was brief, the WFL survived long enough to create a public relations nightmare for the NFL. Despite being in financial trouble from its inception, the WFL had lured several high-profile players away from the NFL with the promise of more money. The upstart league had exposed that NFL players were being underpaid compared to other pro athletes, creating dissent among those still playing for NFL teams.

In 1974 the average NFL player salary of $25,000 had not increased since 1968. So when the latest labor contract between the NFL and the NFL Players Associa-tion—signed after a brief strike in 1970—expired, players wanted a larger portion of NFL revenues. In the first negotiation session between players and owners dur-ing the spring of 1974, the NFLPA articulated fifty-eight demands, including the creation of total free agency. When NFL commissioner Pete Rozelle cautioned that complete, unrestricted free agency could force some teams in smaller markets to fold, the NFLPA replied, "Let those teams go out of business if they can't run a profitable enterprise. That's what happens in American industry."

After submitting an additional thirty-three demands in May, the union became unhappy with the minimal progress being made on the terms of a new collective bargaining agreement. On July 1, 1974, the NFLPA announced that its players would not report to training camp. "Green Bay was targeted by the players as one of the key teams, because the town of Green Bay is a big union town," Devine recalled of disgruntled players picketing outside the training camp facility, wearing T-shirts featuring a clenched fist and the slogan "No Freedom, No Football." "And a lot of hard feelings developed. Because of my dual title as general manager, I squarely was labeled a member of management, and that made me the enemy."

When the dispute dragged into the preseason, the union's fragile stance began to deteriorate as players' unity fragmented. By July 29 almost 20 percent of the striking players had crossed the picket line—including Packers veterans Jim Carter and Chester Marcol—and on August 7 the NFL reported that more than one hundred more players had defected, returning to training camp. Less than a week later, on August 11, the union suspended its forty-one-day strike. When the players returned to camp, they were no closer to free agency and would play without a contract until 1977.

Even before the players' strike, Devine was ready for a change. "Before the 1974 season began, I made up my mind that if somebody contacted me about coaching at the college level again, I definitely would consider it," he admitted in his autobiography, *Simply Devine*. "I remembered before taking the job with the Packers how my friends said the greatest job in football was working as a head coach and general manager in the NFL. After three years, however, I had come to the conclusion that it wasn't all it was advertised to be, at least for me. I had been happier coaching in college, and I couldn't see myself continuing to coach in the NFL for an extended period."

Although a growing faction of fans began calling for Devine's job, the executive committee was committed to supporting him. "I felt that the Dan Devine of 1971 and 1972 was a completely different man from the Devine of 1973 and 1974," Torinus said. "During mid-1973, his wife was diagnosed as having multiple sclerosis, and I have always felt that this had a great effect on Devine's subsequent performance in Green Bay."

Devine, desperate to resolve his quarterback dilemma, jettisoned Del Gaizo and Hunter during the offseason, leaving Tagge as the team's starter and recent offseason acquisition Jack Concannon from the Bears as his backup. By midseason the

ABOVE: During the 1974 preseason, the NFL was crippled by a players' strike that saw rookies and free agents cross picket lines in buses. RIGHT: Packers linebacker Jim Carter (50) chose to cross the picket line against the wishes of fellow veterans (below, left to right) Bill Lueck, Dick Himes, and Gale Gillingham. (ALL PHOTOS MILWAUKEE JOURNAL SENTINEL)

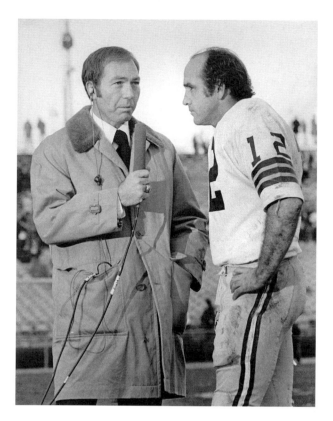

Bart Starr, who went into broadcasting after the 1972 season, interviewed the Packers' recently acquired quarterback, John Hadl. (MILWAUKEE JOURNAL SENTINEL)

duo had completed just one touchdown pass, and "dissension tore the team apart," trainer Domenic Gentile recalled. "Most of the players were down on the coaching staff as a whole and disliked Devine in particular, and it was obvious by their performance on the field."

On October 22, 1974, one day after a 10–9 loss to the Chicago Bears, Devine pulled off a rare mid-season trade. The Packers sent their first-, second-, and third-round picks of the 1975 draft and their first- and third-round selections for 1976 to the Los Angeles Rams for thirty-four-year-old quarterback John Hadl, who was already considered to be on the downward slope of his career. "One of our linebackers, Jim Carter, called it the 'Lawrence Welk trade,' because we had given up 'a 1-2, a 1-2-3,'" Gentile joked.

Devine made the bold move without consulting anybody, including the club's executive committee. "I don't think there was a soul in the organization who knew about the deal other than Dan," Bob Harlan recalled of the trade that mortgaged the Packers' future for several years. "It was a huge mistake on his part, and I knew how the executive committee was going to feel."

Unbeknownst to the executive committee, Devine was already planning his exit strategy out of Green Bay. "If I was leaving, the one thing I wanted to make certain of was that I left the new coach with a better team and a better situation than the one I inherited. And I did," Devine claimed, noting Hadl had been an All-Pro in 1973. "I really thought I had the kind of team that was capable of playing our way into the playoffs. Unfortunately, that didn't happen, and the inner turmoil and politics that were surrounding our franchise partly contributed to our losing our last three games."

After receiving a raise from $90,000 to $400,000, Hadl threw just three touchdown passes in the Packers' final seven games. "The thing I've always said is I didn't make the trade," Hadl remarked in his defense as the Packers' record in that span, 3–4, was no better than it had been before his arrival.

Of the Packers' eight losses that season, two were by 1 point and another by 2 points. Although Green Bay's 6–8 record kept them out of the NFC Central Division cellar that year, "the Committee became more and more disenchanted with Devine as the 1974 season wore on," Torinus recalled. "Devine still had a year to go on his five-year contract, and at the moment, the sentiment of the Committee seemed to be to let him finish it out."

In hindsight, Devine's willingness to say or do whatever it took to get the results he wanted was creating a series of contradictions that signaled his eventual departure. During a taped television interview that aired the Friday night before the Packers' second-to-last game of the 1974 season, Devine revealed that after the 1972 season he had submitted a letter of resignation, which the Packers executive committee rejected. "I had reason to know that there were other clubs that would take my services as head coach. I felt at that time it might be best for me to bow out and go," Devine said. Yet he also claimed he had no thoughts of quitting again. "I didn't put four years into a situation and not want to reap the rewards. The rewards are there to reap next year."

Less than a week later, Devine reiterated his plans to reporters: "I signed a five year contract through the 1975 season and much of my work yesterday involved planning for 1975," he said. "I'm making plans for being here in '75. I'm quite happy and satisfied."

But Devine had other plans as he prepared for the Packers' season finale against the Falcons. "It was strange. When I went to bed Saturday night in Atlanta, I was the head coach of the Packers, [and] the future head coach at Notre Dame," Devine admitted in his autobiography. "It was an unsettling time, but I told myself I was doing the right thing."

"He knew what was coming," assistant coach Perry Moss said of the conversation that occurred the following morning. "We were eating breakfast before the last game of the year. The staff was sitting around the table and Devine asked, 'What's the greatest coaching job in America?' And Devine said, 'Notre Dame.'"

After the Packers lost their season finale, "Devine called President Olejniczak from Atlanta and said he wanted to meet with him when the team got home. He told Olejniczak he had to know what his status was for the 1975 season," Torinus said of the coach's uncharacteristic sense of urgency. "I don't think we had any suspicions that Devine had something up his sleeve, but his intransigence about the following season cemented our opinion that we didn't want to go through another year with him in charge."

After Olejniczak and Fred Trowbridge of the Packers' executive committee arranged the legal details, paying Devine off for the final year of his contract, "the four men shook hands on the deal, and Devine and his attorney left," Torinus said. "It was only a minute later, however, when Devine returned and popped his head into Trowbridge's office, saying, 'Oh, by the way, I am going to Notre Dame.'"

When news of his resignation and subsequent hiring as the next head coach at Notre Dame went public on Monday, December 16, a comment Devine had made

> **"We didn't want to go through another year with [Devine] in charge."**
>
> —EXECUTIVE COMMITTEE MEMBER JOHN TORINUS

a week earlier seemed all the more underhanded. "It would be a damn shame if someone else comes in here and reaps the rewards of all my hard work," he had told to reporters who thought he was about to be fired. "This team is going to win ten games next year."

But to those closest to the Packers, "history will show Dan Devine tore that team up, and he tore up that franchise," wide receiver Barry Smith said of Devine's legacy in Green Bay. "Let's face it, that's what he did."

Dan Devine (hands on head) left Green Bay for Notre Dame after the 1974 season, but not before compiling an overall 25-28-4 record that included one playoff loss in four seasons. (MILWAUKEE JOURNAL SENTINEL)

THE ABYSS
of
MEDIOCRITY

The Packers' inability to recapture Vince Lombardi's winning ways didn't deter fans from supporting the team on a yearly basis. At the team's training camp in 1982, several Packers including Paul Coffman (82), Karl Swanke (67), Rich Wingo (50), Greg Koch (68), John Anderson (59), Del Rodgers (35), Syd Kitson (64), Ron Hallstrom (65), Lynn Dickey (12), and Larry Pfohl—aka professional wrestler Lex Lugar—(66), interacted with fans between practices. (FROM THE GREEN BAY PRESS-GAZETTE ARCHIVES, REPRINTED BY PERMISSION)

The Packers, only seven years removed from their Super Bowl II victory, were now rife with dissension. During the final weeks of the 1974 season, a quiet conspiracy began gaining momentum throughout Green Bay—an underground campaign of whispers to bring back Bart Starr, Vince Lombardi's trusted field general, as the team's next head coach. Once Dan Devine's resignation was made public, even a reluctant Starr understood why he was perceived as the public's romantic solution to fixing a franchise in shambles. "The Green Bay Packers organization had deteriorated to the point where it was one of the worst in pro football," Starr recalled. "I was intrigued by the challenge of fielding an NFL team as well as rebuilding the Packers to the point where they would be as respected as they had been during the Lombardi era."

Although the Packers were rumored to be interested in retired NFL players Jack Pardee and Norm Van Brocklin as possible successors to Devine, Starr set himself apart during his interview with the team's executive committee. "He handed out typewritten brochures, which had been prepared by [former Packers' publicity chief Chuck] Lane, outlining his qualifications and also a rather complete plan of action if he were named to the job," executive committee member John Torinus remembered.

On December 24, 1974, the Packers announced that Bart Starr had signed a three-year contract as their next head coach and general manager. "The decision of the Packer executive committee to appoint me," even Starr admitted, "was based on emotion rather than logic."

Starr had only one year of coaching experience—as an assistant on Dan Devine's staff in 1972—but "Dominic Olejniczak, our team president at the time, told me that the fans really selected this coach, that they almost demanded that he be hired,"

When Bart Starr was named head coach and general manager of the Packers on December 24, 1974, he looked to instill the sense of glory Vince Lombardi had brought to the team fifteen years earlier. (MILWAUKEE JOURNAL SENTINEL)

> "The fans couldn't wait for Bart to take over."
>
> —TEAM EXECUTIVE BOB HARLAN

future team president Bob Harlan recalled. "That was a great description of the situation because the fans couldn't wait for Bart to take over."

Starr was now overextended with the responsibilities of being both the team's head coach and general manager. "This franchise had such incredible success with Lombardi serving in the dual role of coach and general manager that it just seemed that was the way things ought to be done," Harlan explained. "One man coached and also ran all the other football business, answering only to the executive committee."

To assist him in rebuilding the Packers' roster and overall operations, Starr restructured the front office, making Bob Harlan (Devine's assistant general manager) now the corporate general manager and Tom Miller (who had been an assistant general manager under Lombardi) the team's business general manager. Harlan was now in charge of all administrative personnel, the public relations department, and negotiations for all player and assistant coach contracts. Miller became the liaison between the front office and the executive committee, serving as the team's purchasing agent for all phases of the operation and supervising ticket operations in Green Bay and Milwaukee. Starr would have enough support to allow him to focus on fielding a winning team, despite the adverse financial situation he inherited from his predecessor.

Although the Packers hadn't lost money in 1974, as team president Dominic Olejniczak had first feared, their annual profit had dipped to its lowest level in fourteen years. Team treasurer Fred Trowbridge announced to stockholders that the team's 1974 profit amounted to $128,425, compared to $680,242 in 1973. It was the Packers' smallest profit since 1960, when the club made $115,125. "Our operating expenses rose primarily because of higher salaries, number one, and number two, because of keeping more players longer from the time training camp opened until the player strike was called off," Trowbridge told the crowd of 115 stockholders, representing 2,480 of the 4,656 shares in the community-owned, nonprofit corporation. Trowbridge explained that competition for players from the World Football League had inflated salaries, but that this would be offset in the upcoming year by the NFL's new network television contract, providing the team with an increase of $529,974 in income. The Packers would also receive another influx of $241,567 from the NFL's two new expansion franchises.

Earlier that decade, when the NFL announced it would expand from twenty-six to twenty-eight teams, commissioner Pete Rozelle explained that cities would be considered for an expansion team based on their stadium, weather, sports interest, and growth potential. By the spring of 1974, the list of hopeful cities that once included Indianapolis and Jacksonville had been narrowed to five: Honolulu, Memphis, Phoenix, Seattle, and Tampa. That group was thinned to four when NFL owners awarded Tampa, Florida, the twenty-seventh franchise. Less than two months later, the owners welcomed Seattle into the league. The two franchises paid a then-record $16 million entry fee to begin play in 1976.

Back in Green Bay, Bart Starr's return had infused a sense of hope around the Packers' training camp unseen since the early days of Lombardi. "The atmosphere in the organization changed tremendously once Bart Starr arrived. It was almost a feeling of relief because everyone really believed he was the right person for the job," Harlan recalled of the team's fresh start. "The people in our building were as excited as the fans on the street."

Upon taking the job, Starr would have to replenish one of the oldest rosters in the league if the team's fortunes were to turn around. "Right away we began to evaluate the Packers' existing personnel and became very concerned," Starr said of inheriting nine players over the age of thirty and four more at twenty-nine. "The reasons for the Packers' decline after 1968 became more obvious; the organization had failed to adequately plan for the replacement of its quality veteran players."

The NFL's college draft would provide Green Bay with few opportunities over the next two years. The Packers had relinquished the ninth, twenty-eighth, and sixty-first overall picks in the 1975 draft and the eighth and thirty-ninth overall

More than 1,500 fans turned out at the Packers' training camp every day, forming a corridor from Lambeau Field to the Oneida Street practice field, all for the chance to see the return of Bart Starr. (MILWAUKEE JOURNAL SENTINEL)

picks in 1976 as part of the John Hadl trade. Suffering from a lack of talent, "we were no better than most expansion teams and worse than some," Starr remarked.

Starr also eradicated the cancerous personalities from a Packers locker room where losing had become contagious. "Unfortunately, he was unable to replace these people as fast or as quickly as he thought he could," Torinus remarked, "and from his first season on, he suffered from a serious lack of depth in key positions on both offense and defense."

It didn't take long for the Packers' personnel weaknesses to be exposed. In the 1975 season opener, the Detroit Lions blocked three of Steve Broussard's nine punts to set an NFL record; kicker Chester Marcol tore a quadriceps muscle and was lost for the season. The next week, cornerback Willie Buchanon suffered a broken leg against Denver and joined Marcol on the season-ending injured reserve list. Running back John Brockington went into an early season slump and never regained his old swagger. Quarterback John Hadl failed to return to the form that had made him a star with San Diego in the AFL, throwing an NFC-high twenty-one interceptions. When the Packers started the season with four straight defeats, syndicated columnist Steve Harvey

Although Lambeau Field had been sold out consistently since 1960, Bart Starr's return brought added enthusiasm to season-ticket holders. Here (left to right) Kevin Kuehn, Jim Heintzkill, and Chuck Kuehn processed and mailed more than 50,000 sets of season tickets to 1975 Green Bay Packers games. (COURTESY OF THE PRESS-GAZETTE COLLECTION OF THE NEVILLE PUBLIC MUSEUM OF BROWN COUNTY)

Serving as team ambassadors, safeties Steve Luke (left) and Johnnie Gray (right) were two of several Packers who made public appearances in the months leading up to the 1975 season. (COURTESY OF THE PRESS-GAZETTE COLLECTION OF THE NEVILLE PUBLIC MUSEUM OF BROWN COUNTY)

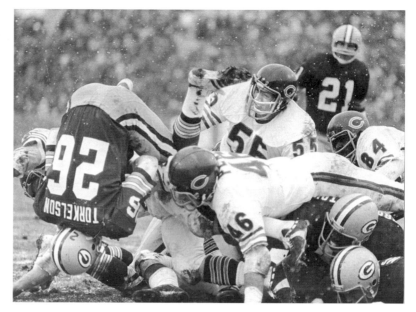

ABOVE: New head coach and general manager Bart Starr was serious about returning honor and re-spectability to the Packers organization, on and off the field. (WHI IMAGE ID 88802)

ABOVE, RIGHT: Running back Eric Torkelson (26) and the rest of the Packers found their 1975 season taking a nosedive as they lost eight of their first nine games. (WISCONSIN STATE JOURNAL)

was unsympathetic when declaring, "Packers coach Bart Starr is off to his worst start since 1955, when he helped quarterback Alabama to an 0–10 season."

After the Packers nipped the Cowboys 19–17 for their first win of the season, they went on to lose four more games. They finished the season on a positive note with a victory over the Falcons. "Winning three of their last five provided reason for hope, even though the Pack had only a 4–10 record on the season," Torinus explained, noting the team's last-place finish in the NFC Central Division.

• • •

The team's future looked brighter during the annual stockholders' meeting that offseason. The Packers reported a net profit of $784,830—the highest since 1970, when it had reached a record $1,139,379. They also announced that for the first time in team history, the franchise's total assets were above the $10 million mark, having reached $10,769,416, up from $9,837,452 in 1974.

Green Bay's annual stockholders' meetings and public disclosures of financial records would become even more relevant that year as they became the last publicly owned NFL franchise. The Patriots franchise, which was formed in 1959 as part of the original American Football League, had been public since William H. Sullivan Jr., along with nine other investors, sold nonvoting public stock to raise capital to help post the franchise fee of $25,000. In 1975 Sullivan became the majority owner, and a year later he purchased the remaining nonvoting stock. Once he acquired control of

The first Green Bay Packers Hall of Fame opened in 1967 as a series of temporary exhibits in the concourse of the Brown County Veterans Memorial Arena. In 1976 President Gerald Ford (holding football, with Bart Starr at left) helped dedicate the hall's new permanent home, just up the street from Lambeau Field. (COURTESY OF GERALD R. FORD PRESIDENTIAL LIBRARY)

the Patriots, he restructured the franchise into a private corporation, no longer required to divulge its operations. That change left the Packers as the only NFL franchise making public annual income statements, a condition under their nonprofit ownership structure. Five years later, when the league adopted new stipulations in 1980 that prevented ownership of a team from comprising more than thirty-two individuals and requiring a primary owner to maintain at least a 30 percent stake in the team, the Packers' unique corporate structure would never be matched again. The new ownership rules prohibited publicly owned franchises, making the grandfathered Packers' corporate structure and annual shareholders' report a unique document, one that provides unusual insight into the often undisclosed economics of professional sports.

Back in Green Bay, Bart Starr decided the Packers needed a fresh arm. Prior to the draft, he dealt third- and fourth-round picks, along with John Hadl and disgruntled defensive back Ken Ellis, to the Houston Oilers for their backup quarterback, Lynn Dickey. The trade did little to change the Packers' immediate fortunes, as they lost their first three games of the 1976 season. However, the Packers recovered, stringing together a three-game winning streak. When their record reached 4–5, there was hope for a .500 season. But when Dickey separated

The Packers were the first NFL team with a Hall of Fame devoted to showcasing its history and honoring players, coaches, and supporters. It quickly became one of Green Bay's most popular and cherished tourist destinations. (WHI IMAGE ID 86639)

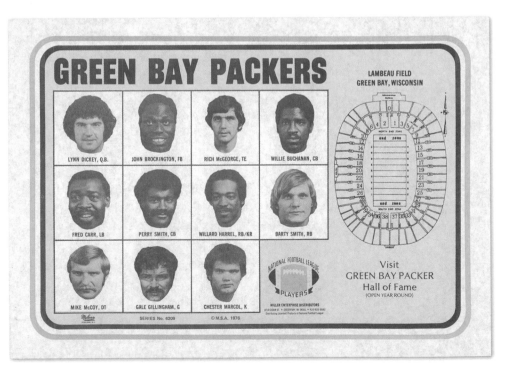

"I know Bart asked us to stop telling it like it is, but I'm going to say they looked good anyway."

10-18-76

ABOVE: Bart Starr (left) surrounded himself with familiar faces and former teammates (left to right) Bill Curry, Zeke Bratkowski, and Dave Hanner as his assistant coaches. (WISCONSIN STATE JOURNAL)

ABOVE, RIGHT: Lyle Lahey's editorial cartoon reflected the fans' and the media's patience with Bart Starr's rebuilding process; as one reporter said to another, "I know Bart asked us to stop telling it like it is, but I'm going to say they looked good anyway." (REPRINTED BY PERMISSION OF THE GREEN BAY NEWS-CHRONICLE)

his shoulder against the Bears in the season's tenth week, the Packers' season unraveled, and they finished last in the Central Division with a 5–9 record. Despite the losing record, Starr told the press he was "pleased with the attitude of the team with respect to the building. Those I know will be with us are smart enough to recognize that we're still a few people away and, until we get them, it's going to be tough sledding." The second-year coach also was appreciative of how accepting the fans were toward what he was trying to accomplish. "I think the fans have been extra good and patient," Starr was quoted as saying in the *Milwaukee Journal*. "They deserve a lot better. I really couldn't have asked for this kind of acceptance."

• • •

Although the Packers won one more game in 1976 compared to their previous campaign, the franchise suffered a 42 percent drop in profits, from $784,830 in 1975 to $455,957 in 1976. Team treasurer Fred Trowbridge explained that the drop in income was due to the team's schedule, pointing out the Packers had large gates on the road in Dallas, Los Angeles, and Cincinnati during the 1975 season. "Where and who we play makes a great deal of difference," Trowbridge remarked. "We had a good schedule in 1975 that we didn't have in 1976 and which we very frankly will not have in 1977." Trowbridge also explained that revenues from television, radio, and program advertising were down. The two new expansion teams in Seattle and Tampa Bay were now part of the shared revenues, but those receipts would increase once the new television contract was negotiated in 1978. The club's total assets, which topped $10 million for the first time in 1975, continued to climb to a figure of $11,114,159 in 1976. "These figures would seem to contradict a commonly held viewpoint of NFL management that the operation of a football team is more a matter of love than a matter of profit," *New York Times* columnist William Wallace claimed.

The NFL Players Association used the Packers' published economic figures to strengthen their demands. And with a lawsuit that was making its way through the U.S. court system, the NFLPA was challenging the league's free-agent compensation clause. The Rozelle Rule, which allowed any team that lost a free agent to another team to receive something of equal value, severely limited player movement. On October 18, 1976, the court ruled that the Rozelle Rule was legal and exempt from the Sherman Antitrust Act liability if free agency was accepted through collective bargaining, further clarifying that player movement should be resolved through the negotiation process. As a result of the ruling, the NFLPA had to bargain with the NFL owners. On February 16, 1977, the two sides came to terms on a collective bargaining agreement that eliminated the Rozelle Rule. A first refusal/compensation system governing free agency was created, where the price of at least a first-round draft choice would be the compensation for signing another team's free agent. The union had obtained improved benefits and grievance procedures, but it hadn't achieved true free agency or reached its goal of winning 55 percent of league revenues for players. The result set the tone for the 1982 negotiations.

The Packers couldn't translate their profits into wins on the field. During the 1977 season, patience ran thin in Green Bay as the Packers showed no improvement and in fact seemed to be getting worse. Born out of the frustration of an offense that generated only eleven touchdowns all season, Packers bashing became fashionable, with jokes like "Why is Lambeau Field a safe place in a tornado? Because there are never any touchdowns there" making the rounds. The Packers scored more than 16 points only once all season. Their 4–10 record—enough for another last-place finish in the Central Division if not for the hapless Tampa Bay Buccaneers—fueled speculation that Starr would resign as coach but stay on as general manager. Executive committee member and

The Packers, decimated by injuries, found themselves unable to catch their rivals, including Walter Payton (34) and the Bears, for most of the 1977 season. (WISCONSIN STATE JOURNAL)

When the Packers traded John Hadl to the Oilers, the team received quarterback Lynn Dickey (10), who had one of the strongest and most accurate arms in the NFL. As long as Dickey had protection and stayed healthy, the Packers had one of the most potent offenses in football. (WISCONSIN STATE JOURNAL)

former Packers star Tony Canadeo came to Starr's defense, exclaiming, "When you had twelve teams in the league, you could build overnight, but with twenty-eight, you can't do that. You have to have confidence in your coach."

When Starr's contract was extended through the 1979 season, despite coaching the Packers to a 13–29 record in his first three seasons, executive committee vice president Richard Bourguignon explained to reporters, "Everyone wanted Bart to get the job and there has been a lot of pressure on him. Now give him a chance."

• • •

The following spring at the Packers' annual stockholders' meeting, treasurer Fred Trowbridge announced that team profits had dipped to just $266,810 for the 1977 season, compared to $455,957 in 1976. The 40 percent decline also represented the lowest net since the $128,425 profit made three years previously, in 1974. "Operating expenses did increase and probably will continue to increase," Trowbridge explained. "But with the assets we have and the television income we can expect, there is no grave concern for the future of the Green Bay Packers financially." The team's total income of $6,567,095 was up $407,025 from 1976 but also showed a $488,238 boost in season expenses of $4,442,800, which included $4.4 million in salaries and bonuses paid to coaches and players—a number that twenty years earlier would have been in the $500,000 range.

To offset the escalating salaries, the Packers, as well as the other twenty-seven NFL franchises, were becoming more dependent on radio and television revenue. In 1977 the Packers received $2,211,122, which Trowbridge explained would increase the following year, when the team would earn $4,842,000 from the networks under the new television contract. The NFL's new broadcast deal was a four-year, $576 million contract that doubled each team's annual revenue from an annual average of just over $2 million to $5.2 million through 1981. For the first time, NFL teams would earn more revenue from the rights to telecast their games than from the ticket sales of the games themselves. The willingness of television networks to pay the increased fees further signified that broadcasting NFL games meant guaranteed television ratings.

> ### "The Pack was back! Then the roof fell in."
> —EXECUTIVE COMMITTEE MEMBER JOHN TORINUS

• • •

A 1978 Harris Poll indicated that 70 percent of the nation's sports fans followed professional football, compared to 54 percent favoring baseball. The continued rise in popularity allowed the NFL to add more games. In 1978 the NFL expanded its regular season from fourteen to sixteen games and also expanded its playoffs from eight teams to ten, adding a second wild-card team from each conference.

Since the Packers stopped dominating the NFC Central Division after 1967, the Minnesota Vikings had filled the vacuum, winning the division from 1968 to 1971 and again from 1973 to 1977—the Packers' 1972 crown being the lone exception. With the revised playoff format, the Packers were now poised to take advantage, since "by 1978, Bart had finally gotten rid of most of the head cases," trainer Domenic Gentile said, referring to Starr's commitment to adding young players and building for the future.

The Packers' 1978 draft class was its best in years, producing wide receiver James Lofton and linebackers John Anderson and Mike Douglass. One of the most poignant indications of the progress made under Starr's direction was that eight of the team's draft choices made the opening day roster that season. The infusion of new talent and a hunger for winning that bordered on starvation helped the Packers win six of their first seven games. All alone in first place, they seemed bound for the playoffs. "Everyone connected with the Packers and the fans were certain their trust and faith in Bart Starr had paid off. The Pack was back!" executive committee member John Torinus exclaimed. "Then the roof fell in."

The Packers went on to lose five of their last seven games, beating only the second-year Buccaneers 17–7 and tying the Vikings 10–10. Because of their tie with

In 1978 Terdell Middleton became the first Packers running back to rush for more than 1,000 yards since John Brockington in 1973. The Packers wouldn't have another 1,000-yard rusher until Edgar Bennett in 1995. (WISCONSIN STATE JOURNAL)

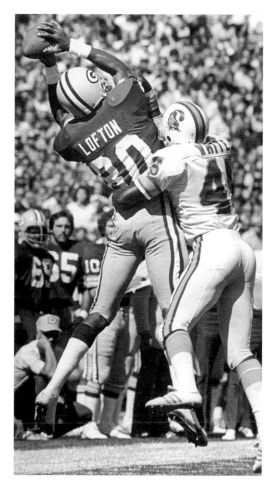

Wide receiver James Lofton helped reinvigorate the Packers' offense in 1978, catching forty-six passes for 818 yards and six touchdowns. (WISCONSIN STATE JOURNAL)

Minnesota, the Packers were eliminated from the playoff picture on the last day of the regular season. Green Bay's 8–7–1 record was identical to the Vikings', but as a result of their loss in Minnesota earlier that year, they didn't own the postseason-deciding tiebreaker. "Most of the state's sportswriters described our performance in the second half of the season as a collapse, or at least a mystery. There was really nothing baffling about it," Starr recalled of how the team had outplayed itself. "We played the second half of the season with little or no chance of sneaking up on opponents."

On the field, the Packers' 1978 performance seemed to vindicate the executive committee's decision to stick with Starr and his rebuilding process. "Packer fans began to have visions of more winning seasons after that fine performance in the early going of 1978," Torinus said. "Another draft and a year of experience for the young players figured to give the Packers a real shot at the playoffs in 1979."

• • •

Despite not making the 1978 playoffs, the Packers still generated a record $1,520,903 profit that season. The seventy-eight stockholders in attendance at the WBAY auditorium for the annual meeting were given a healthy financial outlook that night. The team's $1.3 million increase from the previous season was due to the lucrative new television contract the NFL had put into effect in 1978, which wouldn't expire until 1981. In 1978 the Packers received $5,260,803 from television and radio earnings—a hefty $3,057,681 more than the $2,211,122 derived from the same sources in 1977. Although the team's total income of $9,482,146 was up $2,915,351 from the 1977 season's figure of $6,567,095, the Packers did incur $883,752 more in expenses: $7,610,667, compared to $6,726,915 in 1977. With the latest financial surplus, the team's assets now totaled $15,211,863—up more than $3.5 million from the 1977 figure of $11,823,230.

The Packers hoped their 1979 draft class would continue complementing the team's rebuilding effort. "Of the thirty-three people we've drafted and signed as free agents since 1976, there are twenty-eight still on the roster," Starr explained, noting that twelve of those twenty-eight players were starters. "So we think that is the nucleus of the Packer team of the future."

However, unlike the team's 1978 draft, Green Bay's 1979 draft wouldn't harvest as many immediate-impact players. After the Packers drafted running backs Eddie Lee Ivery and Steve Atkins, their third selection was defensive tackle Charles Johnson. "The player I wanted to pick was Joe Montana," Starr later admitted. "At the risk of sounding arrogant, I was a good judge of talent. My most serious mistakes inevitably occurred when I failed to follow my convictions and deferred to someone with more experience."

Johnson played three seasons in Green Bay but had little impact on the team's fortunes. Meanwhile, Montana was later drafted in the third round by the San Francisco 49ers, where he flourished under the guidance of head coach Bill Walsh, enjoying a Hall of Fame career and winning four Super Bowl rings. Following the 1979 draft, Starr was convinced the Packers "had an excellent shot at another winning record, as long as we stayed healthy and were able to avoid exposing our lack of depth."

Midway through the opening quarter of the first regular-season game, hopes that the Packers would make a serious playoff run began to implode. "For the first time in five years, we finally had a running back, [Eddie Lee] Ivery, who could have the same type of impact on a game as Chicago's superstar, Walter Payton," Starr recalled. But the rookie running back severed a knee ligament when his foot caught on the Bears' Soldier Field Astroturf. Ivery would miss the remainder of the season with what was just one of ten serious injuries that tore apart the team's foundation.

The Packers' 1979 season had few bright spots, but Steve Atkins's (32) run from scrimmage against the Saints got the entire Green Bay sideline excited, including Coach Bart Starr, during the 28–17 victory. (COURTESY OF GREEN BAY PRESS-GAZETTE FROM TOM PIGEON COLLECTION)

The Packers found their 1979 season unraveling as injuries once again decimated the team, including running back Eddie Lee Ivery. (WISCONSIN STATE JOURNAL)

By 1979 the patience of the media and fans had begun to wear thin, as depicted in Lyle Lahey's editorial cartoon. (REPRINTED BY PERMISSION OF THE GREEN BAY NEWS-CHRONICLE)

From there, Green Bay's playoff hopes dissolved. They went on to lose one game in overtime, another by 1 point, a third by 3 points, and a fourth by 5 points. When the Packers finished the season with a 5–11 record, many started to question whether Starr would ever coach a winning team in Green Bay. He was further burdened with the fact that the Packers organization had fallen behind the NFL's elite franchises in many aspects, particularly in the science of evaluating talent. "With the 1980s looming," author Don Gulbrandsen wrote in *Green Bay Packers: The Complete Illustrated History*, "the Packers were nowhere close to the team that Starr had once guided as a quarterback, and the prospects for improvement appeared dim. It was a tough time to be a Packer fan."

• • •

"The Packer office today denied that the team would move to the Philippines and be known as the Manila Folders."

12-4-79

For decades the NFL had prided itself on celebrating "the game." But in recent years, "the money" was overshadowing the sportsmanship being celebrated on the field. By 1980 the corporatization of pro football had made the NFL a multibillion-dollar entity that operated more like Coca-Cola or General Motors than a sports organization. Franchises once struggling to cover payroll were now generating millions of dollars from a variety of revenue streams: tickets, television, merchandise, and advertising. NFL regular-season attendance hit 13 million spectators at the end of the year, marking the third record year in a row and the highest in the NFL's sixty-one-year history. Stadiums were reporting attendance at over 92 percent of total capacity, and television ratings posted all-time highs.

As the NFL grew more popular and powerful, it began leveraging host cities to fund the construction of new, football-exclusive stadiums, complete with moneymaking amenities like luxury boxes.

Cities already hosting franchises were willing to absorb the huge tax burden of building a new football stadium if the alternative was losing their NFL team—a real threat as the demand for NFL teams exceeded the number fielded. During the league's infancy, any prospective team owner with $50 could join. Now the NFL was cultivating potential cities and owners with extreme diligence. As with any good corporate franchisor, the league saw its product thriving in the best new markets available. With the NFL expressing no plans to expand beyond its current twenty-eight-team slate, a city would promise just about anything to lure an existing NFL franchise to relocate. The cutthroat urban arms race to poach franchises from one city to another was about to begin.

Meanwhile, the Packers fumbled their way through the 1980 NFL draft. With the fourth overall pick, they chose Bruce Clark, who was labeled a "can't miss guy" by Dick Corrick, the Packers' director of pro personnel. Clark went on to have a good career, but not for the Packers. He had no interest in playing in Green Bay and chose instead to sign with the Toronto Argonauts of the Canadian Football League before returning to the NFL two years later to play with the Saints and Chiefs. The mishandling of Clark would be considered Starr's biggest blunder as the Packers' general manager, one that was caused by his underestimation of the growing "me first" attitude manifesting itself among athletes.

As the team's head coach, Starr continued feeling some serious heat from the press, which was harping on the team's apparent lack of discipline. He vowed not

> "The logical move, in my opinion, would have been to retain me as the general manager and select a new coach."
>
> —HEAD COACH BART STARR

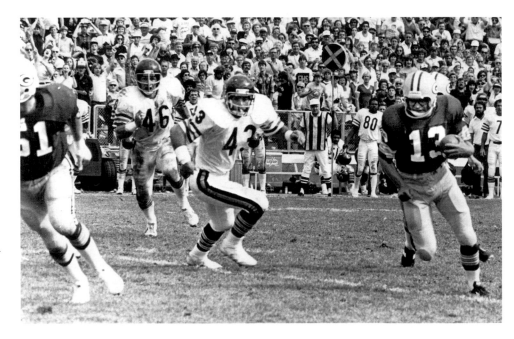

The 1980 season opener at Lambeau Field had a bizarre, happy ending for the home team as kicker Chester Marcol (13) returned his own blocked field goal kick 25 yards for a touchdown, giving the Packers a 12–6 victory. (COURTESY OF GREEN BAY PRESS-GAZETTE FROM TOM PIGEON COLLECTION)

Although the Packers hadn't won a championship in nearly fifteen years, the team was still considered a nostalgic national treasure by many—including presidential candidate Ronald Reagan, who met with Bart Starr at Green Bay's Austin Straubel Airport during a campaign visit in 1980. (AP PHOTO/ CHARLES HARRITY)

to resign after defensive end Ezra Johnson was caught eating a hot dog on the sidelines while his teammates were still on the field in a losing effort. The Packers shook off the hot dog controversy and their winless preseason with a win in their opening game. Three games later, after Green Bay was humiliated in blowout losses to the Lions, Rams, and Cowboys, team president Dominic Olejniczak and the Packers' board of directors provided Starr with a public vote of confidence in a press release. But the low point of the season was a 61–7 loss to the Bears, part of a four-game losing streak to end the season. Overall the Packers had been outscored 127–30.

Green Bay's 5–10–1 record found them tied for last place in the NFC's Central Division. "Packer fans' patience with Bart Starr began to wear thin during the latter part of the 1980 season. The press became much more hostile, and some of this feeling was reflected to some extent by the Packer board of directors," Torinus recalled. The board was called into a special session in late December. "In order to save Starr's job, the committee agreed to proceed immediately with the separation of the responsibilities of head coach and general manager."

On December 27 the executive committee surprised everyone—Starr included—when they kept him on as coach but took away his general manager title. "I was extremely disappointed in their decision," Starr said of being forced to vacate the position, which wouldn't be refilled until 1987. "The logical move, in my opinion, would have been to retain me as the general manager and select a new coach. Our progress in areas most influenced through the general manager's role had been significant, for we were now a solidly structured organization."

The executive committee announced that Bob Harlan and Tom Miller would split the general manager duties, but nobody, including Harlan and Miller, knew what that meant. Starr would continue to oversee the football operation as he had as general manager, answering directly to team president Dominic Olejniczak and the executive committee. The lack of clarity surrounding the announced transfer of responsibilities prompted board member Ted Jamison to proclaim, "There is really nothing different after this decision. Miller and Harlan can continue to do what they always did. I think this team needs a general manager, and the board thinks so, too. We don't have one now, even with this announcement."

• • •

When the Packers held their annual stockholders' meeting in May, the executives announced that team president Dominic Olejniczak would assume the additional title of chief executive officer. He would now have complete authority over the operation of the Packers corporation. "The Executive Committee does not want to hire a general manager, an outsider, and turn everything over to him. Committee members want to continue to have full authority on the hiring and firing of a coach, whether they are good judges of NFL coaching or not," *Milwaukee Sentinel* sportswriter Bud Lea reported. "This was a complete turnabout from the December meeting when the directors voted quickly, and with virtually no study or research, to separate Starr's duties as coach and general manager."

To compensate for the absence of a general manager, the team named Tom Miller as the assistant to the president—business and Bob Harlan as the assistant to the president—corporate, further separating the club's football and non-football operations. "We wanted to free Bart to concentrate on football," Harlan told reporters of how Starr still had complete authority over football operations, including the selection of assistant coaches and player personnel. "Tom will handle the business end of the operation of the club [including ticket offices, accounting and facilities management] and I will handle the league matters and contract negotiations."

Without a general manager or director of player personnel, Starr was responsible for the Packers' 1981 draft. He drafted quarterback Rich Campbell with the sixth overall pick. "There is no question that I made a terrible mistake in passing on Joe Montana in 1979," Starr admitted of his earlier decision to draft Charles Johnson instead, but "our selection of Rich Campbell over Ronnie Lott in 1981 was a colossal blunder." During a forgettable career with the Packers, Campbell went on to throw a grand total of sixty-eight passes. Meanwhile, defensive back Ronnie Lott enjoyed a Hall of Fame career as a key contributor to the San Francisco 49ers championship teams during the decade. It was another personnel move that haunted Starr as the Packers' fortunes continued to founder.

Green Bay's 1981 season opener in Chicago began almost exactly as it had two years earlier. "For Eddie Lee Ivery, the similarities were too much to bear," Starr recalled. "Once again, he got off to a fast start, and once again he found himself planting his left foot to make a sharp cut. He was on the same part of the field and his knee blew out once more, tearing a different ligament."

Again, Ivery was done for the season, exposing the Packers' lack of depth at running back. Following their 16–9 victory over the Bears, Green Bay lost their next two games. To reinvigorate the team's offense, Starr traded three high draft choices to the Chargers for explosive wide receiver John Jefferson. The Packers stumbled to a 2–6 record at midseason before the offense exploded behind a healthy Lynn Dickey and the pass-catching trio of James Lofton, John Jefferson, and tight end

> ## "We wanted to free Bart to concentrate on football."
>
> —TEAM EXECUTIVE BOB HARLAN

LEFT: The Packers' 1981 training camp was a popular destination for fans young and old, as players like James Lofton were popular with autograph seekers. (WISCONSIN STATE JOURNAL)

BELOW, LEFT: The overflow crowds at Packers training camp prompted several youngsters to use their bicycles to get a better view of practice. (MILWAUKEE JOURNAL SENTINEL)

BELOW: Wide receiver James Lofton (80) and quarterback Lynn Dickey (12) partook in one of the Packers most cherished training camp traditions: riding kids' bikes from the practice field back to the Lambeau Field locker rooms. (WISCONSIN STATE JOURNAL)

Packers safety Mark Murphy (37) anchored a defense that featured Mike Douglass (53), John Anderson (59), Mark Lee (22), Casey Merrill (78), and Mike Butler (77). (COURTESY OF GREEN BAY PRESS-GAZETTE FROM TOM PIGEON COLLECTION)

Kicker Jan Stenerud (10), photographed with holder and punter Dave Beverly (11), nailed twenty-two of twenty-four field goals in 1981 to rejuvenate the Packers' lackluster kicking game after the departure of Chester Marcol. (COURTESY OF GREEN BAY PRESS-GAZETTE FROM TOM PIGEON COLLECTION)

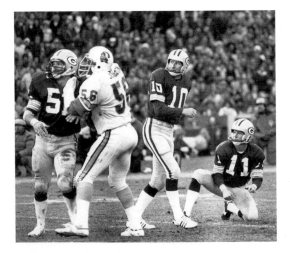

Paul Coffman. "Sure enough, we won six of our last eight games and came within an eyelash of winning the Central Division title," Starr said.

The Packers were within reach of a wild-card playoff spot heading into the season's final week. If Starr's squad beat the Jets and the Giants lost to the Cowboys that afternoon, Green Bay would make the playoffs for the first time in nine years. "A team doesn't realize what getting into the playoffs means until it's been there," Starr said after the Packers' 28–3 loss to the Jets eliminated them from playoff contention. "You talk and talk about it all season, but when it happens, it has a lasting effect on the team. It's an invaluable experience."

The team's improved 8–8 record did little to diffuse the issue of rehiring or dismissing Starr at season's end. "I knew the pressures he felt when we just couldn't get over the hump, and those pressures grew tremendously," Harlan recalled. "The most important thing you do happens on Sunday afternoon when the whole world is there to grade you for three hours. If it doesn't go well, eventually certain people are going to turn on you."

After one of Starr's strongest supporters, Dominic Olejniczak, announced he would step down as team president, the executive committee gave the head coach an

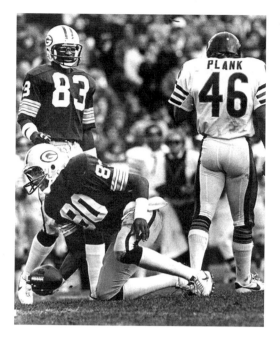

Convinced that the Packers were one impact player away from making the playoffs in 1981, Bart Starr made a rare midseason trade with the San Diego Chargers to acquire wide receiver John Jefferson (83), bolstering the team's already explosive passing game that featured James Lofton (80). (WISCONSIN STATE JOURNAL)

unmistakable win-or-else mandate. "The Packer president, Robert Parins, a former circuit court judge, acted as though we hadn't won a game all year," Starr exclaimed of a growing fear that his days in Green Bay were numbered. "I had to work to get a mere two-year extension from him. I came away with an uneasy feeling."

• • •

Newly elected team president Judge Robert Parins expressed little patience for losing, reinforcing to the press that he had the power to "hire and fire the coach, or anybody else in the organization." He also felt for the team to succeed, "the operation of this franchise clearly calls for a full-time executive officer. By that I mean someone who can take care of the day-to-day business."

The full-time appointment was necessary. The Packers had become a multimillion-dollar corporation, part of a professional sports league that produced record television ratings in 1981 and was finishing up negotiations on a very lucrative television contract. The television networks were also profiting; a *Time* magazine article estimated that CBS made $25 million from the NFL alone in 1981. In March 1982 the NFL signed a then-record $2.1 billion television deal to remain with ABC, CBS, and NBC over the next five years. The 1982 deal was a dramatic increase, with each NFL team garnering on average almost $14.2 million per season, starting with $11.8 million in 1982, up from the $5.8 million per season they had been earning. For some owners, securing a profit was guaranteed before ever selling a single ticket or collecting money from parking or concessions.

The birth of modern franchise free agency occurred on May 7, 1982. The NFL lost a highly publicized lawsuit, which allowed the Oakland Raiders to relocate to Los Angeles. The impact of the court case would be felt throughout the decade, since the league was now unable to stop teams from relocating. "This only reinforced just how important Green Bay's public ownership of the Packers had become. The team might have lagged in adapting to corporate-style management, but at least it would not be guided by the whims of a single owner," author Don Gulbrandsen said of how unhappy owners could now threaten to abandon their home cities for greener pastures. "The saddest example of what NFL fans faced happened in the early morning hours of March 29, 1984, when Colts owner Robert Irsay ordered the team's office and training facility equipment loaded into a convoy of moving vans and driven to Indianapolis."

"When I came into the league in 1978, a rookie could have signed a contract for $22,000, $26,000, $30,000 and $32,000 for his first four years."

—WIDE RECEIVER
JAMES LOFTON

Four days after the Raiders' relocation verdict, pro football made more head-lines. Another rival league—the United States Football League—announced its formation and intention to start play the following season. From its inception, the USFL posed a greater threat to the NFL than the World Football League ever had. The new twelve-team league would play games in the spring, filling the football void between the Super Bowl and preseason games; it planned to lure disgruntled NFL players in search of better salaries; and it was well financed, securing a lucrative television contract with the emergence of cable television and its need for program-ming. ABC would pay the USFL $9 million for the broadcast rights to twenty-one games in the 1983 season. The deal also gave ABC the rights to the 1984 season at $9 million and network options for 1985 at $14 million and 1986 at $18 million. ESPN agreed to televise thirty-four games for $4 million and would pay $7 million for rights in 1984. These television contracts yielded approximately $1.2 million per USFL team in the first year. Understanding that the USFL had achieved instant economic stability through its two television contracts, the NFL recognized that the costs of being in the professional football business were about to rise in a similar fashion to when the league was in intense competition with the AFL.

The NFL's 1982 season began with team owners and players engaged in a brew-ing civil war. The threat of a player walkout had loomed for some time. The current NFL Players Association contract had run out. With no agreement being reached, the NFLPA set a strike date. As in past disputes, the players demanded unrestricted free agency and increased salaries. The league had long fought the concept of one player leaving his team to join another, but NFL players now wanted to enjoy the same success baseball players achieved in their quest for free agency. In 1982 the average salary for an NFL player was $95,000, well below that of Major League Baseball players, who were earning $240,000 apiece, or the NBA's players, who were taking home $215,000 each. "When I came into the league in 1978, a rookie could have signed a contract for $22,000, $26,000, $30,000 and $32,000 for his first four years," wide receiver James Lofton, who also served as the Packers' union represen-tative, explained. "If you talk to guys like Jan Stenerud, when they came into the league, a lot of players were making only $10,000 to $12,000 a year." The NFL of the 1980s would be expected to match its competition.

With the threat of a strike looming, the Packers poised themselves to make a serious run at the playoffs. In the 1982 season opener at Milwaukee County Sta-dium, they displayed their firepower with a spirited second-half comeback victory against the Rams. Their offense had found its stride, becoming as explosive as any in football, which fueled another come-from-behind win the following week against the Giants on Monday night. However, about a half hour before the game, while the Packers ate their pregame meal, the NFL Players Association announced it was going

The Green Bay Packers' locker room sat empty for fifty-seven days in 1982 as a players' strike shortened the regular season to nine games. (MILWAUKEE JOURNAL SENTINEL)

on strike at the conclusion of that evening's game. "I think the strike actually started while the game was still being played, because it was a midnight deadline," Lofton recalled of how the game had been delayed twice by mysterious power outages at Giants Stadium. "You think about the unions who were supporting the players, and you always wonder if they had something to do with it."

That night the NFL Players Association had invoked the first work stoppage that would result in the cancellation of regular-season games. For the next fifty-seven days, the nation went without professional football. The television networks, which had just signed a lucrative broadcast agreement with the league, put tremendous pressure on both warring factions to settle their dispute. In the meantime, NBC tried televising Canadian Football League games but couldn't generate even a fraction of the audience from its NFL counterparts. When the players put on exhibition games to raise money for the union, the television networks refused to broadcast the contests, siding with league management. In an ironic twist, it was the lucrative television contracts that had galvanized the players, causing them to want a bigger percentage of the NFL's revenue. In Green Bay, Packers officials kept a low profile during the players' strike since the organization "always stayed in the background and tried to make the team the most important thing," Lofton recalled.

The strike ended on November 16 when team owners ratified a new collective bargaining agreement that would run through the end of the 1986 season. The new contract guaranteed that owners would pay the players $1.6 billion over four years, including $60 million in immediate bonus money. The "money now" provision meant an increase in team payroll of about $2,250,000 to the Packers, as each active player was to be paid a minimum of $30,000 with a $10,000 increment added for each additional year of service. Other provisions of the CBA increased the minimum salaries from $22,000 to $30,000 for 1982, $40,000 in 1983, and an additional $10,000 per year for successive years of the contract.

In addition to the establishment of a minimum salary schedule, training camp, postseason pay, medical insurance, and retirement benefits were all increased. The players also gained several key concessions from the owners, including the right to obtain copies of every player contract and making salaries public knowledge, which allowed players—and their agents—more leverage in negotiations. A severance-pay system was introduced to aid in career transition, a first for professional sports. The

Behind a solid offensive line anchored by center Larry McCarren (54) and a potent passing attack from Lynn Dickey (12), the Packers finished with the NFC's third best record in 1982. (MILWAUKEE JOURNAL SENTINEL)

owners, despite making numerous concessions, still considered the settlement a victory since there was still no complete system of unrestricted free agency. In reality, "as with any strike, both sides really were the losers," executive committee member John Torinus remarked about how the eight-week strike cost players millions of dollars in unrecouped salaries and the owners an estimated $450 million in lost revenue.

Besides the players and the league, the entire community of Green Bay was affected by the strike. Hotels, restaurants, department stores, and gas stations all suffered severe drops in sales as a result of three Packers games at Lambeau Field being canceled. Each game meant a loss of $1.3 million to area merchants, according to the Green Bay Area Visitor and Convention Bureau. So it was no surprise that the community showed little interest when the NFL scrapped the divisional playoff format in favor of a "Super Bowl Tournament" where the top eight teams from each conference earned playoff berths. The Packers finished the abbreviated season with a solid 5–3–1 record and would host their first playoff game in fifteen years. The fans, instead of expressing unconditional enthusiasm for the Packers, stayed away. For the first time since 1960, Lambeau Field wouldn't host a sellout crowd.

In 1982 Lambeau Field hosted its first playoff game since the 1967 Ice Bowl; the Packers polished off the Cardinals 41-16 behind two touchdowns from Eddie Lee Ivery (40). (WISCONSIN STATE JOURNAL)

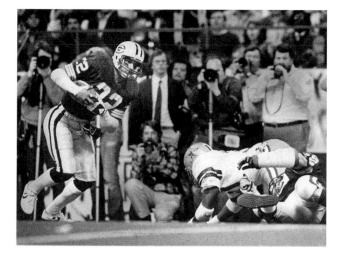

In Dallas, safety Mark Lee (22) returned an interception for a touchdown in the second half, but the Packers couldn't catch up to the Cowboys, losing by a final score of 37-26. (MILWAUKEE JOURNAL SENTINEL)

The 54,282 fans that chose to support the third-seeded Packers were treated to an offensive showcase. Quarterback Lynn Dickey passed for 260 yards and hurled two touchdown passes to John Jefferson and one each to James Lofton and Eddie Lee Ivery in a thunderous 41–16 win against the sixth-seeded St. Louis Cardinals. The next week in Dallas, the Packers racked up 468 yards of offense, but Dickey's three interceptions proved critical as Green Bay lost to the Cowboys 37–26. However, "the press universally declared that the Packers had won great respect in defeat, playing one of the best teams in the league toe-to-toe for sixty minutes," Torinus said.

The NFL had survived the crippling effects of its players' strike, but it continued to be under assault from the rival USFL. That spring, college superstar Herschel Walker and some other notable players spurned the senior circuit, signing lucrative contracts with the upstart league. When Walker and his New Jersey Generals debuted on March 6, 1983, against the Los Angeles Express on ABC, the USFL's opening weekend was considered a success as it received strong television ratings and hosted an average of 39,170 fans in attendance per stadium. Although both of those figures soon declined, the modest successes the league enjoyed during its inaugural season only fueled more spending by its owners. The league's original design for self-imposed fiscal discipline was soon abandoned as team salary structures began exceeding the $1.6 million-per-club limit. To combat the USFL's player poaching, the NFL increased its roster size from forty-five to forty-nine players and began signing its own players to longer-term contracts.

The only significant player the Packers lost to the new league was defensive end Mike Butler. He bolted after Parins, who had taken over negotiating player contracts, failed to close on a new deal. With the Packers' first-ever full-time executive taking a more active role in the team's football operations, "there was a certain amount of power Bart lost," quarterback David Whitehurst recalled. "From a player standpoint, the atmosphere was not as good. The situation in Green Bay changed."

Judge Robert J. Parins made it clear who was running the Packers after he succeeded Dominic Olejniczak as team president. (MILWAUKEE JOURNAL SENTINEL)

• • •

In March, when stockholders arrived for the Packers' annual stockholders' meeting, they were handed a mimeographed balance sheet. It showed the Packers suffering a net loss of $2,153,428 in 1982—not only the largest loss in team history but also its first since 1951. "This isn't a happy report," team treasurer John Stiles explained. The Packers lost ticket revenue from seven of the sixteen scheduled regular-season games canceled because of the strike, plus the corresponding television revenue. They also had to pay out $2.4 million to the players as part of the "money now" portion of the new collective bargaining agreement. "In spite of the losses we've had, we're still in excellent financial position," Stiles said. "We have short-term investments of more than $10 million and long-term investments of close to $5 million for a total of $15 million. We have every expectation that we'll have a good, sound, prosperous year for 1983."

When Starr took the podium, he was armed with statistical proof the Packers were poised to continue their winning ways. "We're on our way up," he told the crowd of 102 stockholders at the Midway Motor Lodge, citing the team's 41 points in its playoff win against the Cardinals and the 466 yards gained on the Cowboys—both the most in the team's postseason history. "It's all coming together at a very good time for us." Before he could return to his seat, Starr was applauded. The audience reaction prompted only a tight grin from Parins as he turned the microphone over to the nominating committee for further business.

Parins's flippant reaction implied that Starr had used up almost all of the goodwill and fond memories he had accrued in his sixteen years as quarterback for the Packers. In the eight years since he had taken over for Dan Devine, Starr had guided the team to just one playoff berth and two winning records. In 1983 his task to return Green Bay to the playoffs was a sobering one. They were scheduled to face eight playoff teams from the year before on their regular-season schedule, but with all the pieces in place to return to the NFL's elite, Starr explained later that the Packers "would have posted a winning record had we avoided a crippling series of injuries."

Green Bay hovered around .500 all season, never winning or losing more than two consecutive games. In one four-game

In 1983, after the Packers' first playoff appearance since 1972, Bart Starr and cohost Gary Knafelc, a former Packers wide receiver, had a devoted following for their weekly *Bart Starr Show*. (MILWAUKEE JOURNAL SENTINEL)

In 1983 tight end Paul Coffman (left, 82) and the Packers' high-octane offense tried outrunning their opponents by generating 6,172 yards, 52 touchdowns, and 429 points. But Green Bay's defense was just as vulnerable, allowing 6,403 yards, 50 touchdowns, and 439 points despite the solid efforts of (right) John Anderson (59), Mike Douglass (53), and Mike McCoy (29). (LEFT: MILWAUKEE JOURNAL SENTINEL; RIGHT: WISCONSIN STATE JOURNAL)

stretch, the Packers posted an almost perfect 55–14 win over the Buccaneers in week five, only to be humbled by the Lions the next week, followed up with an epic Monday night victory over the defending Super Bowl champion Redskins, and then an overtime loss to the Vikings. All season, the team suffered through wild fluctuations from game to game, from quarter to quarter, and sometimes from play to play. Starr would later admit, "Our sixteen-game roller coaster was not the best Packer team I ever played for or coached, but it was by far the most exciting."

As part of one of the most fearsome offenses in the league, quarterback Lynn Dickey threw for an astounding 4,458 yards in 1983 as four receivers—Lofton, Jefferson, Coffman, and Gerry Ellis—each caught at least fifty passes. The Packers' 6,172 yards of total offense set a team record on the way to 429 points. But Starr's league-worst defensive squad surrendered a gluttonous 439 points, holding teams to fewer than 20 points only twice all season. Despite Green Bay's inability to stop anybody on defense, they still had a shot at the playoffs if they could win their season finale against the Bears.

Hosted at Chicago's Soldier Field, the game meant more to the Packers, but the Bears reveled in their role as spoilers. In a contest that seesawed back and forth, Green Bay took a late 21–20 lead with only a few minutes left. As Chicago responded by marching downfield, Starr refused to use any of his available timeouts. With just ten seconds left, the Bears kicked the game-winning 22-yard field goal. The Packers had no time to respond when they got the ball back and suffered the 23–21 loss. Afterward, "I never saw Bart more discouraged," Harlan recalled. "His disappointment was simply that we were right on the verge of getting to the playoffs, and we didn't do it."

The agonizing defeat, which left the Packers with an 8–8 record, eliminated them from the postseason for 1983. Nevertheless, Starr felt good about the direction the Packers were headed. They were four seasons removed from their last losing campaign, showcasing a potent offense. If the defense could get healthy, the team would be on the brink of becoming a consistent contender. "We were no longer a losing ball club, and, more important, we were on the verge of long-term respectability," Starr remarked. "We had rekindled the emotions between the Packer fans and the team. We played exciting, hard-hitting football, and we did so with class."

Less than twenty-four hours after the loss in Chicago, "Starr said that Parins came into his office and said rather bluntly, 'Bart, you are relieved of your duties as head coach.' Parins then turned and walked out, according to Starr, who closed his door, buried his head in his hands and let the emotions of nine losing seasons pour out," trainer Domenic Gentile recalled. "There is no good way to fire a man, but Bart deserved better than that cold slap in the face."

After nine years as head coach, Bart Starr was fired following the 1983 season with an overall 53-77-3 record that included two winning seasons. (WISCONSIN STATE JOURNAL)

"He didn't thank me for my efforts, didn't say a word about my twenty-six-year contribution to the Green Bay Packer organization," Starr recounted. "He didn't even express any regret about having to make the decision. He sounded as though he were delivering a cold, unemotional sentence in his circuit court."

Although Starr had dedicated his life to the Packers, "it is difficult . . . to argue with Judge Parins's decision. Starr did go 21–19–1 in his last three seasons, but it took six bleak seasons to put together that modest run," author David Claerbaut recounted in *Bart Starr: When Leadership Mattered*. "Starr really had only one good year, the strike-shortened '82 season when the team ranked tenth on offense and eighth on defense. In no other season did the team rank in the upper half of the league on both sides of the ball."

When announcing Starr's dismissal to reporters, Parins said the decision was "not made out of emotion or frustration, but on an overall evaluation of the needs of the franchise; we feel the position of head coach needed a fresh look," and while several factors came into play, "if we had had a winning season, in terms of the playoffs, we would not be having this session today."

. . .

Only moments after Starr was fired, the Packers put together an informal list of almost twenty-five candidates for the job—some whom the team was interested in approaching and some who had contacted the team. The organization felt its next coach had to be a disciplinarian and a taskmaster. The executive committee anticipated a long, drawn-out process, one that could allow for a clean break from the team's past and forge a new identity independent of the Vince Lombardi era. At the same time, they couldn't resist the idea of having another one of Lombardi's disciples lead the team. On Tuesday morning, Parins read in a newspaper article that Forrest Gregg was interested in the Packers job but still had two years remaining on his contract as head coach of the Bengals. The Packers contacted Cincinnati and on Wednesday received permission to speak to Gregg. In explaining his haste, Parins said he felt that "this matter involving Forrest came up quite suddenly and in a manner that required us to move rather quickly if we were going to have a satisfactory attempt to offer him this job."

On Thursday Parins discussed the possibility of Gregg as the team's next head coach with the Packers' seven-man executive committee. The next day, Parins and Gregg met in Chicago. Parins would later admit, "He was the only person that we offered the job to."

On Saturday, Forrest Gregg was introduced as the Packers ninth coach in franchise history. "I don't think I would have left Cincinnati for any other job. Ever since I left Green Bay, I always hoped that some day I'd get the opportunity to coach this football team," Gregg told reporters during the introductory conference call. "I spent fourteen years in Green Bay as a player. If I was looking for a college coaching job, I would want to go back to SMU where I played—that's where my roots are. This is where my roots are as a professional football player."

The Packers' executive committee felt Gregg was the perfect person to restore order and the tradition of winning football in Green Bay. "People in the office were sad when Bart left, but Forrest was another Vince Lombardi hero coming home, and so he was very welcome," Harlan recalled. "And it looked like a coup when he came here."

For the first time in team history, the Packers had hired a head coach with previous NFL head coaching experience. Gregg had coached the Cleveland Browns for three years and also led the Bengals to a Super Bowl during his four seasons in Cincinnati. He had earned a reputation as a stern disciplinarian, which was showcased during that initial conference call. "I believe in discipline," Gregg told reporters. "I don't think there's any question it's one of the most important things to a football team. The players have to understand what is expected of them."

> "I believe in discipline. I don't think there's any question it's one of the most important things to a football team."
>
> —HEAD COACH FORREST GREGG

New Packers head coach Forrest Gregg (with arm raised) returned to Green Bay with expectations of leading the Packers— including Dave Drechsler (61) and Larry McCarren (54)—back to the playoffs. (MILWAUKEE JOURNAL SENTINEL)

Forrest Gregg (left) and offensive coordinator Bob Schnelker (wearing glasses) had a brewing quarterback controversy in 1984 as rookie Randy Wright (16) and former first-round draft pick Rich Campbell (19) threatened to take the starter's role away from the often-injured veteran Lynn Dickey (far right). (MILWAUKEE JOURNAL SENTINEL)

After Parins proclaimed to reporters huddled around the phone at team headquarters that "Forrest will have full responsibility of the football operation," Gregg commented, "From the outside I thought I was inheriting a good situation with the Packers."

From the moment he arrived in Green Bay, Gregg decided his training-camp two-a-day practices exposed an inherent weakness. "If I could put my finger on one thing that this team needs," he said of his belief in the full-pad, full-contact practices that players considered pure torture, "this team is really not very strong physically. And that hurts you in two ways—it hurts in consistency and it also makes you more susceptible to injury."

The team was slow to adapt to Gregg's changes and finished the first half of the 1984 season with a lone victory. His decision to trade kicker Jan Stenerud to Minnesota during the offseason was "a move that probably cost us at least one ball game," he later admitted after the Packers lost a 17–14 game to the Broncos in Denver where kicker Eddie Garcia missed three short field goals. "Trading Jan was a move I lamented, one that might have been the difference between us making the playoffs and staying home for the holidays."

During one stretch of heartbreaking defeats, a reporter asked Gregg if he was worried about his players' morale. "I'll never forget his answer," trainer Domenic Gentile remembered: "'Their morale? I'm not worried about their morale. They'd better be worried about mine.'"

When everything started to click, "winning seven of our last eight games was a mixed blessing," Gregg recalled of the Packers' 8–8 finish. "We came very close to the playoffs, but the '84 Packers were an old team. Changes were necessary. We needed to revamp the roster and make the club younger. But I was lulled by the chance to reach the postseason. And I also knew there would have been serious fan repercussions had we torn the team apart after that great finish. So we sat pat and made no major roster changes leading into the 1985 season."

■ ■ ■

Before the start of the NFL's 1985 season, the USFL found itself imploding. The upstart league continued to poach NFL rosters, forcing the escalation of salaries. It also signed some of college football's best players—including Doug Flutie, Jim Kelly, Steve Young, and Reggie White—to lucrative contracts that exceeded the league's revenue streams. Back in 1984, when the USFL had expanded from twelve to eighteen teams, it experienced a decline in television ratings. However, spring football was still sought after by television networks as ABC exercised its option to broadcast the league in the spring of 1985 and even offered a $175 million contract for four additional years beginning in the spring of 1986. ESPN also wanted to stay in business with the USFL, offering a contract worth $70 million over three years. The young league's future looked promising, but its continual straying from the original mission of fiscally responsible, year-round football had taken its toll. On August 27, 1984, the USFL owners—under the urging of New Jersey Generals owner Donald Trump—voted unanimously that after the 1985 spring season the league would resume play in the fall of 1986. The USFL then filed an antitrust lawsuit against the NFL, in hopes of forcing a merger, seeking damages of $1.69 billion and further claiming the NFL was monopolizing the television revenues and creating the inability for the USFL to negotiate a television contract for a fall season. With its lawsuit against the NFL pending, the USFL would suffer through a tumultuous third year.

When the USFL kicked off its third season, the league had contracted to fourteen teams. Several franchises had relocated or suspended operations, knowing they couldn't compete head to head against their counterparts in established NFL cities. Television ratings continued to decline as the league spiraled into greater fiscal and legal turmoil. After the 1985 spring season, franchises continued to merge, relocate, and fold. In 1986 only eight USFL teams remained as the league awaited commencement of its antitrust lawsuit against the NFL. The USFL's survival now rested on the trial's outcome. Following twelve weeks of testimony, the federal court jury rendered the verdict that the NFL was guilty of only one of the minor counts of antitrust violation and awarded the USFL one dollar in damages, tripled to three dollars because it was an antitrust violation. Although the jury found that the NFL's unlawful monopolization of the professional football market had injured the USFL, it cited ample evidence that the USFL had engaged in behavior that contributed to its own demise. The new league's own shortcomings, rather than intentional behavior on the part of the NFL, had caused it to fail because it didn't make the necessary investments and demonstrate the required patience to create a stable and credible professional sports league.

Following the verdict, the USFL suspended operations and never played again. In three short years, it had fielded teams in twenty-two cities with thirty-nine principal owners and amassed fiscal losses estimated at $200 million. Although the NFL was no longer in direct competition with the league, it continued to feel its effects. Besides being the first to use instant replay to challenge officials' calls and instituting professional football's first two-point conversion, the USFL had forced the escalation of NFL salaries. Prior to the USFL, NFL salaries were increasing at a rate of approximately 7 to 10 percent per year. During the first two years of the USFL, NFL salaries jumped 25 percent; they increased another 19 percent in the third season. After the USFL folded, NFL salaries reached a plateau, rising only 5 percent in subsequent years. The USFL's legacy would continue to have an impact over the next decade as well, as many of its players and coaches found success in the NFL.

Meanwhile, the Packers were overseeing the first major upgrade to Lambeau Field since 1970. While earlier expansions had increased the stadium's capacity to 56,263, the facility lacked the moneymaking luxury boxes that had become commonplace in so many other NFL venues. At the start of the 1985 season, the Packers rectified the situation with the debut of seventy-two private suites, increasing the stadium's capacity to 56,926. If the Packers were going to stay competitive in the new world order of generating revenue, the luxury boxes were a good start. For almost two decades, the Packers had survived thanks to the mystique of Lombardi and a devoted fan base determined not to give up on its franchise. Lambeau Field continued to host sellout crowds and maintain a waiting list for season tickets in the tens of thousands, but that patience and dedication came with a price: high expectations.

As the 1985 season approached, optimism prevailed throughout Green Bay. "I'll just say this—this team has been close for several years now, but they've always been that one game away," Gregg said, referring largely to the Packers' 7–1 second-half run to finish at 8–8 for the second consecutive season. "We're going to have to

> "Even Forrest said he was tired of hearing the name Lombardi."
>
> —OFFENSIVE TACKLE GREG KOCH

When Forrest Gregg decided to overhaul the Packers' roster with younger talent, several veterans, including Eddie Lee Ivery (40) and Lynn Dickey (12), found themselves on the sidelines alongside longtime Packers photographer Vernon Biever. (WISCONSIN STATE JOURNAL)

close that gap. A lot of times, that one step is a tough step to take."

Although Gregg had a fiery coaching style compared to the studious Devine and more reserved Starr, his old-school demeanor seemed to only echo the success of his mentor, Vince Lombardi, who still cast a shadow over Green Bay—one that nobody could seem to outrun. The legend of Lombardi was still very much alive in Green Bay. His moving speeches could be heard at the Packers Hall of Fame. His name was plastered all over town: Lombardi Avenue, Lombardi Plaza, Lombardi Middle School. His spirit seemed to pace the Lambeau Field sidelines alongside his failed successors, only fueling further comparisons. "There are paper mills scattered all about Green Bay, a city of fewer than 90,000 people," *Washington Post* columnist Gary Pomerantz wrote. "It's a good thing, too, since you need pages and pages to chronicle the Packers' post-Lombardi failures."

Nothing irritated current Packers players more than hearing about Green Bay's storied past. How often were players hearing the name Lombardi brought up in Green Bay? "After every loss," offensive lineman Tim Huffman said, noting his growing frustration. "The man's been dead for fifteen years, right? I haven't noticed him performing any miracles over the past fifteen years, so he must have been human, right?"

As the losses continued to mount during the 1985 season, "even Forrest said he was tired of hearing the name Lombardi," offensive tackle Greg Koch, who was a nine-year veteran in Green Bay, told the *Milwaukee Sentinel*. "The worst thing is, we've had the players here over the years. We just haven't done anything with them."

After one particularly embarrassing loss, a frustrated Forrest Gregg kicked a garbage can full of ice and soft drinks that sat in the center of the locker room. Because it was full of melting ice, it didn't budge. "You knew it had to hurt," rookie linebacker Brian Noble recalled. When several players stifled laughs, Gregg turned to linebacker Mike Douglass and chastised him in front of the other players for what he considered especially poor play. When Douglass yelled back, the argument escalated into a free-for-all with soda cans and bodies flying back and forth until order was restored. "I was stunned," Noble said as players stood around afterward in quiet shock. "I just put my head down and said, 'This is hell.'"

Meanwhile, the Bears were steamrolling through the regular season en route to their first Super Bowl victory. Chicago's recent success and the Packers' continued failures found their rivalry becoming downright nasty. "During my tenure as coach, the rivalry heated up, to put it kindly," said Gregg of the Bears. "But what stoked the rivalry from my point of view was simply the desire to defeat Chicago. They were the team to beat in the NFC Central, and the 1985 edition of the Bears were the measuring stick for the entire league."

Regardless of whether it stemmed from when the two coaches—the Bears' Mike Ditka and the Packers' Gregg—had collided back when they were players, or because of current personality clashes, their games during the mid-1980s were some of the ugliest ever played. "I don't think the rivalry was ever as full of antics as it was in that period," Noble remarked about how the exchanging of insults and cheap shots before, during, and after plays only seemed to escalate in front of a national television audience. During a Monday Night Football game in Soldier Field, Ditka called for his 320-pound defensive tackle, William "Refrigerator" Perry, to line up at tailback, take a handoff, and plow over linebacker George Cumby for a one-yard touchdown that added insult to an already embarrassing 23–7 Packers loss.

Despite all of their early season disappointments, the Packers won five of their last seven games to finish 8–8 for the third consecutive season but again fell short of the postseason. "It's been that way for us for years," defensive end Ezra Johnson said, noting how injuries continued to plague the team's playoff aspirations. "The bug comes up and bites us." It was a bug that coach Forrest Gregg planned to eradicate that offseason.

■ ■ ■

During the Packers' 1986 training camp, Forrest Gregg was asked what it would take for the Packers to make the playoffs. "Winning another game or two," he replied with a chuckle before providing a more calculated answer. "We've got to get off to a better start and we've got to play consistently well all year long."

In reality he felt that "after two years of mediocrity with an old team, I was tired of sitting still," choosing to replace many of the Packers' experienced veterans with younger players. "Our 7–1 finish in the '84 season had raised expectations for the following year, and had we dismantled the team at that point, I might have been run out of town, but waiting a year to do it was a mistake."

Gregg's overhauling of the roster saw several beloved stars, including Paul Coffman, Mike Douglass, and Lynn Dickey, no longer wearing green and gold. By the start of the 1986 season, only eleven players remained from the fifty-seven Gregg had inherited two years earlier. "What I'm trying to do with this football team is to

Members of the Packers took part in the fabled nut-cracker drill during training camp in 1986, a technique made famous in Green Bay by Vince Lombardi and reintroduced by Forrest Gregg. (MILWAUKEE JOURNAL SENTINEL)

get a fresh start," Gregg told reporters. "We have a lot of inexperience, but we are willing to take the risk. I felt like if we were going to move forward, we had to take some calculated risk."

Relying on younger, less experienced replacements, Green Bay suffered its worst start in franchise history, going winless in its first six games and causing a frustrated fan base to lash out. "When the Extremely Honorable Robert J. Parins hired Gregg as the main man," *Milwaukee Journal* sportswriter Michael Bauman observed, "everyone agreed that Forrest would fix everything. And so far this year, he has—for the Houston Oilers, for the New Orleans Saints and for the Minnesota Vikings. The Chicago Bears are not on this list because they did not need assistance."

The losses piled up as injuries to key players—including offensive lineman Rich Moran, linebacker John Anderson, and cornerback Tim Lewis, who suffered a career-ending neck injury—exposed the team's lack of depth and experience. The Packers' mistake-prone offense struggled to score points. They shuffled through a quarterback merry-go-round of Randy Wright, Vince Ferragamo, and Chuck Fusina while showing interest in upgrading the position. "So the Green Bay Packers have been trying out quarterbacks," Bauman exclaimed after the team failed to acquire the Rams' Jim Everett and Patriots' Doug Flutie. "What they should be holding tryouts for are general managers. The mistakes being made by this particular organization transcend any one particular playing position and go to the nature of the organization itself. The management in Green Bay could qualify for the Olympics because, of course, the Packers brass still has amateur status."

The Packers were also earning a reputation around the league for playing dirty. The worst infraction occurred during a November 23 game in Chicago. "I hated to see us resort to late hits and cheap shots," trainer Domenic Gentile remarked. "Charles Martin's infamous body-slam of quarterback Jim McMahon a full three seconds after the whistle blew was an embarrassment."

The incident, which was witnessed by a large television audience and repeated infinite times in highlight packages broadcast across the country, showed Packers defensive end Charles Martin slamming McMahon into the ground after throwing an interception. The egregious late hit ended McMahon's season with an injured shoulder and got Martin ejected from the game and suspended for two more. Adding to the controversy was that Martin was wearing a hand towel listing the numbers of several Bears offensive players, which he allegedly bragged was a hit list. Afterward, when Ditka accused the Packers of being thugs, Gregg remarked, "I don't think it was a coincidence that the only time we were accused of playing dirty was when we played Chicago. I apologize for nothing. . . . We were out there trying to win and what we did was play the Bears the way the Bears played us."

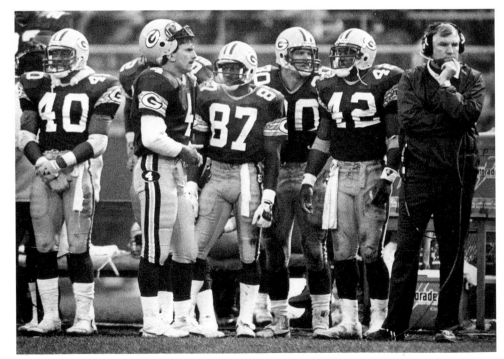

Forrest Gregg (far right) started looking elsewhere for answers as the Packers, including Eddie Lee Ivery (40), Ben Thomas (92), Chuck Fusina (4), Walter Stanley (87), Paul Ott Carruth (30), and Gary Ellerson (42), failed to make the playoffs in 1986. (MILWAUKEE JOURNAL SENTINEL)

During a 4–12 campaign that couldn't end soon enough, several off-the-field indiscretions further soiled the organization's reputation. "Overshadowing our dismal performance was a seemingly endless flood of arrests, accusations, and bad press that would mar the remainder of my stay in Green Bay," Gregg recalled. "For Packer players, life in Green Bay was like living in a fishbowl. And for a period of time it seemed as if everything that could happen did happen. A number of my players ran into trouble with the law for a variety of transgressions."

For decades the Packers had been the symbol of enduring excellence, from their small-town identity to their conservative style. By 1986 they were best known for playing mediocre football with athletes who were spending more time in courtrooms than on the gridiron. Two years earlier, wide receiver James Lofton and running back Eddie Lee Ivery were accused, but never charged, of sexual assault following an incident at a Milwaukee tavern. In 1986 Lofton was again accused of sexual assault stemming from an incident in the stairwell of a Green Bay nightclub. Within weeks, cornerback Mossy Cade was also charged with sexual assault for a separate incident, after allegedly attacking a woman at his house. Both men went on trial in the same week and in the same Brown County Courthouse, but in different courtrooms. Adding to the surreal situation, Gregg and his wife attended Cade's trial while Bart Starr and his wife were at Lofton's trial. In the end, Lofton was acquitted of his charges while Cade was convicted—but the damage had been done. "Some teams are astute enough to trade not simply for size and skill, but character as well," the *Milwaukee Journal's* Michael Bauman wrote in a scathing editorial concerning the Packers' recent legal woes. "The Packers appear to have traded for size and skill and full employment for lawyers."

A *Sports Illustrated* exposé further portrayed Green Bay as a wasteland inhospitable to black athletes, claiming the community had become a relic, too small to compete in the megabucks NFL—an argument that was hard to counter since the Packers had become perennial doormats. "I feel a little hurt and sadness on Sundays now when I hear the Packers' scores on TV or read them in the newspaper," former defensive end Willie Davis said of the franchise's continued downward spiral. "And it seems to have gotten progressively worse."

> "I feel a little hurt and sadness on Sundays now when I hear the Packers' scores on TV or read them in the newspaper."
> —FORMER DEFENSIVE END WILLIE DAVIS

• • •

Many of the franchise's problems could be traced to its archaic organizational structure. The Lombardi-generated concept of a single person having unrestricted authority over the entire football operation had become outdated in Green Bay. "Because Lombardi could do it, we thought everyone could do it. That was our biggest mistake," Harlan said of the Packers' head coaching position no longer being omnipotent. "As the game grew and became more complex, we finally decided it could not be done that way any longer."

During the offseason, team president Parins decided to hire a director of football operations to report directly to him and the executive committee. In January 1987 Parins interviewed Ron Wolf, head of personnel operations for the Los Angeles Raiders, and Tom Braatz, who had been the Atlanta Falcons' general manager between 1982 and 1985 before being demoted to director of college scouting. After an initial interview with Parins, Wolf expressed discomfort over the lack of definition between his potential role and Gregg's. He took himself out of consideration, claiming, "I think it's a tremendous job and a great opportunity, but I wasn't interested."

The position then fell to Braatz, a Kenosha native who had played his college football at Marquette University, who was named Green Bay's executive vice president of football operations in February. "Up to that point I had complete charge of personnel; my job was to hire all coaches, players, and scouts," Gregg said. "The front office had pushed Tom Braatz on me. Though I wasn't the general manager in name, I previously had the responsibilities that came with the job."

For the first time, the team had an executive other than a head coach to build and manage the team. However, Braatz's first draft was a mixture of only a few hits and several misses: running back Brent Fullwood never fulfilled his potential as the draft's fourth overall selection and was traded after a few disappointing seasons; second-rounder Johnny Holland became a fixture at linebacker; and Braatz's tenth-round choice of quarterback Don Majkowski helped revitalize the franchise, if only for a brief moment. Braatz was also burdened after the draft with several well-publicized holdouts, including Fullwood and quarterback Randy Wright. "I don't know how

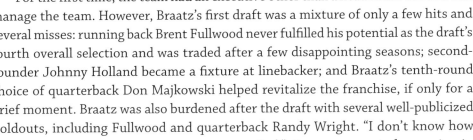

you feel," Gregg was quoted as saying in the *Milwaukee Journal* of the negative publicity surrounding the club. "I know how I feel. I sort of have had enough."

At the annual stockholders' meeting in June, the Packers announced their largest profit ever, $3,081,766, despite suffering through their worst regular season since 1958. With more than $21 million in retained earnings, Parins warned, "I think we've reached a saturation point as far as the money we take in." He feared the team's revenues from television, gate admissions, concessions, and other sources in the upcoming year were in jeopardy.

Forrest Gregg (left) was all smiles at the press conference that introduced Tom Braatz (right) as the Packers' new vice president before the 1987 season. (MILWAUKEE JOURNAL SENTINEL)

Throughout the summer of 1987, talk of another players' strike became a growing distraction. A walkout seemed inevitable since the collective bargaining agreement that had been reached between owners and players in 1982 was set to expire at the end of August. Many of the same issues that had caused the player walkout five years earlier were revisited. Although player salaries, guaranteed contracts, a wage scale, drug testing, and pension benefits were discussed, unfettered free agency became the most prominent and volatile issue between players and owners.

As in 1982, the NFL had just renegotiated its television contracts in January, reaching three-year agreements with ABC, CBS, and NBC totaling $1.43 billion, or $476 million per year. The slight decline from the $490 million the league earned in 1986 was a residual effect from the players' strike five years earlier. Without its usual leverage, the league accepted only a slight increase from ABC for Monday Night Football and slight decreases from its new contracts with CBS and NBC compared to what the league was earning in 1986. To compensate for the lost broadcast revenue, the league signed its first cable-television contract, a three-year agreement with ESPN, for a total of thirteen games—eight games on consecutive Sunday nights covering the last eight weeks of the season and the five prime-time specials that had been on ABC in past years.

In Green Bay, Forrest Gregg was once again optimistic his young roster would produce positive results, but after the Packers started the season 0–1–1, the NFL players walked out. "When the strike came, it took us about a week to put together our roster," Gregg recalled of the league calling in replacement players to cross the picket lines. Many of the replacement players arrived at Lambeau Field carrying nothing more than a backpack. Most expected the experience to last only a few days. But when word came down from the league office that the Packers would be playing on Sunday with the replacement players and that those games would count in the regular-season standings, Gregg described it "as if an electric current went through the room. The news that they would be playing made a marked difference in practice. During the next workout I leaned over to one of my assistants and said, 'Whatever else we'll have, we'll have hungry ballplayers.'"

The NFL canceled its third week of games due to the strike, but then fielded three weeks of mixed-quality football with replacements. Meanwhile, the striking players picketed outside stadiums and team facilities, which exposed the union's shortsighted preparation. No strike fund had been set up to assist players with lost salaries. Cracks in union solidarity soon surfaced. Ten days into the strike, forty-nine players had crossed the picket line. Although no Packers defected, eighty-nine players from around the league eventually did. Regardless of the fact that the replacement games weren't drawing great numbers in ratings or attendance, they were quite effective in bringing the strike to a quick end. On October 15, 1987, the union

When the second players' strike in five years prompted NFL officials to bring in replacement players, regular-season games continued, to mixed fan response. (BOTH PHOTOS MILWAUKEE JOURNAL SENTINEL)

voted to return to work after a twenty-four-day holdout, achieving none of its goals and without a new collective bargaining agreement. During the strike, the Packers fared better than most clubs with their replacement players. They won two of their three games and attracted more than 35,000 fans to each of their two games at Lambeau Field. "Those three contests were memorable," Gregg recalled, "if not for the artistry then for the fervor."

When the regulars returned, so did Green Bay's losing ways. "It was a very, very difficult season," Harlan recalled of how Gregg's bitterness seemed to increase as the Packers' season continued to spiral out of control. "You could see it falling apart the same way you could see Dan Devine's last season falling apart. Things just got worse every week."

Green Bay finished the abbreviated 1987 season with a 5–9–1 record. "After four frustrating years, I felt we had the Packers moving in the right direction. But they were an exhausting four years," Gregg later admitted in his autobiography *Winning*

In four years Forrest Gregg couldn't redirect the Packers toward the playoffs as he compiled a 25-37-1 record. (MILWAUKEE JOURNAL SENTINEL)

in the Trenches. "All the things that had happened had a collective effect on my mind, my attitude. It was constant. Suspensions, arrests, trials, strikes . . . we made the headlines an awful lot but not for the right reasons."

With a year left on his five-year contract, "the prospect of returning to SMU had never crossed my mind before the phone rang," Gregg said of his alma mater's offer to bring him aboard as its athletic director and head coach. "Several weeks passed before I approached Judge Parins, the Packers' president. . . . Not for a moment did he try to talk me out of making the move."

On January 15, 1988, Gregg resigned as head coach of the Packers. "At the time, the organization was very close to releasing him," Harlan recalled. "I think he could see the end was near, and he made his escape before it happened. It was very reminiscent of the Dan Devine thing."

"At this point I was extremely worried about the future of the franchise," trainer Domenic Gentile admitted. "I talked about my fears with Tony Canadeo, a Packers Hall of Famer and a member of the board of directors, and he agreed that the credibility and viability of the franchise had been severely compromised by years of ineptitude." It was a sentiment many Green Bay fans and residents shared. Had the Packers, nearly two decades removed from their last world championship, spent the last of their cultural currency?

■ ■ ■

As the Packers went about finding their next head coach, it was apparent the dead hand of Vince Lombardi still rested on the organization. With an opportunity to make a big splash by hiring a prominent personality, they set their sights on one of college football's hottest coaches. Michigan State's George Perles had just come off leading the Spartans to a Rose Bowl berth, and he had the pedigree the Packers wanted: he was a former defensive coordinator with the Pittsburgh Steelers and a guy who knew what it took to win in the NFL. Word soon leaked out that Perles was going to be named the Packers' next head coach, with a public announcement imminent. When Bob Harlan called to get some final details for the team's press release, Perles informed him he wasn't coming to Green Bay. "Perles, it turned out, was only using our organization to get a sweeter deal at Michigan State," according to Gentile.

Neither of Vince Lombardi's disciples—Bart Starr (15) and Forrest Gregg (75)—had been able to return the Packers to prominence, prompting team officials to look outside the organization for their next coach. (MILWAUKEE JOURNAL SENTINEL)

It didn't matter if Perles backed out because he received a better offer from Michigan State or because he felt the task of coaching in Vince Lombardi's shadow was too daunting. "That was probably the low point for this franchise," Harlan recalled.

At some point, Green Bay had once again become an unappealing place to play football. Regardless of the franchise's ability to post annual profits, claims that the city was too small, the weather too cold, the facilities substandard, and the opportunities for players to earn income outside the game almost nonexistent all fueled rumors that the franchise was in grave danger. When trainer Domenic Gentile approached some members of the executive committee in 1988 to express his concerns, "they hinted that the board of directors might have to get together and start talking about trying to find a corporation to take over the team and possibly even move it."

Threats of franchise relocation were no longer idle. In 1988, when Cardinals owner Bill Bidwell relocated his team to Phoenix, the NFL had endured its third franchise shift in six years. Teams threatening to relocate were now receiving formal approval from fellow owners in an effort to avoid another antitrust lawsuit. Relocation offered a quick fix for even the most ineptly run organization. Franchises could now leverage from prospective cities promises of tax incentives, civically funded stadiums, and lucrative corporate marketing agreements, further escalating the financial benefits of franchise free agency.

Back in Green Bay the Perles debacle forced the Packers to turn to their second choice, hiring Lindy Infante as their new head coach in February 1988. Infante had a long coaching résumé, most recently as the Browns' offensive coordinator, but just one year of head coaching experience—and that was with the USFL's Jacksonville Bulls. He was considered one of the league's leading offensive innovators and would be looked upon to reinvigorate Green Bay's slumping scoring output. "We've got a long way to go," he surmised. "One of the things that will kind of tell us how good we can be and whether or not we can be a contender will be how fast we grasp the new ideas and philosophies and things that we're going to be installing when we go into training camp."

The players struggled to pick up Infante's complex offense as the Packers lost their first five regular-season games in 1988. After a modest two-game winning streak, Green Bay went on to lose its next seven contests, getting shut out three times and outscored 153–53. If not for season-ending victories over the Vikings and Cardinals that left the Packers at 4–12 by season's end, they would have suffered

Team president Robert Parins (right) thought the Packers' prospects were bright when Lindy Infante (left) became the tenth head coach in franchise history. (MILWAUKEE JOURNAL SENTINEL)

through their worst season since Ray "Scooter" McLean's 1–10–1 record three decades earlier.

Before the season, at the Packers' annual stockholders' meeting in May, the team had announced its second-largest profit ever: $3,005,000. "The 1987 players strike disrupted both our football season and our 1987–88 financial plan," Parins said, explaining the slight dip in profits from the previous season. "We had one game canceled and, although we were able to field an exciting replacement team for three games, attendance at home and away suffered. Television, radio, and ticket refunds substantially reduced our gross income."

In just two years, the Packers had made a profit of more than $6 million, with more than $32 million of television revenue filling the team's coffers. Green Bay was no longer hosting a struggling little team with marginal financial prospects. With big cash reserves on hand, the organization was in the position to spend some money in pursuit of making the team a winner—or at least a competitor.

■   ■   ■

In January 1989 the NFL, still without a collective bargaining agreement in place, instituted a limited form of free agency as the NFLPA's lawsuit worked its way through the judicial system. Owners realized that the league's current form of free agency, based on first refusal and compensation, wasn't working. Hoping to avoid a full-blown insurrection by the players, they unilaterally imposed a new form of free agency. Known as "Plan B," the system would allow clubs to protect thirty-seven players on their respective rosters but would provide the remaining players the opportunity to sign with other teams without compensation to the team that lost the player. Although the plan amounted to little more than a shuffling of second-tier players, "we've increased the quality of the bottom part of our football team," Infante remarked. That offseason, Green Bay spent almost $855,000 to sign a league-high twenty players through "Plan B."

The Packers also were in an ideal situation to further rebuild their roster; they had the second overall pick in the upcoming draft. "At that time, Infante and Braatz split the decision making. Neither had authority over the other," future Packers executive Ron Wolf remarked on the inherently flawed arrangement. "Before the

1989 draft, they disagreed on the Packers' first round pick. One wanted Barry Sanders, the other Tony Mandarich. The hierarchy above Braatz and Infante voted for Mandarich, a move that ultimately affected the future of both executives."

By selecting Mandarich, the Packers passed on future Hall-of-Famers Barry Sanders, Derrick Thomas, and Deion Sanders. Mandarich proceeded to hold out the entire preseason. Once he arrived in Green Bay, he struggled, spending most of his rookie season either on the bench or on special teams. After starting just thirty-one games in four years for the Packers, *Sports Illustrated*'s "Incredible Bulk" cover boy would be released. "His failure on the field cast doubt on Tom Braatz's ability to judge NFL talent," author Don Gulbrandsen remarked.

Following the 1989 draft, the Packers held their annual stockholders' meeting in May, reporting the team's smallest annual profit—$1,286,000—since 1982. Several factors caused the $1.5 million decrease from the previous season, including a rise in player salaries, the team's aggressive participation in the NFL's "Plan B" free-agent market, and Green Bay's $622,000 portion of the antitrust settlement reached between the league and the Los Angeles Raiders regarding the franchise's relocation. "If you didn't have the free agent market, the probability is you're looking overall at another one million dollars," Parins explained to stockholders in attendance. At the meeting it was also announced that according to a survey by the NFL Players Association, the Packers ranked twenty-fourth in average salary in 1988 at $213,175 per player—a $35,000 increase from 1987, when the club ranked twenty-sixth.

Following the meeting, Judge Parins retired as the Packers' president and chief executive officer. Although he was disappointed that the team never succeeded on the field during his seven-year tenure, he did oversee the franchise's net worth escalate from $19.5 million to $32 million and its financial reserves rise to a record $18 million. The perception outside of Green Bay was that Parins left behind an organization with a power structure so fragmented there was no clear delineation regarding who answered to whom and that the team's seven-man executive committee was involved in making important football decisions. In reality, the team's personnel and organizational chart had become top-heavy and disjointed, almost by accident, after two decades of mediocre football. In an attempt to remedy the situation, the franchise turned to one of its own.

On June 5, Bob Harlan became the ninth president in team history and the first ever to assume the role from outside the Packers' executive committee. Inheriting an organization still hurting from recent scandals "that totally wiped out the positive things we were doing in the community," Harlan told reporters that marketing was crucial to rebuilding the Packers' image. "This organization has a lot of class, and to lose some of that was a nightmare."

> "This organization has a lot of class, and to lose some of that was a nightmare."
> —TEAM PRESIDENT BOB HARLAN

Not only had the Packers' image been tarnished, but their tradition was getting lost between generations. "None of the young people could relate to the Glory Years," personnel executive Dick Corrick recalled. "Harlan ran some survey on the young people here and found out that at some point we weren't going to have anybody in the stands." At local department stores, Packers clothing was available but hard to find. Local businesses that used to support the team with their logos emblazoned on green and gold calendars, drink coasters, and matchboxes no longer left the freebies on their counters. It was hard even for the most dedicated fan to support a franchise that couldn't field a competitive team. The constant negatives had taken their toll.

Harlan's first priority was to build a winning team. "I thought we needed to find a way to get rid of all those negative perceptions," he remarked in his autobiography, *Green and Golden Moments*. "We're in a very visible business, and it all boils down to those three hours on Sunday."

When Bob Harlan (left) succeeded Robert Parins (right), he was the first team president in franchise history who had not been a member of the executive committee. (MILWAUKEE JOURNAL SENTINEL)

Harlan, also aware that success on the field in professional football correlated to maximizing revenue streams, wasted little time initiating his first major project. "We had looked around at what other teams were doing with their stadiums and decided that we had to develop a way to increase our local revenue," Harlan said of the team's announced $8.3 million expansion of Lambeau Field that would increase the stadium's seating capacity to almost 60,000 patrons. The expansion included 1,920 new club seats and thirty-six private boxes, which would generate millions of dollars in revenue the team didn't have to share with the NFL's twenty-seven other franchises. Following the announcement of their availability, Harlan exclaimed, "We sold them faster than we could build them."

As the 1989 season approached, the entire league was in a state of flux after longtime NFL commissioner Pete Rozelle announced he would retire in November. Since becoming commissioner in 1960, he was instrumental in the league's expansion from twelve to twenty-eight teams, negotiating lucrative television contracts now worth billions of dollars, and developing the Super Bowl into the premier international television event. For the past three decades, the NFL had thrived under Rozelle's "league first" leadership, but new owners such as the Cowboys' Jerry Jones and the Patriots' Victor Kiam epitomized the entrepreneurial spirit of maximizing the changing stadium economics and evolving media marketplace. In the next twenty years, three-quarters of the NFL's teams would build, renovate, or contract for new stadiums. The NFL of the future faced the daunting issues of free agency, league-wide expansion, and the unlimited possibilities of the emerging multimedia revolution. Upon Rozelle's departure, Paul Tagliabue, the league's chief outside attorney since 1969, was named as his successor. In the wake of the announcement, the *New York Times* reported that the decision could mean "that the league may soon be managed more like a $1-billion-a-year entertainment business than a collection of money-losing tax shelters, as many outsiders have viewed it."

During the Packers' training camp, Lindy Infante was reserved in his assessment of his team's potential for the upcoming 1989 season: "We're going to be more solid, more sound and, hopefully, it will be a more productive year in the win column," he explained, declining to make any predictions. "I hope our record's even a little better than we are. Maybe we'll get a little bounce of the ball here or there, or the right kind of break here and there that we win a game maybe we shouldn't have won. That's what turns an average team into a good team. And also those teams that can go out there and win the close ball games. So our challenge is to try to win the close ones. If we can do that, we can be a pretty solid team."

Little did anyone realize, especially after an opening-day 23–21 loss to the Buccaneers, that the Packers would make it fun to watch football in Green Bay again. Behind the swashbuckling heroics of quarterback Don Majkowski, 1989's "Cardiac Pack" went on to win ten games—seven of them by 4 or fewer points—with a knack for pulling out close games. "Those who jumped on the bandwagon needed nerves of steel and a never-say-die attitude as the green and gold came from behind to win seven times and set an NFL record with four one-point wins," author Eric

> ## "Our challenge is to try to win the close ones. If we can do that, we can be a pretty solid team."
> —HEAD COACH
> LINDY INFANTE

Wide receiver Sterling Sharpe (84) became an immediate impact player during his rookie season in 1988. By 1989 he was one of the NFL's most feared offensive threats, catching ninety passes for 1,423 yards and twelve touchdowns. (FROM THE GREEN BAY PRESS-GAZETTE ARCHIVES, REPRINTED BY PERMISSION)

Linebacker Tim Harris (97) and Lindy Infante (right) enjoyed several Gatorade showers on the way to the Packers' 10-6 record in 1989—the team's best since 1972. (MILWAUKEE JOURNAL SENTINEL)

Goska explained in *Green Bay Packers: A Measure of Greatness*.

The season's most memorable comeback occurred against the Bears at Lambeau Field. The Packers were down to their last play after Majkowski directed a frantic last-minute drive that stalled at the Chicago 9. On fourth down, he rolled right and connected with wide receiver Sterling Sharpe for the apparent winning touchdown. But when a line judge threw a penalty flag, signifying that Majkowski had crossed the line of scrimmage, the play was nullified. With the loss of down, the Packers had lost possession of the ball, which would allow the Bears to run out the clock and preserve their victory. That's when the referee turned to instant replay, which was still in its infancy, in hopes of confirming the call on the field was correct. After a five-minute delay, the call on the field was overturned when replay determined that Majkowski had not crossed the line and the touchdown stood, ensuring the Packers a 14–13 upset victory. From there, Green Bay upset the defending Super Bowl champion 49ers in San Francisco and finished the season with a flurry of victories over the Vikings, Buccaneers, Bears, and Cowboys in four of their last five games. "That 1989 season was the first year I believed we could win any game we got into," linebacker Brian Noble recalled. "No one wanted to play us."

The Packers finished the season with a 10–6 record, their best since 1972, and a chance to win the NFC Central Division title outright. If the Bengals could defeat the Vikings the following day in their regular-season finale on Monday night, Green Bay would be headed to the playoffs. But Minnesota won, sharing an identical 10–6 record that would earn them the lone playoff spot, since they owned the deciding tie-breaker of a better divisional record. Once again, the Packers were forced to watch the playoffs from home.

. . .

Despite missing the 1989 postseason, the Pack seemed to be back. "There was real excitement in Green Bay for the first time in a long, long time, and we were all caught up in it," team president Bob Harlan explained. The Packers rewarded Lindy Infante with a two-year contract extension before the start of the 1990 season. "We wanted so desperately to produce a winner here, and we thought we had finally found the coach who was going to get us over the hump."

That summer Green Bay was engulfed in a college-like atmosphere. Hundreds of fans made the pilgrimage to the team's training camp, all in hopes of seeing their new heroes in green and gold. "An awful lot of people in this state waited a long time for this team to come back and be a legitimate contender," Harlan said of the throngs of euphoric fans surrounding the team's practice field. "There's great anticipation."

Veteran linebacker Brian Noble exclaimed, "This is what the city revolves around, the Green Bay Packers. This time of year [football season] is more exciting to this city than anything. They live for this!"

Those spectators noticed several familiar faces missing. On the first day of training camp, eighteen veterans, the majority of them starters, were absent because of contract problems. Offensive linemen Ken Ruettgers, Ron Hallstrom, Rich Moran, and Alan Veingrad missed a combined 101 days of practice. For forty-five days Don Majkowski was engaged in a nasty and protracted holdout, signing a new contract just days before the start of the regular season. Because it was an era before salary caps, signing bonuses, and prorated deals, the Packers could play hardball with their holdouts, and they did. "Lindy wanted to teach these guys a lesson. He wanted to prove to them that they couldn't hold a gun to the Packers," trainer Domenic Gentile recalled. "Lines in the sand were drawn, and they dissected the team. There was a great deal of animosity and bitterness between players and management."

> "They let a lot of good players go. Personalities got in the way."
> —SAFETY GEORGE GREENE

"[Infante] got rid of the 10–6 guys because they were holding out," safety George Greene recalled. "They let a lot of good players go. Personalities got in the way."

Further handicapping the Packers' chances to capitalize on their 1989 success was a failure to upgrade their roster in the draft. With the team's two first-round selections, Tom Braatz selected Tony Bennett, a linebacker who would have a respectable career with the Packers before joining the Colts, and running back Darrell Thompson, who failed to live up to expectations in four lackluster seasons with Green Bay. The underachieving draft class may have been one of Green Bay's worst if not for the later-round selections of cornerback LeRoy Butler and linebacker Bryce Paup, who would both become impact players for the Packers in the upcoming decade.

Despite starting the 1990 season with a stunning win over the Rams, Green Bay was haunted by the residual effects of the player holdouts all season. Their offensive line surrendered a team record sixty-two sacks and contributed to a running game that averaged fewer than 86 yards per game, the worst output in franchise history. Even when Majkowski returned as the team's starting quarterback in week three, he struggled, never regaining his magical form from the previous season.

Following a three-game winning streak in November, the 6–5 Packers found themselves in the thick of the NFL's 1990 playoff race, one that had been expanded

Don Majkowski (7), Tim Harris (97), and Brian Noble (91) found little comfort in the Packers' 1990 season as they fell to a 6–10 record. (MILWAUKEE JOURNAL SENTINEL)

prior to the start of the season with the addition of a third wild-card team in each conference. (Notably, if the expanded playoff format had existed in 1989, the Packers would have made the postseason.) In 1990 the Packers had five games remaining and trailed only the Eagles for the top wild-card spot. But their season began to unravel after Majkowski suffered a season-ending shoulder injury against the Cardinals. Green Bay lost all five of its remaining games, finishing 6–10 and tied for last place in the NFC Central Division. "The situation had reached a crisis point that both the city and the organization were convinced their team probably couldn't be much better," future Packers executive Ron Wolf recalled. "And they had accepted it."

• • •

The Packers certainly had the financial resources available to build a winning team, as their net profit grew by more than four times to $1,859,646 after the 1990 season—a result of the NFL securing a four-year $3.65 billion broadcast agreement that infused $32.6 million into each team's coffers on an annual basis, nearly double the $16.7 million from the previous television contract. But if the organization was going to transform into a winner, it would have to start at the top. During the offseason, team president Bob Harlan debated bringing in a general manager. Instead, he hired Mike Reinfeldt as the team's new chief financial officer. Reinfeldt would assist Tom Braatz with the organization's business side and provide the franchise a savvy contract negotiator. Harlan's resolve to further restructure the team's front office only strengthened after the team's 1991 draft class was deemed another bust. The Packers' first-round selection, cornerback Vinnie Clark, failed to crack the lineup as a rookie and would last only two seasons in Green Bay. Of the seven players the team selected after the sixth round, only one made it through training camp. Three of Braatz's last four number one picks—Mandarich, Thompson, and Clark—were significant disappointments. Despite consistently drafting in high positions, he was criticized for failing to select an impact player other than Sterling Sharpe. When Braatz became the public scapegoat for the Packers' continued regression, he claimed, "I don't think I've ever been in a situation where this much was expected out of a football team and [it] had a breakdown the way we've had."

Entering the 1991 season, Green Bay's forty-seven-man roster featured forty players—including safety Chuck Cecil, kicker Chris Jacke, tight end Jackie Harris,

The Packers' inability to run the ball during the 1991 season left Don Majkowski (7), Tony Mandarich (77), and Rich Moran (57) often exposed and having to pick themselves up off the turf. (COURTESY OF EAU CLAIRE LEADER-TELEGRAM)

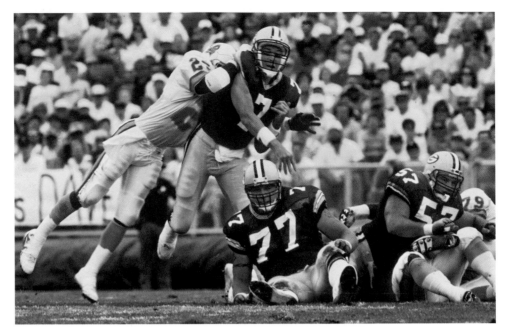

By the end of 1991 the Packers, including Sterling Sharpe (towel on head), Joe Fuller (21), and Perry Kemp (81), were again looking for answers after enduring a disappointing 4-12 campaign. (COURTESY OF ALL-AMERICAN SPORTS, LLC)

nose tackle Esera Tuaolo, and eighteen other draft picks—who were acquired since Braatz arrived. His latest flurry of "Plan B" free agency acquisitions included former Bears quarterback Mike Tomczak, which instilled little confidence in Packerland since their team was now resorting to signing their rival's castoffs. "Year after year of losses and excuses and empty promises piled up like so much garbage in a junkyard," author Don Gulbrandsen conceded. "If the Green Bay Packers were the NFL's measuring stick in the 1960s, then it is fair to say they were the league's laughingstock in the 1970s and 1980s. 'The Pack Will Be Back,' became pro football's version of 'the check is in the mail.'"

Any hope the Packers would enjoy a winning season in 1991 dissipated after they stumbled to a 1–6 start. Inconsistent play and injuries plagued the team all year, but their improved defense kept them competitive and in close games. After a disheartening 10–0 loss to the Bears, Infante told reporters, "I don't have the answers. I wish I did. All I can do is apologize for our performance offensively."

As the losses continued to mount, Braatz held to his reputation for being unflappable, a skill that served him well while speculation swirled that his days in Green Bay were numbered. "I think we're probably three or four players away; maybe five or six," he told reporters of his plans for next year based on projections that the Packers, at worst, would own four of the top forty-four selections in the upcoming 1992 draft. "With our draft picks, we've got a possibility to get there."

"The franchise was floundering and everybody was frustrated," executive committee member John Fabry recalled. "We had to make a bold move. Bob had the guts to make it."

Following a three-game losing streak that left the team at 2–9, the Packers fired Tom Braatz with five games left in the season. "At that point," Harlan recalled, "I had to find the one football guy who could get rid of all those rumors that we didn't care. I needed somebody to come in and say, 'Hey, I'm taking this thing by the neck, and we're going to do it.'"

Lindy Infante (left, standing next to Sterling Sharpe) was fired following the 1991 season after compiling a 24–40 record in four seasons in Green Bay. (FROM THE GREEN BAY PRESS-GAZETTE ARCHIVES, REPRINTED BY PERMISSION)

One week later, Ron Wolf, the same man who had interviewed but taken himself out of the running for the Packers' position that was filled by Braatz in 1987, was named the Packers' executive vice president and general manager. "I knew my timing was strange," Harlan said of his decision to hire Wolf midseason instead of waiting until January or February. "I wanted Ron to be around this team, watch it practice, travel with it and see if something jumped out at him that told him why it wasn't having success."

When Harlan gave Wolf complete control of football operations, allowing him to hire and fire anyone involved with the football side of the organization, "the handwriting was on the wall for Infante, who was forced to coach under a microscope," Gentile remarked.

The Packers responded by losing three straight games after Wolf arrived but rebounded to beat the Vikings in the season finale. The next day, Infante and his entire coaching staff were dismissed. "At the time of Lindy's firing, many longtime Packer fans had become cynical and distrustful of the organization. And who could blame them?" Gentile remarked after Green Bay had suffered through its third 4–12 finish in six years. "Outside of a few fleeting moments of success, we had been losers for nearly twenty-five years. We needed fresh blood, a new start, and a different perspective. In Wolf, we had someone who could give us that."

TITLETOWN'S TURNAROUND

I n the days that followed Lindy Infante's dismissal, Green Bay was abuzz with rumors that retired New York Giants head coach Bill Parcells would be his replacement. The two-time Super Bowl–winning head coach had retired to the television booth but was itching to return to the sidelines. His longtime friendship with Packers executive vice president and general manager Ron Wolf prompted the two to discuss the vacancy, but the conversations never got serious, especially since Parcells had just "strung along the Tampa Bay Buccaneers before stranding them at the altar—turning down a deal worth millions and complete control of the team," Packers trainer Domenic Gentile recalled.

Others rumored to be Infante's possible successor included Pete Carroll, Dave Wannstedt, and a defensive coordinator who received a strong endorsement from one of Wolf's most respected friends. "[Chiefs' head coach] Marty Schottenheimer and I had talked at length about Bill Cowher, who was on his staff in Kansas City," Wolf recalled of the man who would be named head coach of the Pittsburgh Steelers later that offseason. "Marty told me if I brought Bill in for an interview, I would hire him. He was that impressive."

Instead, Wolf pursued his first choice, San Francisco 49ers offensive coordinator Mike Holmgren. Holmgren was a disciple of coaching legend Bill Walsh and as the team's quarterback coach had been instrumental in developing future Hall-of-Famers Joe Montana and Steve Young. When Holmgren became the team's offensive coordinator in 1989, the 49ers won their second consecutive Super Bowl with the NFL's top-ranked offense. By the winter of 1991, Holmgren was considered to be the league's next great coaching prospect, but the Packers weren't the only team looking for a new head coach. While making the rounds to see what each team had to offer,

No image defined the Packers' resurgence during the 1990s more than the Lambeau Leap, a spontaneous celebration that began the day after Christmas in 1993 when safety LeRoy Butler returned a fumble for a touchdown to clinch Green Bay's first postseason berth since 1982. (MILWAUKEE JOURNAL SENTINEL)

Holmgren met with Wolf. "Once I met him, in the first fifteen minutes, I knew this was the guy," Wolf recalled.

"There was a kind of cocky confidence to Mike that reminded Ron of Bill Walsh and what he had done coaching at San Francisco," team president Bob Harlan recalled. "He had everything Ron was looking for: the leadership, the toughness, the charisma and the compatibility."

On January 11, 1992, Mike Holmgren was named the eleventh head coach in Green Bay Packers franchise history. Within a week, the Packers made NFL history by hiring two minority coordinators, ex-49ers assistants Ray Rhodes and Sherman Lewis, to oversee the team's defense and offense, respectively. "We got an idea of the respect Mike had around the league when he put together his first staff. Dick Jauron, Ray Rhodes, Jon Gruden, Steve Mariucci and Andy Reid were on that staff, and all of them became head coaches in the NFL," Harlan recounted. "It was a very dedicated staff, and I always got the impression that they thought it was a real honor to work for Mike Holmgren."

With a new coaching staff in place, Wolf and Holmgren went about rebuilding what had become a dispirited franchise. From the front office to the equipment staff, every crack and crevice of the franchise's psyche reeked of losing. Of the fifty-three players Holmgren inherited, only three had played in a playoff game with Green Bay. The Packers' 1991 squad failed to defeat any opponent that finished with a winning record or send one of its players to the Pro Bowl. It had been twenty-four years since Vince Lombardi paced the Green Bay sidelines, yet Phil Bengtson, Dan Devine, Bart Starr, Forrest Gregg, and Lindy Infante had all failed to outrun his shadow. Instead of trying to compete with the legendary coach's legacy, Holmgren embraced it. "There never will be another Coach Lombardi," he told *Gameday* magazine. "I don't think anyone will ever be able to duplicate his success. I don't hear voices or see ghosts or any of those things. And I don't dwell on the comparisons. I just have to be myself and do the best I can."

The similarities between Holmgren's and Lombardi's rise through the coaching ranks were almost uncanny: Holmgren coached high school football for ten years, college for five, and spent six years as an assistant with the 49ers before coming to Green Bay. Lombardi coached high school for eight years, college for six, and spent five as an assistant with the New York Giants. When Lombardi was named the team's head coach in 1959, he

New Packers head coach Mike Holmgren looked to instill a winning attitude in Green Bay during training camp in 1992. (MILWAUKEE JOURNAL SENTINEL)

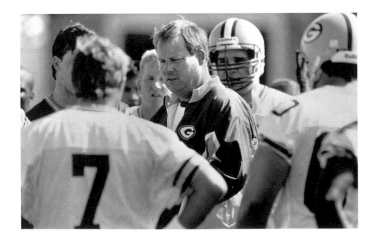

was forty-five years old. Holmgren was forty-three. Similar to Lombardi's "run to daylight" philosophy, Holmgren emphasized a "pass to daylight" attack as part of his complex West Coast offense—which would require a skilled field general. Ron Wolf had the perfect candidate.

Back in the fall of 1991, Wolf had arrived in Atlanta for his first official day on the job as the Packers' executive vice president and general manager. Before the game he excused himself from a conversation with Bob Harlan to watch the Falcons' third-string quarterback during pregame warm-ups. Moments later, Harlan recalled, "he came back to the press box and said he wanted to trade for Brett Favre."

That offseason Wolf discussed acquiring the backup quarterback with the Packers' board of directors and executive committee. "I told them not only did we have a chance to obtain a gifted player but also that this guy would be so good—and I'll always remember this—that he'll make people forget about any player who has ever worn a Green Bay uniform," Wolf recalled. "I told them his number *will* become synonymous with the numbers of all the great players who had ever worn a Green Bay uniform. I even told them he would wear number four, and he would be like what Lou Gehrig meant to the Yankee franchise."

Wolf continued his pitch. "I explained he was a third-string quarterback for the Falcons, but he would be as good as it gets, even if he had done absolutely nothing yet in the NFL," he said, knowing his reputation and the fate of the franchise rested on his decision. "When I said it was Brett Favre, you should have felt the silence and seen the looks."

When the Broncos and Chiefs showed interest in acquiring Favre as well, Wolf offered Atlanta a first-round pick for the quarterback. "The opportunity to acquire Brett Favre, in our opinion, easily outweighed the unknown quantity that might have been available to us," Wolf said of the Packers' willingness to part with their seventeenth overall selection in exchange for the Falcons' thirty-fourth selection from the previous year.

Beginning with the acquisition of Favre, Wolf and Holmgren began the delicate and treacherous process of rebuilding a winner in Green Bay. They considered no player untouchable. That offseason, Wolf initiated dozens of roster transactions. Almost half of the players who were on the roster at the end of Infante's last season were no longer Packers by the time Holmgren coached his first game. The sense of urgency surrounding Wolf's roster purging was fuelled by a conversation he had with Red Cochran, a Packers scout and former Lombardi assistant. "He wanted to win, and he wanted to do it now," Cochran told Wolf about Lombardi's unapologetic approach toward achieving success. "You start talking about winning three or four years from now, and all of a sudden, your thinking changes. You aren't pushing to win as hard and as soon as you should be."

Packers vice president and general manager Ron Wolf (right) greeted his pride and joy, Brett Favre, at the team's mini-camp. (MIL-WAUKEE JOURNAL SENTINEL)

"I think that's my knack—making something happen when nothing is there."

–QUARTERBACK BRETT FAVRE

The club could afford to absorb the costs involved in Wolf's recasting of its roster. During the annual stockholders' meeting, the Packers announced a $2.17 million profit after the 1991 season, despite having to absorb almost $3 million in contract buyouts, including $1.95 million for Infante's three remaining years and his coaches, front-office staff, and scouting personnel. "Considering that we had one large, extraordinary non-recurring event, yeah, it was a good year," treasurer John Underwood said, despite the team's income dropping from a record $5,562,000 the previous year to $1,470,000 because of the buyouts. "The cost of the personnel changes isn't going to be repeated in 1993."

Television revenue continued to keep the Packers in the black, as they collected $28.6 million in the second year of the NFL's four-year television deal. Since the broadcast agreement guaranteed the team $34 million in the upcoming season and $41 million in 1993, Green Bay could afford its personnel makeover—especially since "it was evident we soon would be dealing with a new world of free agency in the NFL, where a decent number of quality players would become available on the market—players good enough to improve our situation immediately," Wolf explained.

Despite an overhauled roster, Green Bay opened the 1992 season with an overtime loss to the Vikings, with Don Majkowski as the team's starting quarterback. The next week in Tampa Bay, while the Packers were being crushed 31–3, Holmgren

During the season's second game, Mike Holmgren benched quarterback Don Majkowski (7) to see what Brett Favre (4) could offer. In the next fourteen games Favre would pass his way to his first Pro Bowl, and the Packers would finish the regular season with a six-game winning streak. (MILWAUKEE JOURNAL SENTINEL)

benched the injury-prone veteran quarterback in favor of his backup, Brett Favre. The highlight of an otherwise error-prone performance occurred when Favre completed his first NFL pass—to himself—after the ball was tipped by a defender at the line of scrimmage. "The ability to improvise is the most important thing," Favre said afterward of his erratic performance. "You can practice something all week and rarely when you get into a game does it go exactly like you practiced it. I think that's my knack—making something happen when nothing is there."

The winless Packers were struggling to grasp Holmgren's new offense. While hosting the Bengals at Lambeau Field in week three, the Packers found their season slipping away. During the first quarter, a tackle by Cincinnati's Tim Krumrie forced Majkowski out of the game with an ankle injury. When Favre took over, he called formations that didn't exist, fumbled four times, and threw to receivers who weren't open. "What people don't remember about that day is that I should have had six or seven interceptions," Favre recalled. "I was all over the place."

The Packers trailed 17–3 going into the fourth quarter until Terrell Buckley returned a punt for a touchdown with 12:43 left to play, cutting the deficit to 7. The Bengals responded with a field goal, but Favre drove the Packers downfield on an eight-play, 88-yard drive that culminated with a 5-yard touchdown pass to Sterling Sharpe. When the Bengals added another field goal, Green Bay trailed 23–17 with 1:07 remaining. Forced to start the game's final drive at their own 8-yard line, the Packers darted upfield. With nineteen seconds left on the clock, Favre took the snap from center at the Cincinnati 35-yard line and hurled a spiral toward the end zone. "I never even saw it," Favre admitted to reporters after the game. "I just threw it up there and waited for the cheers."

Favre's pass found wide receiver Kitrick Taylor in the right corner of the end zone, giving Green Bay a 24–23 victory. "That incredible comeback produced all sorts of wonderful side effects," author Steve Cameron said in *The Packers! Seventy-five Seasons of Memories and Mystique in Green Bay*. "It sent a shock wave of bravado through a young team fighting to find its own identity, and it established beyond a doubt that Favre—however meager the experience he brought to the party—was something very, very special."

As the season progressed, Favre and the Packers continued to show flashes of greatness. "What transpired over the next months was one of the best coaching jobs in the history of the NFL," Wolf exclaimed of Green Bay's second-best record in

Following the 1992 season, general manager Ron Wolf (left) and head coach Mike Holmgren (right) felt the Packers were on the cusp of greatness and in need of a great player to carry them over the threshold. (MILWAUKEE JOURNAL SENTINEL)

twenty years. "Mike Holmgren and his staff took basically the same key players from a 4–12 club and molded them into 9–7 winners."

Despite riding a six-game winning streak into the season finale, the Packers' 27–7 loss in Minnesota eliminated them from the play-offs. "I can't imagine any franchise in NFL history being happier about a 9–7 record," Wolf exclaimed. "The impact this season had on our organization was immeasurable. Now we had reason to be optimistic."

⬛ ⬛ ⬛

In the summer of 1993, the National Football League and its players ended a quarter century of labor strife when reaching a new seven-year collective bargaining agreement. Over the past few years, the owners had lost several legal battles, including "Plan B" free agency being deemed a violation of antitrust law. As a result, unrestricted free agency was introduced in the NFL. "I remember in the mid-80s, everybody would say to me at league meetings, 'Boy, you better hope free agency never comes. It will kill you guys,'" Harlan recalled. "And I can't say we didn't wonder if it would kill us."

To ensure that the NFL maintained its competitive balance in this new era of free agency, the team owners forced the players to agree to a salary cap. The cap would prevent major-market teams from "buying" enough players to win a Super Bowl. Looking back, Harlan admitted, "Total free agency without a salary cap would have devastated us."

The limitations created by the salary cap and escalating salaries dictated a significant change in how NFL personnel directors approached stocking their rosters. The new free agency system indirectly established a way to disperse talent throughout the league and prevent the best clubs from keeping all their top players. In Green Bay, "the timing couldn't have been better for us. It gave us an incredibly important additional tool that we could use to secure frontline, veteran players," Wolf remarked. "For a franchise like the Packers, this new source for acquiring personnel was a welcomed gift."

To traverse the potential financial pitfalls created by the salary cap, Ron Wolf and Green Bay's chief contract negotiator and chief financial officer, Mike Reinfeldt, developed the Packers' "11-player wheel" philosophy of paying higher salaries to eleven key veterans—five on offense, five on defense, and one specialty player—than to most players on the roster. To maintain salary-cap flexibility, the team would fill the rest of its roster with free agents, veteran journeymen, and youngsters playing under rookie contracts. "You no longer can be just a talent evaluator," Wolf said of the economic tug-of-war created by the salary cap. "Instead, you need to forecast the game's financial future."

The Packers' 1992 turnaround resulted in the franchise generating almost $5 million from football operations. Therefore, the team chose to write off its portion of the litigation costs—almost $4.1 million—associated with the NFL's compliance when reaching the latest collective bargaining agreement, which paid the NFLPA $195 million to settle all pending court cases. Although the team reported only a net profit of $860,818, "the interesting thing about this is, if you forget the litigation settlement and just look at total operating revenue and expenses, we had the best year in the history of the Packers," treasurer John Underwood informed stockholders. "What this really did was put us in a position where we could absorb the entire cost of this litigation settlement in the fiscal year that just ended, put it behind us and go ahead—and still show a net profit."

> "You no longer can be just a talent evaluator. Instead, you need to forecast the game's financial future."
> —GENERAL MANAGER RON WOLF

●   ●   ●

The Packers, along with the NFL's twenty-seven other franchises, were preparing to absorb the millions of dollars in escalating salaries free agency was about to generate. Players who had been paid about 30 percent of league revenues in 1982 were now guaranteed twice as much of an even larger pot. Regardless of whether a player changed teams or chose to re-sign, after the first round of signings in 1993 the average salary of an unrestricted free agent more than doubled, from $517,000 to $1,044,000. Restricted free agents fared even better, as their average salary leaped from $293,000 to $780,000. And during those first days of unfettered free agency, no player was more sought after than defensive end Reggie White.

After eight seasons in Philadelphia, Reggie White was considered the NFL's marquee impact player, one whose talent and charisma would invigorate a franchise's fortunes overnight. For a month, the seven-time Pro Bowler sat through boisterous pitches that included limo rides with celebrities, extravagant dinners with politicians, and one team going so far as buying his wife a fur coat. At least a dozen teams courted his services, including Green Bay. Instead of trying to compete with the extravaganzas happening elsewhere, the Packers picked up White at the airport in a Jeep Wrangler and took him to Red Lobster for dinner. "I don't believe in pretenses and gaudy displays, so our courting of Reggie was efficient, serious and sincere—but hardly fancy," Wolf recalled.

Afterward, White was given a tour through the team's practice facilities, Lambeau Field, and the Packers Hall of Fame. Harlan recalled, "Ron told Reggie he could go anyplace and be a hero, but if he came to Green Bay he would be a legend."

Green Bay became the center of the professional football universe after the Packers signed defensive end Reggie White (92) prior to the start of the 1993 season. His impact was immediate as he led the team with thirteen quarterback sacks in 1993. (LEFT: COURTESY OF ALL-AMERICAN SPORTS, LLC; RIGHT: MILWAUKEE JOURNAL SENTINEL)

Many NFL executives assumed that two decades of franchise futility would force the Packers' early exit from the Reggie White Sweepstakes. What they failed to realize was the sincere commitment Harlan, Wolf, and Holmgren expressed to White of their ambitions to build a Super Bowl–caliber team in Green Bay. Of White's three finalists—Washington, San Francisco, and Green Bay—the Packers offered him the most lucrative deal, a four-year contract worth $17.6 million. "When it was finished, there was almost a sense of disbelief—that, and a kind of quiet satisfaction," Reinfeldt said of finalizing White's deal even while the media reported his imminent signing with the 49ers.

The rest of the league was stunned when the Packers announced they had signed White to the league's third highest contract, behind only quarterbacks John Elway and Dan Marino. The perception that no first-rate free agent would voluntarily decide to come to Wisconsin changed overnight. "His presence would do away with all this nonsense about how the football world had passed by Green Bay," Wolf said. "Most of all, he would accelerate everything we wanted to do with the Packers, which alone made him worth the hefty investment."

The enthusiasm generated by White's signing went far beyond the fans and media. "It started out as a murmur between the players," defensive lineman John Jurkovic told the *Green Bay Press-Gazette* about how word first spread through the Lambeau Field locker room. "It was like, 'I think we signed Reggie. I Think We Signed Reggie. HEY, WE SIGNED REGGIE!'"

In White, Ron Wolf had acquired the necessary cornerstone around which he could build a dominating defense. On offense, he and Holmgren felt their young quarterback still needed a strong veteran presence as his backup. During training

> "It was like, 'I think we signed Reggie. I Think We Signed Reggie. HEY, WE SIGNED REGGIE!'"
>
> —DEFENSIVE LINEMAN JOHN JURKOVIC

camp, the Packers brought in several candidates, including Ken O'Brien, who had been traded from the Jets. But they chose to cut the veteran, entering the regular season with backups Ty Detmer and Mark Brunell, neither of whom had played an NFL game. The decision was based on a similar quarterback dilemma the Steelers had faced in 1955 when choosing to keep veterans Jim Finks and Ted Marchibroda along with rookie Vic Eaton. "The guy they cut—" Wolf recalled, pausing for emphasis, "Johnny Unitas. So much for needing the veteran backup quarterback."

All during training camp, the Packers paraded hundreds of players through Lambeau Field—some for a workout, some for a week, some for as long as possible. "I'm sure the players came in every day wondering if the locker next to them would be empty—or how secure their job was," Wolf said of his willingness to try out any player he felt would improve the team.

"In our early seasons, we were executing forty to fifty roster changes per year, an enormous number for the NFL," he said. That included trading for one of the NFL's greatest running backs in hopes of igniting the team's stagnant rushing attack. "We brought in Eric Dickerson, the NFL's No. 2 all-time rusher, hoping he had something left. He didn't, but it was worth the try."

The Packers started the season by clobbering the Rams. "But I kept harking back to 1989 when we were so enthusiastic and then we fell right back down again," Harlan remarked about his guarded optimism. "When we lost three of our first four games in 1993, it took some doing to convince me that we were going to be all right."

Green Bay went on to win their next three games in what became a year filled with as many come-from-behind victories as frustrating losses. In the season's next-to-last game, the Packers clinched a playoff berth with a 28–0 shutout of the Los Angeles Raiders. A season finale loss to the Lions, however, dropped Green Bay's record to 9–7, costing them the division crown. Nevertheless, they would have a chance to avenge the loss in the playoffs the following week in Detroit.

Green Bay's first postseason game in more than a decade escalated into a wild shootout. When the Packers' George Teague ran back an Erik Kramer interception 101 yards for a touchdown, "I was sitting next to Wolf in the press box, and he kept pounding the table with every step the kid took," Harlan said. "He was screaming, 'Run! Run! Run!' at the top of his lungs, which you're not supposed to do in the press box."

With less than a minute remaining, the game's outcome hung in the balance when Favre hurled a 40-yard pass to Sterling Sharpe. "I don't want to say a hope and a prayer, but that's what it really was," Favre said about his game-winning touchdown toss. "I knew where Sterling was going to be and he knew not to give up on me, because who knows where I'll throw it. Sometimes I never know."

A herd of Packers led by Reggie White (92), Tony Bennett (90), Johnny Holland (50), Wayne Simmons (59), and John Jurkovic (64) tackled Lions star Barry Sanders to help secure a 28–24 playoff victory. (MILWAUKEE JOURNAL SENTINEL)

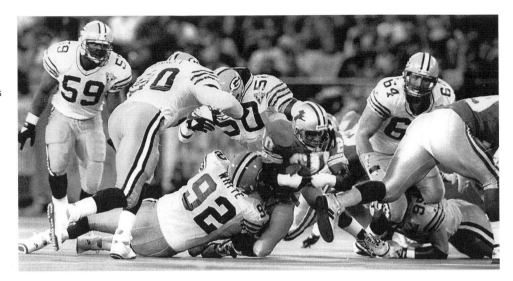

Although LeRoy Butler (36), Johnny Holland (50), and Roland Mitchell (47) couldn't stop Emmitt Smith (22) during a 27–17 playoff loss in Dallas, the Packers felt they were becoming Super Bowl contenders. (MILWAUKEE JOURNAL SENTINEL)

The Packers' road to the Super Bowl brought them to Dallas the next week. For most of the first half, Green Bay kept the game close. But less than a minute before halftime, Corey Harris fumbled a kickoff return that the Cowboys converted into a quick touchdown. Green Bay never recovered from the 17–3 deficit, losing by the final score of 27–17. Despite the loss in Dallas, "the Packers hadn't put together back-to-back winning records like this since 1966–67," Wolf said, explaining the brewing optimism in Green Bay. "We had shown our 1992 accomplishments were no fluke."

●   ●   ●

When the NFL signed new television contracts in December 1993, a significant shift in broadcast partnerships occurred. After thirty-eight years, CBS lost the NFC package to the fledgling Fox Network, which was only seven years old and without a sports division. Fox, understanding that the NFL would bring its network instant credibility, offered $1.58 billion over four years, which was $100 million more a year than CBS's final bid. As a result, the NFL secured a four-year, $4.38 billion package deal with Fox, NBC, ABC, TNT, and ESPN that almost doubled each team's share of television revenue compared to the previous contract.

In Green Bay, the promise of continued television revenue was welcome news. Despite posting a $1 million profit, the cost to maintain a winning club had strained the team's ledger in 1993. "It's not bad when you consider we signed eight free agents the way we did," Harlan said, referring to the signings of Reggie White and other well-paid free agents including offensive lineman Harry Galbreath, nose tackle Bill Maas, safety Mike Prior, and wide receiver Mark Clayton. "In the next few years, we should have a chance to make a good profit every year and still be able to do some things with the roster."

The Packers were benefiting from the NFL's salary cap as the 1994 season approached, but they could no longer ignore the financial ramifications of dividing their home games between Green Bay and Milwaukee. "Every time John Underwood, our treasurer, would make a report to the executive committee or the board of directors, he would tell them that we were leaving $2.5 million on the table by playing four games in Milwaukee," Harlan recounted, describing the projections that had the team losing more than $12 million over a four-year period. "We just had so many more sources of revenue at Lambeau Field than we did at County Stadium that the financial numbers were overwhelming," he continued. "And as I watched the eyes of the executive committee and board of directors getting bigger every time John talked, I knew I didn't have any choice but to come up with a plan."

No one could dispute the essential role Wisconsin's largest city had played in the franchise's survival. For decades Milwaukee had provided the Packers with vital media coverage and an urban fan base, allowing them to compete with the NFL's biggest-city-based clubs. But Milwaukee County Stadium, which had once offered

The Packers' 1994 training camp was full of quarterbacking talent as Brett Favre (4) fended off competition from Ty Detmer (11), Mark Brunell (8), and future Super Bowl MVP Kurt Warner (12). (MILWAUKEE JOURNAL SENTINEL)

higher game attendance and revenue than Green Bay, now lacked the amenities found in modern NFL stadiums, including luxury boxes and club seats. "With no stadium on the horizon and us looking at an overwhelming financial situation, we had to start thinking about leaving," Harlan admitted after several plans to build a replacement for County Stadium were abandoned. "If there had been a new stadium, I'm sure we would have stayed, but the nine years [of waiting] wore us down."

Lambeau Field's latest upgrade, which included ninety new luxury boxes and an overall seating capacity exceeding 60,000, would be completed in time for the 1995 season. As a result, six games into the 1994 season the Packers announced an end to its sixty-two-year tradition of hosting a trio of "home games" at Milwaukee County Stadium. "If anyone had told me in 1989 when I became president of the Packers that I'd have to move the team out of Milwaukee, I wouldn't have believed it was possible," Harlan remarked. He clearly understood that the change could lead to a public relations nightmare. "It was the hardest thing I've ever had to do."

As part of the Packers' exodus out of Milwaukee, they offered County Stadium season-ticket holders three games a year at Lambeau Field—one preseason game and games two and five of the regular season. The particular games were selected before the NFL's schedule was released, because Harlan "wanted the league, not the Packers, to decide who played before the Milwaukee fans and who played before the Green Bay fans."

On the field, enthusiasm that the 1994 Packers were on the verge of becoming an elite NFL team soon quelled. After seven games, they were a disappointing 3–4 following a devastating overtime loss in Minnesota. During the game, Mark Brunell replaced an injured Brett Favre at quarterback. Afterward, Holmgren and his coaching staff discussed the possibility of benching Favre but instead opted to challenge him. "Buddy, it's your job," Holmgren told Favre. "We're joined at the hip.

Brett Favre was already a beloved icon after just two years behind center for the Packers. (MILWAUKEE JOURNAL SENTINEL)

On December 18, 1994, the Packers hosted their final home game at Milwaukee County Stadium. During 126 regular-season contests in their secondary home over forty-two seasons, they compiled a 76–47–3 mark and won their lone playoff game played there versus the Rams in 1967. (COURTESY OF ALL-AMERICAN SPORTS, LLC)

The Packers' Bryce Paup (95) helped hold the Lions' Barry Sanders (20) to minus one yard rushing on thirteen carries in the 16–12 playoff victory. (MILWAUKEE JOURNAL SENTINEL)

Either we're going to the Super Bowl together, or we're going down together."

Favre responded, leading the Packers to a three-game winning streak. But after injuries and inconsistent play resulted in a three-game losing streak, Green Bay was on the brink of postseason elimination. Only after finishing the season with three consecutive wins, including an exciting come-from-behind victory over the Falcons in the last game played at County Stadium, did the Packers earn their second wild-card playoff berth with their third straight 9–7 record. "People throughout the league no longer looked at Green Bay as 'The Frozen Tundra,'" Wolf remarked. "They looked at it as a great place to play football."

Wolf and Holmgren had successfully infused the franchise's storied past into their rebuilding efforts. Their decisions to decorate the team's offices with vintage photos and introduce former players as honorary captains before each home game brought about a renewed sense of pride throughout the organization. "Ron always said if you can't walk onto Lambeau Field and look at the names on the bowl and think of this tradition and the way it grabs you, then you shouldn't be here," Harlan explained.

Twenty-seven years to the day since the Ice Bowl, Lambeau Field hosted its first playoff game in a non-strike season. The Packers were rematched against the Lions, whose offensive attack featured elusive running back Barry Sanders. Since Sanders had rushed for 1,883 yards during the regular season, Green Bay's defensive coordinator, Fritz Shurmur, instructed his squad: "When you've got your shot, take it. The worst thing you can do is sit there and let him juke you because he'll break your ankles."

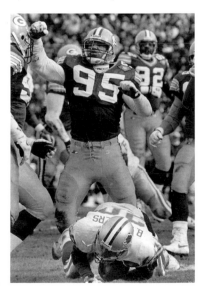

That afternoon, the Packers defense held Sanders to minus one yard rushing on thirteen carries. "I think I saw something I've never seen in my five or six years in the NFL," safety LeRoy Butler said about how Bryce Paup, Doug Evans, Don Davey, Sean Jones, John Jurkovic, Reggie White, and George Koonce harassed and harried Sanders during the Packers' 16–12 victory. "I saw some good hits on Barry Sanders. No one ever gets good shots on him."

The Packers' 1994 season ended abruptly in Dallas—and Reggie White (92), KeShon Johnson (37), LeRoy Butler (36), Terry Mickens (88), Brett Favre (in baseball cap), Ron Wolf, Mark Brunell (8), and Ty Detmer (11) were left dejected—after a 35–9 loss to the Cowboys. (MILWAUKEE JOURNAL SENTINEL)

The following week, the Packers' postseason came to an abrupt end in Dallas. An overpowering Cowboys team scored on four of its first six possessions en route to a 35–9 blowout. Although three straight winning seasons and two straight playoff appearances were a milestone for an organization that had known so much losing since the Lombardi years, "our fans' wish list had changed," Wolf recalled. "At first they had been content with dumping the losing image of the 1970s and 1980s. Now, though, they were restless. The promise of 1992 wasn't evolving as they had hoped. It was nice to win again, but how about a division title or a more competitive showing against the Cowboys?"

●   ●   ●

That offseason began one of the most tumultuous periods in the history of the National Football League. A league famous for stability now found itself in chaos, and the chaos had never been more profitable for team owners. Some of the NFL's most mismanaged franchises found securing a new stadium deal—complete with numerous club seats and luxury boxes—to be the quickest way to resolve their financial problems. When longtime host cities balked at funding or subsidizing the construction of a new stadium, franchise owners followed through on their threats to relocate. The escalating franchise free agency resulted in Los Angeles losing both of its teams in a matter of months before the start of the 1995 season, when the Rams were lured to St. Louis and the Raiders returned to Oakland after thirteen seasons. In 1996 the Browns were uprooted out of Cleveland, placed in Baltimore, and renamed the Ravens. The following year the Houston Oilers relocated to Tennessee and were rebranded as the Titans before their new stadium in Nashville opened in 1999. Meanwhile, owners in New England, Cincinnati, Tampa Bay, Arizona, and Seattle all threatened to move until they extracted new stadium agreements that kept them grounded. "Nearly everyone else is threatening to move unless someone builds them a stadium," Harlan said of how the relocation threats resulted in eighteen teams moving into new stadiums between 1992 and 2006.

Several fertile municipalities showcased their eagerness to host an NFL franchise. The league responded, and in 1995 expansion franchises in Charlotte, North Carolina, and Jacksonville, Florida—the Panthers and Jaguars, respectively—entered the league at a cost of $140 million each, up nearly tenfold from the $16 million paid by Seattle and Tampa Bay in 1976. With Cleveland still outraged over the loss of its team to Baltimore, the league promised the Browns would return in 1998 as an expansion franchise, for the price of $530 million. The next year, Houston was awarded the NFL's thirty-second team as it reentered the league with the Texans at the price of $700 million for its expansion franchise. The inflated franchise fees reflected a new economic reality in the NFL, one that was fueled by the enormous profits created by new stadiums and owners with the leverage to exploit them.

The Packers spent the offseason reevaluating the roster after losing impact players Bryce Paup and Jackie Harris to free agency and Sterling Sharpe to a career-ending neck injury. To compensate for the losses, they traded for tight end Keith Jackson and offered to make Andre Rison the highest-paid wide receiver in the NFL. Instead, Rison signed with the Browns, and Jackson chose not to report to Green Bay until October, almost seven months after the trade. The Packers' apparent inability to replace the lost players left many wondering what direction the team was headed, and Wolf later admitted that "in the days before our 1995 training camp, even some of our players began questioning the status of the team."

Despite a slow start to the 1995 season, the Packers found several of Wolf's earlier draft picks enjoying breakout seasons. Wide receiver Robert Brooks filled the shoes of Sharpe, catching 102 passes. Tight end Mark Chmura caught another 54, and running back Edgar Bennett became Green Bay's first 1,000-yard rusher since Terdell Middleton in 1978. The enigmatic factor that had everyone believing the Packers were destined for great things was Brett Favre. "He's got to know that he's the man to carry us to a championship," Reggie White told the media before the start of the season. "The way he played the last eight games last year, I feel confident he can do it for us."

Favre was living up to expectations by compiling impressive stats for the fourth consecutive season in Green Bay. Yet he felt slighted by the lack of recognition he was receiving from the national media that chose to tout other young quarterbacks, such as Drew Bledsoe, as the league's future stars. "They're going to eat their words,"

Brooks said in defense of his teammate. "They're going to see the numbers over and over and see that Brett Favre is the next great quarterback."

Favre's value to the Packers was never more evident than in their October 22 contest in Minnesota. With Favre and backup Ty Detmer out with injuries, third-string quarterback T. J. Rubley was behind center in the game's final moments with the score tied, 24–24. On third down and one at the Vikings' 38-yard line, the Packers were just outside field goal range when Rubley called an audible on Holmgren's run play. When his pass was intercepted, the Vikings proceeded to kick the game-winning field goal. "It just seemed like we were cursed," Favre told reporters after the disheartening loss, which left the Packers at 5–4 and in need of a spark.

The next week against the Bears, a hobbled Favre threw for 336 yards and five touchdowns in a 35–28 victory. When the Packers won four of their next five, including a 34–23 win in New Orleans, they secured a playoff spot, but a win in their season finale at Lambeau Field would earn them their first NFC Central Division title since 1972. On Christmas Eve 1995 against the Steelers, "it was just one of those games that went back and forth for the whole game," offensive lineman Ken Ruettgers said. Green Bay held a 24–19 lead with sixteen seconds remaining.

The Steelers had driven deep into Packers territory, and on fourth down their quarterback, Neil O'Donnell, rolled out, looking for wide receiver Yancey Thigpen. Thigpen was wide open in the left corner of the end zone, but he bobbled the pass before it fell onto the Lambeau Field turf. His inexplicable drop handed the Packers the Central Division crown. "Winning the division means we have reached another goal set by the team in training camp," Holmgren said of the Packers' 11–5 record. "It also is an indicator we are moving in the right direction."

On New Year's Eve the Packers hosted the Falcons in their playoff opener. After leading 27–10 at the half, Green Bay went on to a decisive 37–20 victory. "In terms of winning this game, so what," defensive end Sean Jones remarked to reporters afterward. "This is a game we expected to win. Let's go to San Francisco and see what they try to do to us."

Against the defending Super Bowl champions, a confident Packers squad expected to play an aggressive and hard-nosed brand of football. On the 49ers' first play from scrimmage, linebacker Wayne Simmons drilled 49ers fullback Adam Walker. The hit forced a fumble that was scooped up by cornerback Craig Newsome, who raced 31 yards for a touchdown, giving Green Bay an early 7–0 lead in the first quarter. "We knew we had to be aggressive. We knew we had to lay the wood on 'em and hit 'em hard," Simmons recalled. "It set the tone for the rest of the day."

The Packers defense went on to enjoy its finest hour, sacking quarterback Steve Young three times and holding the 49ers offense to just 87 yards on the ground during the 27–17 victory. "You have to give all the credit to Fritz [Shurmur]," cornerback

> "They're going to see the numbers over and over and see that Brett Favre is the next great quarterback."
>
> —WIDE RECEIVER ROBERT BROOKS

Doug Evans said of his defensive coordinator's unpredictable schemes that left the 49ers staggering by game's end. "He had a hell of a game plan."

For the third straight season, the Packers' playoff run reached Dallas. "We had one major obstacle keeping us from our Super Bowl goal: the Dallas Cowboys, which had long had our number," safety LeRoy Butler said, referring to the Packers' five losses in the previous two seasons to Dallas. "The Cowboys then was like playing an all-star team."

The Cowboys, who had recaptured their "America's Team" swagger by winning two of the past three Super Bowls, were just as notorious for having one of the game's most maverick owners. Jerry Jones, who had purchased the team along with the Texas Stadium management rights in 1989 for $140 million, had turned the franchise into a financial juggernaut. A year after the team made $25 million from operations in 1993, he challenged the NFL's most sacred cow—revenue sharing—by signing unsanctioned deals with Nike, Pepsi, Dr. Pepper, AT&T, and American Express. By 1995 he claimed the franchise had doubled in value to $300 million. In contrast, the Packers announced a modest $2 million profit in 1995 and were worth considerably less. To many, the NFC championship game was more than a game—it was a classic battle of Green Bay's David versus Dallas's Goliath.

During the game's first thirty minutes, Green Bay contained the big-play capability of Dallas quarterback Troy Aikman, running back Emmitt Smith, and wide receiver Michael Irvin. Although the Cowboys held a 24–17 lead at halftime, the Packers took a 27–24 lead midway through the third quarter on a Robert Brooks touchdown catch. "We had them right there until the end," Favre recalled of the Packers holding the lead into the fourth quarter. "I put us in a position to win, and then I took it away."

In the fourth quarter, "it was three minutes like an avalanche," Butler said, describing the Favre interception that sparked the Cowboys' methodical comeback. "We were ahead, and the next thing I knew, we're down by eleven and they can utilize what they do best, run the ball."

Green Bay's Super Bowl dreams evaporated when Dallas scored twice en route to a 38–27 win. "Afterwards, Coach Holmgren didn't chew us out," Butler recalled. "In fact, he told us not to be upset by the loss. 'I'm glad you got a taste of this. It's going to make you hungry to get back,' he told us."

For Bob Harlan, "that was three years in a row that the Cowboys had knocked us out, and I was so sick and tired of going into that Dallas press box and walking out of the stadium after a loss." At that moment, the Packers decided their goal for the 1996 season would be for the road to Super Bowl XXXI to go through Green Bay.

■ ■ ■

Despite the loss in Dallas, a fervor swept over Packerland during the offseason. The notion that Green Bay was a Super Bowl contender had gone from idle chatter to the Packers being recognized as one of the league's elite teams. In August *Sports Illustrated* predicted the Packers would face the Chiefs in Super Bowl XXXI, which prompted defensive lineman Sean Jones to declare, "What people outside Green Bay don't understand is that for us to be validated as a great team, we've got to exorcise all these ghosts—like Willie Woods, the Willie Davises, the Bart Starrs," he said. "The pressure that America puts on us is tiny compared to that."

Nobody felt the pressure to produce a winner in Green Bay more than Ron Wolf. During an active offseason, he assembled the last pieces of what he thought was a championship-caliber roster. Through trades and free-agent signings, he added veteran safety Eugene Robinson, defensive tackle Santana Dotson, wide receiver Don Beebe, and kick return specialist Desmond Howard. By the start of the 1996 season, only LeRoy Butler, Chris Jacke, and Ken Ruettgers remained from the original fifty-six-man roster Wolf and Holmgren had inherited in 1992. Even with a roster stockpiled with talent, "[Wolf] always made it a point, no matter how well the team was doing, to have some free agents parade through the locker room on Tuesdays," Harlan recalled of his general manager's strategy to keep the Packers from becoming complacent.

The franchise's ability to meld the current Packers squad with the Lombardi-era players brought about an even richer resolve to return the Lombardi Trophy to Green Bay. "Almost every Packer of the old days has some identification for the current Packers," Hall of Fame defensive end Willie Davis said. "I find the current players saying, 'These are the guys who did it then, let's go do it now and be a part of this rich tradition.' I don't think every team shares that sense of past and present."

The Packers' recent success helped football fans all over the world rediscover the team's rich tradition, many of them making the pilgrimage to Lambeau Field. During the first week of the 1996 NFL season, President Bill Clinton brought his reelection campaign to Green Bay, giving a speech in nearby De Pere. Afterward, he insisted on seeing Lambeau Field. The president received a tour of the stadium, was introduced to Harlan, Wolf, and Holmgren, and talked football with players on the field. While posing for photographs, he looked into the empty stands and with the enthusiasm of a child exclaimed, "Boy, I never thought I'd get a chance to see this place!"

Even the biggest football cynic had trouble denying what made Lambeau Field special. It was the most tangible symbol representing the Green Bay Packers franchise. The team's undeniable attraction as a quaint oddity in the industry of professional sports continued to thrive as the NFL grew into more of a corporate conglomerate than a league of sportsmen. At the annual stockholders' meeting, team

President Bill Clinton could be seen smiling ear to ear while visiting Lambeau Field during a 1996 reelection campaign stop in Green Bay. (LEFT: COURTESY OF WILLIAM J. CLINTON PRESIDENTIAL LIBRARY; RIGHT: WHS MUSEUM #1996.153.5)

officials released the only publicly distributed team balance sheets in the four major sports leagues—NFL, MLB, NBA, and NHL—and did so while answering questions from an inquiring crowd of about two hundred citizens, who, in effect, served as their bosses. In 1996 a motion from the floor underscored the importance of the Packers' public ownership structure when stockholder and Green Bay lawyer Robert Schaefer proposed an amendment to the team's bylaws challenging the process of dissolution in the event the franchise moved or was sold. "When the corporation was formed in 1923, the original articles said that the net proceeds of any sale would go to the Sullivan-Wallen American Legion Post in Green Bay in order to build 'a proper soldiers' memorial,'" Harlan explained. Schaefer suggested that the Green Bay Packers Foundation, founded in the 1980s as the team's charitable arm, be inserted as the replacement for the Legion Post to distribute assets to area charities. Back when the Packers were reporting modest earnings of $75,208 in 1959, the Legion Post was an adequate recipient of the funds. But by 1996 team assets and stockholders' equity totaled more than $68 million, far more than any Legion Post needed to build "a proper soldiers' memorial." The bylaws would soon be amended, but not before the Packers announced a record profit of $5,440,628 for the 1995 season. Despite shattering the previous record of $3.33 million after the 1993 season, the team needed to continue raising additional revenue. In 1995 the Packers' estimated $62 million in income ranked them twenty-second in the league with few outlets for growth. "It's absolutely critical for this franchise to build and replenish cash rather than invest money in facilities," treasurer John Underwood announced of the team's upcoming financial strategy to stay competitive. "Cash is king. Why should we build our cash? Well, our strategy is to win. We've said many times our job description is the preservation of the national treasure."

The Packers were falling behind when it came to generating stadium and merchandising revenue. Lambeau Field, which was already filled to capacity and guaranteed to sell out every game, had a season-ticket waiting list of at least 23,000 and another 200 fans waiting for luxury boxes. Entertaining no plans to expand, the Packers could generate more revenue at Lambeau Field only by raising ticket prices. With Packermania at an all-time high, team officials expected a 25 percent increase in sales—which in 1995 totaled almost $2.4 million—at the team's pro shop and through licensing receipts and marketing projects. But even that revenue-sharing stream was in jeopardy.

Back in 1995, the NFL had filed a lawsuit that challenged the licensing and sponsorship agreements Cowboys owner Jerry Jones signed outside of NFL jurisdiction on behalf of Texas Stadium with Nike, AT&T, Dr. Pepper, American Express, and Pepsi. The suit contended that those arrangements violated the NFL's centralized licensing and marketing role. The Cowboys countersued, charging that the NFL's centralized role violated antitrust laws and stating that the Texas Stadium sponsorships didn't involve Cowboys trademarks. In December 1996 the league settled with Jones, allowing him to continue negotiating his own stadium sponsorship agreements without having to share the revenue with the NFL's other twenty-nine teams. While this meant that the Packers were now allowed to secure their own individual sponsorship agreements, it ultimately would only expose a growing revenue gap in the next few years. Not only did Green Bay anticipate signing much smaller agreements compared to those arranged in the NFL's larger cities, but Lambeau Field lacked the revenue-generating amenities necessary to keep pace with fellow NFL stadiums.

Meanwhile, under the preexisting licensing agreement, all thirty NFL teams took an even split of the revenue generated by licensing and sponsorship agreements. During the 1995 season, the Packers received $3.15 million in NFL Properties income. Overall, almost 60 percent of football's revenue was shared (compared to 30 percent in baseball), and that source of income was vital in maintaining the league's competitive balance. In Green Bay, "eighty-four percent of the Packers' income comes from revenue sharing," Harlan said at the time. "If we would ever lose that, we simply could not be competitive and would cease to exist. There is no team that needs those twenty-nine other partners more than Green Bay."

League-wide revenue sharing was the legacy of former commissioner Pete Rozelle, one that had launched the NFL on its path toward financial euphoria. Even after he retired as commissioner in 1989 to be succeeded by Paul Tagliabue, Rozelle's "league first" philosophy not only brought competitive balance to the league but increased the average value of an NFL franchise from about $2 million in 1960 to somewhere in the $150 million to $200 million range by 1996. When Rozelle died of a brain tumor on December 6, 1996, the NFL lost one of its greatest champions. To honor him, the league announced that team helmets in Super Bowl XXXI would have the name "Pete" inscribed on them.

■ ■ ■

The Green Bay Packers' road to Super Bowl XXXI began with a 34–3 thrashing of the Buccaneers to start the 1996 season. The next week, they dominated the Eagles 39–13 during the first Monday Night Football game hosted at Lambeau Field in a decade, prompting defensive end Sean Jones to proclaim, "What I saw tonight was a team that realized it can be great."

But when disheartening losses in Kansas City and Dallas planted fears that the season would start unraveling, Mike Holmgren remarked, "In this league, very rarely can you just win on talent . . . straight out-and-out talent. And I think you need—it's an overused word, probably—but chemistry, or feeling . . . whatever you want to call that. . . . You need that team feeling."

The Packers resurrected their Super Bowl dreams during a 24–9 win in St. Louis and finished the season on a five-game winning streak. "The way it is right now, it's really contagious," safety Eugene Robinson said of the Packers' late-season surge. "We've got like a disease of wanting to make plays. It's sticking with this team. They want to continue to do that, to be part of making a play. It's a lot of fun."

The 1996 Packers scored more points on offense—a team record 456—and gave up the fewest on defense—210—to become the first team to lead the NFL in both categories since the 1972 Dolphins, who went undefeated through an entire season before winning Super Bowl VII. "Everybody will always talk about the offense and how formidable they were," defensive tackle Santana Dotson recalled. "But the thing that sticks out in my mind was how strong the defense was. Gilbert Brown, Reggie White, Sean Jones, those were great players and we loved looking at the offensive line and seeing the looks on their faces every play as they tried to decide who they were going to double-team. It was almost like a lion walking through a slaughterhouse. You knew somebody was going to eat."

In the third-to-last game of the season, the Packers clinched their second straight Central Division title by beating up on the Broncos. The celebration seemed to defuse the brief stir caused by Brett Favre's mention of being unsure how much longer he wanted to play football. "I don't want to get to a certain age and not be able to play with my kids because I'm so beat up," he disclosed to a Mississippi television station reporter late in the season around his twenty-seventh birthday. "I don't want someone telling me when it's time to go. I want to leave on my own terms."

> "You need that team feeling."
>
> –HEAD COACH
> MIKE HOLMGREN

The Packers' NFC-best 13–3 record guaranteed that the road to the Super Bowl would go through Lambeau Field. "I think everybody's scared to death to come in here and play," Wolf said of Green Bay's going 8–0 at home in 1996 and 15–1 over the past two seasons, "and that's the way we want it."

However, the Packers' home field advantage wasn't a guaranteed moneymaking proposition. "The league really takes control of the game," Harlan said, acknowledging that the NFL establishes ticket prices for all playoff games and reduces the split of gate receipts and concession revenue for the home team from 60 percent during the regular season to 50 percent, with the rest going to the visiting team and the league. "While the playoffs aren't the money-machine you might imagine, the Super Bowl is actually a money-loser. With all the travel expenses involved in having an entire team spend a week at the site of the game, and with most of the people in the organization spending four days there, the bill is quite substantial." But it was one bill Harlan was willing to pay. "It might be expensive, but it would be worth every dollar to get to New Orleans this year," he said.

After enjoying its week-one bye, Green Bay hosted a 49ers squad looking to avenge its playoff loss from the year before. As kickoff approached, "I heard the rain coming down," Dotson recalled of the cold and miserable weather conditions. "Then I decided this was Lambeau weather, Green Bay weather, so I might as well go out and have some fun with it."

The game's first score came when the Packers' Desmond Howard ran a punt back 71 yards for a touchdown. Howard returned San Francisco's next punt 46 yards to the 49ers' 7-yard line, setting up a Favre-to-Andre Rison touchdown. "It's gotten to the point where it's almost ridiculous. Why kick it to him?" wide receiver Don Beebe asked reporters after the game. "If I'm the special teams coach playing the Green Bay Packers, I'd just [punt] it out of bounds."

An Edgar Bennett touchdown run gave the Packers a 21-point lead before San Francisco cut the deficit to 21–7 by halftime. When the 49ers lined up for the first play from scrimmage in the second half, several of them had changed into clean uniforms during halftime, including wide receiver Jerry Rice. "We made a point on the first play of the second half to get him dirty again," Dotson recalled of cornerback Craig Newsome and linebacker Wayne Simmons knocking the future Hall-of-Famer to the ground just to make sure he was filthy. "It was the mud bowl."

San Francisco closed the score to 21–14 on an Elvis Grbac touchdown run, but the Packers brought about an onslaught of rushing power and defensive domination that left the entire 49ers squad in disarray. "There are so many things we can do to attack you," Wolf said after the Packers' 35–14 victory. "We said all along: You let us play up here in December and January, our guys can run in this stuff. It was proven again today. We're built exactly for this."

> "I decided this was Lambeau weather, Green Bay weather, so I might as well go out and have some fun with it."
>
> —DEFENSIVE TACKLE SANTANA DOTSON

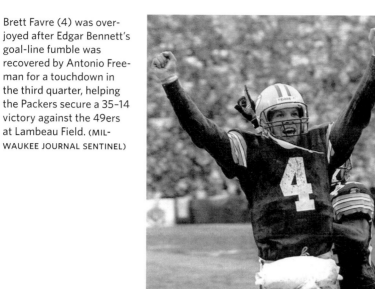

Brett Favre (4) was overjoyed after Edgar Bennett's goal-line fumble was recovered by Antonio Freeman for a touchdown in the third quarter, helping the Packers secure a 35–14 victory against the 49ers at Lambeau Field. (MILWAUKEE JOURNAL SENTINEL)

Despite the steady downpour throughout the game, "we had a record crowd of 60,787, and it was announced that we had only three no-shows," Harlan said of the dedicated Lambeau Field crowd that braved a nine-degree windchill. "I have some doubts about that no-show count, but I can tell you the fans stuck with us to the very end. Nobody left the stadium because people were so hungry for playoff football in Green Bay."

The next week Green Bay hosted its first NFC championship game. The Carolina Panthers arrived after having eliminated the defending Super Bowl champion Cowboys the previous week. Led by head coach and defensive wizard Dom Capers, the second-year franchise featured an exotic zone blitz where linebackers swarmed in from anywhere on the field to wreak havoc on even the most talented offense. "The week before Carolina came to play us, all the magazines talked about the possibility of the two expansion teams, Carolina and Jacksonville, playing each other in the Super Bowl," safety LeRoy Butler recalled. "All the attention given to the Panthers and Jaguars was a slap in the face that we took personally."

Before the Lambeau Field public address system echoed with Gary Knafelc's introduction of the Packers' starting lineup, "we could hear the Carolina Panthers trying to psych themselves up during warm-ups. Their players would be saying things like, 'Oh, it's not that cold,'" defensive tackle Gilbert Brown recalled of the game-day forecast for windchills nearing thirty below zero. "We knew anybody coming to Green Bay in January was going to feel it. That's why we worked so hard all season to get home-field advantage."

The pregame momentum Green Bay felt from the 60,216 fans packed into Lambeau Field was halted in the game's opening minutes. The Panthers scored first on a touchdown that was set up on a Brett Favre interception. "He still goes brain-dead every once in a while," backup quarterback Jim McMahon said of Favre. "I don't think it'll change. Not when you've got confidence in yourself like he does."

The Packers responded with a 29-yard touchdown pass from Favre to Dorsey Levens, but a Favre fumble resulted in a field goal that gave Carolina its second lead of the game. "They had us on our heels," safety LeRoy Butler said of the 10–7 deficit. "No one had done that to us all season."

Behind a dominating offensive line led by Bruce Wilkerson, Aaron Taylor, Frank Winters, Adam Timmerman, and Earl Dotson, the Packers marched down the field 71 yards, using nearly eight minutes, to tie the game. The last time a Green Bay offensive line dominated opponents with such brute force was during the fateful Ice Bowl drive. But back then, the offensive line in front of Starr averaged just 244 pounds a man, and overall the Packers' 1967 roster didn't list a single player at more than 260 pounds, with only ten players at or taller than six-foot-four. The Packers' 1996 roster featured ten Packers listed at more than 300 pounds, with sixteen at six-foot-four or taller. Physical comparisons aside, "end zone to end zone, sideline to sideline, nothing has changed. You still need a great defense, a great offensive line, and a great running game to get to the Super Bowl," Jerry Kramer proclaimed in the *Super Bowl XXXI Official Game Program*, going on to joke, "I'm a little prejudiced about that offensive line part."

On a Favre-to-Freeman touchdown pass, the Packers took a 17–10 lead into halftime. Despite being dominated on both sides of the ball, the Panthers felt they still held the advantage by keeping the game close. In the third quarter, Bennett scored on a 4-yard run, giving the Packers a 27–13 advantage just as their running game began to overwhelm the Panthers' defense. "Our biggest motivation was that all year, everyone has been saying our weakest point was our running game," running back Dorsey Levens said after the Packers rushed for 201 yards that afternoon. "We wanted to prove our point. We didn't ask anybody to give us respect. I guess we had to go out and take it."

The Packers extended their lead in the fourth quarter with a 28-yard field goal from Chris Jacke, giving the Packers a 30–13 lead. "As you sat in the stadium with four or five minutes left knowing the Packers were going to the Super Bowl in

New Orleans, I never felt anything like it," WTMJ radio announcer Jim Irwin recalled of the spine-tingling experience of the Lambeau Field crowd surging, rolling, and screaming in anticipation of what was about to happen. "We just wanted to stay there and soak in everything."

When the clock reached zero, "our fans didn't rush the floor like they do in basketball; we rushed the fans," safety LeRoy Butler recalled. "We jumped in the stands and walked around the stadium, giving high-fives to the people who had supported us for so long."

"You can't imagine how emotional it was unless you were standing down there looking at it," Harlan said about how the crowd stayed for the postgame celebration when the Packers were awarded the George Halas Trophy as NFC Champions. "As cold as it was, people just didn't want to leave. They stayed and stayed and stayed, cherishing the moment."

The Packers were now bound for New Orleans and Super Bowl XXXI. Their roster, comprising "twenty-two of our draft choices, four players who arrived through trades, six unrestricted free agents, one Plan B player, five players claimed off waivers, and thirteen street free agents," according to Wolf, was the culmination of a five-year rebuilding effort that saw only LeRoy Butler and Chris Jacke still remaining from the Infante regime. "Our success evolved in much the way we had envisioned during the initial days of our revitalization program," Wolf said.

Green Bay spent the two weeks leading up to the Super Bowl comprehending and preparing for the magnitude of what it meant to win the big game. Their opponents, the New England Patriots, found themselves caught up in a media storm focused around head coach Bill Parcells' leaving to become head coach of

> "Our fans didn't rush the floor like they do in basketball; we rushed the fans."
>
> —SAFETY LEROY BUTLER

During the 1996 season, Super Bowl fever swept through Green Bay and all of Wisconsin as fans twirled Title Towels in support of their Packers. (WHI MUSEUM #1997.34.1)

the New York Jets after the Super Bowl. But once inside the New Orleans Superdome, after the Macarena dancers cleared the field and Luther Vandross belted out the national anthem, none of those distractions mattered. What happened on the gridiron would determine the winner of Super Bowl XXXI and pro football's next world champion. "When I was warming up, I had knots in my stomach, and that's the first time I've ever had knots," wide receiver Andre Rison recalled. "That let me know how big a game this was."

Following the opening kickoff, Green Bay forced the Patriots to punt on their opening possession. Desmond Howard then returned the punt 32 yards to the Packers' 46-yard line, and Green Bay scored on its second play of the game. After Favre threw a 54-yard touchdown pass to Andre Rison, the quarterback "took off his helmet and ran off the field like a kid running to his mom and dad in a Little League game," Harlan recalled. "It was like, 'Look what I did, Mom!'"

Chris Jacke added a field goal before New England responded with two touchdown drives to take the lead, 14–10, in the first quarter. The teams exchanged punts before Favre threw a Super Bowl–record 81-yard touchdown pass to receiver Antonio Freeman. Regaining the lead, Green Bay stonewalled the Patriots and further extended their margin going into halftime, 27–14, on a 2-yard touchdown run from Favre. After the second half began with a series of punts, the Patriots' Curtis Martin scored on an 18-yard touchdown run to cut the Packers' lead to 27–21. "The Patriots came right back at us and the game went back and forth and back and forth," Butler remarked. "The game was tight."

But on the ensuing kickoff, Howard returned the ball 99 yards for a touchdown. When Favre completed a pass to tight end Mark Chmura for the successful 2-point conversion, the Packers led 35–21. From there, Green Bay's defense took over, preventing New England's offense from advancing past its own 32-yard line and intercepting Bledsoe twice—once by Craig Newsome and once by Brian Williams. "I don't know where he comes up with some of those schemes," linebacker Ron Cox marveled at Fritz Shurmur's defensive strategy. "Maybe he sits out in his ice-fishing shed and draws in the ice, I don't know. But they sure work."

When the game was over, Holmgren was hoisted onto his players' shoulders and led off the field in triumph. "It's like we reinstated the legacy," fullback William Henderson said of bringing the Lombardi Trophy back to Green Bay. "It's the sweetest feeling in the world. It's like bringing a family heirloom back that's been gone for so many years."

As the purple and yellow Mardi Gras–themed confetti rained down on the field, "Vince Lombardi would have to be excited," Freeman remarked. "We set our goals in July. We knew that we had what it takes to go all the way, and we kept the faith, we kept together, and now, we're world champions."

> **"We kept the faith, we kept together, and now, we're world champions."**
> —WIDE RECEIVER ANTONIO FREEMAN

The Packers celebrated early and often during Super Bowl XXXI thanks to (above) touchdown catches from Antonio Freeman (86) and Andre Rison (84); (above, right) Super Bowl MVP Desmond Howard's 99-yard kickoff return for a touchdown; and (right) Reggie White's (92) three quarterback sacks of the Patriots' Drew Bledsoe (11). (ALL PHOTOS FROM THE GREEN BAY PRESS-GAZETTE ARCHIVES, REPRINTED BY PERMISSION)

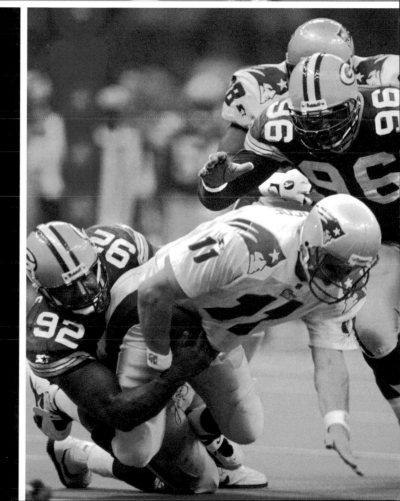

Both of the Packers' marquee stars, Brett Favre and Reggie White, were outstanding in the big game, but the Super Bowl MVP award went to Desmond Howard, who accumulated 244 return yards, including the 99-yard kickoff return for a touchdown that sealed the 35–21 victory. "That's why Ron Wolf is Ron Wolf," running back Edgar Bennett remarked to reporters, referring to the Packers' general manager bringing in Howard on a bargain, $300,000 free-agent contract that year. "He takes chances on players when other teams give up on them. He knows talent when he sees it and he isn't afraid to do whatever it takes to help the team."

For winning Super Bowl XXXI, the Packers received $48,000 apiece, $33,000 more than their Super Bowl I counterparts earned. Money aside, "there's nothing like being a world champion," Harlan remarked later. "It's a high that doesn't end in a hurry, which was why 1265 Lombardi Avenue was a great address for a long time after we won Super Bowl XXXI."

When the Packers returned to Green Bay, an estimated 200,000 fans escorted them from the airport to the stadium in a parade that should have taken an hour. Instead, the Return to Titletown celebration took three hours as the motorcade weaved through the crowded streets of Green Bay to its final destination at Lambeau Field, where 60,000 ticket holders paid $5 each to honor their heroes. Despite the subzero windchills, neither the players nor the fans seemed to notice the frosty weather conditions during the celebration. As Harlan later exclaimed, "People talk about ticker tape parades, but there was never anything warmer than the welcome we got on that cold day."

The Packers' unbridled fan support led to unparalleled merchandise sales. "Our national fan phenomena and Super Bowl victory resulted in NFL Properties recording its highest level overall in Super Bowl merchandise sales ever," Harlan remarked. "I'm told there was $70 million in Packers merchandise sold across the country in January alone."

The NFL reported sales of Super Bowl XXXI merchandise soaring to a record $130 million. Fans bought 650,000 Packers locker room hats—the same ones worn by the players after their victory—breaking the record of 400,000 set by the NBA champion Chicago Bulls the previous spring. More than 125,000 copies of the Packers' highlights video were sold within two weeks of going on sale. The Packers Pro Shop saw its annual revenue rise from $2.47 million in 1995 to $5.82 million in 1996 as a result of the victory.

Beyond the record sales figures, the Packers' Super Bowl run provided Green Bay with the immeasurable benefit of being rechristened Titletown USA and providing the community with an immense economic impact. During 1996 it was estimated the area made $3 million for each home game played at Lambeau Field. The team's twelve games—two preseason, eight regular-season, and two playoff

Retailers were quick to capitalize on the Packers' Super Bowl resurgence, offering fans abundant opportunities to display their support. (LEFT: WHS MUSEUM #1997.116.3; RIGHT: WHS MUSEUM #1997.116.14)

games—meant the Packers were responsible for generating $36 million in just one year. "Commissioner Paul Tagliabue came to town about three months after the game to talk to our Executive Committee, and he said that the Green Bay Packers winning the Super Bowl was the best thing to happen to professional sports in years," Harlan recalled. "He said this was small town America, blue collar America, and it took everybody back to simpler times."

What wasn't being waxed over with nostalgia was the Packers' projected financial future. The team's overall value had escalated toward $200 million following their Super Bowl XXXI victory while posting the highest annual profit—$5,877,061—in the franchise's seventy-eight-year history. Although the team posted subsequent profits of $5.4 million for fiscal 1996, $2.33 million in 1995, and $3.33 million in 1994, the cost of staying competitive in the NFL was growing. Operating expenses were also up, with player costs rising by $5.2 million to $46.7 million. Although operating income was up $7.87 million from the previous year to $78.16 million, the team's share of the league's television contract—$41.41 million—represented only 53 percent of the Packers' income. Because of the rapidly changing economic structure of the National Football League, the team had to generate a cash reserve if it hoped to remain on equal footing with its competitors. With few options available, the Packers contemplated the fate of their forty-year-old stadium.

• • •

Even though Lambeau Field remained structurally sound, it lacked the capacity, the luxury box seating, and the amenities of newer and recently proposed stadiums around the league. Other than television money, stadium revenue had emerged as the primary source of income for NFL teams. By 1997 Lambeau Field and its 60,790 capacity was the fifth smallest stadium in the NFL, failing to satisfy ticket demand with 34,000 people on a waiting list for season tickets, another 265 on a waiting list for luxury boxes, and about 700 on a waiting list for club seats. While other NFL franchises with more favorable leases, fewer capital costs, and owners with deep pockets stockpiled cash in greater quantities, the Packers turned to a familiar solution when Harlan, as he noted in his autobiography, "started getting calls and letters from people who wanted to buy stock in the Green Bay Packers."

As a result, the Packers began organizing their fourth stock drive in team history. In hopes of raising as much as $80 million, they offered 400,000 new shares at a price of $200 per unit. Support from the franchise's initial 1,728 shareholders was overwhelming, especially after the Packers announced that the original 10,000 shares of common stock would be split on a 1,000-to-1 basis. As with past stock drives, shareholders would not receive dividends; the new stock wouldn't appreciate; and no one would be allowed to own more than 200,000 shares, preventing any shareholder from assuming control of the club.

In a letter addressed to shareholders, Harlan stressed that without the stock sale, the Packers feared they would not have the economic wherewithal to be a viable NFL force in the upcoming decade and into the next century. Although the team had close to $25 million in cash reserves, they had already committed more than $19 million of it in signing bonuses to just three players—quarterback Brett Favre, defensive end Reggie White, and safety LeRoy Butler—in the past year. However, the Packers had to reassure the rest of the league's owners that the money raised in the stock sale would be used exclusively for stadium renovations and not for subsidizing player salaries or signing bonuses. "I acknowledged to them that there was no one in the room who needed his [twenty-nine] partners as much as the Green Bay Packers," Harlan recalled of receiving the league's permission to conduct the sale. "When [Pittsburgh Steelers owner] Dan Rooney stood up and said that the Green Bay Packers are 'vitally important' to the NFL, that meant a lot to me."

When the stock sale launched in November, the Packers' designated clearinghouse received 55,000 phone calls within the first twenty-four hours. In the first eleven days, $7.8 million worth of stock was sold. Throughout December, paid orders came in at the rate of 3,500 shares, or $700,000, a day. The seventeen-week sale sold 120,010 shares to 105,989 new shareholders from all fifty states plus Guam and the Virgin Islands. "I never dreamed we'd reach $24 million. In fact, if people had told me when we started that we'd go over $20 million, I would have told them they were insane," Harlan recalled. With control of the franchise now spread across over 4.7 million shares, he said the sale "did exactly what we had hoped it would do. We made a lot of friends, and we were able to set some money aside to help us with our facilities."

Packers stockholders voted to split the team's stock in 1997, offering 400,000 new shares at a price of $200 per unit.
(FROM THE GREEN BAY PRESS-GAZETTE ARCHIVES, REPRINTED BY PERMISSION)

GREEN BAY PACKERS, INC.

COMMON STOCK

OFFERING DOCUMENT

COMMON STOCK DOES NOT CONSTITUTE AN INVESTMENT IN "STOCK" IN THE COMMON SENSE OF THE TERM.
PURCHASERS SHOULD NOT PURCHASE COMMON STOCK WITH THE PURPOSE OF MAKING A PROFIT.

GP01   CH00000060   5000029043

Green Bay Packers, Inc.

SEE REVERSE FOR CERTAIN DEFINITIONS

A NONPROFIT CORPORATION ORGANIZED UNDER THE LAWS OF THE
STATE OF WISCONSIN

This Certifies that

is the owner of   **ONE**

SHARES OF THE NO PAR VALUE COMMON STOCK OF
GREEN BAY PACKERS, INC.,

fully paid and nonassessable, transferable on the books of the Corporation in person or by duly authorized Attorney upon surrender of this certificate properly endorsed, but only in compliance with, and to persons permitted to hold stock according to, the regulations of the Corporation.
The Holder hereof understands and agrees:
    That no dividend shall ever be paid on said stock;
    That if the Corporation is dissolved all the assets shall go to charitable causes;
    THAT SAID STOCK IS SUBJECT TO TRANSFER RESTRICTIONS DESCRIBED ON THE REVERSE SIDE.
    In Witness Whereof, the said Corporation has caused this Certificate to be signed by its duly authorized officers and sealed with the Seal of the Corporation.

Dated   NOVEMBER 26, 1997

GREEN BAY PACKERS, INC.
CORPORATE SEAL
GREEN BAY, WIS.

Secretary

President

COUNTERSIGNED AND REGISTERED
FIRSTAR TRUST COMPANY
TRANSFER AGENT AND REGISTRAR
BY
AUTHORIZED SIGNATURE

027054

AMERICAN BANK NOTE COMPANY.

The stock sale was a success, but the Packers would still have to be savvy with their finances—especially in the NFL's new world order of unrestricted free agency, where the only thing more challenging than building a championship team was being able to maintain it. Less than six weeks after his Super Bowl MVP performance, free agent Desmond Howard accepted a $6 million contract offer to join the Oakland Raiders. Impact players Keith Jackson and Sean Jones retired. And key contributors Andre Rison and Chris Jacke weren't re-signed. Despite all this, "we were strong favorites to go back to the Super Bowl following the 1997 season because we had just about everybody back," safety LeRoy Butler remarked, "something that is pretty unusual in this era of free agency."

The core of the Packers' roster wasn't affected, thanks to the team's architect, Ron Wolf, whose contract was extended through the 2002 season. "He was the best general manager in the National Football League, and I wanted to make sure we were paying him that way," Harlan said, noting the team's desire to prevent other clubs from trying to poach Wolf out of Green Bay. "I didn't need someone coming in here and destroying us. We had a great partnership with Mike and Ron, and I didn't want it to end."

When training camp commenced, Holmgren adamantly expressed his fear of complacency and a potential letdown after the Packers' Super Bowl XXXI victory. "I think winning it the first time is a very difficult task," Holmgren said of living up to heightened expectations. "But repeating—winning it a second time—requires even more work and dedication. It will take even more sacrifices than it did last year."

The Packers opened their 1997 season on Monday night with a victory over the Bears and went on to win eight of their first ten games. In week eleven, "we were humbled in a big way by the Indianapolis Colts who at that point were 0–10," safety LeRoy Butler said of the 41–38 loss that gave Colts head coach Lindy Infante his first win of the season.

The Packers responded by routing the Cowboys 45–17 the following week at Lambeau Field, further demonstrating that the balance of power had shifted in the NFC. Green Bay closed out the season on a five-game winning streak and repeated as NFC Central Division champions with a 13–3 record.

Securing the NFC's number two seed, Green Bay hosted a resurgent Tampa Bay squad in the playoffs' second round. The Packers defense compensated for an error-prone offense that dropped a half dozen passes, committed three turnovers, and incurred multiple penalties during crucial situations. "It really felt like we hadn't played in two weeks," wide receiver Antonio Freeman told reporters after the 21–7 victory. "It was a different type of football, but guys were able to overcome that feeling and push through it."

The following week, the Packers traveled to San Francisco for what many considered the marquee playoff matchup of the year. For thirteen straight years, NFC teams had won the Super Bowl, and the two teams battling that afternoon were considered to be the NFL's strongest. A rain-soaked, sloppy field assisted Green Bay's defense in stonewalling the 49ers' running attack, allowing them only 33 yards on the ground. Safety Eugene Robinson's 58-yard interception return led to Favre finding Freeman in the end zone for a 27-yard touchdown pass and an early 10–0 Packers' lead. The game remained within striking distance for the 49ers late in the fourth quarter, but with four minutes left in the game linebacker Keith McKenzie sacked quarterback Steve Young on fourth down. The Packers, taking over on downs at the San Francisco 11-yard line, secured the 23–10 victory when Dorsey Levens ran in for a 5-yard touchdown. "They can say what they want," wide receiver Antonio Freeman said afterward of the 49ers' pregame rhetoric, "but champions know how to win on the road."

After the game, a stage was quickly erected in the middle of San Francisco's 3Com Park. "It was still pouring when Ron and I went out onto the field for the trophy presentation, and that was just spooky," Harlan recalled of seeing all the empty stands. "Everybody had gone home. It was a real contrast from the previous year when we were at Lambeau Field and nobody wanted to go home."

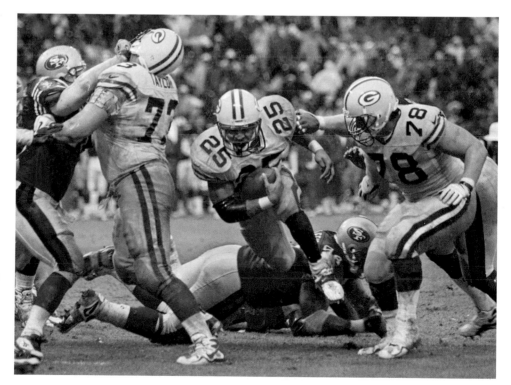

Offensive linemen Aaron Taylor (73) and Ross Verba (78) helped running back Dorsey Levens (25) rush for 114 yards against the 49ers during the Packers' 23-10 victory in the 1997 NFC championship game. (WISCONSIN STATE JOURNAL)

Green Bay's Super Bowl XXXII opponent would be the Denver Broncos after they beat Jacksonville, Kansas City, and Pittsburgh. Because Denver was an AFC wild-card team and failed to win in their four previous Super Bowl appearances, "the danger was that we were already arrogant, thinking we were unbeatable just for coming back to the Super Bowl," safety LeRoy Butler remarked. "Being fourteen-point favorites swelled our heads even further and put us in the position to get our butts kicked."

"One thing that made the atmosphere very different for us at this Super Bowl was that we weren't the sentimental favorites anymore," Harlan remarked. "It was just strange to see how the sentiment had switched over to [Broncos quarterback John] Elway because of what he had meant to the league and to his franchise and how he was nearing the end of his career."

In the days leading up to the game, reporters with little to write about hounded Holmgren about an offhand comment he had made earlier in the year about his interest in someday adding the title of general manager to his coaching duties. When Holmgren refused to deny he had an interest, the innocuous remark exploded into a full-scale controversy, and "we had to deal with rumors that the Seattle Seahawks wanted him to be both coach and director of their football operations," Wolf recalled.

When Denver kicked off to start Super Bowl XXXII, the Packers scored on their opening drive. The Broncos stormed right back with a touchdown of their own. On the second play of Green Bay's next possession, Favre threw an interception, leading to another Denver touchdown. Although the Packers would cut the Broncos' lead to 17–14 at halftime, "I remember thinking as I watched our players come out of the locker room for the third quarter that there wasn't a lot of spirit on the team," Harlan recalled. He had a brief conversation with Ron Wolf and Mike Reinfeldt at the time: "We didn't talk about it much, but it didn't seem to any of us that there was much spark there."

On Denver's first offensive play of the second half, the Packers' Tyrone Williams forced and recovered a Terrell Davis fumble, which allowed Green Bay to tie the game on a Ryan Longwell field goal. Later in the third quarter, the Broncos marched down the field on a thirteen-play, 92-yard drive that culminated in the defining moment of Super Bowl XXXII: two Packers defenders hitting Elway so hard that he spun sideways through the air while holding onto the ball, then fell forward for a first down to keep the Denver drive alive. Two plays later, Davis scored on a one-yard touchdown run, giving Denver a 24–17 lead. "The Broncos had scouted us so well that they knew what we were going to do practically before we did," Butler recounted. "We kept trying to make adjustments throughout the game, but the Broncos made corrections based on whatever we did."

Dejected tight end Mark Chmura stepped off the gridiron after the Broncos defeated the Packers in Super Bowl XXXII. (WISCONSIN STATE JOURNAL)

On the ensuing kickoff, Denver recovered an Antonio Freeman fumble, but the Packers defense responded when Eugene Robinson picked off an Elway pass in the end zone. After the interception, Green Bay marched 85 yards in just four plays to tie the score at 24 with 13:32 remaining in the fourth quarter. On the Broncos' final drive, the Packers couldn't stop Elway or Davis, "and for the first time I felt a little bit of panic. We were in trouble, and we were running out of time," Harlan recalled. Denver was on the one-yard line with just 1:47 left in the game. "The clock was getting away from us, and we weren't going to get it done. It's an awful feeling."

To prevent the Packers from running out of time, Holmgren ordered his players to let Denver score on the next play. When Davis ran into the end zone for his third rushing touchdown of the game, the Broncos took a 31–24 lead. Holmgren's clock strategy almost worked. With 1:04 left to play, the Packers had a first down on the Denver 35-yard line. But after picking up 4 yards on the next play, Green Bay's hopes of repeating as Super Bowl champions ended after Favre threw three straight incomplete passes. "When it was over, I just sat there staring at the field and watching everyone walk off. It was such a terrible loss, and I was feeling it," Harlan remarked. "They played an exceptional game, and they deserved to win. But as I watched the Broncos going up on that stage to get the trophy, I kept thinking that was us last year, and it should be us today."

It was a sentiment shared by the Packers players as the Broncos hoisted the Lombardi Trophy. "We felt that we were the best team," Freeman said. "But for one day the Denver Broncos were better than us and they're the champs."

"You just have that empty feeling," linebacker Bernardo Harris said of the Packers' lost opportunity. "You had a chance to go down in history as being one of the teams to win it back to back."

Despite failing to win their second straight Super Bowl, the Packers found themselves greeted by 35,000 loyal fans upon their return to Green Bay the next day. Always the optimist, team president Bob Harlan reassured the crowd: "The most important thing we should remember is that there are thirty teams in the National Football League. Only two were playing on [Super Bowl] Sunday, and one of them was the Green Bay Packers."

■ ■ ■

In the days preceding Super Bowl XXXII, the NFL announced that its new broadcast agreements with Fox, CBS, ABC, and ESPN would guarantee the league $17.6 billion over the next eight years with an average of $2.275 billion per year. Since the previous deal had paid the league $1.075 billion a year over four years, both NBC and TNT balked at the increased license fees, allowing CBS to acquire the AFC television package and ESPN to acquire the full slate of Sunday night games.

The coming influx of new television revenue was of little comfort to the Packers organization and its dedicated fans who spent the offseason trying to cope with the team's Super Bowl XXXII defeat. "It was the most disappointing loss I've had since I've been with the Packers," Harlan remarked. "In many ways, 1997 was a great season, but we let the game we should have won slip away from us."

The Packers' offseason was further burdened with the loss of several key contributors who chose to sign lucrative free-agent contracts elsewhere. "The bottom line," future president of finance Andrew Brandt remarked, "is this: the salary-cap makes it harder for successful teams to stay successful, and the system allows for teams that have struggled to get better, quicker."

When defensive end Gabe Wilkins, cornerback Doug Evans, safety Eugene Robinson, offensive guard Aaron Taylor, and punter Craig Hentrich signed elsewhere, Ron Wolf was unfazed. "If you're a good football team, you're going to lose good football players," he remarked. He was ready to replace the players lost in free agency with developed players from the draft who were younger and cheaper. "Ever since the first year of free agency, we've kind of established a modus operandi that we're going to concentrate on two things, signing and developing our own players."

It was a strategy Wolf felt would prevent the Packers from suffering the salary cap pitfall that had decimated the Cowboys dynasty earlier in the decade. "When the salary cap was developed, no one anticipated the credit-card spending that occurred," Brandt recalled of Dallas creating short-term cap room by deferring player salaries at the expense of its future. "The ramifications were rollercoaster-type [win-loss] periods" that engulfed the Cowboys', 49ers' and Jaguars' championship-caliber teams in later years.

The Packers looked to avoid a similar fate while preparing for their upcoming annual stockholders' meeting in July. As a result of their recent very successful stock drive, they had to consider a new venue for the meeting. In the past Green Bay's Midway Motor Lodge had served as an adequate location, since attendance was only a few hundred at most. With attendance anticipated to be in the thousands, the team chose Lambeau Field as the new location. "It's the first time, I think, that a professional sports franchise ever held a meeting in a stadium," public relations director Lee Remmel remarked of accommodating the 18,707 shareholders and their guests in attendance that year.

Despite the initial party atmosphere generated by eager first-time stockholders, the stadium served as nothing more than an oversized boardroom. "You could tell what they had really come for was to see Lambeau Field," Harlan said of the stockholders' reaction to Ron Wolf giving his football report, John Underwood presenting his treasurer's report, and all business aspects of the Packers' football operation being discussed at the outdoor meeting. "The next year attendance dropped to 7,064."

At the meeting Underwood declared fiscal year 1997 as the best ever for the Packers, due in large part to the team's raising $24 million from the stock sale. "The beauty of the stock offering is that we can use that money for our facility projects and we can deal with the other side from a different equation," he said, referring to Favre, Butler, and linebacker Brian Williams being signed to recent contract extensions. The Packers had also benefited from raising ticket prices to an average of $37, up from $32.75, which accounted for an additional $1.7 million in revenue from home games and helped mark the third consecutive year that the Packers pulled a profit of more than $5 million.

> "We knew Coach Holmgren's time to leave was coming."
> —SAFETY LEROY BUTLER

On the field in 1998, Green Bay's 4–0 start served as only a temporary distraction from growing uneasiness that the Packers were about to lose their head coach. "It seemed to me that he knew it was about to end for him in Green Bay," Harlan said of Mike Holmgren during the 1998 season. "He was quieter than he'd been in the past, not as outgoing. He'd get on the team plane and kind of be by himself. There was a different demeanor and a different personality there."

Enthusiasm surrounding the Packers' great start died after a week five loss to the Vikings on Monday night, which also ended their twenty-five-game winning streak at Lambeau Field. As the season wore on, the offseason pillaging of Green Bay's roster and subsequent lack of depth were exposed. Dorsey Levens missed the first nine games with a broken leg as a running-back-by-committee platoon served up anemic rushing numbers in his absence. The receiving corps was just as crippled by injuries, with Robert Brooks, Corey Bradford, Tyrone Davis, and Bill Schroeder all missing time with nagging injuries. Although the Packers finished the season with three straight wins, "we knew Coach Holmgren's time to leave was coming," Butler recalled.

Earlier in November, an otherwise tight-lipped Wolf even acknowledged that he thought Holmgren would be departing at season's end. "I'm sure he can handle the general manager's duties," he told reporters, "but as long as I'm at Green Bay, Mike won't run the football operation here. That's my job. So if he feels coaching no longer completely satisfies him and he wants to expand his responsibilities, he'll have to go elsewhere."

After navigating a season filled with distractions and setbacks, Green Bay conceded the NFC Central Division crown to the Vikings, who finished with a league-best 15–1 record. The Packers' 11–5 record earned them their sixth straight playoff berth and the opportunity to face the 49ers in San Francisco. "This wasn't the Super Bowl, it was a wild-card game, but it sure felt like the Super Bowl," Favre said, describing the overwhelming intensity surrounding the postseason contest.

It was the fourth consecutive year the two franchises had faced each other in the playoffs. That sense of familiarity kept the game close all afternoon, with no team holding more than a 7-point lead. When Favre found Freeman in the end zone, Green Bay took a 27–23 lead with 1:56 remaining in the game. With less than two minutes to engineer a comeback, San Francisco's Steve Young began traversing 76 yards of gridiron by carving up the Packers' secondary. Green Bay could do little to stop the offensive juggernaut. Even when rookie safety Scott McGarrahan forced a fumble out of the hands of Jerry Rice that Bernardo Harris recovered, officials ruled the 49ers receiver was down before the ball spilled out. Four plays later and with three seconds remaining, Young connected with Terrell Owens on an improbable 25-yard touchdown catch that even hard-hitting safeties Darren Sharper and Pat Terrell couldn't jar loose. "You just don't lose a game like this," Holmgren said of the Packers' 30–27 loss, which marked his first opening-round exit from the playoffs since arriving in Green Bay. "It's the worst thing that can happen. This is a hard one. The Super Bowl loss last year was very difficult, but the way this one ended was startling."

The Packers' sudden playoff departure was immediately overshadowed by the uncertainty of Mike Holmgren's future in Green Bay. The suspense didn't last long. Just five days later, he answered all the persistent questions and rumors by accepting an offer from the Seattle Seahawks to become their head coach and executive vice president of football operations. "If I had gone into the locker room after we beat the Patriots to win Super Bowl XXXI and told the players that within two years, Mike would be gone and we wouldn't even be the best team in our division, they would have laughed me out of the place," Wolf lamented. "When you are giddy with victory, it is tough to seriously contemplate the downside of success."

Prior to his departure, Holmgren turned down an offer from Wolf that would have made him the highest-paid coach in the NFL, instead opting for the omnipotence the Seahawks could give him with the titles of coach, general manager, and executive vice president. Even Brett Favre didn't feel he could have done much to persuade Holmgren to stay. "I understood why he was leaving," the quarterback said years later. "It happened so fast. The next thing I know, he's gone."

Holmgren's sudden departure fractured the Packers organization. "When Mike left, he took a lot of his assistant coaches with him. He also took Mike Reinfeldt and Ted Thompson. He wanted Reinfeldt to oversee his salary cap and do his contracts, and he wanted Thompson to come in and build a ball club for him," Harlan recalled.

"Ted was a key guy for Ron. He was his right-hand man, and he had promoted him twice.

"Reinfeldt, meanwhile, was a very big loss for me," Harlan continued. "When I'd hired him eight years earlier I had told him that he was part of my succession plan. But I couldn't compete with the money that he was being offered in Seattle."

The Packers were forced to look to their future for comfort but found the recent past casting a dubious shadow over the organization. "I believe to this day that that was a team that probably should have won two and maybe three Super Bowls. I really thought 1996 was just the beginning," Harlan recounted. "You look back and you're upset with yourself because it's so tough to get there and you don't know how hard it's going to be to get back."

Mike Holmgren left Green Bay for Seattle following the 1998 season, but not before returning the Packers to perennial Super Bowl contention while compiling an overall record of 84–42, which included a 9–5 postseason record and the Super Bowl XXXI championship victory.
(WISCONSIN STATE JOURNAL)

GREEN BAY'S GOLDEN TICKET

O n the cusp of the new millennium, the Green Bay Packers were at a crossroads. The franchise that had exemplified excellence within professional football's new era of unrestricted free agency was now struggling to keep pace. Escalating player salaries were evaporating even the largest of team profits, and economic forecasts projected a grim future. "When we looked at it, even though we would have our fifth consecutive record year for income, we were going to have a negative cash flow," team president Bob Harlan explained. "The atmosphere in the league has changed. We did sign everybody that Ron wanted to sign this year, but it cost us over $30 million [in signing bonuses]."

The Packers were becoming a victim of the growing financial gap between teams created by the recent construction boom, in which almost two-thirds of franchises received new or renovated stadiums full of revenue-producing luxury suites, club seats, and advertising. During the past decade, the percentage of league revenues that went unshared was growing at an alarming rate, from 12 percent in 1994 to 21 percent by 2003. Although there was no direct tie between a team's economic value and its ability to generate wins and losses on the field, unshared stadium revenue affected a franchise's worth. Furthermore, the more revenue a stadium could generate, the more an organization could spend on coaches, scouting staff, and training facilities—all of which could directly affect a team's fortunes on the field.

As a result, the Packers were forced to find new and creative sources of revenue from their existing stadium after calculating that raising ticket prices and leasing the stadium's eighty-eight luxury boxes wouldn't close the gap. At first they considered a modest renovation of Lambeau Field, which carried a $75 million price tag but generated just $5 million in extra revenue on an annual basis. That plan

Quarterback Brett Favre (4) and wide receiver Donald Driver (80) celebrated often in the first decade of the 2000s as the Packers continued to be one of the NFL's elite teams. (COURTESY OF CHIP MANTHEY)

was soon shelved as the team considered whether a more expansive renovation of Lambeau Field—featuring more revenue-producing amenities—would be feasible. The Packers also weighed the option of building a new stadium that could provide all new sources of income through signage for advertisements, luxury boxes, club seats, food courts, restaurants, and expanded parking. "We need to make money here more than ten days a year to support this franchise," Harlan remarked.

Placing the franchise deeper in a state of flux was the fact that it was without a head coach for the first time in seven years. Many of the familiar faces who had brought a Super Bowl championship to Green Bay just two years earlier were gone after head coach Mike Holmgren and most of his assistants, along with chief financial officer Mike Reinfeldt, left for Seattle. "We all came in here together and we were all part of something—when you really sit back and think about it—that was tremendous," executive vice president and general manager Ron Wolf explained. "But I think change is inevitable."

Wolf had prepared for Holmgren's inevitable departure. "During the [1998] season, Ron told me that if we were going to make a coaching change, he was going to go after Ray Rhodes," Harlan recalled. "He had known almost that whole season who he was going to bring in, although he did talk about some other people. Steve Spurrier's name was mentioned, for example."

Without interviewing anybody else for the position, Wolf hired Rhodes to be the Packers' twelfth head coach just three days after Holmgren departed. Rhodes seemed to be a logical choice, having spent two successful years as the Packers' defensive coordinator under Holmgren and four years as head coach of the Philadelphia Eagles. He had a reputation for being tough, and that's what Wolf wanted. At his introductory news conference, Rhodes exclaimed, "When you look at the football team and everything around it, you are in awe."

Wolf felt the franchise didn't need to be rebuilt, just refined, a sentiment shared by Rhodes, who compared the Packers to an older car that just needed a few spark plugs and an oil change. Following an undefeated preseason, it seemed the franchise had been reinvigorated by Rhodes's arrival. Expectations continued to grow as Brett Favre led the Packers to three thrilling comeback victories in the regular season's first four games, despite injuring his thumb during an exhibition game. But as the season progressed, the injury never healed, hampering his play, which was evident as he threw twenty-three interceptions to just twenty-two touchdowns. "It's been a factor every game," new quarterbacks coach Mike McCarthy told reporters about the injury in November, "but we're not going to make excuses."

The Packers went on to win four of their first six games, but they suffered through two separate three-game losing streaks that season. Some attributed the poor performance to Rhodes's management style. "We would be going through

> "[Favre's injury has] been a factor every game, but we're not going to make excuses."
> —QUARTERBACKS COACH MIKE MCCARTHY

Ron Wolf (left) hand-picked Ray Rhodes (right) to be Mike Holmgren's successor as head coach. But after the Packers posted an 8-8 record, Rhodes was fired after one season. (FROM THE GREEN BAY PRESS-GAZETTE ARCHIVES, REPRINTED BY PERMISSION)

losing streaks and not playing good football, and when I'd walk through the locker room in the middle of the week, he'd be sitting at a table playing dominoes with the players," Harlan recalled.

When it came to discipline, Rhodes "thought we should take responsibility for ourselves," safety LeRoy Butler said. "Unfortunately, our team had too many young players who were used to walking into college team meetings thirty minutes to an hour late without repercussions."

By December, Wolf determined the effects of Rhodes's lack of leadership had spread throughout the locker room. "The team was dead," he remarked. "For whatever reason, the players just didn't respond to Ray. The team had no life and it had to change."

"He had lost his authority," Harlan recalled of Rhodes. "It was almost like what Ron [Wolf] had seen when he'd gone onto Lindy Infante's practice field and called it a country club atmosphere."

The deciding factor Wolf needed to prove he'd made the wrong choice came in December when the Packers dropped a crucial contest to Carolina on the game's final play. As the Panthers drove downfield for an eventual winning score, Rhodes refused to call any of the Packers' three remaining timeouts. When Carolina waited for the clock to run down and called a timeout before scoring on the game's last play to pull out the 33–31 win, Wolf watched Rhodes's coaching blunder in stunned disbelief. Within hours of the season finale three weeks later, Rhodes was fired. "I'd have made the same decision even if we'd made the playoffs," Wolf remarked. "It couldn't continue like this. It was horrible. Those things are not pleasant, but somebody had to do it."

Wolf's swift action underscored that the Packers' 8–8 record, tying them for third place in the NFC Central Division, wasn't good enough. "I think we have to have a disciplined, hard-nosed football team here," Wolf explained. "That's how you're successful in this business, and we didn't have that this year."

• • •

The National Football League entered the twenty-first century as both America's most popular and most lucrative professional sports league, with annual revenues exceeding $3.6 billion. Its eight-year, $17.6 billion television deal delivered

$2.2 billion on an annual basis, which equated to $70 million a year for each team. By comparison, Major League Baseball's television contract was worth just $570 million per season, providing each team with $19 million. The NFL's free agency era, which was less than ten years old, succeeded in creating greater parity among teams, but it also escalated team salaries from $14.6 million in 1988 to $64 million by 2000. As pro football's economic model shifted away from shared revenue, it left many poor teams lagging behind the rich ones. On average, in 1994 non-shared revenue—which was primarily stadium-related, from parking, concessions, pro shop sales, private boxes, and club seats—accounted for 12 percent of a team's total revenues. By 2003 non-shared stadium-related revenue was projected to account for almost a quarter of a team's total revenue.

As glorious as their recent success was on the field, the Packers found themselves facing a long-term and steep financial slide. Back in 1997, they ranked ninth in the NFL in terms of team revenues, but they dropped to sixteenth by 1999 and were predicted to decline to twenty-fifth place by 2003. Furthermore, team treasurer John Underwood projected that the team's reserve fund, which had a $49.8 million balance in 2000, would fall to $7.9 million in 2004 and would evaporate by 2005. After making a profit of just over $7 million in 1998 and just under $7 million in 1999, the Packers had lost $419,000 in the 2000 fiscal year—their first operating loss in more than a decade. "As more and more teams play in new venues, we slide closer and closer to the bottom of the NFL," Underwood explained. "Without new sources of stadium revenue, projections tell us we will be among the two or three poorest teams in the league."

By 2000 Lambeau Field—which first hosted the Packers in 1957—was the longest continuously occupied stadium in the NFL. In pro sports as a whole, only the Boston Red Sox's Fenway Park, the Chicago Cubs' Wrigley Field, and New York's Yankee Stadium had longer active home field tenures. As a result, Lambeau Field had fallen far behind other NFL stadiums in how much money it could generate for the franchise. The Packers, without the ability to turn to a wealthy owner, had to devise new ways to produce capital. For most teams in the NFL, that meant building a new stadium while simultaneously taking a wrecking ball to their history. In Green Bay, that was a very sensitive subject. "It's a slippery slope," explained senior vice president John Jones, who had been brought in by Harlan as the Packers' senior vice president of administration to replace Mike Reinfeldt when he left for Seattle with Holmgren. "Other teams usually leverage moving to green pastures [to get new stadiums], but that's not an option for us. We have to be creative to remain viable."

When Packers executives initiated feasibility studies to explore potential options, which included the possibility of constructing a new stadium to replace Lambeau Field, fans were outraged. The team proposed a plan that emerged from

> "Do you want to remain a winner or do you want to go back to the dark days of the 1970s and again become mediocre?"
>
> —GENERAL MANAGER RON WOLF

the studies to satisfy, in part, everyone's goals. "We asked engineers to test that bowl to see how long it would last," Harlan explained. "When they told us it would last for another fifty years, we knew we wanted to renovate instead of building a new stadium. Our goal all along was to keep Lambeau Field as it was."

The Packers unveiled their plan to the public in January 2000 with a statewide tour. The proposal was a dramatic expansion and renovation that promised to make Lambeau Field a facility on par with—or surpassing—even the newest NFL stadiums. Now the organization had to convince the public how desperate they were to stay solvent. "It's about money if you want to become a winning team, if you want to stay a winning team," Ron Wolf declared. "Do you want to remain a winner or do you want to go back to the dark days of the 1970s and again become mediocre? We need your help to maintain the level of excellence associated with the Packers in the 1990s."

One of the key contributors to the Packers' stadium renovation plan was John Underwood, the team's treasurer. At the annual shareholders' meeting in 2000, Underwood emphasized that the Packers were facing their greatest challenge since Curly Lambeau and the Hungry Five had passed the hat to keep the team viable in the mid-1920s. "This is when John became famous for his three-legged-stool talk," Harlan recalled. "He said the long-term viability of the franchise depended on three legs. The first leg was a substantial level of revenue sharing in the NFL. The second was a hard salary cap. And the third was an ability to generate new revenue from the stadium. We had the first two legs, but we needed the third to succeed."

With the proposed expansion, Lambeau Field's capacity would increase to 72,922, allowing the Packers to offer more tickets to both the general public and to the thousands waiting for season tickets. Most aspects of the hallowed ground inside the stadium, from the bleacher seats to the natural grass, would not change, since architect John Somerville's original design from 1956 had made it possible to expand seating capacity without compromising the bowl. The renovation's top feature was a five-story, 366,000-square-foot atrium that would turn Lambeau Field into a year round attraction for the community, offering restaurants, bars, and space for meetings, weddings, and parties. Plus, the new and expanded Packers Hall of Fame and team Pro Shop would become part of the stadium. However, the team couldn't afford to pay for this themselves and proposed that residents in Green Bay's Brown County pay a half-percent sales tax to provide $160 million toward the $295 million project.

Levying the tax required passage of both legislation in the Wisconsin statehouse and a referendum in Brown County. The idea of initiating a tax increase and public support for a private entity—even for one as beloved as the Packers—quickly became a contentious issue. At the state's capitol in Madison, Harlan and Jones spent numerous hours, days, and months lobbying politicians for support and received the endorsement of Governor Tommy Thompson. "The Green Bay Packers have come to us with an exciting and well-thought-out plan for their future viability," he said during his State of the State address in 2000. "Stadium issues aren't easy and they're not fun. It's like being on the one-yard line, down by three points and deciding whether to go for the win or settle for the tie. In Wisconsin, we always go for the win."

In May 2000 the Packers received the reluctant approval from lawmakers, but they still had to convince Brown County residents, who were scheduled to vote on the tax referendum in September. When poll numbers suggested residents would not only reject the tax but do so by a huge margin, Harlan was shocked. So he and Jones went door to door like old-time politicians soliciting votes. In the months leading up to the referendum, they spoke at dozens of factories, department stores, and community gatherings in hopes of persuading the public. In their stump speeches, they emphasized the Packers would provide a huge economic impact for Brown County, estimated at $144 million annually, in return for the small tax increase. But the opposition was well organized, and the Packers were coming off a disappointing 8–8 season. "Hopefully, people will see it's much bigger," defensive end Vonnie Holliday remarked. "This is about tradition, about pride, about history, the past and Green Bay Packer football."

As the 2000 season approached, the franchise was also overcome with a sense of urgency to win games. "One of the factors driving the Packers' need to turn around quickly was the possible retirement of star quarterback Brett Favre," author Don Gulbrandsen explained in *Green Bay Packers: The Complete Illustrated History*. "It is unclear exactly when the rumors of Favre's retirement surfaced, or who started them, but speculating about how much longer Favre would play became an annual rite for the media and fans."

The organization was left without a head coach after Ron Wolf's handpicked successor to Mike Holmgren, Ray Rhodes, had been dismissed after just one disappointing season. Refusing to make the same mistake again, Wolf had interviewed half a dozen high-profile coaches and coordinators immediately after the 1999 season, with Marty Schottenheimer, the former Cleveland Browns and Kansas City Chiefs head coach, believed to be the front-runner. "Marty was the one person who was really prominent in Ron's picture during most of that time. They were talking back and forth to each other, and I really felt the offer was going to go to Marty," Harlan noted. However, despite Schottenheimer's rumored $4 million per-year salary demand, "he just didn't seem overly anxious to get the job, and I think it bothered Ron that he wasn't."

One of the other prospective coaching candidates Wolf met with was Seattle Seahawks offensive coordinator Mike Sherman, who had been a tight ends coach in

"I want some of Coach Lombardi to rub off on me."

–HEAD COACH MIKE SHERMAN

During training camp in 2000, new head coach Mike Sherman (right) already expected Brett Favre and the Packers to return to the playoffs. (COURTESY OF CHIP MANTHEY)

Green Bay under Holmgren. During their interview, Sherman impressed Wolf with his unwavering dedication and sense of organization, despite having no head coaching experience and just three years of NFL seasoning on his résumé. "Marty never showed that kind of enthusiasm. And then Mike Sherman came in and showed all kinds of enthusiasm, not only for the job but for the tradition, and that swayed Ron tremendously," Harlan said. "If Marty had shown the same excitement as Mike, there's a good possibility that he would have been hired. But he never displayed any warmth for the job."

The morning after interviewing Sherman, Wolf approached Harlan about Schottenheimer's substantial financial demands, while admitting, "Tell you what, if I had any guts I'd hire Mike Sherman right now." When Harlan replied, "Why not?" it wasn't five minutes later that Wolf returned to say, "It's done."

When Mike Sherman was introduced on January 18, 2000, as the Packers' thirteenth head coach, he immediately embraced the team's rich history, saying, "I want some of Coach Lombardi to rub off on me." The sentiment resonated throughout the locker room, and as the 2000 season approached, Sherman brought an added sense of discipline to the team. Although it would take both the new coach and his team time to adjust, there was reason for optimism throughout Green Bay.

On September 12, 2000, Brown County voters approved the sales tax referendum by a margin of 53 percent to 47 percent, providing $160 million toward the Lambeau Field renovation. The balance of the project's $295 million price tag was covered by the state of Wisconsin, which contributed $9.1 million for stadium infrastructure improvements, and the Packers, who paid their $125.9 million portion with money raised in the 1997 stock sale and a onetime seat license fee for season-ticket holders. Although many longtime fans grumbled at the license fee of as much as $1,400 per seat, and some even dropped their season tickets, "most realized it was a worthwhile investment that would help ensure the future of football in Green Bay," author Don Gulbrandsen noted. "Again the fans had come to the rescue."

Green Bay started the 2000 season by dropping their first two games but ended with four straight wins to secure a 9–7 record. The Packers' third-place

ABOVE: In 2000 Packers president Bob Harlan (right) and executive John Jones (left) proposed renovating Lambeau Field. They helped secure a Brown County sales-tax referendum that assisted in financing the renovation. (FROM THE GREEN BAY PRESS-GAZETTE ARCHIVES, REPRINTED BY PERMISSION)

ABOVE, RIGHT: Harlan celebrated after Brown County residents voted in September 2000 to help finance Lambeau Field's renovation. (AP PHOTO/ MIKE ROEMER)

finish in the NFC Central Division kept them out of the playoffs, but they had discovered a ground game with the acquisition of running back Ahman Green, who rushed for nearly 1,200 yards. "We were playing our best football at the very end, and I thought that was a great tribute to Mike [Sherman]," Harlan remarked. "Then Brett Favre had made the comment that this was the best team chemistry he had seen since he'd come to Green Bay. I thought that was pretty heavy coming from a player who had been on two Super Bowl teams."

One month after the Packers' strong finish, Ron Wolf retired as the team's executive vice president and general manager. During Wolf's nine-year tenure in Green Bay, the Packers had enjoyed the NFL's best regular-season record (83–45), eight winning seasons, six straight playoff appearances, back-to-back NFC titles, 101 total victories including eight in the playoffs, and a Super Bowl victory. Wolf's ability to build a champion after 1993's advent of free agency may have also attributed to his sudden retirement. "I think one of the main things that really drove him out of the game was what he called 'the new football,' brought on by free agency and the salary cap," Harlan said of Wolf. "He hated to think about the money rather than thinking about the talent of the player he wanted to go after."

Upon announcing his retirement, Wolf recommended that Sherman fill his vacancy, and the Packers made Sherman the team's first head coach with the GM title since Bart Starr in 1980. "I believed that was what was most beneficial for the corporation right then," Harlan explained. "I was also worried that if I brought somebody in over Mike, they wouldn't get along."

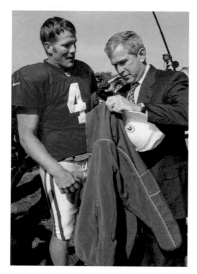

In September 2000 presidential candidate George W. Bush talked with Brett Favre (left) and completed a pass to tight end Bubba Franks (right) during a visit to the team's practice. (BOTH PHOTOS FROM THE GREEN BAY PRESS-GAZETTE ARCHIVES, REPRINTED BY PERMISSION)

■ ■ ■

After a four-month transition period, Ron Wolf officially retired on June 1, 2001, but he continued to help the team in a consulting role. Ironically, Sherman now possessed the authority Holmgren had sought and wielded more power within the organization than any Packers head coach since Vince Lombardi. Sherman made sure to offset his relative lack of experience by giving more power to talented administrators within the organization, including Reggie McKenzie and John Dorsey, and by hiring Mark Hatley away from the Bears to make him the Packers' vice president of football operations.

As the 2001 season approached, many prognosticators felt the Packers were on the downward slide toward mediocrity. In recent years, free agency had proven to be a double-edged sword for successful franchises. Once a team achieved greatness, it was next to impossible to keep its roster intact for any length of time. The decade was soon littered with a legacy of Super Bowl teams that failed to even make the playoffs the following season. Outside of Green Bay, critics perceived Sherman to be incapable of being both head coach and administrator. But once again, the Packers succeeded in doing what most NFL teams had failed to do in recent years: reload and flourish. The previous year the Packers acquired Ahman Green and a fifth-round pick from the Seahawks, giving up a sixth-round pick and underachieving cornerback Fred Vinson. Green became an immediate impact player for the Packers, rushing for 1,175 yards in 2000 and 1,387 in 2001, the second-highest single-season total in team history. "You can hit him and stop him all ten times," Favre remarked about Green's tenacity and determination. "On the eleventh carry he'll take it and go all the way. That's the type of explosive back he is."

Wide receiver Bill Schroeder and the Packers raced to a 12–4 regular-season record in 2001. (COURTESY OF CHIP MANTHEY)

"People on the plane will say if we would have done this or we wouldn't have done that. Like I always say, if a chicken had lips, he could whistle."

–QUARTERBACK BRETT FAVRE

With Favre under center and Green's commanding presence in the backfield, the Packers dominated their opening-day opponent, the Detroit Lions, 28–6 to start the 2001 season. Two days later, the 9/11 attacks on America prompted NFL commissioner Paul Tagliabue to postpone the fifteen games that were scheduled for the following weekend, marking the first time in the history of the league that games were canceled for reasons other than a players' strike. The following week, games resumed and so did the Packers' dominance as they shut out the Redskins 37–0 and throttled the Panthers 28–7 to start the season with a 3–0 record. The Packers, featuring one of the league's most potent offenses and stingiest defenses, posted an impressive 12–4 record to finish second in the NFC Central Division behind the 13–3 Chicago Bears.

The Packers returned to the playoffs for the first time since 1998 to face a familiar foe: the San Francisco 49ers. Despite home field advantage, Green Bay was behind 7–6 at halftime, but they opened up the passing game in the second half, scoring 19 points in the 25–15 win. The Packers sealed their victory when cornerback Mike McKenzie, a third-year pro who signed a five-year, $17.1 million contract extension the Friday before the game, deflected a Jeff Garcia pass intended for Terrell Owens to stall the 49ers' drive. Favre then drove the Packers 93 yards in eight plays, with the payoff coming on Ahman Green's 9-yard touchdown run.

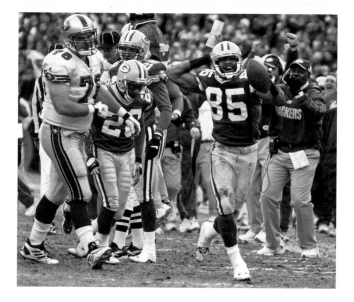

Corey Bradford (85) celebrated after stripping the ball from San Francisco's Paul Smith during the Packers' 25-15 victory over the 49ers. (WISCONSIN STATE JOURNAL)

When Green Bay's Corey Bradford stripped Paul Smith of the ball on the ensuing kickoff return and recovered it, the Packers ran out the clock for their first playoff victory since the 1997 NFC championship game in San Francisco. The victory made the Packers 11–0 at Lambeau Field and Favre 31–0 at home when the game-time temperature was thirty-four degrees or lower. "It's do or die in the playoffs," Favre remarked after the game, "and I don't ever want to look back and say we left something on the field."

The following week the Packers suffered when Favre failed to manufacture plays out of nothing or complete throws no one else could make. Against the Rams, he hurled six interceptions—the most in an NFL playoff game since 1955—that included three returned for St. Louis touchdowns. The error-prone Packers committed a total of eight turnovers during the crushing 45–17 defeat. "It's not one of my better days," Favre explained. "People on the plane will say if we would have done this or we wouldn't have done that. Like I always say, if a chicken had lips, he could whistle."

Favre's poor performance was even more disheartening because he had become such a prominent symbol of the Packers' resurgence in recent years. His daring playmaking and last-second heroics had captured the imaginations of fans nationwide, and "people would do anything to make sure he stays a Green Bay Packer," Harlan remarked. "In 2001 we signed him to a ten-year, $100 million contract extension that made him the highest-paid player in the NFL, and the negotiations were easy."

■ ■ ■

Before the start of the 2002 season, the NFL expanded to thirty-two teams with the inclusion of the Houston Texans. Since the league was first challenged by the AFL in 1960, the NFL had expanded more than two and a half times its size and was now at the ideal size first envisioned as far back as 1969 by then–NFL commissioner Pete Rozelle: "If the economics of professional football were such that it would be feasible, the ideal number [of teams] would be thirty-two. Then we could have two conferences, sixteen teams in each, broken down into four four-team divisions."

The Packers broke ground for the renovation of Lambeau Field on May 19, 2001. (FROM THE GREEN BAY PRESS-GAZETTE ARCHIVES, REPRINTED BY PERMISSION)

In accordance with Rozelle's vision, starting with the 2002 season the sixteen teams in each conference were divided into four divisions of four teams each, with the Packers preserving their rivalries with the Vikings, Bears, and Lions in the NFC North Division. Each of the four division winners were guaranteed to host a play-off game, and the two best teams without division-winning records earned playoff berths as wild-card teams.

Thanks to its latest expansion, the NFL had reason to be optimistic. The era of wholesale franchise relocation seemed to be a thing of the past, despite rumblings from cities like Los Angeles that still wanted to host professional football. From a financial perspective, NFL teams averaged just over $35 million from ticket sales in 2002, but that number comprised only 23 percent of total team revenue. Television revenue alone, totaling more than $2 billion per year and shared equally among the NFL's thirty-two franchises—about $77 million per team—brought in more than double the revenue earned from gate receipts. Higher television ratings also kept pushing up the price that networks were willing to pay to broadcast games. And the league made even more money from licensing agreements, with products grossing $3.1 billion, putting it fourth in licensing revenue among world companies, behind Disney, Warner Bros., and Bonjour.

Bob Harlan (right) and John Jones (left) oversaw every aspect of Lambeau Field's renovation. (FROM THE GREEN BAY PRESS-GAZETTE ARCHIVES, REPRINTED BY PERMISSION)

> "You look around and typically, that's Green Bay Packer weather. That's when Brett Favre shines."
>
> —DEFENSIVE END VONNIE HOLLIDAY

On the strength of the league's heightened business profile and the twenty new stadiums built or refurbished since 1993, total NFL revenues had doubled in the span of five years to nearly $5 billion in 2002. The league had also navigated the minefield of player free agency with relative ease. Although escalating salaries and liberal player movement bothered both owners and fans, the league enjoyed a long period without labor strife, the importance of which was made apparent by ongoing player-owner disputes in baseball, basketball, and hockey. Fans, growing tired of what they saw as unnecessary bickering between perceived rich owners and spoiled players, flocked to the stable NFL in greater numbers and with stronger allegiances. Another benefit of free agency could be summed up simply as "parity," because it allowed for more liberal player movement, creating teams that were more evenly matched, and the road from the bottom of the league standings to the top could be traveled in just one or two seasons. Now every fan had hope that his or her team could be a winner.

In Green Bay, the Packers rebounded from the previous season's humbling in the playoffs by starting the 2002 season winning eight out of their first nine games, which included their first seven-game winning streak since 1963. But injuries robbed the team of several starters and key role players. Even Brett Favre suffered a severe sprained thumb that jeopardized his streak of consecutive starts. He stayed the course, throwing for 3,658 yards and twenty-seven touchdowns, as the Packers, further aided by Ahman Green and his 1,240 yards on the ground, stormed to another 12–4 season. Clinching their first division title since 1997, Green Bay needed a win over the Jets in the season finale to secure a first-round playoff bye. Instead, they looked awful in the 42–17 loss and seemed to have lost momentum as they entered the postseason.

Green Bay would now host the Atlanta Falcons in their first-round playoff matchup. Playing under the Lambeau Field lights, the Packers were a solid favorite, especially since the franchise had never lost a playoff game at home in eleven previous contests. But on a snowy Saturday evening, the Falcons ignored the mystique and dominated the injury-ravaged Packers, who were without one of their defensive leaders, safety Darren Sharper. In the first half Green Bay gave up an early touchdown on a blocked punt and never found an answer for quarterback Michael Vick as Atlanta rolled to a 24–0 halftime lead. Many of the 65,358 fans in attendance actually booed the Packers off the field at halftime, and by game's end the stands were half-empty as frustrated fans headed for an early exit. For the rest of the evening, the Packers never offered anything resembling a legitimate comeback attempt in the 27–7 loss where injuries, ineptitude, and questionable coaching decisions haunted them all evening. "You look around and typically, that's Green Bay Packer weather. That's when Brett Favre shines," defensive end Vonnie Holliday said of the reversal of fortune. "They took a page out of our history book."

That playoff loss brought a sour end to a season that saw the Packers go unbeaten at home in the regular season—the only team in the NFL to accomplish that in 2002. Over the past two seasons, they had won twenty-four regular-season games followed by early and embarrassing exits from the postseason. "There's a lot of guys that put that [consecutive-playoff wins streak at Lambeau Field] together, guys that were playing here when I was in Little League," safety Matt Bowen said of the potential fallout from the loss. "It's important to a lot of people, and I'm sure we let some people down." The Packers' long, lonely winter pondering the Atlanta loss began with Favre bolting from the facility. For just the third time in his career, and the first time at home, Favre didn't talk to reporters after the game, leaving many to wonder if the Packers' latest defeat would hasten his retirement, which he had raised as a possibility all season regardless of his consecutive-starts streak.

■ ■ ■

As the 2003 season began, the Packers, who had lost only one regular-season home game during the past two years, found that their traumatic playoff loss to the Falcons had shattered Lambeau Field's aura of invincibility. In what would be the team's first of three losses at home that season, on Sunday, September 7, 2003, Brett Favre and the Packers were on the short end of a 30–25 contest at the hands of the Vikings. The defeat cast a shadow over an otherwise joyous week of ceremonies and celebration. Lambeau Field's $295 million renovation had been completed on time, within budget, and without the Packers having to play home games anywhere else, despite the construction site enveloping the stadium for almost two years. Lambeau Field's redevelopment included almost 6,000 more bowl seats, and 11,600 additional seats overall, increasing its capacity to 72,928. The block of new seats helped the Packers remove almost 1,500 names from their season-ticket waiting list (which still had more than 74,000 names on it; those at the bottom of the list had an estimated thirty-year wait before they would have the opportunity to buy season tickets). During halftime of the season opener, the Packers held a brief rededication ceremony for the stadium that included NFL commissioner Paul Tagliabue telling the 70,505 fans that "the NFL would not be what it is today without the Green Bay Packers."

> "We have the best of both worlds now. We have the tradition, but now we have the amenities to go along with it."
>
> –KICKER RYAN LONGWELL

Lambeau Field was now celebrated as the perfect combination of maximizing economic potential to stay competitive in the NFL while preserving the franchise's storied history. "We have the best of both worlds now," kicker Ryan Longwell exclaimed. "We have the tradition, but now we have the amenities to go along with it."

The previous Sunday at a gala hosted inside the stadium's brand-new atrium, Packers executive vice president and chief operating officer John Jones spoke of the true significance of the Lambeau Field renovation when he proclaimed: "The Packers

NFL commissioner Paul Tagliabue (at microphone) joined Packers executives and other dignitaries on the field on September 7, 2003, to commemorate the completion of the Lambeau Field renovation. (FROM THE GREEN BAY PRESS-GAZETTE ARCHIVES, REPRINTED BY PERMISSION)

will be here in Green Bay for our children and our grandchildren, just as they were here for our parents and grandparents."

Lambeau Field's increased economic impact on the community was immediate that first year, as almost 35 percent of special events booked at the Atrium came from outside Brown County. Furthermore, the Packers had added more than three thousand club seats priced at $200 each, which over the course of a season generated an additional $8 million in revenue that the team wouldn't have to share with the NFL's thirty-one other teams. "I don't think facilities win football games, but they certainly bring players to your team that can help you win football games," Sherman concluded.

Despite the stadium facelift, the Packers sputtered to a 3–4 start before a 30–27 road victory over the Vikings sparked their 7–2 finish. For the second straight year, Favre found his consecutive-starts streak jeopardized after he broke his right thumb on the helmet of teammate Mike Wahle during a loss to St. Louis. For the rest of the season, he could never quite grip the ball, but he continued building his legacy as one of the NFL's greatest quarterbacks, especially during a late-December Monday Night Football performance against the Oakland Raiders. The night before the game, Favre's father died, leaving many to wonder if Green Bay would be without its quarterback in a game they had to win to keep pace with the division-leading Vikings. Favre decided to play, throwing for 399 yards and four touchdowns in a 41–7 victory that added another chapter to his growing legacy. The next week the Packers' emotional regular season concluded with a decisive 31–3 win over the Broncos at Lambeau Field. However, they would make the playoffs only with a Minnesota loss. The Vikings had dominated the division from the start that season but had also dropped six of their last nine games heading into their season finale against the Cardinals. Minnesota, who was heavily favored to win, now had to beat the Cardinals to make the playoffs and keep the Packers out. In Green Bay, following the season-finale victory, the Lambeau Field crowd was captivated by what was being broadcast on the stadium's scoreboard from Arizona. On the last play of the game, the Cardinals scored on a 25-yard touchdown pass, giving them the 18–17 upset victory to knock the Vikings out of the playoffs and put the Packers in. "It was an unbelievable feeling to see our fans and everyone just kind of seize the moment," Favre told reporters after the game. "To say I'm shocked that we not only got in, but we're division champs would be an understatement."

■ ■ ■

The Packers' 10–6 record in 2003 might have been perceived as something of a step backward for the team after having posted consecutive 12–4 campaigns, but the team's gutsy finish with four consecutive wins had raised the team out of its mediocre 6–6 start to become the NFC's Super Bowl favorite heading into the play-offs. "The way we're playing right now, I know this team is capable of going all the way," Favre commented. "We just had to get in first. We've done that, and now anything's possible."

After winning their second straight North Division title, Green Bay would host Mike Holmgren's Seattle Seahawks in the playoffs' first round. The game's first sixty minutes were a seesaw battle, with the teams tied at 3, 13, 20, and 27 along the way. It seemed whoever got the ball to start the sudden-death overtime period would drive for the winning score. So when Seattle won the toss and chose to receive the ball, quarterback and former Packers backup Matt Hasselbeck declared to the Lambeau Field crowd, "We want the ball, and we're going to score."

Moments later, the Seahawks were driving when Hasselbeck threw a pass toward wide receiver Alex Bannister, who was being covered by Packers cornerback Al Harris. "I was just praying that he did throw the ball," Harris explained later, "because I was going to gamble on that play."

> "I was just thinking, 'Don't drop the ball.' I anticipated it, and I know the quarterback ain't going to catch me."
> —CORNERBACK AL HARRIS

When Harris jumped the route, he intercepted the pass and returned the game's only turnover for the game-winning touchdown. "I was just thinking, 'Don't drop the ball,'" he recalled of the first defensive score ever to win an NFL playoff game in overtime. "I anticipated it, and I know the quarterback ain't going to catch me."

The Packers' stunning 33–27 victory meant they'd have to travel to Philadelphia for a divisional playoff game the following Sunday against the NFC East Division champion Eagles. The Packers took an early 14–0 lead in the first quarter on touchdown passes of 40 and 17 yards from Favre to wide receiver Robert Ferguson. By

Cornerback Al Harris raced toward the end zone after intercepting the Seahawks' Matt Hasselbeck in the Packers' 33-27 overtime victory. (WISCONSIN STATE JOURNAL)

halftime the lead had shrunk to 14–7 due in part to Ahman Green having been stopped on a fourth-and-one situation at the goal line late in the second quarter. For the remainder of the game, Green Bay outplayed the Eagles. Ryan Longwell's 31-yard field goal with just over ten minutes left gave the Packers a 17–14 lead, which they held onto until there was 2:30 left in regulation. Green Bay's defense seemed to have the game wrapped up as the Eagles struggled, facing fourth down and 26. But that's when quarterback Donovan McNabb saved the Eagles' season with one pass, hitting wide receiver Freddie Mitchell for a 28-yard gain and the first down. "I guess we didn't have enough people in the right spot," safety Darren Sharper explained. "We still had a chance to keep them from scoring, but it would have been nice to end it there." A few plays later, the Eagles' David Akers kicked a 37-yard field goal with five seconds remaining to send the game into overtime.

On the first offensive play of the sudden-death period, Favre launched a pass toward wide receiver Javon Walker that was intercepted by the Eagles' Brian Dawkins and returned 35 yards to the Packers' 34-yard line. Less than five minutes into overtime, Akers kicked a 31-yard field goal to give the Eagles the 20–17 victory. "I was as devastated as I've ever been at a football game," Harlan said. It was the quietest locker room he had ever seen after a loss: "Nobody said a word. There was just shock on their faces, like, 'What the heck just happened here? How did this get away?'"

After the game, neither Favre nor Green talked to reporters. Sherman did, but he didn't point fingers at his players. "I'm very disappointed for them rather than at them," he admitted. "You would think you would win a fourth-and-twenty-six. We didn't get that done."

The repercussions of the Packers getting that close to an NFC championship berth brought mounting pressure on Sherman. During the offseason he fired defensive coordinator Ed Donatell. "When you're the head coach of the Packers," Sherman confessed, "you never finish the season totally fulfilled unless you win the Super Bowl."

■ ■ ■

Despite the Packers' heartbreaking exit from the playoffs, the renovated Lambeau Field was exceeding even the most optimistic economic models for infusing the franchise with additional revenue. The new Packers Pro Shop inside the Atrium had become the NFL's top single-team retail store, recording $15.4 million in sales in 2003, up from $11.1 million the previous year. Just four years earlier, the Packers had done just $1.5 million in retail sales. The Packers Hall of Fame, which had been moved to the stadium and expanded after being located across the street for many years, admitted more than 76,000 visitors in the first eight months at the stadium, compared to 72,500 visitors in all of 2002. Over that same time period, 28,000 people toured the new Lambeau Field, at $8 per person, compared to just 18,600 tours in all of 2001. The biggest financial impact of Lambeau Field's renovation, however, came from special events, ranging from corporate gatherings and business meetings to weddings; the Atrium brought in $3.1 million, mostly from special events, during its first seven months. "We've been very pleased with the response from people wanting to hold events at Lambeau," John Jones noted. "There always seems to be something going on here."

In just one mid-April weekend, more than 2,000 Packers fans paid $20 each to cram into the Lambeau Field Atrium for the team's first-ever "Draft Day" party to watch the NFL draft. While that special event went late into the evening, several

Fans flocked to the renovated Lambeau Field and its newly added Atrium, which quickly became both year-round tourist stop and revenue generator for Green Bay and surrounding communities. (AP PHOTO/DAVID STLUKA)

hundred Green Bay high school students attended their prom in the stadium's Legends Room. Just twelve hours later, several hundred children took part in a karate tournament on Lambeau Field's third floor. That weekend was just the latest example of how the Packers had turned their historic stadium into a year-round destination, one that generated almost $30 million in additional revenue for the team. "What we did was very unique and other teams are noticing," team treasurer John Underwood said of the renovation's importance for maintaining the team's tenth-place ranking in revenue of all thirty-two NFL teams.

As a result, Packers officials reported to shareholders that the team had a net income of $20.8 million after the 2003 season. In 2001, when the stadium was used for just ten home games a year, the team's net income was a comparatively meager $3.7 million. If not for the renovation, "we were running the risk of falling into financial oblivion," Underwood explained, noting that the renovation also helped the team grow its financial reserve, which had shrunk to $2.9 million in 2000. As of June 2004 the reserve was at $84.5 million, with team officials working toward building the reserve to equal the cost of one year of football operations—$113 million based on 2003 figures. "We are making good headway to reaching that goal," Underwood said. "That is important because it gives us a cushion to do things we have to do as a football team to remain competitive."

The renovation further benefited the team as marketing brought in $14.1 million, up from $10.5 million, which included corporate sponsorships of the five Lambeau Field gates. The Packers' gate receipts also climbed to $26.5 million, compared to $20.5 million the previous year. "We are exceeding the targets we set for ourselves when we developed the plan for renovation," Underwood remarked.

What made the revenue generated by the renovation all the more crucial was that the NFL's salary cap, which was $75.7 million during the 2003 season, was set to increase to $80.5 million for 2004. No longer could shared revenue alone from the league's lucrative television contract—$81.2 million as of the 2003 season—offset the Packers' growing expenses, which rose to $149.9 million. "The whole purpose of the renovation project was to create enough additional revenue to keep us on solid financial ground and able to compete against any team in the NFL," Underwood explained. "If you were to diagnose the financial health of this company, it is very favorable, very positive."

Back when Mike Sherman was named the Packers' general manager, his vice president of football operations, Mark Hatley, had managed the Packers' growing player costs, which had risen from $77.9 million to $96.1 million in just one year. But in July Hatley suffered a fatal heart attack, and Sherman was now without one of his key personnel executives. His loss would be felt throughout the 2004 season as Sherman struggled through an extended contract dispute with cornerback Mike

McKenzie. McKenzie, who still had three years left on a five-year extension, began his holdout during training camp, and Sherman refused to negotiate. "All Mike [Sherman] could talk about was McKenzie," Harlan explained of the situation that only worsened when the cornerback ended his holdout to become a disgruntled cancer in the locker room. "Seeing Mike so preoccupied with general manager duties . . . convinced me that that dual role was too big a burden to put on one guy."

The Packers had opened the 2004 season with a win in Carolina but proceeded to drop their next four games, including three at Lambeau. "We had no motivation, no enthusiasm, and the fans were letting us hear it," kicker Ryan Longwell recalled of the team's 1–4 start. "They were screaming about Coach Sherman, even yelling things about number 4, saying it was time to move on."

Although the McKenzie situation was resolved when the Packers traded him to New Orleans in October for a conditional sixth-round draft choice, Sherman's performance as general manager had become the focal point for the team's losing streak. The fact that the Packers were underachieving on the field brought growing criticism that Sherman was failing to maintain the talented team he had inherited. His personnel moves were further scrutinized because most of his free-agent signings had been busts. In addition, several of his draft classes had underachieved as a whole, leaving the Packers' pool of young talent relatively shallow. Yet when all looked hopeless, Green Bay went on a six-game winning streak that put them back into playoff contention. After finishing the season with consecutive road wins against the rival Vikings and Bears, the 10–6 Packers clinched their third consecutive NFC North Division title.

Going into their first-round playoff game against the Vikings, the Packers were heavy favorites. They were playing at home and had swept the regular-season series. Plus, the Vikings had stumbled into the playoffs with an 8–8 record after losing seven of their final ten games. But when Minnesota scored on each of its first three possessions, jumping out to a quick 17–0 lead, the deficit was too much to overcome. The penalty-prone Packers, who also lost wide receiver Javon Walker to a shin injury in the first half and left tackle Chad Clifton in the third quarter, fell short and for the second time in three years lost a postseason game at Lambeau Field. Favre, who threw four interceptions in the 31–17 defeat, fueled speculation that he would retire when he refused to guarantee that he would be back in Green Bay for a fifteenth season. "It would be easy to walk off the field after that game and say, 'I've had enough,'" Favre admitted afterward. "But I'm going to try to be as fair to myself and my team as possible. I've had a lot of great games. This obviously was not one of them."

The Packers' early playoffs exit only strengthened Bob Harlan's resolve to once again divide the head coach and general manager duties between two people, which

> "I'm going to try to be as fair to myself and my team as possible. I've had a lot of great games. This obviously was not one of them."
>
> —QUARTERBACK BRETT FAVRE

RIGHT: Wide receiver Javon Walker became Brett Favre's favorite target in 2004, catching eighty-nine passes for 1,382 yards and twelve touchdowns. (COURTESY OF CHIP MANTHEY)

BELOW, RIGHT: The Packers' Ahman Green (30) rushed for more than 1,000 yards in six of seven seasons between 2000 and 2006, including a franchise record 1,883 in 2003. (COURTESY OF CHIP MANTHEY)

BELOW: Safety Darren Sharper had thirty-six career interceptions with the Packers between 1997 and 2004, including five that he returned for touchdowns. (COURTESY OF CHIP MANTHEY)

he said "is what I would have liked to have done in 2001 if I hadn't been so worried about bringing in somebody who could work with Mike. I was still concerned about that, and ironically the thing that I had feared then proved to be a legitimate concern. He did have trouble co-existing with a new man."

Earlier in the season, Harlan had asked Ron Wolf to suggest a name. Without hesitation, Wolf suggested Ted Thompson, who had worked in Green Bay as assistant director of pro personnel for eight years before moving to Seattle to be Holmgren's vice president of football operations for the Seahawks. With both the Packers and the Seahawks eliminated from the postseason, Harlan approached Thompson about the position. Within forty-five minutes of requesting permission from the Seahawks to talk with Thompson, "I got a copy of Ron Wolf's contract, and I basically offered Ted the same perks and the same responsibilities that Ron had had and assured him that he would have total authority over the football operation," Harlan explained. "Ted was the only one I had in mind for our job, and if he hadn't been available, Mike Sherman probably would still have been the general manager the next year." Thompson accepted the job the next morning.

Head coach Mike Sherman (left) and general manager Ted Thompson (right) conferred during the Packers' 2005 training camp.
(FROM THE GREEN BAY PRESS-GAZETTE ARCHIVES, REPRINTED BY PERMISSION)

When Harlan told Sherman his plans, "I'm sure he took it personally," he recalled. "He wasn't pleased about it, but there was not a big argument or anything like that. He said he could make it work with Ted. Then we shook hands, and I left his office."

When Ted Thompson was introduced as Green Bay's new executive vice president, general manager, and director of football operations, he was only the fourth general manager in team history to serve exclusively from the front office, joining Verne Lewellen (1954–58), Lombardi (1968), and Wolf (1992–2001). His hiring, despite having been based on the need to separate the general manager and head coach responsibilities and not on Sherman's performance, caused an immediate rift between the Packers' head coach and team president. "I was probably as close to him at that time as I'd been to Mike Holmgren," Harlan recalled. "But that definitely cooled after I gave the general manager's duties to Ted. We rarely talked in that last year after Ted got here."

■ ■ ■

Casting an even bigger shadow over the Packers' future during the offseason were the NFL's ongoing negotiations to secure a new television contract and settle on a new collective bargaining agreement with its players' association. First, the league announced that it had extended its contracts with Fox, CBS, and DirecTV for the next six years. *Monday Night Football,* which had been a fixture on ABC since its inception in 1970, would be televised by ESPN beginning in 2006. Subsequently, the Sunday night package moved to NBC, which hadn't broadcast an NFL game since the Packers' Super Bowl XXXII loss to the Broncos. The NFL's annual revenue generated from the television contracts would grow from $2.4 billion per season to $3.75 billion. "Television continues to this day to be our largest single source of operating income," Harlan recalled. "It was worth $87.3 million in 2006, which was 41.9 percent of our total operating income. Every time we negotiate a television contract, I think it's never going to be this good again."

As the 2005 season approached, the NFL was the envy of every other professional sports organization on the planet. League-wide revenues totaled almost $5.2 billion, up from $3.6 billion in 2000. Even the Packers, playing in a metro area one-fortieth the size of New York, were worth $911 million, ranking them thirteenth of thirty-two teams, according to *Forbes* magazine.

The Packers also continued to benefit from the Lambeau Field renovation, reporting a profit of $25.4 million after the 2004 season. The 10.9 percent increase from the previous year meant the franchise was ranked in the NFL's top ten in revenue for the third year in a row. However, the Packers were still on fragile financial footing, despite accumulating more than $97 million in reserves. "[The reserve] allows us to have the funds necessary to maintain the Packers as a viable and competitive team in the NFL," team treasurer Larry Weyers explained. "With all that is going on in the NFL nowadays, we need to be prudent with our finances."

The Packers' goal of developing reserves to equal the cost of one year of football operations, which in 2005 was estimated at $119 million, would help it survive if there was ever a work stoppage or drastic shift in the league's economic structure. However, without access to an owner with deep pockets, "it seems the Packers are a victim of their own success," suggested a *Green Bay Press-Gazette* editorial. "By building their state-of-the-art facilities—both the Lambeau Field improvements and the practice facilities—the Packers accomplished two things. They set the pace for progressive action in today's professional sports market. But they also showed everyone else how to do it."

Team president Bob Harlan was largely responsible for the Packers' recent financial renaissance, but the organization was also benefiting from the financial wizardry of John Jones, its executive vice president and chief operating officer. Jones, who had been associated with the team as far back as 1974, when he was the editor of *The Packer Report*, joined the Packers' front office in 1999 after working for the NFL's management council, where he was one of the developers of salary cap computer software. He was also part of the league's negotiating team that secured a global settlement of player lawsuits in 1993, which led to the creation of a collective bargaining agreement and salary cap. Upon arriving in Green Bay, Jones concentrated on improving the team's business operations and became a vital factor in the success of Lambeau Field's renovation. Under his financial guidance, the organization was no longer just running a football team; it was running a tourist destination. "We had to evolve into a year-round operation and implement many business practices that we had never done before," Jones explained, noting that the Packers' workforce had expanded from about 50 to more than 150 full-time employees after the Lambeau Field renovation was completed. "League economics continue to shift, and the intensity of NFL business competition speaks for itself. It's an environment in which only the best franchises can succeed."

The Packers' continued success on and off the field was a direct result of their ability to manage their salary cap—a skill that prevented them from being forced into the money-saving roster purges afflicting many teams that had won or challenged for titles in recent years. "We're proud we've had the best record in the salary cap era in the NFL," said Andrew Brandt, the Packers' vice president of player finance. "We've prepared ourselves with Brett [eventually retiring] cap wise, and always on our mind when managing the Packers' cap is the effect of Brett's contract. We feel we've prepared well. Hopefully, he'll play forever, but assuming he stops at some point, we'll have a net gain on our cap to help replace him."

Ted Thompson spent the majority of his first few months as the Packers' general manager trying to coax a commitment out of Brett Favre to be in Green Bay for the 2005 season. Thompson exchanged phone calls with Favre almost every week. He and Sherman took individual trips to Favre's home in Hattiesburg, Mississippi, to visit with the quarterback in hopes of harvesting an answer. It wasn't until March 10 that Favre called Sherman and proclaimed, "I want to come back and have fun and help this team win and have a shot for another Super Bowl." But he reiterated, "You know as well as I do that I may not be any better next year than I was last year."

Now that Thompson no longer had to wonder about Favre's immediate future in Green Bay, he set the tone for his tenure in Green Bay. He let several popular players leave via free agency—including offensive guards Marco Rivera and Mike Wahle and safety Darren Sharper—after refusing to meet their contract demands. Instead, Thompson wanted to develop younger talent, building the franchise's roster through the draft and placing a premium on character. "You have to do what you

> **"I'm just excited about learning from Brett. I'm kind of looking forward to being in his shadow until my time comes."**
>
> **–QUARTERBACK AARON RODGERS**

Brett Favre (4) sensed Aaron Rodgers (12) over his shoulder during 2005's training camp. (AP PHOTO/ MORRY GASH)

think is best for the organization," he explained. "You have to take the best player available. And I think history will bear me out in that when you stray from that, that's when you make mistakes."

Overseeing his first NFL draft in Green Bay, Thompson found Aaron Rodgers still available when the Packers were to make their selection with the first round's twenty-fourth pick. "We were a little surprised that he got all the way to us," Thompson said about the quarterback prospect, who was projected by many experts to be the draft's top pick. "But we were prepared for it, and we felt like we made the right decision."

Rodgers was not only Green Bay's first quarterback taken in the first round since 1983, he also would serve as a wise insurance plan if Favre continued to debate his future in Green Bay. Over the years the Packers had drafted and acquired numerous skilled quarterbacks, such as Ty Detmer, Mark Brunell, Jim McMahon, Rick Mirer, Doug Pederson, Steve Bono, Kurt Warner, Danny Wuerffel, Craig Nall, Aaron Brooks, and Matt Hasselbeck, but Favre continued to retain his starting position. So it was no surprise the Packers' current starting quarterback shunned reporters who asked if he planned on mentoring his heir apparent. "He can figure it out like everybody else," Favre said. "I don't have time to teach him."

The controversy surrounding the pick wasn't lost on Thompson, who explained, "You make draft choices and draft-day decisions based on the long-term best interest of your organization."

Upon arriving in Green Bay, Rodgers relished his role as a rookie. "I totally recognize the fact that Brett is the guy back there and he's a legend, and my goal for this next year is to tap into his resources as a player," Rodgers explained. "I'm just excited about learning from Brett. I'm kind of looking forward to being in his shadow until my time comes."

As the Packers' training camp approached, Mike Sherman struggled with his reduced role, but he was gracious when explaining it to the press. "When you work in Titletown it's pretty obvious what's expected," he remarked. "I've always considered myself on a one-year contract regardless of my situation. This year is no different than any preceding year I've ever coached."

In August Thompson announced that Sherman had accepted a two-year contract extension through the 2007 season, but that did little to resolve the growing rift between the two men. As a result, the Packers' 2005 season was in trouble, immediately. "I don't know that anyone saw that 0–4 start coming," Harlan remarked. "It was a feeling this organization hadn't had since 1991, and it was scary."

Each game seemed to include a disastrous mistake or injury that would lead to another loss. Wide receiver Javon Walker blew out his knee just thirty-seven minutes into the season. Running back Ahman Green and his top backup, Najeh Davenport, were also lost to season-ending injuries. Several other key contributors, such as tight end Bubba Franks, wide receiver Robert Ferguson, and center Mike Flanagan, were hampered by injuries almost all season. Almost every week, the Packers had a chance to win but couldn't get it done, losing eight games by 7 or fewer points. Favre tried to compensate, but his risky plays often resulted in him throwing one of his league-leading twenty-nine interceptions. Of the sixteen games he played, Favre threw at least one interception in fourteen of them and managed just one touchdown pass in his final five games. Although running back Samkon Gado emerged as the season's brightest note by leading the team's rushing attack with 582 yards on the ground and six touchdowns, the Packers crashed to a 4–12 record—their worst since Lindy Infante's 1991 season. "The system with free agency and the salary cap is set up so that one day it's going to hit you," Harlan remarked. "You know the system is going to get you, but it's still a jolt when it does."

The Packers' 4–12 finish ended thirteen straight years of not fielding a losing club in Green Bay. "It started during free agency when people were saying that the Packers were going to suffer because the franchise was small, and the weather was too cold and nobody would want to come here," Harlan said of the streak. "The franchise record is fourteen [years], set between 1934 and 1947 when Curly Lambeau was coach, and I thought it would be a great accomplishment if we could tie or break that record."

After the season finale, a 23–17 win over the Seahawks, Favre stepped off the Lambeau Field gridiron in a subdued manner that suggested he was done. In the locker room, he was presented with the game ball from Sherman before breaking down in tears. Then he bailed on his traditional postgame news conference, leaving even the most optimistic Favre fans to speculate that he was done playing football. "It's hard to imagine a team running out there without a No. 4," kicker Ryan Longwell told reporters after the game. "It's weird to think of the Green Bay Packers without him."

A couple of days before the Packers' contest against Seattle, Thompson had approached Harlan about making a change at head coach. "He just said it hadn't worked out the way he'd expected it would, and that the team needed to go in a different direction," Harlan said of the season-long strain between Sherman and

> "It's hard to imagine a team running out there without a No. 4. It's weird to think of the Green Bay Packers without him."
> —KICKER RYAN LONGWELL

Mike Sherman was fired as head coach of the Packers following the 2005 season. During his six years in Green Bay, he went 59–43, which included a 2–4 record in the postseason. (COURTESY OF CHIP MANTHEY)

Thompson. "It was more a matter of where we were then and where we needed to go."

The day after the season finale victory over the Seahawks, Mike Sherman was fired. "It was a sad end to a head-coaching tenure in which Sherman had compiled a very good [57–39] record, but critics pointed to his relatively weak 2–4 mark in the postseason and the fact that his teams never made it to the NFC championship game—let alone the Super Bowl," author Don Gulbrandsen remarked in *Green Bay Packers: The Complete Illustrated History*. "It promised to be a very trying offseason for Packers fans, who were demoralized by Green Bay's worst season since the Lindy Infante era."

■ ■ ■

To fill their vacant head coaching position, the Packers considered several candidates. Ted Thompson's recruiting process was detailed and measured. For nine days he undertook a grueling and exhaustive series of interviews that included San Francisco offensive coordinator and former Packers quarterbacks coach Mike McCarthy, Cleveland offensive coordinator Maurice Carthon, New York Giants defensive coordinator and former Packers defensive back Tim Lewis, Dallas offensive coordinator and assistant head coach Sean Payton, San Diego defensive coordinator Wade Phillips, and Chicago defensive coordinator Ron Rivera. The last person he met with was the Packers' defensive coordinator under Sherman, Jim Bates. Afterward, Thompson confided in Harlan that they had a great interview. "I honestly felt that he was going to go with Jim Bates," Harlan recalled. "I didn't see Ted the rest of the day, but he came in the next morning and said he'd made his decision. He was going to hire Mike McCarthy."

On January 12, 2006, Mike McCarthy was named the fourteenth head coach of the Green Bay Packers. He was considered by many to be a surprise choice. Critics pounced on Thompson's decision, claiming McCarthy was not one of the league's elite assistant coaches, despite his having served as an offensive coordinator for the Saints and the 49ers. Plus, they claimed he was too young, at forty-two, to be a head coach. Thompson ignored the second-guessing at McCarthy's introductory news conference and touted the Packers' new head coach as someone who could return the franchise to a championship level. "What stood out to me in the interview process was Mike's leadership ability and the comfort level that he and I had on a personal level," Thompson told reporters. "That appealed to me very much. And he is all about football."

Mike McCarthy (right), who became the four-teenth head coach in franchise history prior to the start of the 2006 season, was familiar with Brett Favre (4), having served as the Packers' quarterbacks coach in 1999 under Ray Rhodes. (AP PHOTO/MIKE ROEMER)

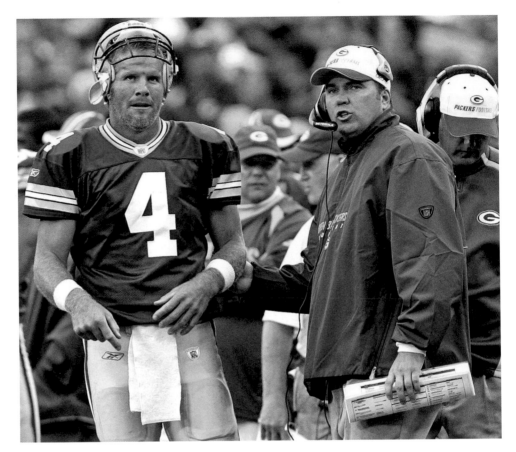

McCarthy was well respected throughout the league for being an expert when it came to working with quarterbacks and running the West Coast offense. He also had a reputation for being tough, hard-nosed, and devoted to football. "There will be an unconditional commitment from Ted and myself to bring a World Champion-ship back to Green Bay," McCarthy declared. "I think that's very important to state that right up front."

McCarthy had also forged a friendship with Brett Favre during his one year as the Packers' quarterbacks coach under Ray Rhodes. But that meant little as Favre watched in silence, giving no indication if he would retire or return to Green Bay for the 2006 season. For the next five months, Favre let the team fish for assurances while providing no guarantees. As his summer of indecision wore on, his former teammate and friend, tight end Mark Chmura, went on a Milwaukee radio station to reveal another side of the Packers icon. "People who don't think it's all about him are fooling themselves," he revealed about Favre. "He's a selfish guy. He's a very selfish guy."

Chmura's enlightening comments were supported when Favre was asked later that summer if he were taking too long to decide his future. "What are they going to do?" he asked. "Cut me?" When he realized that all the goodwill he had built up over the years was in danger of slipping away, Favre decided to announce his return just before the start of training camp.

Favre's decision came after the NFL was at risk of coming to a screeching halt back in March, when the past two decades of relative harmony between the NFL and the NFL Players Association fell into serious jeopardy. The league's collective bargaining agreement with its players was about to expire, and the window to negotiate a new deal was closing. The threat of a strike or lockout put professional football on the brink of suffering through a similar public relations disaster as its counterparts in hockey, basketball, and baseball had in recent years. But before the owners could resolve the pending financial issues with their players, they had to settle several contentious issues among themselves. A rift was forming among the NFL owners, often along generational lines, with some of the oldest families facing off against the newest—and most entrepreneurial—team owners. A small group, including the Cowboys' Jerry Jones and the Redskins' Daniel Snyder, had mastered the art of making money that wasn't eligible for league-wide revenue sharing. The issue proved more contentious than anyone had anticipated as concerns grew that the disparity between higher- and lower-revenue teams—a difference that in some cases exceeded $100 million annually—wouldn't be resolved before the labor contract expired.

Shared revenue guaranteed profits for any well-managed franchise. As far back as 1970, just 4 percent of league revenue was not shared among the teams, and that figure had changed little over the next two decades. Yet any team achieving success struggled to maintain it because of free agency. When the NFL introduced unrestricted free agency and its corresponding salary cap in 1993, the growing financial disparities between clubs were unforeseen. As a result, the parity loved by the league had shifted. Players too costly to retain were oftentimes lost to the financial lure of another club. Coaching geniuses were now forced to evaluate their rosters based not only on talent but also on available cap space. The changing economics of the game threatened to undermine the "capitalistic socialism" on which the NFL had thrived since the first national television contract in 1962. Owners like Jones and Snyder began harvesting unshared local revenue derived from luxury boxes, club seats, seat licenses, naming rights, sponsorships, and local advertising to circumvent the salary cap. They could afford to offer players huge signing bonuses, which resulted in wealthier clubs widening the gap between the haves and have-nots, and by 2005 estimates of unshared revenues ranged between 10 and 20 percent and amounted to more than $1 billion of income that was not shared among the owners or players.

"What are they going to do? Cut me?"

QUARTERBACK
BRETT FAVRE

The Green Bay Packers hosted more than 10,000 stockholders at their annual meeting in 2006 at Lambeau Field. (FROM THE GREEN BAY PRESS-GAZETTE ARCHIVES, REPRINTED BY PERMISSION)

On March 7, 2007, the NFL and its players' association announced that their collective bargaining agreement had been extended, ensuring labor peace through the completion of the 2010 season. "This agreement is not about one side winning or losing," Gene Upshaw, executive director of the NFL Players Association, said in a statement. "Ultimately, it is about what is best for the players, the owners and the fans of the National Football League. As caretakers of the game we have acted in the manner the founders intended. While they could not possibly have predicted the economic growth and revenue streams, they clearly saw the structure."

The deal immediately raised the salary cap by $7.5 million, to $102 million for the 2006 season. Additional terms of the agreement also resolved the growing financial disparity between teams by including a new revenue-sharing model that forced the league's top fifteen revenue-producing teams to contribute to a fund that would be dispersed to lower-revenue teams, guaranteeing that lower-revenue clubs could afford to comply with the 59.5 percent of total football revenues now earmarked for player salaries. In total, about $3 billion of the league's $5.2 billion revenue stream would now be shared equally among teams. Ironically, the Packers contributed an estimated $4 million to the NFL's revenue sharing pool that first year. "It seems odd that Green Bay, with the smallest market in the NFL, is paying into the fund," team treasurer Larry Weyers remarked, "but we've been able to do well here over the past several years."

Less than two weeks later, Paul Tagliabue announced he would step down as the NFL's commissioner. By resolving his last piece of unfinished business with the newest collective bargaining agreement, he had cemented his legacy of unprecedented labor peace during his seventeen years as commissioner. He had also positioned the league to continue thriving in a considerably more complex media environment than the one he had inherited back in 1989. When Tagliabue replaced Rozelle, the league took in $975 million in revenue and the average franchise was worth about $100 million. By 2006, those figures, calculated by *Forbes* magazine, were $6.2 billion and $898 million, respectively. The average franchise's value had risen at eleven times the growth rate of the S&P 500 since 1998 while Tagliabue was commissioner.

Soon after Tagliabue's announcement, the Packers' Bob Harlan, who had been the team's president since 1989, decided to retire. To ensure a smooth transition, he planned to hand the presidency to John Jones in May 2006 but would remain with the club as its chief executive officer until May 2007, at which time Jones would fulfill those responsibilities as well. "He was someone I thought would do well in our organization because of his background in Green Bay and with the league," Harlan said of his heir apparent. "It is my job to make sure that when I leave, the club is in good hands."

Since his arrival in 1999, Jones had been an essential part of the Packers' financial revitalization, but he would be again tasked with finding ways for the franchise to generate new revenue. Although the team had climbed to seventh of thirty-two NFL franchises in terms of revenue—the highest point the Packers had reached in more than a decade—their net income of $18 million was almost a 30 percent drop from the previous year, because Lambeau Field's revenue had plateaued. "The history of a new stadium is that revenue peaks up when you open and then trails off," team treasurer Larry Weyers explained. "There are a lot of deep pocketed owners out there and we have to continue to work hard to make sure we have the financial resources to put a winning team on the field."

Despite having the funds available to re-sign several established veterans, Thompson chose to replace them with younger, unproven players. His belief that a team's successful core can be built through the draft brought first-round selec-

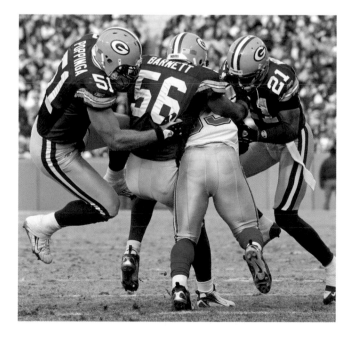

Cornerback Charles Woodson (21), along with Nick Barnett (56) and Brady Poppinga (51), helped the Packers to a 8-8 record in 2006. (COUR-TESY OF CHIP MANTHEY)

tion A. J. Hawk and second-rounder and wide receiver Greg Jennings to Green Bay. Thompson was not one to spend money arbitrarily on free agents, but when he did his decisions were motivated by more than making headlines. When the Packers signed cornerback Charles Woodson, whose eight injury-plagued years in Oakland generated criticism that Thompson was spending money on a player who was washed up, the Packers' general manager was quick to defend his decision. "He's a good football player, and he thinks he's a good player, which is a good thing in my opinion," Thompson said of Woodson. "He knows how to play the game."

Fielding the youngest roster in the NFL, the Mike McCarthy era in Green Bay began with a 26–0 shutout loss to the Bears at Lambeau Field. The Packers' 2006 season plummeted as their record dropped to 1–4, even though they were showing steady improvement. When a devastating 38–10 loss to the Jets left the Packers with a 4–8 record, fears of incurring a second consecutive 4–12 record began to mount. "That's when Mike McCarthy really stepped forward and proved himself," Harlan explained. "Mike knows what he's doing, he believes in what he's doing, and he has convinced the players that what he's doing is the right thing."

The Packers went on to win their last four games and by season's end were downright feared. In a season of highs and lows, they saved their best performance for the season finale in Chicago, despite having already been eliminated from the playoffs by mere percentage points. The Packers forced six turnovers during the 26–7 victory to finish the season with an 8–8 record, but as was the case the previous season, the big question loomed: Had Brett Favre played his last game in Green Bay? As he stepped off the Soldier Field gridiron, he waved to the crowd, in tears. "If this is my last game, I want to remember it," Favre hinted to reporters after the game. "It's tough. I love these guys. I love this game. What a great way to go out against a great football team. I couldn't ask for a better way to get out."

■ ■ ■

In the months that followed, Favre stayed silent about his potential return. When it was reported that the Packers refused to trade for veteran wide receiver Randy Moss during the NFL draft, anonymous sources claimed Favre's agent had called Thompson to request a trade. The situation simmered a few days later when McCarthy got Favre to admit he didn't want to play elsewhere. "The big thing with him is January football," McCarthy said of his veteran quarterback. "You look in his eyes, and you can see the wars he's been through, trying to get to more January football. It's all he cares about."

When Favre agreed to return for his sixteenth season in Green Bay, wide receiver Donald Driver explained, "He's not only our leader—he's the symbol of the franchise, of the whole town. There's a generation of fans in Green Bay who don't know this team ever existed without Brett."

Nevertheless, Favre's ongoing indecision brought about a keen awareness he was entering the twilight of his career in Green Bay. "It's going to be a sad, sad day when he walks down the tunnel at Lambeau Field and disappears for the last time because you don't recover from losing a Brett Favre very quickly," Harlan explained. "To lose his presence will be like losing a John Elway in Denver or a Dan Marino in Miami. Those men were icons in the game, and that's what Brett has meant to us."

The Packers' renewed stability at quarterback did little to settle the uncertainty of the franchise's future in the front office. A week before John Jones was supposed to succeed Bob Harlan in May, the organization announced that Harlan would delay his retirement as the team's chief executive officer. At first the reasons for the decision were vague. Peter Platten, speaking on behalf of the team's executive committee, would say only that it was "mutually beneficial for John to take a leave of absence while we continue our evaluation of the situation and collectively determine next steps."

Health concerns soon surfaced as the major reason. Back in June 2006 Jones had undergone heart surgery to correct a dissected aorta and had suffered a stroke that was reported to have affected his short-term memory and physical stamina, which affected some of his day-to-day management duties. Ultimately, the Packers bought out Jones in late July and named a search committee to find his replacement. In the interim, Harlan began his nineteenth and final season as the Packers' team president and CEO.

Under Harlan's leadership, the Packers continued to thrive as one of the NFL's healthiest franchises financially. The team's late surge in 2006 helped generate a net income of $22 million, a 22 percent increase from the previous season. The team was in the NFL's top ten in terms of revenue for the fourth consecutive year, ranking seventh, and therefore could afford to add $10 million to the Packers Franchise Preservation Fund, putting the total at $125.5 million. Among the team's largest revenue sources were its Pro Shop, Lambeau Field Atrium, and marketing department, which together generated $40.7 million that year. Back in 1993 the Packers' retail operation had consisted of a four-hundred-square-foot store with one hundred different products, five employees, and $350,000 in annual sales. By 2007 the retail operations, which included the Pro Shop at Lambeau Field, Internet sales, and a mail-order catalog, encompassed eight thousand square feet in four stadium stores and employed ten managers and one hundred part-time employees. Sales totaled $17.5 million, and according to team officials, the Packers Pro Shop was the top-selling single retail operation in the NFL, selling more than six thousand Packers items.

The Packers saw their tumultuous offseason culminate with the loss of running back Ahman Green to free agency. Green had been the cornerstone of the team's rushing attack since 2000, eclipsing 1,000 yards six of the past seven seasons. Without a prominent successor to replace him, the Packers relied on Brett Favre more than ever at the beginning of the 2007 season. By season's end, he had started 252 consecutive games at quarterback, making him the only player to start every game for the same team since September 27, 1992. During that time, Favre overcame several injuries to keep his streak alive. He played with a separated left shoulder in 1992, a deep thigh bruise in 1993, a severely bruised left hip in 1994, right elbow tendonitis in 2000, a left foot sprain in 2000, a sprained knee ligament

> "There's a generation of fans in Green Bay who don't know this team ever existed without Brett."
>
> —WIDE RECEIVER DONALD DRIVER

Mark Murphy (right) was named Bob Harlan's (left) successor as the Packers' team president on December 3, 2007, and formally assumed the position on January 28, 2008. (FROM THE GREEN BAY PRESS-GAZETTE ARCHIVES, REPRINTED BY PERMISSION)

in 2002, and a broken thumb in 2003. "Initially, you'll be remembered by statistics, how many yards you throw, touchdowns and things like that," Favre said about his pending legacy. "But in the long run what I hope and what people will remember me by is durability and wins—which is the bottom line in this business, especially for a quarterback."

In 2007 Favre added to his legendary status in Green Bay after engineering several game-winning drives and last-second heroics, including an 82-yard game-winning touchdown pass to wide receiver Greg Jennings on the first play of overtime against the Broncos. As the season progressed, running back Ryan Grant—whom Thompson acquired from the Giants for a sixth-round draft pick—emerged as one of the NFL's most productive running backs, finishing the season with 956 rushing yards despite starting just ten games. "When he got the opportunity, he made the most of it," Favre said of Grant. "It sure turned us from one-dimensional into something totally different."

The Packers captured the NFC North Division title with a 13–3 record. By securing the NFC's second-best record, Green Bay earned a first-round bye before facing the Seattle Seahawks in the divisional playoff round. Inside the snow globe that was Lambeau Field that Saturday evening, the Seahawks got off to an early 14–0 lead after Ryan Grant fumbled twice on the Packers' first three offensive plays. As the snow continued to fall, Favre and Grant seemed impervious to the conditions. The quarterback tossed three touchdowns and no interceptions, while the

Running back Ryan Grant made up for two early fumbles in the 2007 divisional playoff game against the Seahawks by rushing for 201 yards and three touchdowns. (AP PHOTO/CHARLIE NEIBERGALL)

Brett Favre raised his hands triumphantly after throwing three touchdown passes in the snow at Lambeau Field in the 42–20 victory against the Seahawks. (AP PHOTO/MIKE ROEMER, FILE)

running back gained 201 yards on the ground and scored the Packers' three other touchdowns in the 42–20 victory. Green Bay was now just one victory away from reaching Super Bowl XLII. "Did I ever think we'd be in this position?" Favre asked after the win against Seattle. "In the past, I knew every game what would work and how'd we win. Now I really have no idea week to week what's going to go well and what isn't. I'm thrilled about it, but it is a strange year. I'm just riding the wave."

The Packers found their road to the Super Bowl routed through Lambeau Field after the wild-card New York Giants knocked off the top-seeded Cowboys. A week later, the NFC championship game was played in dangerous conditions. The temperature at kickoff was minus-one with a windchill of twenty-three below zero, making it the second-coldest game played in Lambeau Field's history, behind only the infamous Ice Bowl. In the game's first quarter, the weather didn't seem to affect Giants quarterback Eli Manning, who engineered two scoring drives to give New York an early

6–0 lead on a pair of field goals. After Koren Robinson's fumble of the ensuing kick-off left the Packers on their own 10-yard line, Favre, with his back up against his own end zone, connected with wide receiver Donald Driver for a 90-yard touchdown pass that gave Green Bay an early 7–6 lead. But the Packers' 10–6 halftime advantage was short-lived, and the Giants retook the lead, 13–10, at the start of the third quarter. Moments later, the Packers' Tramon Williams, seemingly trapped along the left sideline, cut right and returned the kickoff 49 yards to the New York 39. A few plays later, Favre froze the Giants' defense on a brilliant play-fake that sprung tight end Donald Lee free in the back of the end zone for a 12-yard touchdown reception and a 17–13 Green Bay lead. Early in the fourth quarter, Green Bay kicker Mason Crosby tied the game at 20 before both defenses buckled down. With a Super Bowl berth hanging in the balance, the game came down to Giants kicker Lawrence Tynes, who hadn't attempted a big fourth-quarter field goal all season. With 6:49 remaining, he missed a 43-yard attempt. Then as the game clock expired, he shanked a 36-yarder, sending the game into overtime.

The Packers' defensive unit, which featured Kabeer Gbaja-Biamila (94), Nick Barnett (56), and Corey Williams (99), kept a tight grasp around the Giants' Eli Manning. (COURTESY OF CHIP MANTHEY)

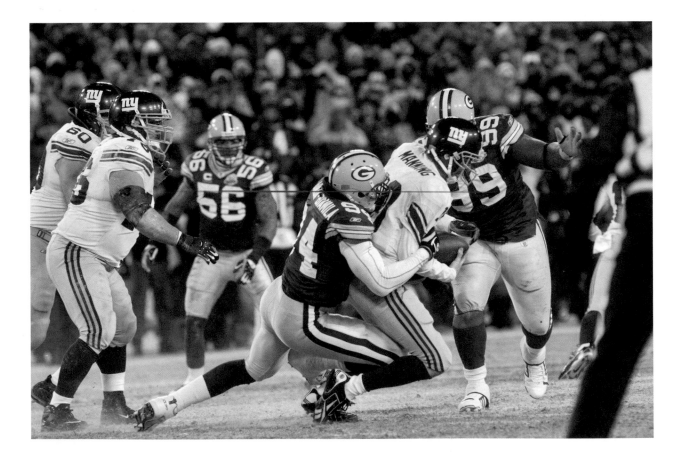

The Packers won the coin toss to start the sudden-death session. On their second play of overtime, Favre threw an errant pass that was picked off by the Giants' Corey Webster, who returned the interception to Green Bay's 34-yard line. Four plays later, Tynes nailed a 47-yard kick to win the game 23–20, giving the Giants the improbable win to become the first NFC team to ever reach the Super Bowl by winning three straight playoff games on the road. It also marked the end of the Packers' storybook season. "Any season, when you're together for 180 straight days and then all of a sudden, bang, it's over, it's a shock to your system," running back coach Edgar Bennett said of the loss.

At his season-ending news conference, Mike McCarthy was blunt, giving no excuses for the Packers' failure to make it to the Super Bowl. "We did not play our best football in a time when we needed to play our best football," he explained. When asked what changes the Packers could make to ensure that it wouldn't happen again, he replied, "We've shown in the last two years we've been here we're not afraid to change if it's going to make our football team better." The upcoming offseason would test the validity of his statement to the franchise's core.

Brett Favre's last pass as quarterback for the Green Bay Packers was intercepted in overtime of the 2007 NFC championship game and helped secure the Giants' 23–20 victory. (COURTESY OF CHIP MANTHEY)

SECURING the LEGACY

The disappointment Green Bay endured after falling short of the Super Bowl in 2008 didn't dissipate as winter melted into spring. At the same time, quarterback Brett Favre—whose ill-advised throw in the NFC championship game's sudden-death overtime period became the decisive play in the Packers' heartbreaking 23–20 loss—wrestled with his future. When he had flirted with retirement, he walked off the field to fans chanting "One more year." After the sudden defeat to the eventual Super Bowl–champion Giants, Favre—along with many Packers fans—was left stunned and silenced. Over the next forty-four days, Mike McCarthy reached out to Favre almost once a week to discuss the quarterback's future. The Packers' head coach had engaged in a similar process the previous offseason when Favre contemplated retirement, but this year the quarterback's demeanor was different. Insisting he was "at peace" with his decision, Brett Favre announced his retirement from professional football on March 4. "I've given everything I possibly can give to this organization, to the game of football, and I don't think I've got anything left to give," Favre confessed two days later during a tear-filled press conference. "And that's it. It's been a great career for me, and it's over. As hard as that is for me to say, it's over."

After sixteen seasons in Green Bay, Brett Favre was not only the face of the Packers franchise but also professional football's most recognizable ambassador. He was leaving the game as its all-time leader in touchdown passes (442), completions (5,377), attempts (8,758), yards (61,555), and wins (160). He had won a Super Bowl and three MVP awards with the Packers, but his most enduring legacy was as the model of toughness, starting an NFL-record 275 consecutive games that included the playoffs. Although he earned roughly $101 million playing professional football,

Head coach Mike McCarthy hoisted the Lombardi Trophy after the Packers won Super Bowl XLV. (WISCONSIN STATE JOURNAL)

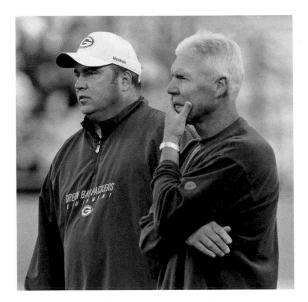

Packers head coach Mike McCarthy (left) and general manager Ted Thompson (right) prepared for the 2008 season without Brett Favre. (FROM THE GREEN BAY PRESS-GAZETTE ARCHIVES, REPRINTED BY PERMISSION)

Favre often looked as if he was playing just for the fun of it. "I'm not going to sit here like other players maybe have said in the past that I won't miss it," he admitted to reporters at the press conference. "Because I will. But I just don't think I can give anything else, aside from the three hours on Sundays. And in football, you can't do that."

With Favre's retirement official, the Packers committed to Aaron Rodgers, who had spent the past three years as the legend's understudy. "I got to learn the offense, study the offense and become an expert on our offense," Rodgers remarked after the 2008 season. "So when my time did come, I expected to play well."

In 2008 Rodgers provided the Packers with a solid future, but without Favre Green Bay went from being a Super Bowl contender to being a team in transition—far from the finished product Ted Thompson had envisioned when he arrived in 2005. So Thompson continued implementing his team-building philosophy of stockpiling talent through the draft. "I'm not opposed to moving up [in the draft order], but I do value draft picks," Thompson explained before choosing wide receiver Jordy Nelson in the second round, tight end Jermichael Finley in the third, and reserve quarterback Matt Flynn and wide receiver Brett Swain in the seventh. "I think they're great long-term investments for the organization."

When critics ridiculed him for not signing any prominent free agents during recent offseasons, Thompson kept quiet. "There are a lot of general managers and coaches around the league who are not maybe as warm as people would like them to be. It's almost a bashfulness on Ted's part," Harlan remarked. "It's his nature. I knew exactly what I was getting when I got him. I knew what his personality would be like and how he would work with the football operation."

With Thompson, Harlan was confident the Packers' football operation was in good hands, and he retired on January 28, 2008, to become the organization's chairman emeritus. Back in November the organization had hired Mark Murphy as Harlan's successor to become president and chief executive officer of the Packers. The former NFL player and athletic director at Northwestern University was inheriting one of the most coveted jobs in the NFL and a franchise worth more than $1 billion according to *Forbes* magazine. The respected financial periodical ranked the Packers sixteenth among the NFL's thirty-two franchises but expected the ranking to dip in the post-Favre era, because his jersey sales alone had helped push marketing revenue up 23 percent to more than $50 million. *Forbes* also reported that the Packers had recorded a net income of $23.3 million following the 2007 season, almost a 6 percent increase from the previous year. But it wasn't as big as team officials had hoped. "We had a good year, but not as strong as you might have anticipated," Murphy explained. "There are some trends that are really concerning us."

The team's profits from football operations fell 37 percent from 2006 to $21.4 million due to rising player costs. The average NFL player's salary had reached $1.5 million, pushing total operating expenses from $184 million to $220 million in the past fiscal year. In hopes of expanding its financial footprint, the team purchased fifteen acres adjacent to Lambeau Field with plans to develop it for retail and entertainment ventures. "We're looking at ways to generate additional revenue," Murphy explained. "We knew [buying the land] would be a good investment as we look to the future."

The Packers were placing their gridiron future squarely atop the shoulders of Aaron Rodgers, who had already shown glimpses of his potential. "I think we saw it a year before he was starting," tackle Chad Clifton said, recalling Rodgers' 2007 performance in Dallas. "Brett went out [with an injury] and Aaron came in. You could see then he had the poise." Although the Packers lost that game, Rodgers completed eighteen of twenty-six passes for 201 yards and one touchdown. More important, he won a lot of locker room respect. As wide receiver Greg Jennings recalled, "I think guys understood that this guy is something special."

> "I think guys understood that this guy [Rodgers] is something special."
>
> —WIDE RECEIVER GREG JENNINGS

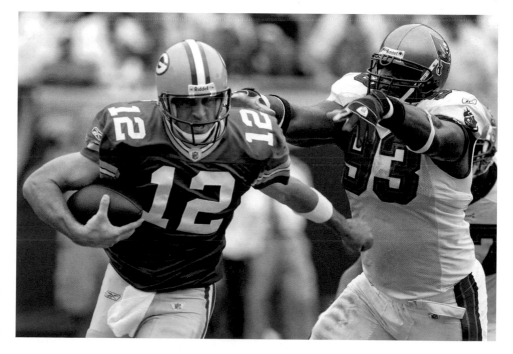

Aaron Rodgers found himself being chased by aggressive defenders and by critics who felt he was ill-prepared to replace Brett Favre as the Packers' next franchise quarterback.
(AP PHOTO/REINHOLD MATAY)

By July the Packers were confident Aaron Rodgers was their quarterback for the future. Meanwhile, Brett Favre had become restless, just four months into his announced retirement, and he expressed to head coach Mike McCarthy a renewed interest in returning to the Packers as their starting quarterback. This time team officials weren't receptive to his sudden change of heart. Favre's desire to return seemed only to strengthen as the Packers' commitment to Rodgers remained unshaken. In early August the Packers offered Favre the opportunity to compete for the team's starting quarterback position—but for the first time in over a decade wouldn't guarantee it was his. In response, the legendary quarterback took his private conversations with the club into the very public forum of national news programs to plead his case. That's when Mike McCarthy decided that Favre couldn't get past the emotional wounds created in recent weeks. "The train has left the station, whatever analogy you want," he told reporters about his "brutally honest" conversations with Favre, adding "if we can't get past things that have happened, I have to keep the train moving."

By the time Favre submitted his reinstatement papers to the league, his relationship with the Packers had deteriorated beyond repair, leaving the team with only one option: to trade him, which they did, to the New York Jets for a conditional fourth-round draft pick. Favre's tumultuous divorce from the Packers would now define Ted Thompson's tenure in Green Bay. Thompson had stayed silent during most of the incident, but he became the scapegoat for impassioned fans, angering season-ticket holders and blustery critics who second-guessed the direction the team would now take. Harlan put the situation into perspective: "When we went through the Favre situation, it was just a love affair with Brett Favre. Anybody who would have [cut ties with Favre] would have been in trouble."

Thompson remained steadfast despite the mounting criticism. "I think in terms of what's best for the team right this second," he explained. "You would like for all of them to agree with you most of the time, but they're not, that's not the way it works. And you can't run the team trying to be a politician. You can't try to get votes. You have to do what you have to do."

Throughout Favre's messy departure from Green Bay, Aaron Rodgers never spoke ill of Favre or the situation. Whether he was facing reporters pressuring him with questions about replacing the legend or isolated fans yelling insults at him through the cyclone fence during training camp, he remained poised. "I just think it's been part of my story—waiting for my opportunity," Rodgers remarked. "And trust in God that my time was coming, knowing at the same time that when it does come I have to make the most of it."

When Rodgers was introduced to the Lambeau Field crowd before the Packers' 2008 season opener, he was greeted by 71,004 fans with the kind of delirium that

> "You can't run the team trying to be a politician. You can't try to get votes. You have to do what you have to do."
>
> —GENERAL MANAGER TED THOMPSON

Ted Thompson (left) and former Packers general manager Ron Wolf (right) had a lot to smile about during 2008's training camp. (FROM THE GREEN BAY PRESS-GAZETTE ARCHIVES, REPRINTED BY PERMISSION)

in the past had been reserved for his predecessor. His debut resulted in a 24–19 season-opening victory over the Minnesota Vikings, extinguishing any doubts that he was capable of replacing such an icon. Rodgers continued to play smart football throughout the season, and the Packers entered their bye week with a 4–3 record. His command of the offense had him finishing fourth in the league in passing yards (4,038), fourth in passing touchdowns (28), and sixth in passer rating (93.8), having thrown only thirteen interceptions. But after winning just two of their last nine games, the Packers finished the season with a disappointing 6–10 record, losing seven of those ten by 4 points or fewer. Their defense, despite benefiting from seven interceptions apiece from Charles Woodson and Nick Collins, and Aaron Kampman's 9.5 sacks, was unable to come up with important stops at critical times. As a result, McCarthy gutted his defensive staff following the season finale in a twenty-four-hour period unlike any other in the Packers' long history. "I mean, it's shocking," defensive tackle Ryan Pickett said. "I never thought there'd be this many changes. But going from one of the top defenses like we did to this year, that's pretty horrible." The move proved that if there was one thing Mike McCarthy wasn't satisfied with, it was being average.

■   ■   ■

As the 2009 season approached, the U.S. economy was in the grips of a major economic recession. However, the NFL remained unscathed as revenues from the league's thirty-two teams rose 7 percent to $7.6 billion that year due to the league's latest television deals with CBS, Fox, NBC, and ESPN, which combined to pay each team $94 million for the 2008 season. Ticket and concession revenue increased as well, providing an average of $59 million per team.

In summer 2009 the Packers released their long-awaited financial report for the preceding fiscal year—a report that drew a lot of attention and interest in the ongoing labor dispute between the NFL and the NFLPA. "The former Executive Director of the NFLPA, the late Gene Upshaw, used to treat the Packer financials like the Magna Carta, saying that if tiny Green Bay—the smallest NFL market—could show profit, imagine how well the rest of the league fares?" former vice president of player finance Andrew Brandt noted.

The economic downturn did affect the team's ledger, resulting in a modest net income of $4 million following the 2008 season. It was the lowest since the completion of Lambeau Field's renovation and a dramatic drop from the $23.3 million recorded a year earlier. "We were still able to turn a small profit, but we are no different than many other businesses that have been impacted by the economy," Mark Murphy explained. "We've been able to weather it okay. We have a strong foundation here and have been able to continue to maintain the quality of our football team."

The two biggest areas of impact were the team's investments and marketing, which included merchandise sales in its Pro Shop. Murphy said the Packers lost $16 million from the organization's investment portfolio (a mixture of stocks, bonds, and real estate) after making $8 million the previous fiscal year. The team didn't release specific Pro Shop sales figures, but overall revenue from sales and marketing, including retail sales, was $43.7 million, down from $50.2 million. With total operating expenses jumping 4 percent to $227.8 million and player expenses increasing 11 percent to $138.7 million, "when you really dig in and look at the numbers, it shows the issues," Murphy explained. "Just the last two years, our player costs have gone up $14 million—at a much higher rate than our revenues."

As the only NFL team to release financial information publicly, the Packers were held up by the league as a symbol of what was wrong with the current collective bargaining agreement. The trend of salaries exceeding revenues had prompted the Packers' leadership and fellow NFL owners to unanimously vote to opt out of their collective bargaining agreement with the players union a year earlier. Although the agreement would remain in effect through the conclusion of the 2010 season, NFL commissioner Roger Goodell, who succeeded Paul Tagliabue in August 2006, hoped a new deal could be negotiated that would allow the owners to retain a larger share of overall revenue. "It is extremely important that we protect the mechanisms the NFL has in place today," Murphy explained. "The salary cap is very important and it allows us to compete against teams in much larger markets. The system does need to be tweaked a bit and that is what we are working on."

If a new agreement between owners and players wasn't reached before the start of the 2011 season, the Packers were prepared for a potential lockout or players' strike, able to rely on the Packers Preservation Fund created several years earlier to ensure the franchise had the necessary funds to stay solvent in trying economic times. (Because of the Packers' modest profit in 2008, they didn't contribute any money to the fund, maintaining its balance at $127.5 million.) Another factor in the Packers' favor in the event of a work stoppage was its relative lack of debt compared to other NFL teams, especially those that had built new stadiums in recent years. "I think that's one of our real advantages, and one of the main reasons we've been so successful," Murphy remarked. "We give football operations, and Ted in particular, the resources they need to be successful. Even though our profits were down this year, we're not reducing in any way the support we provide them."

Nevertheless, following a 6–10 season and the Favre drama, Ted Thompson was under a microscope during the 2009 NFL draft. His previous drafts had provided a mixed bag of results, but that did little to deter him from his philosophy. "He says he's going to take the top guy on the draft board and he does," Harlan explained. "He told me one time, 'I know some people are going to criticize us when we do this,' but he said, 'My job is to build the entire team. If the top guy on my board is a wide receiver and we're deep at wide receiver and I pass him up, to dip to somebody at another position where we have a need and in the first game we lose two wide receivers to injuries, I'm going to kick myself the entire year for not taking that guy.'"

With the ninth pick in the first round, Thompson drafted nose tackle B. J. Raji, considered by most experts to be the second-highest-rated defensive player in the draft. When a potential impact player still remained late in the first round, Thompson traded three picks to the Patriots to move up to take linebacker Clay Matthews III. "I thought, 'I can't believe Ted Thompson would ever try something like that. It was a huge move for this franchise,'" Harlan explained. "I don't know if we've had many better first rounds than what he did that day."

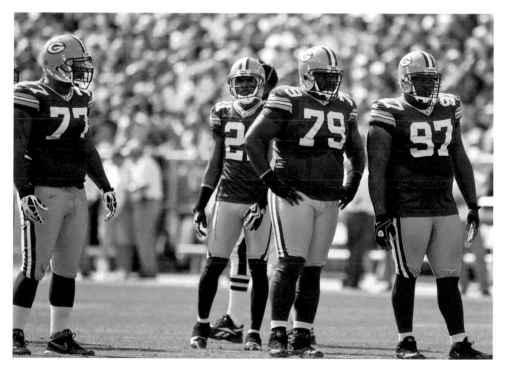

The 2009 Packers featured one of the NFL's best defenses, behind an aggressive scheme initiated by defensive coordinator Dom Capers and executed by Cullen Jenkins (77), Charles Woodson (21), Ryan Pickett (79), and Johnny Jolly (97). (COURTESY OF CHIP MANTHEY)

With the additions of Raji and Matthews, the Packers defense improved to second best in the NFL by season's end. Defensive coordinator Dom Capers's aggressive defensive schemes attacked the ball and forced opponents to make mistakes, resulting in the squad's most impressive statistic for the year: an NFL-best takeaway differential of plus-24. On offense, the only thing that seemed to keep the team from scoring on every drive was its depleted offensive line that allowed Rodgers to be sacked fifty times. When the regular season concluded, the Packers were playing their best football. Their 11–5 record earned them a playoff berth as a wild-card team, and many thought they had the makings of an improbable Super Bowl contender.

After winning seven of their last eight regular-season games, the Packers were heavy favorites in Arizona against the defending NFC champion Cardinals. But on the game's first play from scrimmage, Rodgers threw an uncharacteristic interception that led to the Cardinals' first touchdown. On the Packers' next possession, wide receiver Donald Driver had the ball ripped away, and less than six minutes into the game the Packers found themselves trailing 14–0. Despite being behind 31–10 early in the third quarter, Rodgers and the resilient Packers mounted an epic comeback. When the shootout ended in regulation, the game was tied 45–45. But on the third play of overtime, Cardinals cornerback Michael Adams hit Aaron Rodgers's arm as Rodgers tried to avoid a sack. When the ball popped free and bounced off Rodgers's foot, it landed in the arms of linebacker Karlos Dansby, who raced the 17 yards for the game-winning touchdown and a Cardinals 51–45 victory. "If you'd have told me

Aaron Rodgers (getting tackled) and the Packers suffered a devastating playoff loss to the Cardinals despite a valiant second-half comeback. (FROM THE GREEN BAY PRESS-GAZETTE ARCHIVES, REPRINTED BY PERMISSION)

this morning our offense is going to score 45 points," defensive end Cullen Jenkins remarked, "I'd be like, 'Yeah, we're gonna win.' We just couldn't stop them. For whatever reason, we couldn't get it done. So we get to sit at home now and watch the playoffs."

Three days after the Packers' stunning exit from the postseason, cornerback Charles Woodson, whose nine interceptions and four forced fumbles were career highs, was named the NFL's Defensive Player of the Year. "To get this award, I've done everything an individual can do," Woodson said, knowing the honor paled in comparison to his ultimate career goal. "I'm just going to keep taking shots until I get back to the Super Bowl—and win it."

ABOVE, LEFT: Rookie linebacker Clay Matthews III became an immediate impact player for the Packers in 2009, with ten sacks and three fumble recoveries, one for a touchdown. (COURTESY OF CHIP MANTHEY)

ABOVE, RIGHT: Cornerback Charles Woodson (21) earned NFL Player of the Year honors after intercepting nine passes, scoring three touchdowns, and forcing four fumbles in 2009. (COURTESY OF CHIP MANTHEY)

LEFT: Wide receiver Greg Jennings enjoyed his second consecutive 1,000-plus-yard season (1,292 yards in 2008 and 1,113 yards in 2009) while also scoring thirteen touchdowns over those two seasons. (COURTESY OF CHIP MANTHEY)

∎ ∎ ∎

As the Packers distanced themselves from their playoff loss to the Cardinals, there was a feeling of genuine optimism throughout Green Bay. "Every year as a head coach, you have exit interviews, and that Monday after the Arizona loss . . . it was different," head coach Mike McCarthy recalled. "I went home, and I was actually at peace with the conversations I had with so many of our players. Our players were disappointed, but they were excited because they knew they had a good team."

As the next football season approached, the 2010 squad and the 1996 Super Bowl championship team were being compared extensively. Both had come off 11–5 records for the previous season. McCarthy, like Holmgren, had just completed his fourth year as head coach. And quarterback Aaron Rodgers, like Favre, was twenty-six years old. However, critics were quick to claim that Ted Thompson had failed to properly fill the holes on his 2010 roster by adding several prominent free agents as his mentor Ron Wolf had done prior to the start of the 1996 season. When those same critics prognosticated that would be the Packers' undoing, Thompson was quick to retort: "I disagree. I think we got guys that can come in and make an impact."

From the beginning of his tenure in Green Bay, Thompson placed tremendous value on draft choices. His approach had required patience, which some shortsighted fans and critics were unwilling to offer. What they didn't account for was that,

The 2010 Packers never trailed an opponent by more than 7 points all season. They also chased down their NFC North opponents—including Clay Matthews III sacking the Vikings' Brett Favre— during a 10-6 campaign. (WISCONSIN STATE JOURNAL)

The Packers refused to use injuries as an excuse, with role players such as John Kuhn (30) and Tom Crabtree (83) becoming key contributors throughout the season. (FROM THE GREEN BAY PRESS-GAZETTE ARCHIVES, REPRINTED BY PERMISSION)

barring any unforeseen disasters, Green Bay was projected to have twenty-one of its twenty-two preferred starters back for the upcoming season. "We're a better football team in 2010 today than we have been in the past in my opinion," McCarthy said before the start of training camp. "I really like the way our football team looks on paper."

The Packers also looked good on paper financially. Their revenue for the 2009 season was an all-time high of $258 million. However, their annual profits from operations fell from $20.1 million the previous year to $9.8 million. "I think a lot of people are looking at these numbers," team president Mark Murphy said. "We want to be very fair and balanced, but I do think it shows some of the issues with the current system."

For years, NFL owners had showcased the Packers organization, and its publicly released financial figures, as the poster child for why their agreement with the Players Association was no longer sustainable. According to Murphy, "It's really the continuing growth of our player's salaries. For the past four consecutive years, player costs have grown at twice the rate as what the team was bringing in."

Despite the foreboding financial forecast, the Packers' value as a franchise remained steady at $1.02 billion in 2010, making them the fourteenth most valuable in the NFL, according to *Forbes* magazine. In Green Bay, their value was even more evident, especially after the most comprehensive study of the economic impact of both the Packers franchise and the redeveloped Lambeau Field in almost a decade was released in September. The report estimated that for each game hosted at Lambeau Field, the Packers generated almost $12.3 million in economic impact for the community. In 2009 alone the franchise was estimated to have brought $282 million into the community and to have supported 2,560 jobs.

All of Green Bay was abuzz during the preseason, with the Packers a popular pick for the Super Bowl. But a staggering 3–3 start to the regular season and a roster hampered with fifteen players on the injured reserve list—including six starters—soon quelled any talk of the Packers winning their thirteenth NFL championship. Such adversity would have doomed most teams, but the Packers' ability to replace linebacker Nick Barnett with Desmond Bishop, cornerback Al Harris with Sam Shields, safety Morgan Burnett with Charlie Peprah, tackle Mark Tauscher with Bryan Bulaga, and linebacker Brad Jones with rookie Frank Zombo defined

Former U.S. president and Georgia native Jimmy Carter shook hands with Packers president Mark Murphy prior to kickoff of the Packers versus Falcons regular-season contest at the Georgia Dome in 2010. (AP PHOTO/JOHN BAZEMORE)

"We'll play anybody, anytime, anywhere. Trust me. We'll be ready when we get to Philadelphia."

—HEAD COACH
MIKE MCCARTHY

how the team handled adversity. "I think the guys upstairs have done an outstanding job of bringing in guys with high character," wide receiver Greg Jennings remarked, "but at the same time guys that can get it done on Sundays."

Because of Thompson's patient approach to building the Packers' roster, it began blossoming at the top and budding at the bottom as the season progressed. It seemed whenever a blossom fell and a player was lost to injury, there was a bud ready to bloom and take its place. "Success in the NFL is obviously a multi-pronged strategy, but there does appear to be an operational philosophy that endures," Brandt explained. "Drafting well, developing young players, and having a deep and talented infrastructure coming through the pipeline are the most proven plan for sustained success."

The Packers also benefited from the parity that was alive and well in the NFL in 2010. For the first time since 1959, every NFL team had lost at least two of its first eight games. As a result, the Packers were still alive in late December, needing to win their final two regular-season games at Lambeau Field just to make the playoffs. They crushed the Giants 45–17 and followed up with a 10–3 win over the rival Bears, giving them a 10–6 regular-season record and the NFC's final playoff berth. "We've had a very difficult road we've traveled this year and we've met every challenge," McCarthy said of the Packers' having to play all their playoff games on the road as the NFC's sixth seed. "We feel very good about our chances. We'll play anybody, anytime, anywhere. Trust me. We'll be ready when we get to Philadelphia."

Regardless of how far the Packers advanced into the postseason, it wouldn't be a moneymaking proposition. All playoff ticket revenue went to the NFL. Unless a team hosted a playoff game and made money from concessions, parking, and merchandise sales, its only game-day income was from NFL reimbursements. In 2010 division-winning teams received $650,000 from the league to offset expenses for the first round of playoff games. Wild-card teams got $590,000. In the second round, each team would get $650,000, and in the conference championship round each received $1.01 million. The Super Bowl winner would receive just over $4.1 million, and the runner-up got nearly $2.9 million. If a wild-card team were to win the Super Bowl, it would receive $6.4 million in total. But according to the Packers' vice president of administration and general counsel, Jason Wied, "we spend more than we are reimbursed, and we are happy to pay it because it means we are in the playoffs. I would say it's a fine price to pay for that."

Before the Packers arrived in Philadelphia, McCarthy emphasized to his players the goal of playing sixteen strong quarters of football—with the final four being Super Bowl XLV. The Packers' defense rose to the occasion against the Eagles, making critical plays at critical times. They contained quarterback Michael Vick with the right mix of playmakers, blitzes, and coverages, sacking him three times and limiting him to just 33 yards on the ground. Thanks to Dom Capers's strategy to confine Vick, "he didn't hurt us that much," cornerback Tramon Williams said. "That was the main thing. The D-line did a great job holding their lanes and kind of limiting what he could do."

The Packers' offense, which was criticized for being one-dimensional, handed the ball off to rookie James Starks, who ran for 123 yards in the game after amassing just 101 yards all season. At quarterback, Aaron Rodgers played mistake-free football, leading the Packers to a late 21–16 advantage. But he was helpless as the game's final moments wound down with Vick and the Eagles driving for the game-winning score. Deep in Green Bay territory and with just thirty-three seconds to play, Vick threw a spiral toward the end zone that cornerback Tramon Williams jumped in front of to intercept, securing the Packers' victory. "That interception saved our postseason hopes," defensive end Cullen Jenkins told reporters after the game.

Running back James Starks (below) rushed for 123 yards against the Eagles, and cornerback Tramon Williams (below, right) intercepted a Michael Vick pass in the game's final moments to secure the Packers' 21–16 wild-card game victory in Philadelphia. (BOTH PHOTOS FROM THE GREEN BAY PRESS-GAZETTE ARCHIVES, REPRINTED BY PERMISSION)

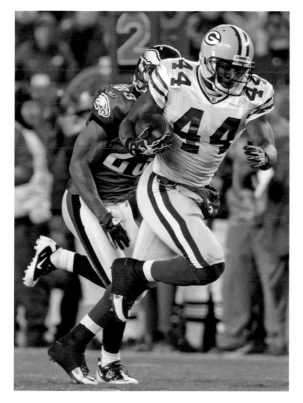

As the NFC's lowest seed in the playoffs, Green Bay faced the top-seeded Falcons in Atlanta. The Packers had to overcome an inherent disadvantage playing at the Georgia Dome, since the number one seeds in the NFC had an 18–2 record at home in the divisional round of the playoffs. The Falcons, who had twelve days of rest since their season finale, jumped out to an early lead by taking advantage of two huge Green Bay mistakes in the first half: a lost fumble by wide receiver Greg Jennings that was converted for a score and a 102-yard kickoff return for a touchdown that put Atlanta ahead 14–7 early in the second quarter. Looking very much at home, however, the Packers stayed focused and retaliated against a proud Atlanta defense. As the Falcons blitzed relentlessly, Rodgers completed thirty-one of thirty-six passes for 366 yards, connected for three touchdown passes, and ran for another. Green Bay scored 35 consecutive points, including Tramon Williams's 70-yard interception return for a touchdown on the final play of the first half. The Packers' stunning 48–21 rout of the Falcons marked the first time in history that they won two playoff games on the road. "You never feel invincible," fullback John Kuhn explained. "I won't say we're world-beaters. But it's confidence. It's that snowball effect."

Green Bay's dominating win against the Falcons meant they were headed to Chicago to face the Bears in the NFC championship game. Never in their ninety-year-old rivalry and 181 previous meetings had the stakes been higher. The game had an added sense of urgency for several Packers players who still felt their defeat to the Giants in the 2007 NFC championship game was a lost opportunity. "That's one thing you have to take with you, the feeling you had or we had coming off that field at home and seeing another team celebrating on our field, on our turf," wide receiver Greg Jennings told reporters before the game. "It's been three years since we've been in this position and we're fortunate to be in this situation and we'll try to make the best of it."

In the week leading up to the game, Chicago prepared for a championship party that included a promise from President Barack Obama that if the Bears won, he'd attend Super Bowl XLV in person. The Windy City fervor was soon silenced when Aaron Rodgers marched the Packers downfield on a seven-play, 84-yard opening drive that ended with him scrambling

Quarterback Aaron Rodgers eluded Atlanta defenders all evening, throwing for 366 yards and three touchdowns while rushing for another in the 48-21 NFC divisional playoff victory. (FROM THE GREEN BAY PRESS-GAZETTE ARCHIVES, REPRINTED BY PERMISSION)

The Packers' defense sacked Falcons quarterback Matt Ryan (2) five times, intercepted him once, and recovered two fumbles while allowing just 194 yards of total offense. (FROM THE GREEN BAY PRESS-GAZETTE ARCHIVES, REPRINTED BY PERMISSION)

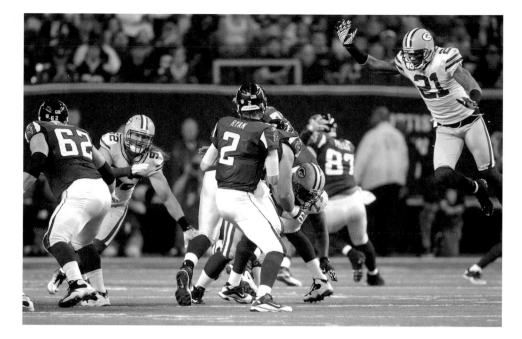

> ## "I don't get paid to tackle, but that was probably one of my better plays of the game."
>
> —QUARTERBACK
> AARON RODGERS

for a touchdown. Early in the second quarter, James Starks extended the Packers' lead to 14–0 on a 4-yard run. Maintaining that lead through halftime, Green Bay's defense forced a three-and-out to begin the second half before Rodgers went back to marching the offense down the field. On third and goal with the Packers poised to put the game away, Rodgers instead tossed the ball to Bears linebacker Brian Urlacher, who had a clear path to return the interception for a touchdown. But when Rodgers chased him down near midfield, he managed to trip him up and prevent the touchdown. "I don't get paid to tackle," Rodgers remarked to reporters after the game, "but that was probably one of my better plays of the game."

On the ensuing set of downs, the Packers preserved the shutout, but to the Bears' credit, they never gave up. Even when starting quarterback Jay Cutler exited in the third quarter with a knee injury and backup Todd Collins was pulled for being ineffective, Chicago rallied behind third-stringer Caleb Hanie, who generated an improbable touchdown drive early in the fourth quarter. With six minutes left in the game and the Packers holding onto their 14–7 lead, defensive coordinator Dom Capers made his fateful call when Chicago faced third and 5 at its 15-yard line. "B. J. has dropped a handful of times this season, maybe five or six," Capers said about the play, which resulted in nose tackle B. J. Raji jumping in front of Hanie's pass and returning the interception for a touchdown. "For once it worked the way we drew it up."

The defensive score gave Green Bay a 21–7 lead, but the Bears rallied with a quick touchdown in response. Just when it mattered most, the Packers defense rose to the occasion. With Chicago down to its last play on fourth and 5 at Green Bay's 27-yard line, undrafted rookie cornerback Sam Shields picked off his second pass of the day, thwarting the Bears' last chance to tie the game. The Packers and their fans claimed a 21–14 victory and ultimate bragging rights over their foes to the south. "Main thing is, we got the win," wide receiver James Jones said of the Packers moving on to Super Bowl XLV. "That's all that matters."

In the Packers' locker room after the game, cornerback Charles Woodson addressed more than eighty teammates, coaches, and administrators about how he felt slighted by Obama's promise to attend the Super Bowl only if the Bears advanced. "The President don't want to come watch us at the Super Bowl. Guess what. . . . We'll go see him!" Woodson stated, alluding to the Super Bowl winner's traditional trip to the White House.

When the Green Bay Packers arrived in Dallas as the NFC's representative for Super Bowl XLV, they had defied the odds with a roster that included thirty-one players missing a total of 206 games. "This was the path that was chosen for us, and I think it's really shaped a hell of a football team," McCarthy remarked. "We've always felt that we are a very good football team. Now we have the opportunity to achieve greatness."

Even though the Packers would face the Pittsburgh Steelers—who were looking to win their third Super Bowl in six years—McCarthy had so much faith in his players that he had them fitted for championship rings the night before the game. "We loved

BELOW: Nose tackle B. J. Raji scored on an interception return for a touchdown to give the Packers a commanding 21-7 lead in the fourth quarter. (WISCONSIN STATE JOURNAL)

BELOW, RIGHT: Wide receiver Donald Driver was overwhelmed with emotion after Green Bay's 21-14 victory over the Bears in the 2010 NFC championship game. The Packers were headed to Super Bowl XLV. (FROM THE GREEN BAY PRESS-GAZETTE ARCHIVES, REPRINTED BY PERMISSION)

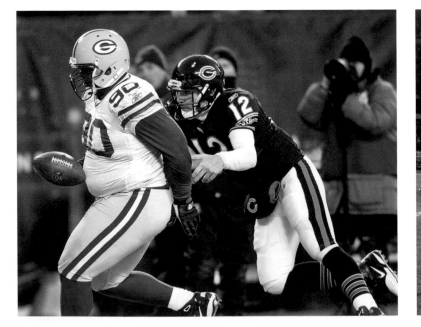

When President Barack Obama visited Green Bay following the Packers' victory over the Bears in the NFC championship game, Green Bay Mayor Jim Schmitt presented him with an autographed Charles Woodson jersey. (AP PHOTO/MIKE ROEMER)

it. That showed the confidence Coach McCarthy has in us," defensive tackle Ryan Pickett explained. "He had us believing in ourselves all year—even when everybody else didn't."

Following an action-packed pregame celebration, the first three drives of Super Bowl XLV ended with punts. Then Green Bay scored when Aaron Rodgers connected with wide receiver Jordy Nelson on a 29-yard touchdown pass. On the first play after the ensuing kickoff, Steelers quarterback Ben Roethlisberger was hit by nose tackle Howard Green while trying to throw a pass. The ball projected well short of its intended target, and Packers safety Nick Collins intercepted it and returned it 37 yards for a touchdown, giving Green Bay a 14–0 lead. The Packers extended the lead to 21–3 with a 21-yard touchdown throw from Rodgers to Jennings. With 2:24 left until halftime, they seemed to be well on their way to their thirteenth NFL championship. But the second quarter had been a costly one for the Packers as wide receiver Donald Driver limped off the field with a high ankle sprain, cornerback Sam Shields left the game with a bruised shoulder, safety Nick Collins suffered from dehydration, and cornerback Charles Woodson broke his collarbone just two plays after Jennings's touchdown.

After the Steelers cut the lead to 21–10 by halftime, Woodson addressed the team during intermission. As he fought through the pain of his broken collarbone, "he tried to give a pep talk and he broke down in tears," defensive line coach Mike Trgovac recalled. "He got so emotional it was unreal. It was from the heart."

Woodson's impassioned speech "kind of defines our season," Jennings remarked. "We are a team with a certain dynamic that a lot of teams don't have. What separated us from the other thirty-one teams was that dynamic and that will to overcome adversity."

Following halftime, the Packers were unable to regain any momentum in the third quarter, compiling four straight three-and-outs on offense. Meanwhile, the Steelers responded with another touchdown to shrink Green Bay's lead to 21–17. On the first play of the fourth quarter, and with the Steelers on the verge of driving toward another score, Roethlisberger handed off to running back Rashard Mendenhall as Green Bay's Clay Matthews and Ryan Pickett penetrated the backfield. Their hit on Mendenhall popped the ball free, and Desmond Bishop pounced on it for the Packers' third of three takeaways in the game. "That's what we've been doing all season long—creating turnovers," Matthews explained. "We know if we can create turnovers, give the ball back to our offense, it's going to be hard to beat us."

ABOVE: The Packers' defense prepared to face the AFC champion Pittsburgh Steelers in Super Bowl XLV. Left to right: Clay Matthews (52), Tramon Williams (38), Cullen Jenkins (77), Charles Woodson (21), A. J. Hawk (50), Frank Zombo (58), and Sam Shields (37). (FROM THE GREEN BAY PRESS-GAZETTE ARCHIVES, REPRINTED BY PERMISSION)

LEFT: Wide receivers James Jones (89) and Jordy Nelson (87) celebrated after Nelson scored the first touchdown of Super Bowl XLV. Nelson finished the game with nine catches for 140 yards and a touchdown. (FROM THE GREEN BAY PRESS-GAZETTE ARCHIVES, REPRINTED BY PERMISSION)

BELOW: Safety Nick Collins (36) celebrated with Clay Matthews (52) in the end zone after returning a Ben Roethlisberger interception for a touchdown that gave the Packers an early 14–0 lead. (WISCONSIN STATE JOURNAL)

Linebacker Desmond Bishop (55) recovered the fumble from the Steelers' Rashard Mendenhall during the first play of the fourth quarter of Super Bowl XLV. (FROM THE GREEN BAY PRESS-GAZETTE ARCHIVES, REPRINTED BY PERMISSION)

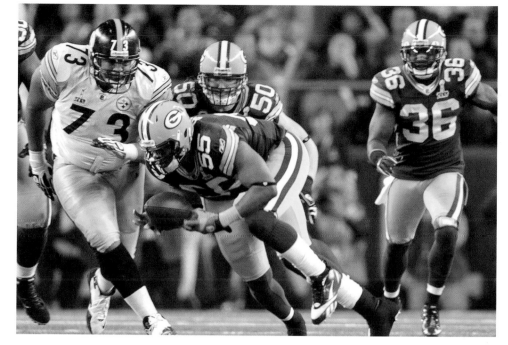

"We know if we can create turnovers, give the ball back to our offense, it's going to be hard to beat us."
—LINEBACKER CLAY MATTHEWS

Before that play, Green Bay appeared to be on the wrong end of the biggest Super Bowl comeback ever, letting a 21–3 first-half lead slip way. Instead, Rodgers converted the turnover into a touchdown by picking apart the Steelers' secondary with precision completions to James Jones, Jordy Nelson, and an 8-yard touchdown strike to Greg Jennings, extending the Packers' lead to 28–17. Their 11-point lead was short-lived as Roethlisberger brought the Steelers back to within 3 points on a 25-yard touchdown pass to wide receiver Mike Wallace followed by a 2-point conversion. "The NFL is a quarterback's league," president Mark Murphy said of the Steelers' tenacity. "The reason they were right there with us was Roethlisberger."

With just over seven minutes left in the game, the Packers marched downfield in hopes of putting the game out of reach. But their drive stalled after Rodgers's third-down pass skimmed off Jordy Nelson's fingertips in the corner of the end zone. They settled for a Mason Crosby field goal and a 31–25 lead that now forced Pittsburgh to play for the end zone. The Steelers got the ball back on their 13-yard line with just two minutes remaining, a dangerous amount of time. Two years earlier, in Super Bowl XLIII, Roethlisberger had marched the Steelers 88 yards in a two-minute drill to beat the Arizona Cardinals. And in December 2009 against the Packers, he had driven for scores at the end of each half for the victory. "I'm thinking, Oh God—two minutes left, Ben's got the ball, here we go," safety Charlie Peprah exclaimed to reporters after the game. "Seen this before."

Roethlisberger opened the drive with a 15-yard pass to tight end Heath Miller and a 5-yard pass to Hines Ward. Then, on second down, A. J. Hawk forced him to throw the ball away. His third-down pass sailed over the head of Mike Wallace after being under considerable pressure. On fourth and 5 at the 33—with just fifty-six seconds remaining—Roethlisberger threw to Wallace on a 12-yard curl pattern that cornerback Tramon Williams broke up. "We just never gave Ben a chance to get anything going," Williams said of the Packers' successful last stand. "That's confidence in the guys on the field and the scheme you're playing."

Aaron Rodgers took the final snap and kneeled as the game clock expired. The Packers had won Super Bowl XLV. Although it was Rodgers's first NFL championship, "I think people are going to write stories about him ten years from now that he's pretty special," general manager Ted Thompson said afterward. "Even though he's done so much, he's sort of just getting started."

In Super Bowl XLV Rodgers was twenty-four of thirty-nine for 304 yards, three touchdowns, and no interceptions against a Steelers defense that had allowed an average of only 14.5 points per game all season. After accepting the Super Bowl MVP award, Rodgers said, "The organization stood by me, believed in me, and that's what I did on the podium. I thanked Ted [Thompson], Mark [Murphy, the president and CEO] and Mike [McCarthy] for really believing in me and giving me the opportunity. I told Ted in 2005 that he wouldn't be sorry with his pick. I told them in 2008 I would repay their trust and give them this opportunity."

BELOW: Safety Nick Collins held up a celebratory towel proclaiming the Packers Super Bowl XLV champions. (FROM THE GREEN BAY PRESS-GAZETTE ARCHIVES, REPRINTED BY PERMISSION)

BELOW, RIGHT: Clay Matthews (left) and Aaron Rodgers (right) celebrated the Packers' Super Bowl XLV victory. (FROM THE GREEN BAY PRESS-GAZETTE ARCHIVES, REPRINTED BY PERMISSION)

As the confetti rained down on the Packers players' black Super Bowl XLV champion hats, their improbable championship run was complete. A team that had made the playoffs on the strength-of-victory tiebreaker over Tampa Bay and the Giants had risen to the football mountaintop. "The smallest city in the league has won the biggest game," NFL commissioner Roger Goodell announced to the 103,219 fans in attendance at Cowboys Stadium.

Afterward in the Packers' locker room, current stars like Rodgers, Woodson, and Matthews celebrated their Super Bowl victory alongside franchise icons Bart Starr, Ron Wolf, and Bob Harlan. Their sharing of the franchise's thirteenth NFL championship was like a family passing down its traditions from one generation to the next. Mike McCarthy embraced that sentiment by echoing Vince Lombardi's coaching philosophy after the Super Bowl victory: "Chasing perfection and catching excellence on the way is something I think exemplifies everything that every football team, particularly ours, is trying to accomplish."

While the Packers celebrated their fourth Super Bowl title, everyone in the locker room knew their history of financial stress was far from over. As a small-market team, the franchise would have to continue to be proactive and assertive if it expected to stay solvent in the increasingly competitive National Football League. "We've got some difficult times ahead, but I have great confidence in the organization," team president Mark Murphy said to explain the franchise's enduring legacy. "The Packers have withstood the test of time."

Head coach Mike McCarthy (holding trophy), team president Mark Murphy (left), and general manager Ted Thompson (right) celebrated the Packers' fourth Super Bowl title with announcer Terry Bradshaw. (FROM THE GREEN BAY PRESS-GAZETTE ARCHIVES, REPRINTED BY PERMISSION)

EPILOGUE
The Championship Culture

For generations to come, the Green Bay Packers' story will continue building on its legendary foundation. Although the Packers have been part of the National Football League for over nine decades, they continue to strive for that perfect season, break franchise records, and depend on the unconditional support of their fans to stay competitive. In the meantime, the team's Hall of Fame will have plenty of options when it comes to choosing new inductees, mementos, and highlight reels to display, especially with Green Bay's recent success. "When you come in, you can't help but see the winning tradition," running back John Kuhn said. "You're expected to win here, you're expected to compete, and you're expected to play at a very high level."

"It's a culture that Mike [McCarthy] and Ted [Thompson] have brought here," safety Charlie Peprah noted. "It's working well."

Following the 2010 regular season, the Packers met those high expectations, winning three playoff games en route to becoming Super Bowl XLV champions. The team's coffers boasted a net income of $17.1 million in fiscal year 2011. Success on the field translated directly to the ledger as excited fans paid to be part of something special. "We saw a big jump in our [Lambeau Field] Atrium businesses and our Pro Shop with apparel sales throughout the playoff run," Packers' CEO Mark Murphy explained. "We are seeing a lot of interest in our merchandise, especially anything with 'Super Bowl' on it."

In early December 2011, the Packers turned to their devoted fans again when announcing plans to raise at least $22 million through a stock sale to help finance a $143 million Lambeau Field expansion. The team anticipated selling up to 250,000 shares—more than double the 120,000 stock shares sold in 1997. At $250 each, the shares would help pay for adding more than 6,600 seats, new video boards, and a rooftop viewing platform to the iconic stadium. Optimistic team president Mark Murphy said, "We are hoping to match what we did last time [in 1997]. Our fans are excited about this opportunity."

The response to the Packers' fifth-ever stock offering was overwhelming. The team sold more than 1,600 in the sale's first eleven minutes. Less than a month later, the Packers announced they would offer another 30,000 shares after the initial 250,000 sold out—even though the stock pays no dividends, cannot be sold or traded on a stock exchange, and provides no preferential treatment in terms of tickets to Lambeau Field. Murphy was quick to explain the truest benefit of owning stock in the Packers: "significant bragging rights."

The public interest in Packers' stock came less than five months after a tumultuous offseason for the National Football League that prevented the team from enjoying all the perks of being reigning champions. The NFL was embroiled in a 132-day work stoppage imposed by the owners. Between March 11, 2011, and July 25, 2011, players and teams were prevented from interacting. But as soon as a new collective bargaining agreement was reached, players reported to training camp. "In Green Bay, Super Bowl definitely trumps the lockout," Murphy told reporters before the start of the 2011 regular season.

As they kicked off the 2011 season, the Packers found themselves defending their fourth Super Bowl title and thirteenth overall NFL championship against the thirty-one other NFL franchises looking to dethrone them. Head coach Mike McCarthy used that championship status as motivation. "We refuse to be hunted. We're always going to be the hunter. We've been talking about it since Day 1," he said. "The nice part about it, our football team stayed right on pace in accordance with that message."

> "We refuse to be hunted. We're always going to be the hunter."
> —HEAD COACH MIKE MCCARTHY

Following a preseason visit to the White House to meet with President Barack Obama, the Packers started the season as the NFL's pacesetters with thirteen straight victories. Experts and fans alike wondered if this team would join the 1972 Dolphins as the only team in league history to go undefeated throughout the regular season and playoffs. On a weekly basis, franchise and individual records were being shattered as the team's explosive offense compensated for its suspect defense, which ranked last in the league in several categories. Although the Packers' chase for perfection was halted by a confounding 19–14 loss in Kansas City, they finished the season with two more victories and a 15–1 regular-season record. The team set nineteen franchise records in 2011, including regular season victories (15), points scored (560), offensive yards (6,482), fewest penalties (76), and fewest turnovers (14). "I'm proud of the performance and the production of our football team through the regular season," McCarthy told reporters during his season-ending press conference. "It's something that I'll probably appreciate more once I'll be able to step away from this evaluation process I'm in the middle of. But, the reality is you put yourself in position to make a run into the playoffs—we did that very well—but then once the second season started, we did not play to the identity that we were able to formulate all season."

Green Bay entered the 2011 playoffs with home field advantage and a first-round bye. The team had won twenty-one of its previous twenty-two games dating back to the 2010 regular season and playoffs. It seemed the league's highest scoring offense and Super Bowl MVP signal-caller were able to overcome anything—but not everything. Almost all that the 2011 Packers were striving to achieve fell apart on a blustery late Sunday afternoon when they faced the New York Giants in the playoffs' divisional round. Green Bay's defense conceded big plays to quarterback Eli Manning and the Giants' offense all afternoon. The Packers' receivers dropped passes. Their running backs put the ball on the ground. Even Rodgers missed open receivers. As a result, the Packers watched their season end in a 37–20 loss to the Giants that was as emotionally heart wrenching as the NFC championship game loss four years earlier on the same Lambeau Field turf. "Everything that happened during the regular season, all the records that different guys were setting, . . . when it comes down to it, we didn't do it in the playoffs," Packers' linebacker A. J. Hawk told reporters after the game. "It's almost like college basketball. You get in the [NCAA] tournament, and it's how far you go in there. It's the same feeling. It almost erases what you did in the regular season."

Green Bay had become the latest victim of the NFL's hottest team coming into the playoffs. Despite a 9–7 regular season record, the Giants defeated the Packers on their way to winning Super Bowl XLVI. "That's the way the game goes," cornerback Charles Woodson said, noting the irony of losing to the hottest team when just a year earlier the Packers were in a similar situation as playoff darlings. "A team gets hot, and they're hard to stop. They [the Giants] are getting hot at this particular time to get themselves another shot at a trophy."

The loss stung all the more because "we play to win championships," quarterback Aaron Rodgers said, lamenting the season's sudden end. "You win a championship, have kind of the top of the mountain, and you forget how bad this feeling is."

Although the Packers fell short of securing another Super Bowl trophy, team president Mark Murphy brought perspective to how the team's championship culture will persevere in the years to come. "We have a lot to build on. We have a young talented team, a great head coach, a great general manager and a great quarterback. I'm very confident we'll be right back in the playoffs next year and, hopefully, we'll win another Super Bowl," he told guests at the forty-seventh annual Red Smith Sports Award Banquet, just days after the team's loss to the Giants. "You learn from things like this. The future is very bright."

The Green Bay Packers—with their strong nucleus of talented players, enhanced financial stability created by the latest stock offering, and having secured general manager Ted Thompson and head coach Mike McCarthy in long-term contract extensions—are poised to continue building on their championship culture. "I think it all starts with the organization," fullback John Kuhn said. "They do such a great job of keeping your eye on the prize and what the goal around here really is. It's more about the team, coming together, trying to achieve something that will last for longer than money ever will."

A R T I C L E S. O F I N C O R P O R A T I O N

OF THE

GREEN BAY FOOTBALL CORPORATION

KNOW ALL MEN BY THESE PRESENTS that we, the
undersigned, adult persons, residents of the State of
Wisconsin, have associated ourselves and do hereby
associate ourselves for the purpose of forming a corporation, under the provisions of Chapter Eighty-six
of the Statutes of the State of Wisconsin, and for that
purpose, do hereby adopt the following:

ARTICLES OF INCORPORATION

ARTICLE 1. The name of said corporation shall be
"Green Bay Football Corporation", and its principal
office and place of business shall be located in the
City of Green Bay, Brown County, Wisconsin.

ARTICLE 11. The business of said corporation shall
be the carrying on of professional football and other
athletic sports incidental to such business at the City
of Green Bay and elsewhere and to buy, lease and sell
real estate and personal property for the carrying on of
the purposes of the corporation.

ARTICLE 111. The capital stock shall consist of Five
Thousand Dollars ($5,000.00) divided into one thousand
shares of the par value of Five ($5.00) Dollars each.

ARTICLE 1V. The general officers of said corporation
shall be a president, a vice-president, a secretary, and
a treasurer, of which any two offices may be held by the
same person, and the Board of Directors shall consist of
fifteen stockholders.

ARTICLE V. The Board of Directors shall appoint an
executive committee of five members from their body, who
shall have charge of the general affairs of the corporation,
subject, however, to the control of the Board of Directors.

ARTICLE Vl. The principal duties of the president
shall be to preside at all meetings of the Board of Directors and of the stockholders, and to have general supervi-
sion of the affairs of the corporation.

The principal duties of the vice-president
shall be to discharge the duties of the president in the
event of the absence or disability for any cause whatsoever
of the latter.

The principal duties of the secretary
shall be to countersign all deeds, leases and conveyances
executed by the corporation; to affix the seal of the corporation thereto, and to such papers as shall be required
or directed to be sealed; to keep a record of the pro-
ceedings of meetings of the Board of Directors, and of
the stockholders, and to safely and systematically keep
all records, papers, and documents belonging to the corporation, or in any wise pertaining to the business thereof;

The principal duties of the treasurer
shall be to keep and account for all moneys, credits, and
properties of the corporation, of every kind and nature
which shall come into his hands, and to keep an accurate
account of all moneys received and disbursed, and proper
vouchers for money so disbursed, and to render such ac-
counts, statements, and inventories of moneys and proper-

ties received and disbursed, and money and property on hand generally of all matters pertaining to his office, as shall be required by the Board of Directors.

The Board of Directors may provide for the appointment of such additional officers as they may deem for the best interests of the corporation and may prescribe the duties thereof.

The office of president and treasurer, or secretary and treasurer may be held by the same person.

In addition to the duties above prescribed, such officers shall perform such additional or different duties as may from time to time be imposed or required by the Board of Directors, or as may be prescribed from time to time by by-laws.

ARTICLE V11. Only persons holding stock according to the regulations of the corporation shall be members to it.

ARTICLE V111. These articles may be amended by resolution in writing, setting forth such amendment or amendments adopted at any regular meeting of the stockholders, or at any special meeting of the stockholders called upon ten (10) days notice in writing, stating the purpose of such meeting, by a vote of not less than two thirds (2/3) of all the stock of said corporation then outstanding.

ARTICLE 1X. This corporation shall be operated without cost to the stockholders and any earnings, if any shall be donated to the Sullivan Post, of the American Legion, Green Bay, Wisconsin.

IN WITNESS WHEREOF, we have hereunto set our hands and seals this 14 day of August, 1 9 2 3.

E. H. Joannes (SEAL)

A. B. Turnbull (SEAL)

John A. Kittell (SEAL)

IN THE PRESENCE OF

E. Lambeau

J. W. Calhoun

STATE OF WISCONSIN)
) SS
BROWN COUNTY   )

Personally came before me this ‾14‾ day of August,
1923, the above named ‾L H Joannes‾. ‾O B Turnbull‾
and ‾John C Kittell‾, to me known to be the persons who executed the foregoing instrument and acknowledged
the same.

                              ‾E L Everson‾
                         NOTARY PUBLIC, WISCONSIN.

                         My commission expires
                         ‾Nov 7, 1926‾

STATE OF WISCONSIN)
) SS
BROWN COUNTY   )

‾L H Joannes‾ and ‾A B Turnbull‾
being first duly sworn, on oath each for himself says that
they are two of the signers of the foregoing original Articles
of Incorporation of the Green Bay Football Corporation, as
adopted and acknowledged by said signers.

                              ‾L H Joannes‾
                              ‾A B Turnbull‾

Subscribed and sworn to
before me this ‾14‾
day of August, 1923.
‾E L Everson‾
NOTARY PUBLIC, BROWN CO, WIS.

ACKNOWLEDGMENTS

Green Bay Packers: Trials, Triumphs, and Tradition has benefited from the personal generosity and cooperation of dozens of individuals who contributed their time, knowledge, and resources. From the Green Bay Packers: Craig Benzel, Shea Greil, and Aaron Popkey; from the Green Bay Packers Hall of Fame: Kristine Zegers; from the *Green Bay Press-Gazette*: John Dye and Jeff Ash; from the *Wisconsin State Journal*: John Smalley and Dennis McCormick; from the *Milwaukee Journal-Sentinel*: Alan King, Don Walker, and Judy Berger, who helped me research the paper's vast photo archives; from the *Eau Claire Leader-Telegram*: Steve Kinderman; from the Neville Public Museum of Brown County: Louise Pfotenhauer; from the University of Wisconsin–Milwaukee Library: Ellen Engseth; from the Marquette University Library: Matt Blessing and Phillip Runkel; from the William J. Clinton Presidential Library: John Keller; from the Gerald R. Ford Presidential Library: Nancy Mirshah; from the Richard Nixon Presidential Library: Pamla Eisenberg; from the Dwight D. Eisenhower Presidential Library:

Kathy Struss; the Vernon Biever family; and the collections of Chris Nerat, Chip Manthey, Tom Pigeon, and Artie Rickun. My candid interviews with several current and former players and executives, including Bob Harlan, John Underwood, and Bart Starr, helped bring an even greater personal perspective to this Packers' story, and I am grateful for their cooperation. Special thanks also go to Cooper Greil, Kiana and Leila Schiegg, and Jade Schiegg.

This book also benefited from the cooperation of the entire Wisconsin Historical Society Press team, including Michael Stevens, Kathy Borkowski, Kate Thompson, John Nondorf, Melanie Roth, Mike Nemer, Andrew White, and all their dedicated colleagues. Finally, only with the generosity of my entire family—from Milwaukee to Coloma—have many of my ambitions become a reality. Thanks to my wife, Kate, and sons Jackson and Cameron, this book's epic conclusion with Super Bowl XLV became a family experience that will provide fond memories to last a lifetime.

FURTHER READING

Hundreds of books, magazine articles, newspaper stories, and documentary films have chronicled the Green Bay Packers. Below is a brief list of works that were cited as direct sources or that served as valuable resources within *Green Bay Packers: Trials, Triumphs, and Tradition.*

BOOKS

Barber, Phil. *The Official Vince Lombardi Playbook*. Guilford, CT: Lyons Press, 2009.

Bauer, David, ed. *The Champions: Green Bay Packers 1996*. New York: Sports Illustrated, 1997.

Beebe, Don, with Bob Schaller. *More Than a Ring: Don Beebe's Unlikely Path to the NFL and a Super Bowl Championship*. Wautoma, WI: Angel Press of Wisconsin, 1998.

Bengtson, Jay, and Len Wagner. *Launching the Glory Years: The 1959 Packers*. N.p.: Coach's Books, 2001.

Bengtson, Phil, with Todd Hunt. *Packer Dynasty: The Saga of the Championship Green Bay Teams*. New York: Doubleday, 1969.

Berger, Phil. *Championship Teams of the NFL*. New York: Random House, 1968.

Berghaus, Bob. *Black & Blue: A Smash-Mouth History of the NFL's Roughest Division*. Cincinnati: Clerisy, 2007.

Bie, Michael. *It Happened in Wisconsin*. Guilford, CT: Morris, 2007.

Biever, John, with George Vecsey. *Young Sports Photographer with the Green Bay Packers*. New York: W.W. Norton, 1969.

Biever, Vernon J. *The Glory of Titletown: The Classic Green Bay Packers Photography of Vernon Biever*. Lanham, MD: Taylor Trade, 1997.

Butler, LeRoy, and James J. Keller. *The LeRoy Butler Story: From Wheelchair to the Lambeau Leap*. Neenah, WI: JJK Sports Entertainment, 2003.

Bynum, Mike, ed. *Vince Lombardi: Memories of a Special Time*. Chicago: October Football, 1988.

Cameron, Steve. *The Packers! Seventy-five Seasons of Memories and Mystique in Green Bay*. Dallas: Taylor, 1993.

Carlson, Chuck. *Brett Favre: America's Quarterback*. Chicago: Triumph, 2007.

———. *Game of My Life: Memorable Stories of Packers Football*. Champaign, IL: Sports Publishing, 2004.

———. *Green Bay Packers: Yesterday & Today*. Lincolnwood, IL: West Side, 2009.

———. *Tales from the Packers Sideline: A Collection of the Greatest Stories Ever Told*. Champaign, IL: Sports Publishing, 2003.

———. *Titletown Again: The Super Bowl Season of the 1996 Green Bay Packers*. Lenexa, KS: Addax, 1997.

Christl, Cliff, and Dale Hofmann. *The 25 Greatest Moments in Lambeau Field History*. Stevens Point, WI: KCI Sports, 2007.

Claerbaut, David. *Bart Starr: When Leadership Mattered*. Lanham, MD: Taylor Trade, 2004.

Coenen, Craig R. *From Sandlots to the Super Bowl: The National Football League, 1920–1967*. Knoxville: University of Tennessee Press, 2005.

Collins, Tom. *The Green Bay Packer Hall of Fame: The Tradition Lives On!* Green Bay, WI: Green Bay Packer Hall of Fame, 1995.

Cope, Myron. *The Game That Was: The Early Days of Pro Football.* New York: World, 1970.

Curry, Bill. *Ten Men You Meet in the Huddle: Lessons from a Football Life.* New York: ESPN Books, 2008.

D'Amato, Gary, and Cliff Christl. *Mudbaths & Bloodbaths: The Inside Story of the Bears-Packers Rivalry.* Black Earth, WI: Prairie Oak, 1997.

Daley, Art, and Jack Yuenger. *The Lombardi Era and the Green Bay Packers.* Milwaukee: Inland, 1968.

Davenport, Don. *Green Bay Packers Titletown Trivia Teasers.* Black Earth, WI: Prairie Oak, 1997.

Devaney, John. *Bart Starr.* New York: Scholastic, 1968.

Devine, Dan, with Michael R. Steele. *Simply Devine: Memoirs of a Hall of Fame Coach.* Champaign, IL: Sports Publishing, 2000.

Eisenberg, John. *That First Season: How Vince Lombardi Took the Worst Team in the NFL and Set It on the Path to Glory.* New York: Houghton Mifflin Harcourt, 2009.

Epstein, Eddie. *Dominance: The Best Seasons of Pro Football's Greatest Teams.* Washington, DC: Brassey's, 2002.

Everson, Jeff. *This Day in Green Bay Packers History.* Wautoma, WI: Angel Press of Wisconsin, 1997.

Favre, Brett, and Bonita Favre. *Favre.* New York: Rugged Land, 2004.

Favre, Brett, with Chris Havel. *Favre: For the Record.* New York: Doubleday, 1997.

Felser, Larry. *The Birth of the New NFL: How the 1966 NFL/AFL Merger Transformed Pro Football.* Guilford, CT: Lyons Press, 2008.

Fishman, Marv, with Tracy Dodds. *Bucking the Odds: The Birth of the Milwaukee Bucks.* Milwaukee: Raintree, 1978.

Fitzgerald, Francis J., ed. *Heir to the Legacy: The Memorable Story of Mike Holmgren's Green Bay Packers.* Louisville, KY: AdCraft Sports Marketing, 1996.

Flynn, George. *The Vince Lombardi Scrapbook.* New York: Gross & Dunlap, 1976.

———, ed. *Vince Lombardi on Football.* 2 vols. New York: New York Graphic Society, 1973.

Fortunato, John A. *Commissioner: The Legacy of Pete Rozelle.* New York: Taylor Trade, 2006.

Gentile, Domenic, with Gary D'Amato. *The Packer Tapes: My 32 Years with the Green Bay Packers.* Madison, WI: Prairie Oak, 1995.

Goska, Eric. *Green Bay Packers: A Measure of Greatness.* Iola, WI: Krause, 2003.

Green Bay 1997 World Champions. Northbrook, IL: H&S Media, 1997.

Green Bay Packers. *Green Bay Packers Super Bowl XLV Championship Commemorative Edition.* Big Lake, MN: GameDay Sports Media & Marketing, 2011.

Green Bay Press-Gazette. *Green, Gold & Glorious: The Green Bay Packers' Magical Run to Super Bowl XLV.* Green Bay: Pediment, 2011.

———. *Lambeau Field: Green Bay's National Treasure.* Green Bay: Pediment, 2003.

———. *Titletown's Team: A Photographic History of the Green Bay Packers.* Green Bay: Pediment, 2009.

———. *Titletown: The Unforgettable Story of the Green Bay Packers' Road to Super Bowl XXXI.* Louisville, KY: AdCraft Sports Marketing, 1997.

Gregg, Forrest, and Andrew O'Toole. *Winning in the Trenches: A Lifetime of Football.* Cincinnati: Clerisy, 2009.

Gruver, Ed. *The Ice Bowl: The Cold Truth about Football's Most Unforgettable Game.* Ithaca, NY: McBooks, 1998.

———. *Nitschke.* Lanham, MD: Taylor Trade, 2002.

Gulbrandsen, Don. *Green Bay Packers: The Complete Illustrated History.* St. Paul, MN: Voyageur, 2007.

Gullickson, Denis J. *Vagabond Halfback: The Life and Times of Johnny Blood McNally.* Madison, WI: Trails, 2006.

Gullickson, Denis J., and Carl Hanson. *Before They Were the Packers: Green Bay's Town Team Days.* Black Earth, WI: Trails, 2004.

Gutman, Bill. *Brett Favre: Leader of the Pack*. Brookfield, CT: Millbrook Sports World, 1998.

Hand, Jack. *Great Running Backs of the NFL*. New York: Random House, 1966.

Hanrahan, Phil. *Life after Favre: A Season of Change with the Green Bay Packers and Their Fans*. New York: Skyhorse, 2009.

Harlan, Bob, with Dale Hofmann. *Green and Golden Moments: Bob Harlan and the Green Bay Packers*. Stevens Point, WI: KCI Sports, 2007.

Havel, Chris. *A Year of Champions: The 1996 Green Bay Packers; Remembered by Gilbert Brown*. Green Bay: Petasek Promotions, 2006.

Herskowitz, Mickey. *The Golden Age of Pro Football: A Remembrance of Pro Football in the 1950s*. New York: Macmillan, 1974.

Heuman, William. *Famous Pro Football Stars*. New York: Dodd, Mead & Company, 1967.

Hofmann, Dale, and Cliff Christl. *365: The Best Wisconsin Sports Stories Day by Day*. Stevens Point, WI: KCI Sports, 2010.

Hornung, Paul, as told to Al Silverman. *Football and the Single Man: A Candid Autobiography*. Garden City, NY: Doubleday, 1965.

Hornung, Paul, as told to William F. Reed. *Golden Boy*. New York: Simon & Schuster, 2004.

Hornung, Paul, with Billy Reed. *Lombardi and Me: Players, Coaches and Colleagues Talk about the Man and the Myth*. Chicago: Triumph, 2006.

Isaacson, Kevin, with Tom Kessenich. *Return to Glory: The Inside Story of the Green Bay Packers' Return to Prominence*. Iola, WI: Krause, 1996.

Johnson, Chuck. *The Great Packers of Them All*. New York: G.P. Putnam's Sons, 1968.

———. *The Green Bay Packers: Pro Football's Pioneer Team*. New York: Thomas Nelson, 1961

Korth, Todd. *Greatest Moments in Green Bay Packers Football History*. Lenexa, KS: Addax, 1998.

Kramer, Jerry. *Jerry Kramer's Farewell to Football*. Edited by Dick Schaap. New York: World, 1968.

———, ed. *Lombardi: Winning Is the Only Thing*. New York: World, 1970.

Kramer, Jerry, and Dick Schaap. *Distant Replay*. New York: Jove, 1985.

———. *Instant Replay: The Green Bay Diary of Jerry Kramer*. New York: New American Library, 1968.

Kramer, Ron, with Dan Ewald. *That's Just Kramer! From Michigan Legend to Lombardi's "12th Man."* Ann Arbor, MI: Sports Media Group, 2007.

Lazenby, Roland. *The Pictorial History of Football*. San Diego: Thunder Bay Press, 1987.

Lea, Bud. *Magnificent Seven: The Championship Games That Built the Lombardi Dynasty*. Chicago: Triumph, 2002.

Lefebvre, Hank, and Ray O. Wanek. *50 Years of Professional Football: A Complete Picture History of the Green Bay Packers*. Green Bay: Green Bay Packer Alumni Association, 1968.

Leuthner, Stuart. *Iron Men: Bucko, Crazylegs, and the Boys Recall the Golden Days of Professional Football*. New York: Doubleday, 1988.

Lombardi, Vince, with W.C. Heinz. *Run to Daylight*. New York: Tempo, 1963.

Lombardi, Vince, Jr. *The Lombardi Rules: 26 Lessons From Vince Lombardi—the World's Greatest Coach*. New York: McGraw-Hill, 2005.

MacCambridge, Michael. *America's Game: The Epic Story of How Pro Football Captured a Nation*. New York: Anchor, 2004.

Maraniss, David. *When Pride Still Mattered: A Life of Vince Lombardi*. New York: Simon & Schuster, 1999.

Maxymuk, John. *Packers by the Numbers*. Black Earth, WI: Prairie Oak, 2003.

McCullough, Bob. *My Greatest Day in Football: The Legends of Football Recount Their Greatest Moments*. New York: Thomas Dunne, 2001.

McDonell, Chris. *The Football Game I'll Never Forget: 100 NFL Stars' Stories*. Buffalo, NY: Firefly, 2004.

McGinn, Bob. *The Road to Glory: The Inside Story of the Packers' Super Bowl XXXI Championship Season.* Louisville, KY: AdCraft Sports Marketing, 1997.

Milwaukee Journal Sentinel. *The Pack Is Back! How the Green Bay Packers Won Their 13th NFL Championship.* Stevens Point, WI: KCI Sports, 2011.

Mishler, Todd. *Cold Wars: 40+ Years of Packer-Viking Rivalry.* Black Earth, WI: Prairie Oak, 2002.

Names, Larry. *Green Bay Packers Facts & Trivia.* Wautoma, WI: E.B. Houchin, 1992.

————. *The History of the Green Bay Packers: The Lambeau Years, Part One.* Wautoma, WI: Angel Press of Wisconsin, 1987.

————. *The History of the Green Bay Packers: The Lambeau Years, Part Two.* Wautoma, WI: Angel Press of Wisconsin, 1989.

————. *The History of the Green Bay Packers: The Lambeau Years, Part Three.* Wautoma, WI: Angel Press of Wisconsin, 1990.

————. *The History of the Green Bay Packers: The Shameful Years, Part Four.* Wautoma, WI: Angel Press of Wisconsin, 1995.

National Football League Properties. *The First Fifty Years: A Celebration of the National Football League in Its Fiftieth Season.* New York: Ridge / Benjamin, 1969.

————. *The Official NFL Encyclopedia of Pro Football.* 3rd ed. New York: New American Library, 1982.

New York Times. *Sports of the Times: A Day-by-Day Selection of the Most Important, Thrilling and Inspired Events of the Past 150 Years.* Edited by William Taaffe and David Fischer. New York: St. Martin's, 2003.

Nitschke, Ray, as told to Robert W. Wells. *Mean on Sunday: The Autobiography of Ray Nitschke.* Garden City, NY: Doubleday, 1973.

O'Brien, Michael. *Vince: A Personal Biography of Vince Lombardi.* New York: Quill, 1987.

Oriard, Michael. *Brand NFL: Making & Selling America's Favorite Sport.* Chapel Hill: University of North Carolina Press, 2007.

Parins, Jerry, with Mike Dauplaise. *Bodyguard to the Packers: Beat Cops, Brett Favre, and Beating Cancer.* Green Bay: TitleTown, 2008.

Peterson, Robert W. *Pigskin: The Early Years of Pro Football.* New York: Oxford University Press, 1997.

Plimpton, George. *One More July: A Football Dialogue with Bill Curry.* New York: Harper & Row, 1977.

Poling, Jerry. *After They Were Packers: The Super Bowl XXXI Champs & Other Green Bay Legends.* Madison, WI: Trails, 2006.

————. *Downfield: Untold Stories of the Green Bay Packers.* Black Earth, WI: Prairie Oak, 1996.

Povletich, William. *Green Bay Packers: Legends in Green and Gold.* Charleston, SC: Arcadia, 2005.

Quirk, James, and Rodney D. Fort. *Pay Dirt: The Business of Professional Team Sports.* Princeton, NJ: Princeton University Press, 1992.

Rainbolt, Richard. *The Green Bay Packers: A Pictorial Drama.* Minneapolis: Nodin, 1975.

Reischel, Rob. *Packers Essential: Everything You Need to Know to Be a Real Fan!* Chicago: Triumph, 2006.

Reynolds, Neil. *Pain Gang: Pro Football's Fifty Toughest Players.* Washington, DC: Potomac, 2006.

Robinson, Eugene, with Kevin Isaacson and Rocky Landverk. *Diary of a Super Bowl Season.* Iola, WI: Krause, 1998.

Rosenthal, Harold. *The Big Play: Exciting and Dramatic Plays from Big Games of the N.F.L. That Made or Broke Champions.* New York: Random House, 1965.

Ross, Alan. *Packer Pride: For the Love of Lambeau, Lombardi and Cheeseheads.* Nashville: Cumberland House, 2004.

Rubin, Bob. *Green Bay's Packers Return to Glory.* New York: Stuart L. Daniels, 1973.

Sauerberg, George, and Vernon Biever. *The Pack Fights Back: Can Fresh Faces Turn Things Around? 1986–1987 Green Bay Packers.* Chicago: Bonus, 1987.

Schaaf, Phil. *Sports, Inc.: 100 Years of Sports Business.* Amherst, NY: Prometheus, 2004.

Schaap, Dick. *Green Bay Replay: The Packers' Return to Glory*. New York: Avon, 1997.

Schoor, Gene. *Football's Greatest Coach: Vince Lombardi*. Garden City, NY: Doubleday, 1974.

Sports Illustrated. *Brett Favre: The Tribute*. New York: Sports Illustrated Books, 2008.

Starr, Bart, with Murray Olderman. *My Life in Football: Starr*. New York: William Morrow, 1987.

Stotts, Stuart. *Curly Lambeau: Building the Green Bay Packers*. Madison, WI: Wisconsin Historical Society Press, 2007.

Sullivan, Sandy. *Green Bay Love Stories and Other Affairs*. Bloomington, IN: AuthorHouse, 2004.

Taylor, Jim, with Kristine Setting Clark. *The Fire Within: Jim Taylor*. Chicago: Triumph, 2010.

Torinus, John B. *The Packer Legend: An Inside Look*. Neshkoro, WI: Laranmark, 1982.

Towle, Mike. *I Remember Vince Lombardi: Personal Memories of and Testimonials to Football's First Super Bowl Championship Coach as Told by the People and Players Who Knew Him*. Nashville: Cumberland House, 2001.

Ward, Arch. *The Green Bay Packers: The Story of Professional Football*. New York, G.P. Putnam's Sons, 1946.

Wells, Robert W. *Lombardi: His Life and Times*. Madison, WI: Wisconsin House, 1971.

White, Reggie, with Jim Denny. *In The Trenches: The Autobiography*. Nashville: Thomas Nelson, 1996.

Whittingham, Richard. *Sunday's Heroes: NFL Legends Talk about the Times of Their Lives*. Chicago: Triumph, 2003.

———. *What a Game They Played: An Inside Look at the Golden Era of Pro Football*. New York: Simon & Schuster, 1987.

Wiebusch, John, ed. *The Official NFL Pro Set Card Book*. New York: Workman, 1991.

Wolf, Ron, and Paul Attner. *The Packer Way: Nine Stepping Stones to Building a Winning Organization*. New York: St. Martin's, 1998.

Yost, Mark. *Tailgating, Sacks, and Salary Caps: How the NFL Became the Most Successful Sports League in History*. Chicago: Kaplan, 2006.

Ziemba, Joe. *When Football Was Football: The Chicago Cardinals and the Birth of the NFL*. Chicago: Triumph, 1999.

Zimmerman, David. *In Search of a Hero: Life and Times of Tony Canadeo*. Hales Corners, WI: Eagle, 2001.

———. *Lambeau Legends: Packer Profiles of Courage*. Hales Corners, WI: Eagle, 2008.

———. *Lambeau: The Man Behind the Mystique*. Hales Corners, WI: Eagle, 2003.

Zimmerman, David, and Stephen Zimmerman. *The Scrapbook History of Green Bay Packer Football*. 2 vols. Hales Corners, WI: Eagle, 2005–6.

FILMS

America's Game: Green Bay Packers Collection. NFL Productions / Warner Home Video, 2007.

The Complete History of the Green Bay Packers: 1919–2003. NFL Productions / Warner Home Video, 2003.

Green Bay Packers: The Grandstand Franchise. Wisconsin Public Television, 1989.

The Legend of Lambeau Field: The Heroes, the Highlights, the History. Frozen Tundra Films, 2003.

NFL Greatest Games Series: Green Bay Packers. NFL Productions / Warner Home Video, 2008.

GREEN BAY PACKERS MEMORABILIA

Media Guides 1950–2010

Yearbooks 1960–2010

Prospectus Guides 1973–1993

1996 Postseason Guide

Super Bowl XXXI Guide

Super Bowl XXXI Program

1997 Postseason Guide

Super Bowl XXXII Guide

Super Bowl XXXII Program

Super Bowl XLV Program

WORKS CITED

PROLOGUE

xi *I always tell people*: Green Bay Press-Gazette. *Lambeau Field: Green Bay's National Treasure* (Green Bay: Pediment, 2003), 13.

xi *a community project and a regional religion*: Johnson, Chuck. *The Green Bay Packers: Pro Football's Pioneer Team* (New York: Thomas Nelson & Sons, 1961), 140.

xi *There is no parallel*: Johnson. *Green Bay Packers*, 7.

xii *is like playing for a college or university*: Johnson. *Green Bay Packers*, 142.

xii *If you want to go on a wild goose chase*: Bengtson, Phil, with Todd Hunt. *Packer Dynasty: The Saga of the Championship Green Bay Teams* (New York: Doubleday, 1969), 142.

xii *You can't really compare*: Cameron, Steve. *The Packers! Seventy-five Seasons of Memories and Mystique in Green Bay* (Dallas: Taylor, 1993), 86.

xiii *It's not so much*: Bauer, David, ed. *The Champions: Green Bay Packers 1996* (New York: Sports Illustrated, 1997), 76.

CHAPTER ONE

3 *The big step had been taken*: 1969 Green Bay Packers Official Press Book, 6.

4 *In 1919, no one in Green Bay*: Names, Larry. *The History of the Green Bay Packers: The Lambeau Years, Part One* (Wautoma, WI: Angel Press of Wisconsin, 1987), 44.

4 *he had a lingering ache to play football*: Torinus, John B. *The Packer Legend: An Inside Look* (Neshkoro, WI: Laranmark, 1982), 13.

5 *just wanted to play for the love of football*: Johnson, Chuck. *The Green Bay Packers: Pro Football's Pioneer Team* (New York: Thomas Nelson & Sons, 1961), 43.

6 *I talked my boss*: Whittingham, Richard. *What a Game They Played: An Inside Look at the Golden Era of Pro Football* (New York: Simon & Schuster, 1987), 14.

6 *All they wanted was the name*: Johnson. *Green Bay Packers*, 43.

6 *Too bad there isn't a place in the Hall of Fame*: Cameron, Steve. *The Packers! Seventy-five Seasons of Memories and Mystique in Green Bay* (Dallas: Taylor, 1993), 141.

7 *the twenty-one 'regulars' divided up the profits*: Johnson. *Green Bay Packers*, 44.

8 *Marcel Lambeau directed volunteers*: Gulbrandsen, Don. *Green Bay Packers: The Complete Illustrated History* (St. Paul, MN: Voyageur, 2007), 18.

8 *Like so many other successful town teams*: Gullickson, Denis J. *Vagabond Halfback: The Life and Times of Johnny Blood McNally* (Madison, WI: Trails, 2006), 58.

8 *Spreading the Acme name around the Midwest*: Names. *History of the Green Bay Packers: The Lambeau Years, Part One*, 51.

10 *Of all the gentlemen*: Ward, Arch. *The Green Bay Packers: The Story of Professional Football* (New York: G.P. Putnam's Sons, 1946), 69.

10 *In the 1950s, a writer by the name of Roger Treat*: Torinus. *Packer Legend*, 29.

11 *he ran everything*: Associated Press. "Agree to Disagree: Pennsylvania Congressman Disputes Packers' Coaching History," *SportsIllustrated.com*, January 9, 2004, http://sportsillustrated.cnn.com/2004/football/nfl/specials/playoffs/2003/01/09/packers.coach.history.ap/.

11 *You're supposed to be a college graduate*: Lea, Bud. "The Great Packer-Bear Rivalry," *1986 Green Bay Packers Yearbook*, 24.

12 *Joe Carr was proving himself*: Ward. *Green Bay Packers*, 53.

12 *Again the matter of the Green Bay franchise came up*: Daley, Art. "The Green Bay Blues: Formerly Packers," *1983 Green Bay Packers Yearbook*, 22.

12 *George Halas, owner of the Chicago Bears*: Coenen, Craig R. *From Sandlots to the Super Bowl: The National Football League, 1920–1967* (Knoxville: University of Tennessee Press, 2005), 22.

13 *You can't do anything*: Daley, Art. "The Packer Fan . . . by Far the Best," *1984 Green Bay Packers Yearbook*, 2.

13 *Calhoun used to call us*: Johnson. *Green Bay Packers*, 48.

14 *Nate Abrams deserves to be recognized*: Names. *History of the Green Bay Packers: The Lambeau Years, Part One*, 214, 215.

14 *You go on with that game*: Christopulos, Mike. "Profitably Nonprofit: Packer Setup Is Unique," *Milwaukee Sentinel*, September 20, 1969.

14 *Lambeau will tell you that*: Ward. *Green Bay Packers*, 57.

14 *They knew that a professional football team*: Names. *History of the Green Bay Packers: The Lambeau Years, Part One*, 213.

15 *The American Legion supplied the team*: Torinus. *Packer Legend*, 25.

15 *The Hungry Five and their man Calhoun*: Ward. *Green Bay Packers*, 71.

15 *although it was written in red ink*: Names. *History of the Green Bay Packers: The Lambeau Years, Part One*, 114.

17 *the franchise reported a loss of $13,000 and was forced to relocate*: Coenen. *From Sandlots to the Super Bowl*, 38.

18 *Carr and large-city owners refused*: Coenen. *From Sandlots to the Super Bowl*, 24.

18 *The franchise was free of all debts*: Names. *History of the Green Bay Packers: The Lambeau Years, Part One*, 122.

20 *Grange was estimated to have earned $100,000*: Ward. *Green Bay Packers*, 78.

22 *In those days when professional football*: Torinus. *Packer Legend*, 27.

22 *Always a perfectionist*: Ward. *Green Bay Packers*, 91.

22 *I know the whole town is behind us*: Ward. *Green Bay Packers*, 92.

23 *He had an unmatched talent*: Johnson. *Green Bay Packers*, 84.

23 *Over the years, Lambeau would deal*: Gullickson. *Vagabond Halfback*, 60, 61.

23 *I countered with an offer to take the $100*: Whittingham, Richard. *Sunday's Heroes: NFL Legends Talk about the Times of Their Lives* (Chicago: Triumph, 2003), 15.

24 *For all purposes, Lambeau was through*: Johnson. *Green Bay Packers*, 53.

24 *the first time that I really got the feeling*: Gullickson. *Vagabond Halfback*, 68.

24 *In those days a team carried*: Lewellen, Verne. "The Game I Will Never Forget," *Milwaukee Sentinel*, September 20, 1969.

24 *Oh, how we hated to see the substitute*: Johnson. *Green Bay Packers*, 56.

25 *That left an open area*: Bengtson, Phil, with Todd Hunt. *Packer Dynasty: The Saga of the Championship Green Bay Teams* (New York: Doubleday, 1969), 196.

25 *The result was that the bout ended*: Ward. *Green Bay Packers*, 107.

25 *Green Bay residents threw a civic celebration*: Coenen. *From Sandlots to the Super Bowl*, 30.

26 *I am especially grateful*: Whittingham. *Sunday's Heroes*, 17.

26 *Some of the early years were lean ones*: Names. *History of the Green Bay Packers: The Lambeau Years, Part One*, 178.

26 *Green Bay may be the 241st city*: Coenen. *From Sandlots to the Super Bowl*, 31.

27 *The Portsmouth Spartans lost more than $43,000*: Coenen. *From Sandlots to the Super Bowl*, 35.

27 *Between 1920 and 1925, small-city teams dropped out*: Coenen. *From Sandlots to the Super Bowl*, 66.

27 *Pro football's carnival like atmosphere*: Ziemba, Joe. *When Football Was Football: The Chicago Cardinals and the Birth of the NFL* (Chicago: Triumph, 1999), 167.

27 *There were a lot of good times in Green Bay*: Whittingham. *What a Game They Played*, 37.

29 *I agreed to go to Green Bay for $4,000*: Johnson. *Green Bay Packers*, 59.

29 *When the smallest city in the league can win*: Ward. *Green Bay Packers*, 119.

30 *the court assessed the football corporation $2,500*: Names. *History of the Green Bay Packers: The Lambeau Years, Part Two*, 34.

31 *Ever since he had taken over the town team*: Names. *History of the Green Bay Packers: The Lambeau Years, Part One*, 193.

31 *Without the extra game, the Spartans found themselves*: Coenen. *From Sandlots to the Super Bowl*, 35.

32 *No other small city will be admitted*: Coenen. *From Sandlots to the Super Bowl*, 25.

32 *In 1930 and 1931, D. C. Haderer*: Coenen. *From Sandlots to the Super Bowl*, 44.

33 *I had gone into the 1932 season surrounded*: "Bears Once Owed Packers $1,500," *1986 Green Bay Packers Yearbook*, 29.

33 *The next year when the Bears played*: "Bears Once Owed Packers $1,500," *1986 Green Bay Packers Yearbook*, 29.

33 *Between Calhoun's publicity*: Zimmerman, David. *Lambeau: The Man behind the Mystique* (Hales Corners, WI: Eagle, 2003), 95.

CHAPTER TWO

35 *The trip to Hawaii and California*: Names, Larry. *The History of the Green Bay Packers: The Lambeau Years, Part Two* (Wautoma, WI: Angel Press of Wisconsin, 1989), 35.

35 *the Packers were now $12,300 in debt*: Johnson, Chuck. *The Green Bay Packers: Pro Football's Pioneer Team* (New York: Thomas Nelson & Sons, 1961), 64.

35 *Willard J. Bent was finally awarded a $5,200 judgment*: Names. *History of the Green Bay Packers: The Lambeau Years, Part Two*, 34.

36 *Joannes then loaned the corporation $6,000*: Names. *History of the Green Bay Packers: The Lambeau Years, Part Two*, 35.

38 *the Green Bay Packers will move to Milwaukee*: Coenen, Craig R. *From Sandlots to the Super Bowl: The National Football League, 1920–1967* (Knoxville: University of Tennessee Press, 2005), 45.

38 *in spite of Joe Carr's many efforts*: Names, Larry. *The History of the Green Bay Packers: The Lambeau Years, Part One* (Wautoma, WI: Angel Press of Wisconsin, 1987), 213.

39 *Green Bay residents accepted the fact*: Coenen. *From Sandlots to the Super Bowl*, 48.

39 *I guess Curly was a human guy after all*: Whittingham, Richard. *What a Game They Played: An Inside Look at the Golden Era of Pro Football* (New York: Simon & Schuster, 1987), 41.

39 *League officials gave the city one last chance*: Coenen. *From Sandlots to the Super Bowl*, 45.

39 *Word of their meeting went round the town*: Ward, Arch. *The Green Bay Packers: The Story of Professional Football* (New York: G.P. Putnam's Sons, 1946), 127.

40 *during the Depression, toilet paper and paper towels*: Coenen. *From Sandlots to the Super Bowl*, 47.

40 *By early February more than 154 boosters*: Coenen. *From Sandlots to the Super Bowl*, 46.

40 *Before we had the Packers*: "Green Bay Proud of Gridiron Team," *Palm Beach Post*, December 10, 1939.

41 *Curly Lambeau once told me*: Cope, Myron. *The Game That Was: The Early Days of Pro Football* (New York: World, 1970), 148.

41 *It's lucky I sent my letter*: Johnson. *Green Bay Packers*, 73.

41 *When I got to Green Bay, Curly told me*: Whittingham. *What a Game They Played*, 122.

41 *Curly Lambeau may not have been the greatest coach*: Michalske, Mike. "The Game I Will Never Forget," *Milwaukee Sentinel*, September 20, 1969.

42 *The best way I can describe Hutson*: Whittingham. *What a Game They Played*, 95.

42 *With a cunning eye for talent*: Zimmerman, David. *Lambeau: The Man behind the Mystique* (Hales Corners, WI: Eagle, 2003), 121.

43 *This league would never survive*: Yost, Mark. *Tailgating, Sacks, and Salary Caps: How the NFL Became the Most Successful Sports League in History* (Chicago: Kaplan, 2006), 54.

43 *Contract negotiations with Curly*: Zimmerman. *Lambeau*, 125.

43 *I was getting $150 a game*: Gullickson, Denis J. *Vagabond Halfback: The Life and Times of Johnny Blood McNally* (Madison, WI: Trails, 2006), 116.

44 *with Hutson and myself as receivers*: Whittingham. *What a Game They Played*, 39.

45 *Although 29,545 fans were in attendance*: Johnson. *Green Bay Packers*, 77.

45 *hell, the whole town was there to greet us*: Whittingham. *What a Game They Played*, 126.

46 *The fans told the truth*: Cope. *Game That Was*, 101.

47 *That was the only game I can remember*: Whittingham. *What a Game They Played*, 126.

47 *I felt we were a better team*: Whittingham. *What a Game They Played*, 126.

47 *It generated $68,332 in gross income*: Coenen. *From Sandlots to the Super Bowl*, 88.

47 *the most lucrative gate in NFL history to date*: Johnson. *Green Bay Packers*, 79.

48 *The play for the full sixty vibrant minutes*: Whittingham. *What a Game They Played*, 182.

48 *With the possible single exception of George Halas*: Names. *History of the Green Bay Packers: The Lambeau Years, Part Two*, 137.

48 *NBC-TV approached the NFL's Brooklyn Dodgers*: Coenen. *From Sandlots to the Super Bowl*, 152.

48 *When the sun crept behind the stadium*: Whittingham. *What a Game They Played*, 193.

49 *Green Bay fans overlook the great debt*: Coenen. *From Sandlots to the Super Bowl*, 48.

50 *It was very windy that day*: Whittingham. *What a Game They Played*, 126.

50 *We broke their hearts*: Goska, Eric. *Green Bay Packers: A Measure of Greatness* (Iola, WI: Krause, 2003), 387.

50 *State Fair Park's capacity crowd of 32,279*: Coenen. *From Sandlots to the Super Bowl*, 88.

50 *a winner's share of $703*: Johnson. *Green Bay Packers*, 85.

50 *Green Bay will retain its franchise*: Ward. *Green Bay Packers*, 147.

51 *Mutual Broadcast Company paid the league $2,500*: Coenen. *From Sandlots to the Super Bowl*, 111.

51 *In a good year, with all incentives paid off*: Zimmerman. *Lambeau*, 143–44.

52 *As the team grew more successful*: Zimmerman. *Lambeau*, 24.

52 *Shake hands! That would have been a lie*: D'Amato, Gary, and Cliff Christl. *Mudbaths & Bloodbaths: The Inside Story of the Bears-Packers Rivalry* (Black Earth, WI: Prairie Oak, 1997), 22.

52 *I lose money every time I play at Green Bay*: Names. *History of the Green Bay Packers: The Lambeau Years, Part Two*, 168.

53 *In his early days*: Cope. *Game That Was*, 101.

53 *To combat it, Lambeau*: Whittingham. *What a Game They Played*, 100.

53 *It put about a four-inch gash*: Whittingham. *What a Game They Played*, 100.

55 *Any football fan will agree*: Ward. *Green Bay Packers*, 154.

55 *the Packers organization invested $10,000*: Torinus, John B. *The Packer Legend: An Inside Look* (Neshkoro, WI: Laranmark, 1982), 45.

55 *It is possible our club won't be*: Names. *History of the Green Bay Packers: The Lambeau Years, Part Two*, 185.

56 *The community responded by purchasing*: Names. *History of the Green Bay Packers: The Lambeau Years, Part Two*, 187.

57 *Sports' main obligation*: Ziemba, Joe. *When Football Was Football: The Chicago Cardinals and the Birth of the NFL* (Chicago: Triumph, 1999), 243.

57 *Prior to the war, 40 to 50 percent*: Coenen. *From Sandlots to the Super Bowl*, 101.

57 *Primary among the teams*: Names. *The History of the Green Bay Packers: The Lambeau Years, Part Two*, 193.

57 *despite estimates the team would lose $25,000*: Torinus. *Packer Legend*, 47.

57 *Curly's idea was to house the team*: Torinus. *Packer Legend*, 59.

58 *Lambeau's stated intention*: Gulbrandsen, Don. *Green Bay Packers: The Complete Illustrated History* (St. Paul, MN: Voyageur, 2007), 52.

60 *for the first time this year*: Goska. *Green Bay Packers*, 388.

61 *record gate receipts of $146,205.15*: Ward. *Green Bay Packers*, 165.

61 *If I ever play on this field again*: Johnson. *Green Bay Packers*, 87.

61 *They believed professional football*: Names. *History of the Green Bay Packers: The Lambeau Years, Part Two*, 222.

61 *five franchise applications*: Coenen. *From Sandlots to the Super Bowl*, 114.

61 *He was beginning to believe*: Names. *History of the Green Bay Packers: The Lambeau Years, Part Two*, 237.

61 *Lambeau had built a fantasy world*: Names. *History of the Green Bay Packers: The Lambeau Years, Part Two*, 234.

62 *he was never the same*: Whittingham. *What a Game They Played*, 96.

62 *I was born in and have lived in Green Bay*: Names. *History of the Green Bay Packers: The Lambeau Years, Part Two*, 231.

62 *the most devastating quarter*: Ward. *Green Bay Packers*, 178.

64 *It was damn near impossible*: Whittingham. *What a Game They Played*, 128.

64 *an annual $15,000 salary*: Zimmerman. *Lambeau*, 115.

65 *there is nothing for the National Football League*: Ward. *Green Bay Packers*, 209.

65 *Teams say their payrolls*: Ward. *Green Bay Packers*, 213.

65 *The national league will bring a team*: Ziemba. *When Football Was Football*, 291.

66 *Lambeau stubbornly stuck to his single-wing*: Zimmerman, David. *Lambeau Legends: Packer Profiles of Courage* (Hales Corners, WI: Eagle, 2008), 178.

67 *Cal's long and intimate association*: Torinus. *Packer Legend*, 29.

67 *We took all the grief and criticism*: Johnson. *Green Bay Packers*, 92.

67 *he married another woman*: Torinus. *Packer Legend*, 60.

68 *In an attempt to regain control*: Johnson. *Green Bay Packers*, 89.

68 *Jerry Clifford called an executive board meeting*: Johnson. *Green Bay Packers*, 93.

68 *I believe these men*: Johnson. *Green Bay Packers*, 93.

68 *this proved impossible*: Johnson. *Green Bay Packers*, 89.

69 *Green Bay's Packers, rumors to the contrary*: Names, Larry. *The History of the Green Bay Packers: The Lambeau Years, Part Three* (Wautoma, WI: Angel Press of Wisconsin, 1990), 47.

69 *Back in 1941 only a few star players*: Coenen. *From Sandlots to the Super Bowl*, 128–30.

69 *the number of homes with television sets*: Coenen. *From Sandlots to the Super Bowl*, 153.

70 *If Curly was successful*: Names. *History of the Green Bay Packers: The Lambeau Years, Part Three*, 11.

70 *The game kind of passed Curly by*: Poling, Jerry. *Downfield: Untold Stories of the Green Bay Packers* (Black Earth, WI: Prairie Oak, 1996), 178.

70 *the fact that Lambeau paid*: Zimmerman, David. *In Search of a Hero: Life and Times of Tony Canadeo* (Hales Corners, WI: Eagle, 2001), 124.

71 *He claimed we hadn't been trying*: Whittingham. *What a Game They Played*, 219.

71 *The team was pretty much done*: Poling. *Downfield*, 179.

72 *By the end of the 1948 season*: Coenen. *From Sandlots to the Super Bowl*, 132.

72 *Incurring estimated total losses of $155,000*: Coenen. *From Sandlots to the Super Bowl*, 147.

73 *In the inglorious years*: Zimmerman. *Lambeau*, 25.

73 *This is only one game*: Zimmerman. *In Search of a Hero*, 141.

73 *Everybody was thinking*: Zimmerman. *In Search of a Hero*, 149.

74 *the financial situation became critical*: Torinus. *Packer Legend*, 63.

75 *That's the only game we ever played*: Zimmerman. *In Search of a Hero*, 152.

75 *Green Bay's troubles today are many*: Kuechle, Oliver. "Packer Troubles Due to Jealousies," *Milwaukee Journal*, November 22, 1949.

75 *it was easily surmised*: Torinus. *Packer Legend*, 63.

75 *The Packers had now hit rock bottom*: Zimmerman. *In Search of a Hero*, 155.

77 *The Packers have successfully passed*: Names. *History of the Green Bay Packers: The Lambeau Years, Part Three*, 169.

78 *When Curly failed*: Names, Larry. *The History of the Green Bay Packers: The Shameful Years, Part Four* (Wautoma, WI: Angel Press of Wisconsin, 1995), 11.

78 *While local patronage*: Coenen. *From Sandlots to the Super Bowl*, 115.

78 *No group of twelve men*: "Lambeau Asks Action from Packers' Board: New Contract Never Issued," *Milwaukee Journal*, January 11, 1950.

79 *I didn't set the Rockwood Lodge fire*: Coenen. *From Sandlots to the Super Bowl*, 149.

79 *it was no surprise*: Torinus. *Packer Legend*, 63.

79 *We've had two good breaks*: Johnson. *Green Bay Packers*, 97.

79 *I don't see*: Johnson. *Green Bay Packers*, 97.

CHAPTER THREE

81 *We're not taking a chance*: Torinus, John B. *The Packer Legend: An Inside Look* (Neshkoro, WI: Laranmark, 1982), 69.

82 *some thought the whole thing*: Johnson, Chuck. *The Green Bay Packers: Pro Football's Pioneer Team* (New York: Thomas Nelson & Sons, 1961), 98.

82 *the Packers organization made 9,500*: Names, Larry. *The History of the Green Bay Packers: The Shameful Years, Part Four* (Wautoma, WI: Angel Press of Wisconsin, 1995), 23.

82 *That night more than one thousand shares*: Coenen, Craig R. *From Sandlots to the Super Bowl: The National Football League, 1920–1967* (Knoxville: University of Tennessee Press, 2005), 150.

82 *There were shares*: Ledbetter, D. Orlando, and Cliff Christl. "Packers Get League Approval for Stock Sale," Packers Plus Online, November 12, 1997, www2.jsonline .com/packer/sbxxxii/news/stock111297.stm (accessed December 4, 2008; site discontinued).

82 *A lot of people didn't think*: Ledbetter and Christl. "Packers Get League Approval."

82 *It is impossible*: Names. *History of the Green Bay Packers: The Shameful Years, Part Four*, 26.

83 *We want Milwaukee*: Larson, Lloyd. "Milwaukee Definitely in Future Plans," *Milwaukee Sentinel*, February 8, 1950.

83 *When we were at about $80,000*: Ledbetter and Christl. "Packers Get League Approval."

83 *the team raised roughly $50,000*: "Shareholder & Financial History," *Green Bay Packers Gameday*, 2007, 128.

83 *bringing in $105,825*: Coenen. *From Sandlots to the Super Bowl*, 150.

83 *All those rumors*: Schaap, Dick. *Green Bay Replay: The Packers' Return to Glory* (New York: Avon, 1997), 159.

83 *out of the financial woods*: Coenen. *From Sandlots to the Super Bowl*, 150.

85 *By 1949 total NFL television rights*: Yost, Mark. *Tailgating, Sacks, and Salary Caps: How the NFL Became the Most Successful Sports League in History* (Chicago: Kaplan, 2006), 67.

85 *More people have seen the Bears*: Peterson, Robert W. *Pigskin: The Early Years of Pro Football* (New York: Oxford University Press, 1997), 196.

85 *You can't give a game to the public*: Rubin, Bob. "The Men and Events Behind the Boom," *Sport*, August 1968, 29.

85 *Gene Ronzani had little respect*: Gulbrandsen, Don. *Green Bay Packers: The Complete Illustrated History* (St. Paul, MN: Voyageur, 2007), 61.

86 *He was trying*: Whittingham, Richard. *What a Game They Played: An Inside Look at the Golden Era of Pro Football* (New York: Simon & Schuster, 1987), 219.

86 *one of the most exceptional*: Miller, Mike. "Jack Vainisi: The Drafting Genius behind the Packers Dynasty," *Wisconsin State Journal*, April 23, 2009, http://host.madison.com/sports/article_3965e117-959a-524a-8e98-8de214462d21.html.

86 *not only pay all expenses*: Associated Press. "Green Bay Packers in N.F.L. to Stay," *Lewiston Daily Sun*, December 7, 1950.

87 *They don't have to worry*: Associated Press. "Green Bay Packers in N.F.L. to Stay."

87 *The gossip intensified*: Names. *History of the Green Bay Packers: The Shameful Years, Part Four*, 50.

87 *This move was taken solely*: Names. *History of the Green Bay Packers: The Shameful Years, Part Four*, 69.

89 *When the Wisconsin Network*: Torinus. *Packer Legend*, 85.

89 *During the 1952 season*: Torinus. *Packer Legend*, 70.

90 *If Coach Gene Ronzani*: Larson, Lloyd. "Looks Like Packers Are Here to Stay," *Milwaukee Sentinel*, February 5, 1953.

91 *When he stepped down*: Names. *History of the Green Bay Packers: The Shameful Years, Part Four*, 264.

91 *He treated the Packers*: Names. *History of the Green Bay Packers: The Shameful Years, Part Four*, 264.

92 *All of us want to see*: Names. *History of the Green Bay Packers: The Shameful Years, Part Four*, 90.

92 *Situations in the past*: Johnson. *Green Bay Packers*, 141.

92 *Every Tuesday in Green Bay*: Johnson. *Green Bay Packers*, 100.

92 *Bogda took a well-oiled ship*: Names. *History of the Green Bay Packers: The Shameful Years, Part Four*, 264.

92 *The fall of Gene Ronzani*: Names. *History of the Green Bay Packers: The Shameful Years, Part Four*, 107.

94 *The situation has grown so serious*: Names. *History of the Green Bay Packers: The Shameful Years, Part Four*, 121.

94 *Despite the tumultuous season*: Coenen. *From Sandlots to the Super Bowl*, 156.

95 *That allowed the DuMont Broadcasting Network*: Schaaf, Phil. *Sports, Inc.: 100 Years of Sports Business* (Amherst, NY: Prometheus, 2004), 88.

95 *DuMont paid $95,000*: Peterson. *Pigskin*, 197.

95 *In 1955 NBC assumed*: Fortunato, John A. *Commissioner: The Legacy of Pete Rozelle* (New York: Taylor Trade, 2006), 11.

95 *The first year I was doing*: Flynn, George. *The Vince Lombardi Scrapbook* (New York: Gross & Dunlap, 1976), 151.

96 *The Executive Committee wanted*: Gulbrandsen. *Green Bay Packers*, 65.

96 *Blackbourn was hired*: Associated Press. "Marquette Mentor Is Surprise Choice; Fills Spot Vacated by Gene Ronzani," *Pittsburgh Post-Gazette*, January 8, 1954.

96 *The 13-man executive committee*: Johnson. *Green Bay Packers*, 104.

96 *Nobody realizes any more*: Goska, Eric. *Green Bay Packers: A Measure of Greatness* (Iola, WI: Krause, 2003), 110.

97 *Despite their losing record*: Coenen. *From Sandlots to the Super Bowl*, 156.

97 *The locker room was horrendous*: Zimmerman, David. *In Search of a Hero: Life and Times of Tony Canadeo* (Hales Corners, WI: Eagle, 2001), 53.

98 *Green Bay boosters had to fend off*: Coenen. *From Sandlots to the Super Bowl*, 169.

99 *Their good intentions*: Names. *History of the Green Bay Packers: The Shameful Years, Part Four*, 136.

100 *Blackbourn's modest success*: Names. *History of the Green Bay Packers: The Shameful Years, Part Four*, 176.

100 *Old friends like Gene Ronzani*: Torinus. *Packer Legend*, 96.

100 *If the question doesn't win*: Names. *History of the Green Bay Packers: The Shameful Years, Part Four*, 195.

101 *golden era is going to be*: Names. *History of the Green Bay Packers: The Shameful Years, Part Four*, 196.

101 *The stadium contract*: Green Bay Press-Gazette. *Lambeau Field: Green Bay's National Treasure* (Green Bay: Pediment, 2003), 21.

101 *I well remember getting a telegram*: Torinus. *Packer Legend*, 95.

101 *When I first came here*: Bauer, David, ed. *The Champions: Green Bay Packers 1996* (New York: Sports Illustrated, 1997), 13.

102 *I actually felt sorry*: Johnson. *Green Bay Packers*, 106.

102 *the Packers still reported a profit*: Names. *History of the Green Bay Packers: The Shameful Years, Part Four*, 210.

102 *The Packers had a $142,993*: Coenen. *From Sandlots to the Super Bowl*, 184.

103 *In those days any time*: Leuthner, Stuart. *Iron Men: Bucko, Crazylegs, and the Boys Recall the Golden Days of Professional Football* (New York: Doubleday, 1988), 18.

103 *The NFLPA went to the owners*: Coenen. *From Sandlots to the Super Bowl*, 182.

104 *Bell was adamant*: Torinus. *Packer Legend*, 87.

105 *He is a natural athlete*: Schaap, Dick. "The Rough Road Ahead for Paul Hornung," *Sport*, November 1961, 64.

105 *I went to the University of Michigan*: Gulbrandsen. *Green Bay Packers*, 65.

105 *It just wouldn't*: Gulbrandsen. *Green Bay Packers*, 65.

106 *when the team was losing*: Johnson. *Green Bay Packers*, 106.

106 *He was a very good coach*: Reischel, Rob. *Packers Essential: Everything You Need to Know to Be a Real Fan!* (Chicago: Triumph, 2006), 17.

106 *If anything is coming up*: Names. *History of the Green Bay Packers: The Shameful Years, Part Four*, 234.

106 *Blackbourn wasn't run out of town*: Names. *History of the Green Bay Packers: The Shameful Years, Part Four*, 239.

107 *A board certainly can fire*: Kuechle, Oliver. "The Record Will Speak in Liz's Dismissal, but It Will Not Show Extra Manipulations," *Milwaukee Journal*, January 7, 1958.

108 *also a possibility*: Names. *History of the Green Bay Packers: The Shameful Years, Part Four*, 238.

108 *But coaching good or bad*: Kuechle. "Record Will Speak."

108 *advisable to hire McLean*: Kuechle. "Record Will Speak."

108 *The people of Green Bay*: Johnson. *Green Bay Packers*, 109.

108 *Blackbourn's firing*: Names. *History of the Green Bay Packers: The Shameful Years, Part Four*, 242.

109 *Olejniczak inherited a team*: Names. *History of the Green Bay Packers: The Shameful Years, Part Four*, 246.

109 *Milwaukee is a good football town*: Names. *History of the Green Bay Packers: The Shameful Years, Part Four*, 247.

109 *We're shooting for the moon*: Names. *History of the Green Bay Packers: The Shameful Years, Part Four*, 243.

109 *the players will be on their honor*: Johnson. *Green Bay Packers*, 109.

109 *Scooter would play poker*: Reischel. *Packers Essential*, 14.

109 *The players just didn't*: Reischel. *Packers Essential*, 18.

110 *If they had spent*: Torinus. *Packer Legend*, 81.

110 *Those days were just miserable*: Reischel. *Packers Essential*, 14.

110 *the executive committee didn't want*: Names. *History of the Green Bay Packers: The Shameful Years, Part Four*, 268.

110 *the hurt was made worse*: Bengtson, Phil, with Todd Hunt. *Packer Dynasty: The Saga of the Championship Green Bay Teams* (New York: Doubleday, 1969), 3.

110 *Why a board of directors*: Johnson, Chuck. "Packer Director Calls for 'House Cleaning,'" *Milwaukee Journal*, November 6, 1958.

111 *The Packers overwhelmed*: Johnson. *Green Bay Packers*, 110.

111 *the Siberia of pro football*: Gruver, Ed. *The Ice Bowl: The Cold Truth about Football's Most Unforgettable Game* (Ithaca, NY: McBooks, 1998), 75.

111 *The situation was pretty hopeless*: Berger, Phil. *Championship Teams of the NFL* (New York: Random House, 1968), 113.

111 *As 1959 began*: Names. *History of the Green Bay Packers: The Shameful Years, Part Four*, 268.

CHAPTER FOUR

113 *What we lacked*: McCullough, Bob. *My Greatest Day in Football: The Legends of Football Recount Their Greatest Moments* (New York: Thomas Dunne, 2001), 218.

113 *how many stripes*: Bengtson, Phil, with Todd Hunt. *Packer Dynasty: The Saga of the Championship Green Bay Teams* (New York: Doubleday, 1969), 10.

113 *One of the notable applicants*: Torinus, John B. *The Packer Legend: An Inside Look* (Neshkoro, WI: Laranmark, 1982), 112.

113 *when the board of directors met*: Zimmerman, David. *Lambeau: The Man behind the Mystique* (Hales Corners, WI: Eagle, 2003), 234.

113 *You had to like him*: Zimmerman, David. *In Search of a Hero: Life and Times of Tony Canadeo* (Hales Corners, WI: Eagle, 2001), 198.

114 *All I have to do is win*: Wagner, Len. *Launching the Glory Years: The 1959 Packers* (Green Bay: Coach's Books, 2001), 9.

114 *My number one job*: Green, Bob. "Vince's Toughest Job? Leaving Green Bay," *Owosso Argus-Press*, September 3, 1970.

114 *Since the club grossed only $836,000*: Bynum, Mike, ed. *Vince Lombardi: Memories of a Special Time* (Chicago: October Football, 1988), 49.

114 *There's no room for sentiment*: Bengtson with Hunt. *Packer Dynasty*, 15.

114 *And he wasn't kidding*: Bengtson with Hunt. *Packer Dynasty*, 13.

114 *Where many ladles*: Kuechle, Oliver. "Time Out for Talk: One Ladle Stirs Where Many Once Stirred," *Milwaukee Journal*, July 5, 1959.

115 *Go ahead and quit*: Berger, Phil. *Championship Teams of the NFL* (New York: Random House, 1968), 116.

115 *Billy was probably*: Biever, Vernon J. *The Glory of Titletown: The Classic Green Bay Packers Photography of Vernon Biever* (Lanham, MD: Taylor Trade, 1997), 17.

115 *Everybody involved*: Bengtson with Hunt. *Packer Dynasty*, 31.

116 *Had our fast start*: Hornung, Paul. *Golden Boy* (New York: Simon & Schuster, 2004), 96.

116 *It did indeed seem*: Bengtson with Hunt. *Packer Dynasty*, 40.

116 *the franchise had made a net profit*: Associated Press. "Packers Become $ Million Business," *Milwaukee Sentinel*, May 2, 1960.

117 *I think Vince took care*: Flynn, George. *The Vince Lombardi Scrapbook* (New York: Gross & Dunlap, 1976), 83.

117 *The NFL's refusal to expand*: Coenen, Craig R. *From Sandlots to the Super Bowl: The National Football League, 1920–1967* (Knoxville: University of Tennessee Press, 2005), 188.

118 *establishing an entrance fee of $100,000*: Felser, Larry. *The Birth of the New NFL: How the 1966 NFL/AFL Merger Transformed Pro Football* (Guilford, CT: Lyons Press, 2008), xv.

119 *Rozelle was the genius*: Hornung. *Golden Boy*, 108.

119 *His background as a PR man*: Hornung. *Golden Boy*, 148.

119 *The NFL had just sold*: Fortunato, John A. *Commissioner: The Legacy of Pete Rozelle* (New York: Taylor Trade, 2006), 26.

119 *The clubs' individual television deals*: MacCambridge, Michael. *America's Game: The Epic Story of How Pro Football Captured a Nation* (New York: Anchor, 2004), 171.

119 *And CBS, which had contracts*: Fortunato. *Commissioner*, 28.

120 *For the four league games*: Johnson, Chuck. *The Green Bay Packers: Pro Football's Pioneer Team* (New York: Thomas Nelson & Sons, 1961), 143.

120 *[Vainisi] had suffered*: Maraniss, David. *When Pride Still Mattered: A Life of Vince Lombardi* (New York: Simon & Schuster, 1999), 249.

120 *Their squad was*: Bengtson with Hunt. *Packer Dynasty*, 47.

121 *With time for only one play*: Bengtson with Hunt. *Packer Dynasty*, 49.

121 *[Lombardi] told us we hadn't*: Carlson, Chuck. *Game of My Life: Memorable Stories of Packers Football* (Champaign, IL: Sports Publishing, 2004), 22.

121 *The Packers found little comfort*: Johnson. *Green Bay Packers*, 150.

121 *We were in the dressing room*: Leuthner, Stuart. *Iron Men: Bucko, Crazylegs, and the Boys Recall the Golden Days of Professional Football* (New York: Doubleday, 1988), 20.

122 *Vince wanted to take the Giant job*: Bynum, ed. *Vince Lombardi*, 167.

122 *I've got news for you*: Lea, Bud. *Magnificent Seven: The Championship Games That Built the Lombardi Dynasty* (Chicago: Triumph, 2002), 2.

123 *The single network contract legislation*: Schaaf, Phil. *Sports, Inc.: 100 Years of Sports Business* (Amherst, NY: Prometheus, 2004), 68.

123 *The whole thing was equalizing*: Yost, Mark. *Tailgating, Sacks, and Salary Caps: How the NFL Became the Most Successful Sports League in History* (Chicago: Kaplan, 2006), 75.

123 *On January 10, 1962, CBS*: Coenen. *From Sandlots to the Super Bowl*, 220.

123 *The TV package deal*: Rubin, Bob. "The Men and Events behind the Boom," *Sport*, August 1968, 74.

123 *If there was any danger*: Associated Press. "Lombardi Gets 5-Year Contract, Salary Boost," *Milwaukee Sentinel*, August 8, 1961.

123 *First-stringers [Paul] Hornung*: Bengtson with Hunt. *Packer Dynasty*, 51.

124 *It was a cold day*: McCullough. *My Greatest Day in Football*, 59.

124 *He built it up*: Lea. *Magnificent Seven*, 3.

124 *I listened as Lombardi explained*: Gentile, Domenic, with Gary D'Amato. *The Packer Tapes: My 32 Years with the Green Bay Packers* (Madison, WI: Prairie Oak, 1995), 19.

125 *Paul Hornung isn't going to win*: Lea. *Magnificent Seven*, 6.

125 *Our offensive line was devastating*: McCullough. *My Greatest Day in Football*, 59.

125 *Nine of the guys*: Berger. *Championship Teams of the NFL*, 138.

126 *You're the greatest team*: Bengtson with Hunt. *Packer Dynasty*, 56.

126 *It was a two-thousand-dollar expenditure*: Bengtson with Hunt. *Packer Dynasty*, 57.

126 *the first to earn a million-dollar gate*: Lefebvre, Hank, and Ray O. Wanek. *50 Years of Professional Football: A Complete Picture History of the Green Bay Packers* (Green Bay: Green Bay Packer Alumni Association, 1968), 75.

126 *With an estimated 55 million fans*: Gulbrandsen, Don. *Green Bay Packers: The Complete Illustrated History* (St. Paul, MN: Voyageur, 2007), 77.

126 *the club cleared a net profit*: Associated Press. "Packers Have Huge Surplus," *Gettysburg Times*, May 3, 1962.

126 *Lombardi probably did not have*: Flynn. *Vince Lombardi Scrapbook*, 74.

126 *There was no way*: Leuthner. *Iron Men*, 20.

127 *were tired, strained*: Bengtson with Hunt. *Packer Dynasty*, 59.

127 *The momentary lapse*: Bengtson with Hunt. *Packer Dynasty*, 60.

127 *the character of our team surfaced*: Starr, Bart, with Murray Olderman. *My Life in Football: Starr* (New York: William Morrow, 1987), 93.

127 *It seemed that both teams*: McDonell, Chris. *The Football Game I'll Never Forget: 100 NFL Stars' Stories* (Buffalo, NY: Firefly, 2004), 142.

127 *The Giants were playing angry*: Lea. *Magnificent Seven*, 35.

129 *You have to remember*: Cameron, Steve. *The Packers! Seventy-five Seasons of Memories and Mystique in Green Bay* (Dallas: Taylor, 1993), 95.

129 *One commentator*: Wells, Robert W. *Lombardi: His Life and Times* (Madison, WI: Wisconsin House, 1971), 125.

129 *When the writers and commentators*: Bengtson with Hunt. *Packer Dynasty*, 58.

129 *Here we are*: Bengtson with Hunt. *Packer Dynasty*, 58.

129 *The wind was so ferocious*: Carlson. *Game of My Life*, 40.

129 *Our philosophy was move the chains*: McCullough. *My Greatest Day in Football*, 237.

130 *Probably the biggest moment*: Lea. *Magnificent Seven*, 50.

130 *It's got to give you*: McDonell. *Football Game I'll Never Forget*, 143.

130 *We can hold our heads high*: Johnson. *Green Bay Packers*, supplement, 7.

130 *there remained, however*: Bengtson with Hunt. *Packer Dynasty*, 61.

131 *posting an all-time net profit*: Associated Press. "Packer Profit of $255,501 in 1962 Is Record," *Chicago Tribune*, May 4, 1963.

131 *Most teams would have been*: Starr with Olderman. *My Life in Football*, 106.

131 *Someone once figured out*: Gruver, Ed. *The Ice Bowl: The Cold Truth about Football's Most Unforgettable Game* (Ithaca, NY: McBooks, 1998), 35.

132 *The frustration of finishing second*: Starr with Olderman. *My Life in Football*, 108.

132 *He disclosed a profit*: Journal Special Correspondence. "Nontitle Packers Collected Less, Paid Less, Kept Less." *Milwaukee Journal*, May 5, 1964.

132 *With television income up*: Journal Special Correspondence. "Nontitle Packers Collected Less."

133 *At the moment we have*: Journal Special Correspondence. "Nontitle Packers Collected Less."

133 *the NFL's fourteen franchises had grossed*: Oriard, Michael. *Brand NFL: Making & Selling America's Favorite Sport* (Chapel Hill: University of North Carolina Press, 2007), 4.

133 *Today we take for granted*: Gulbrandsen. *Green Bay Packers*, 84.

133 *I remember I sat down*: Devaney, John. "The Inner Workings of the NFL," *Sport*, December 1964, 71.

135 *Each franchise was estimated to earn*: Fortunato. *Commissioner*, 60.

135 *paying the league $36 million*: Fortunato. *Commissioner*, 61.

135 *In the space of seven days*: Gruver. *Ice Bowl*, 33.

136 *an estimated 21 million viewers*: Gruver. *Ice Bowl*, 32.

136 *A different outcome*: Bengtson with Hunt. *Packer Dynasty*, 65.

136 *gave you the sense of reality*: McCullough. *My Greatest Day in Football*, 238.

137 *We didn't make*: Bengtson with Hunt. *Packer Dynasty*, 66.

137 *The difference [between*: Lombardi, Vince, Jr. *The Lombardi Rules: 26 Lessons from Vince Lombardi—the World's Greatest Coach* (New York: McGraw-Hill, 2005), 23.

137 *It seemed the more successful*: Zimmerman. *Lambeau*, 238.

137 *The city of Green Bay*: Associated Press. "Packers Founder's Funeral Saturday," *Sarasota Herald-Tribune*, June 3, 1965.

137 *Few men anywhere*: Zimmerman. *Lambeau*, 28.

137 *After two winning*: Lea. *Magnificent Seven*, xii.

138 *So far this season*: Bengtson with Hunt. *Packer Dynasty*, 69.

138 *I'm very happy to stay*: Bengtson with Hunt. *Packer Dynasty*, 76.

138 *The reporters were asking us*: Carlson. *Game of My Life*, 124.

139 *The Colts can say what they want*: Andrews, Tom. "40th Anniversary of Mud and Men: '65 Title Game Re-kindled Packers Dynasty," *2005 Green Bay Packers Yearbook*, 81.

139 *In the exhibition season*: Andrews. "40th Anniversary of Mud and Men," *2005 Green Bay Packers Yearbook*, 80.

139 *The Browns bus eventually arrived*: Gregg, Forrest, and Andrew O'Toole. *Winning in the Trenches: A Lifetime of Football* (Cincinnati: Clerisy Press, 2009), 110.

140 *They were all over him*: Andrews. "40th Anniversary of Mud and Men," *2005 Green Bay Packers Yearbook*, 82.

140 *The snow and mud were our allies*: National Football League Properties. *The Official NFL Encyclopedia of Pro Football*, 3rd ed. (New York: New American Library, 1982), 368.

141 *In June 1965 the NFL recruited*: Rubin. "The Men and Events," 29.

141 *As general manager*: Andrews. "40th Anniversary of Mud and Men," *2005 Green Bay Packers Yearbook*, 98.

141 *struggled with the thorny problem*: Fishman, Marv, with Tracy Dodds. *Bucking the Odds: The Birth of the Milwaukee Bucks* (Milwaukee: Raintree, 1978), 12.

141 *the Packers were so strong*: Fishman with Dodds. *Bucking the Odds*, 10.

143 *Challenging Lombardi*: Fishman with Dodds. *Bucking the Odds*, 20.

143 *We might have overcome*: Fishman with Dodds. *Bucking the Odds*, 16.

143 *I wouldn't do anything*: Fishman with Dodds. *Bucking the Odds*, 16.

143 *If I couldn't get the stadium*: Fishman with Dodds. *Bucking the Odds*, 20.

144 *My kids have this ball*: Whittingham, Richard. *Sunday's Heroes: NFL Legends Talk about the Times of Their Lives* (Chicago: Triumph, 2003), 176.

144 *Congressman Boggs, I don't know*: Felser. *Birth of the New NFL*, 98.

144 *we were determined*: Bengtson with Hunt. *Packer Dynasty*, 93.

145 *Yet, Green Bay's annual income*: Coenen. *From Sandlots to the Super Bowl*, 222.

145 *The next year one of our players*: Gentile with D'Amato. *Packer Tapes*, 18.

145 *In 1946 an average annual*: Schaap, Dick. "Why Pro Football Players Revolt," *Sport*, January 1964, 74.

145 *If there was one small spot*: Bengtson with Hunt. *Packer Dynasty*, 94.

146 *Standing in the Packer locker room*: Gruver. *Ice Bowl*, 29.

146 *was one of the most exciting*: Bengtson with Hunt. *Packer Dynasty*, 100.

146 *there was nothing we could do*: Lea. *Magnificent Seven*, 93.

147 *I had his [Meredith's] left arm*: Goska, Eric. *Green Bay Packers: A Measure of Greatness* (Iola, WI: Krause, 2003), 391.

147 *The toughest coaching job*: Bengtson with Hunt. *Packer Dynasty*, 104.

147 *We had to win*: Bengtson with Hunt. *Packer Dynasty*, 105.

147 *Here you had new guys*: Green Bay Press-Gazette. *Titletown: The Unforgettable Story of the Green Bay Packers' Road to Super Bowl XXXI* (Louisville, KY: AdCraft Sports Marketing, 1997), 131.

147 *we didn't know a thing*: Cameron. *Packers!*, 125.

149 *Pressure?*: Izenberg, Jerry. "Behind the Scenes at the Super Bowl: The Winning Packers," *Sport*, April 1967, 31.

149 *We will win this game*: Izenberg. "Behind the Scenes," 31.

149 *Fortunately, those were the last*: Rozelle, Pete. "Truly the Biggest Game," *Super Bowl XXXI Official Game Program*, 96n.

149 *We talked for almost five minutes*: Felser. *Birth of the New NFL*, 131.

149 *It was the only time*: Cameron. *Packers!*, 125.

150 *The Packers played probably*: McCullough. *My Greatest Day in Football*, 62.

150 *He said, "Okay*: McCullough. *My Greatest Day in Football*, 62.

150 *That, for all purposes, was the end*: Bengtson with Hunt. *Packer Dynasty*, 108.

151 *It was almost as if*: Bengtson with Hunt. *Packer Dynasty*, 109.

151 *the Packers players each received*: United Press. "Great to Be a Packer, Pretty Profitable, Too," *Reading Eagle*, February 21, 1967.

151 *It just goes to show*: United Press. "Great to Be a Packer."

152 *When I finished my first year*: Bynum, ed. *Vince Lombardi*, 125.

152 *the team's gross operating income*: "Record $827,439 Profit for Packers," *Milwaukee Sentinel*, June 6, 1967.

152 *Green Bay's City Stadium Commission*: Associated Press. "Lambeau Field Profit: $58,059," *Milwaukee Sentinel*, March 16, 1967.

152 *Within two years, some team*: Felser. *Birth of the New NFL*, 157.

153 *all fans could talk about*: Gulbrandsen. *Green Bay Packers*, 92.

153 *Some of you people are fat*: Bynum, ed. *Vince Lombardi*, 79.

153 *This is the price*: Gruver. *Ice Bowl*, 105.

153 *were down to bare bones*: Lea. *Magnificent Seven*, 160.

154 *We weren't quite the ballclub*: Lea, Bud. "Packers Three-Peated" *1997 Green Bay Packers Yearbook*, 91.

154 *They were a dominant team*: Gruver. *Ice Bowl*, 133.

154 *Few teams in NFL history*: Bengtson with Hunt. *Packer Dynasty*, 115.

154 *Everybody's been saying*: Gruver. *Ice Bowl*, 127.

155 *I don't know why*: Whittingham. *Sunday's Heroes*, 44.

155 *I think I'll have another bite*: Gruver. *Ice Bowl*, 139.

155 *Weather won't beat the team*: Bengtson with Hunt. *Packer Dynasty*, 242.

155 *Then the "breaks"*: Bengtson with Hunt. *Packer Dynasty*, 120.

155 *we got our last chance*: Bengtson with Hunt. *Packer Dynasty*, 121.

155 *I knew instantly*: Carlson. *Game of My Life*, 150.

156 *That was the point*: Gruver. *Ice Bowl*, 190.

156 *it would have meant*: Gruver. *Ice Bowl*, 212.

156 *the most beautiful sight*: Gruver. *Ice Bowl*, 215.

156 *This was it*: Gruver. *Ice Bowl*, 218.

157 *after the emotional peaks*: Bengtson with Hunt. *Packer Dynasty*, 126.

157 *I've never been around*: Cameron. *Packers!*, 122.

157 *I've never been so proud*: Felser. *Birth of the New NFL*, 165.

159 *play the last thirty minutes*: Bengtson with Hunt. *Packer Dynasty*, 130.

159 *One more time, Coach*: Bengtson with Hunt. *Packer Dynasty*, 131.

CHAPTER FIVE

161 *Because of the nature*: Meyers, Harold B. "Packers' Operation Is Nonprofit but Profitable," *Milwaukee Journal*, November 8, 1968.

161 *the survey calculated*: Bengtson, Phil, with Todd Hunt. *Packer Dynasty: The Saga of the Championship Green Bay Teams* (New York: Doubleday, 1969), 138.

162 *an extreme example of the separation*: Meyers, Harold B. "The Profitable Nonprofit in Green Bay," *Forbes*, November 1968, 142.

162 *He's always told us*: Chicago Daily News. "Lombardi Decision Hinges on Owner-Coach 'Pact,'" *Pittsburgh Press*, February 5, 1969.

162 *You know, the pressures*: Gentile, Domenic, with Gary D'Amato. *The Packer Tapes: My 32 Years with the Green Bay Packers* (Madison, WI: Prairie Oak, 1995), 22.

162 *Anybody who had been around*: Lea, Bud. *Magnificent Seven: The Championship Games That Built the Lombardi Dynasty* (Chicago: Triumph, 2002), 184.

162 *He was physically whipped*: Cameron, Steve. *The Packers! Seventy-five Seasons of Memories and Mystique in Green Bay* (Dallas: Taylor, 1993), 102.

162 *Let's face it*: Torinus, John B. *The Packer Legend: An Inside Look* (Neshkoro, WI: Laranmark, 1982), 177.

162 *He made a real mistake*: Towle, Mike. *I Remember Vince Lombardi: Personal Memories of and Testimonials to Football's First Super Bowl Championship Coach as Told by the People and Players Who Knew Him* (Nashville: Cumberland House, 2001), 155.

162 *he was sort of lurking about*: Towle. *I Remember Vince Lombardi*, 155.

163 *I was starting with a mixed bag*: Bengtson with Hunt. *Packer Dynasty*, 249.

163 *With television paying the Packers*: Crittenden, John. "Profit and Loss in Camelot," *Miami News*, November 13, 1968.

163 *probably approaching $2 million*: Meyers. "Profitable Nonprofit in Green Bay," 142.

163 *I'm very unhappy*: Gregg, Forrest, and Andrew O'Toole. *Winning in the Trenches: A Lifetime of Football* (Cincinnati: Clerisy, 2009), 137.

163 *Fortunately, a compromise settlement*: Bengtson with Hunt. *Packer Dynasty*, 252.

164 *He felt lost*: Cameron. *Packers!*, 102.

164 *The evening of our first exhibition*: Bengtson with Hunt. *Packer Dynasty*, 278.

164 *Lombardi never interfered*: Lea. *Magnificent Seven*, 184.

164 *Vince that one year*: Flynn, George. *The Vince Lombardi Scrapbook* (New York: Gross & Dunlap, 1976), 84.

164 *nobody, probably not even Phil*: Gentile with D'Amato. *Packer Tapes*, 22.

166 *it was obvious he wasn't happy*: Towle. *I Remember Vince Lombardi*, 158.

166 *Vince Lombardi asked*: Christl, Cliff. "Don't Dump Too Much on Brett Favre without Knowing History of Lambeau, Lombardi," *Green Bay Press-Gazette*, October 21, 2010.

166 *the reaction among Packers fans*: Gulbrandsen, Don. *Green Bay Packers: The Complete Illustrated History* (St. Paul, MN: Voyageur, 2007), 101.

166 *They could have condemned me*: Wells, Robert W. *Lombardi: His Life and Times* (Madison, WI: Wisconsin House, 1971), 131.

166 *Phil is being given*: United Press International. "Packers Pick Phil Bengtson to Take Over," *Windsor Star*, March 6, 1969.

166 *some of the Green Bay citizens*: Wells. *Lombardi*, 130.

167 *It was an impossible situation*: Carlson, Chuck. *Tales from the Packers Sideline: A Collection of the Greatest Stories Ever Told* (Champaign, IL: Sports Publishing, 2003), 45.

167 *the Packers posted a net profit*: United Press International. "Packers Sign Top Draft Choice," *Windsor Star*, May 27, 1969.

167 *At that point, Phil probably*: Gentile with D'Amato. *Packer Tapes*, 113.

168 *There was some interest*: Salituro, Chuck. "Super Coach: Suppose Shula Had Come to Green Bay . . . ," *Milwaukee Journal*, January 27, 1983.

169 *the television audience increased*: Felser, Larry. *The Birth of the New NFL: How the 1966 NFL/AFL Merger Transformed Pro Football* (Guilford, CT: Lyons Press, 2008), 205.

169 *The 1960s will be remembered*: Wagner, Len. "Bart Starr: Figures to Pass Football . . . Not Put It," *1971 Green Bay Packers Yearbook*, 20.

170 *sadly, even with more slots*: Gulbrandsen. *Green Bay Packers*, 103.

170 *in a marathon twenty-two hour session*: Goska, Eric. *Green Bay Packers: A Measure of Greatness* (Iola, WI: Krause, 2003), 174.

170 *It wasn't a strike*: Felser. *Birth of the New NFL*, 206.

170 *They gave us what they wanted*: Fortunato, John A. *Commissioner: The Legacy of Pete Rozelle* (New York: Taylor Trade, 2006), 151.

171 *The power of Vince Lombardi's personality*: Gentile with D'Amato. *Packer Tapes*, 25.

171 *Few people knew then*: Gentile with D'Amato. *Packer Tapes*, 25.

171 *an overall profit of $653,109*: United Press International. "Green Bay Lists Profit For '69," *Beaver Country Times*, June 9, 1970.

171 *Bengtson went into the hospital*: Torinus. *Packer Legend*, 178.

171 *I encountered a new experience*: Starr, Bart, with Murray Olderman. *My Life in Football: Starr* (New York: William Morrow, 1987), 164.

171 *After our last Super Bowl*: Kiester, Edwin, Jr. "Starr & Unitas: Why the Old Quarterbacks Won't Quit," *Sport*, July 1970, 20.

171 *That wasn't good enough*: Torinus. *Packer Legend*, 178.

172 *Because of a very disappointing season*: Greene, Bob. "New Packers Era Unfolds as Team Hunts for Coach," *Portsmouth Times*, December 23, 1970.

172 *the whole social mood of the city*: Flynn. *Vince Lombardi Scrapbook*, 144.

172 *We got the veterans here*: Dowling, Tom. "The Pack Is Devine . . . ," *Sport*, July 1971, 53.

172 *We never really knew*: Torinus. *Packer Legend*, 182.

173 *the executive committee's route*: Gulbrandsen. *Green Bay Packers*, 105.

173 *I can answer your questions*: Remmel, Lee. "Meet Dan Devine . . . He Defies Type Casting," *1971 Green Bay Packers Yearbook*, 5.

173 *I was the only man*: Remmel, Lee. "Dan's Plans for the Pack," *1971 Green Bay Packers Yearbook*, 9.

173 *Green Bay is a good organization*: Remmel. "Dan's Plans for the Pack," 10.

173 *There are certain guys*: Remmel. "Dan's Plans for the Pack," 11.

174 *He'd tell us that the Green Bay sweep*: Bie, Michael. *It Happened in Wisconsin* (Guilford, CT: Morris, 2007), 117.

174 *there was all sorts of turmoil*: Reischel, Rob. *Packers Essential: Everything You Need to Know to Be a Real Fan!* (Chicago: Triumph, 2006), 69.

174 *We don't have as good a football team*: Remmel. "Dan's Plans for the Pack," 11.

174 *People say it's a difficult transition*: Dowling. "The Pack Is Devine . . . ," 78.

174 *At the annual stockholders' meeting*: Daley, Art. "Dollars and Cents," *1971 Green Bay Packers Yearbook*, 42.

175 *I couldn't do all of the administrative*: Devine, Dan, with Michael R. Steele. *Simply Devine: Memoirs of a Hall of Fame Coach* (Champaign, IL: Sports Publishing, 2000), 100.

175 *the first reporter I talked to*: Harlan, Bob, with Dale Hofmann. *Green and Golden Moments: Bob Harlan and the Green Bay Packers* (Stevens Point, WI: KCI Sports, 2007), 49.

175 *There was something prophetic*: Torinus. *Packer Legend*, 181.

177 *Devine never could learn*: Reischel. *Packers Essential*, 68.

178 *The $766,361 profit for 1971*: Slocum, Jim. "Packer Profits Down $373,018: Devine Steals Show by Signing Lane," *Milwaukee Sentinel*, May 16, 1972.

178 *It was a team that played*: Cameron. *Packers!*, 215.

178 *We flat-out ran over everybody*: Cameron. *Packers!*, 214.

178 *I remember we'd be leading*: Cameron. *Packers!*, 214.

179 *He was different*: Carlson. *Tales from the Packers Sideline*, 58.

179 *I was named the NFC coach of the year*: Devine with Steele. *Simply Devine*, 107.

179 *Washington coach George Allen*: Torinus. *Packer Legend*, 183.

180 *I thought, "If they stay*: Poling, Jerry. *Downfield: Untold Stories of the Green Bay Packers* (Black Earth, WI: Prairie Oak, 1996), 94.

180 *Devine tried to take over*: Poling. *Downfield*, 95.

180 *Bart and Devine were fifty feet apart*: Poling. *Downfield*, 95.

180 *By the third quarter*: Poling. *Downfield*, 95.

180 *We'd run into that five-man front*: Carlson, Chuck. *Game of My Life: Memorable Stories of Packers Football* (Champaign, IL: Sports Publishing, 2004), 111.

180 *the story came out that Starr*: Torinus. *Packer Legend*, 184.

181 *With the nucleus we had*: Carlson. *Game of My Life*, 16.

181 *I think one of Devine's biggest mistakes*: Gentile with D'Amato. *Packer Tapes*, 114.

181 *We had managed to overcome*: Devine with Steele. *Simply Devine*, 107.

181 *I could have coached better*: Devine with Steele. *Simply Devine*, 107.

181 *presumably by an irate fan*: Torinus. *Packer Legend*, 185.

182 *In 1974 the average NFL player salary*: Fortunato. *Commissioner*, 153.

183 *Let those teams go out of business*: Fortunato. *Commissioner*, 154.

183 *Green Bay was targeted*: Devine with Steele. *Simply Devine*, 110.

183 *Before the 1974 season began*: Devine with Steele. *Simply Devine*, 110.

183 *I felt that the Dan Devine*: Torinus. *Packer Legend*, 184.

185 *dissension tore the team apart*: Gentile with D'Amato. *Packer Tapes*, 115.

185 *One of our linebackers*: Gentile with D'Amato. *Packer Tapes*, 115.

185 *I don't think there was a soul*: Harlan with Hofmann. *Green and Golden Moments*, 53.

185 *If I was leaving*: Devine with Steele. *Simply Devine*, 114.

185 *The thing I've always said*: Reischel. *Packers Essential*, 71.

185 *the Committee became more and more*: Torinus. *Packer Legend*, 189.

186 *I had reason to know*: "Devine Attempted to Quit 2 Years Ago," *Milwaukee Journal*, December 7, 1974.

186 *It was strange*: Devine with Steele. *Simply Devine*, 118.

186 *He knew what was coming*: Reischel. *Packers Essential*, 70.

186 *Devine called President Olejniczak*: Torinus. *Packer Legend*, 189.

186 *the four men shook hands on the deal*: Torinus. *Packer Legend*, 189.

187 *It would be a damn shame*: Associated Press. "Devine Goes to ND; Starr May Get Nod," *Sarasota Journal*, December 17, 1974.

187 *history will show Dan Devine*: Reischel. *Packers Essential*, 70.

CHAPTER SIX

189 *The Green Bay Packers organization*: Starr, Bart, with Murray Olderman. *My Life in Football: Starr* (New York: William Morrow, 1987), 170.

189 *He handed out*: Torinus, John B. *The Packer Legend: An Inside Look* (Neshkoro, WI: Laranmark, 1982), 213.

189 *The decision of the Packer*: Starr with Olderman. *My Life in Football*, 173.

189 *Dominic Olejniczak*: Harlan, Bob, with Dale Hofmann. *Green and Golden Moments: Bob Harlan and the Green Bay Packers* (Stevens Point, WI: KCI Sports, 2007), 57.

190 *This franchise had such*: Cameron, Steve. *The Packers! Seventy-five Seasons of Memories and Mystique in Green Bay* (Dallas: Taylor, 1993), 217.

190 *Our operating expenses*: "Profit for Packers Lowest in 14 Years," *Milwaukee Journal*, April 29, 1975.

191 *The atmosphere in the organization*: Harlan with Hofmann. *Green and Golden Moments*, 58.

191 *Right away we began*: Starr with Olderman. *My Life in Football*, 172.

192 *we were no better*: Starr with Olderman. *My Life in Football*, 181.

192 *Unfortunately, he was unable*: Torinus. *Packer Legend*, 216.

193 *Packers coach Bart Starr is off*: Gentile, Domenic, with Gary D'Amato. *The Packer Tapes: My 32 Years with the Green Bay Packers* (Madison, WI: Prairie Oak, 1995), 118.

193 *Winning three of their last five*: Torinus. *Packer Legend*, 215.

193 *The Packers reported a net profit*: "Packer Profits Up, Highest Since 1970," *Milwaukee Journal*, April 20, 1976.

195 *pleased with the attitude*: Kupper, Mike. "Slowly but Surely? Starr Hopes Packers' Progress Will Lead to More Victories Next Season," *Milwaukee Journal*, December 17, 1976.

195 *Where and who we play*: "Packers' Profit Dropped," *Milwaukee Sentinel*, May 10, 1977.

196 *These figures would seem*: Wallace, William. "Packers' Profits Challenge Owners' Sob Story," *Sarasota Herald-Tribune*, June 5, 1977.

197 *When you had twelve teams*: Hofmann, Dale. "Packer Profit Dips after Suit," *Milwaukee Sentinel*, May 9, 1978.

197 *Everyone wanted Bart*: United Press International. "Says Starr Won't Resign," *Sarasota Herald-Tribune*, November 8, 1977.

197 *Operating expenses did increase*: Hofmann. "Packer Profit Dips after Suit."

197 *In 1977 the Packers received*: Hofmann. "Packer Profit Dips After Suit."

198 *The NFL's new broadcast deal*: MacCambridge, Michael. *America's Game: The Epic Story of How Pro Football Captured a Nation* (New York: Anchor, 2004), 332.

198 *by 1978, Bart had*: Gentile with D'Amato. *Packer Tapes*, 119.

198 *Everyone connected with the Packers*: Torinus. *Packer Legend*, 217.

199 *Most of the state's sportswriters*: Starr with Olderman. *My Life in Football*, 188.

199 *Packer fans began to have*: Torinus. *Packer Legend*, 217.

199 *the Packers still generated*: Christopulos, Mike. "Packers Show Record Profit," *Milwaukee Sentinel*, May 15, 1979.

199 *Of the thirty-three people*: Christopulos. "Packers Show Record Profit."

200 *The player I wanted to pick*: Starr with Olderman. *My Life in Football*, 192.

200 *had an excellent shot at*: Starr with Olderman. *My Life in Football*, 192.

200 *For the first time in five years*: Starr with Olderman. *My Life in Football*, 192.

201 *With the 1980s looming*: Gulbrandsen, Don. *Green Bay Packers: The Complete Illustrated History* (St. Paul, MN: Voyageur, 2007), 115.

201 *NFL regular-season attendance*: Yost, Mark. *Tailgating, Sacks, and Salary Caps: How the NFL Became the Most Successful Sports League in History* (Chicago: Kaplan, 2006), xii.

202 *can't miss guy*: *1980 Packer Prospectus*, 21.

203 *Packer fans' patience*: Torinus. *Packer Legend*, 220.

203 *I was extremely disappointed*: Starr with Olderman. *My Life in Football*, 198.

203 *There is really nothing different*: Wolf, Bob. "Harlan, Miller Veterans of Packers Front Office," *Milwaukee Journal*, January 9, 1981.

204 *The Executive Committee does not*: Lea, Bud. "No One Challenged Aging Packer Leadership," *Milwaukee Sentinel*, May 6, 1981.

204 *We wanted to free Bart*: "Packers Reorganize," *Milwaukee Journal*, May 4, 1981.

204 *There is no question*: Starr with Olderman. *My Life in Football*, 199.

204 *For Eddie Lee Ivery*: Starr with Olderman. *My Life in Football*, 201.

206 *Sure enough, we won six*: Starr with Olderman. *My Life in Football*, 201.

206 *A team doesn't realize*: Torinus. *Packer Legend*, 228.

206 *I knew the pressures he felt*: Harlan with Hofmann. *Green and Golden Moments*, 63.

207 *The Packer president, Robert Parins*: Starr with Olderman. *My Life in Football*, 205.

207 *hire and fire the coach*: "Judge Parins Voted President of Packers Corp.," *Milwaukee Sentinel*, May 4, 1982.

207 *The television networks were also*: Fortunato, John A. *Commissioner: The Legacy of Pete Rozelle* (New York: Taylor Trade, 2006), 116.

207 *This only reinforced*: Gulbrandsen. *Green Bay Packers*, 121.

208 *ABC would pay the USFL*: Fortunato. *Commissioner*, 177.

208 *In 1982 the average salary*: Fortunato. *Commissioner*, 159.

208 *When I came into the league*: Christopulos, Mike. "United Front Helped Pack," *1983 Green Bay Packers Yearbook*, 27.

209 *I think the strike*: Carlson, Chuck. *Game of My Life: Memorable Stories of Packers Football* (Champaign, IL: Sports Publishing, 2004), 117.

209 *always stayed in the background*: Christopulos. "United Front Helped Pack."

209 *The "money now" provision meant*: Torinus. *Packer Legend*, 251.

210 *as with any strike*: Torinus. *Packer Legend*, 251.

210 *Each game meant a loss*: Christopulos. "United Front Helped Pack."

211 *the press universally declared*: Torinus. *Packer Legend*, 249.

211 *there was a certain amount of power*: Poling, Jerry. *Downfield: Untold Stories of the Green Bay Packers* (Black Earth, WI: Prairie Oak, 1996), 80.

212 *It showed the Packers suffering a net loss*: Lea, Bud. "Packers Run a Cozy Annual Meeting," *Milwaukee Sentinel*, March 8, 1983.

212 *We're on our way up*: Lea. "Packers Run a Cozy Annual Meeting."

212 *would have posted a winning record*: Starr with Olderman. *My Life in Football*, 207.

213 *Our sixteen-game roller coaster*: Starr with Olderman. *My Life in Football*, 207.

214 *I never saw Bart more discouraged*: Harlan with Hofmann. *Green and Golden Moments*, 65.

214 *We were no longer*: Starr with Olderman. *My Life in Football*, 210.

214 *Starr said that Parins came*: Gentile with D'Amato. *Packer Tapes*, 120.

214 *He didn't thank me*: Starr with Olderman. *My Life in Football*, 210.

214 *it is difficult*: Claerbaut, David. *Bart Starr: When Leadership Mattered* (Lanham, MD: Taylor Trade, 2004), 224.

214 *not made out of emotion*: United Press International. "Starr: I'm Leaving Good Team to My Successor," *Telegraph Herald*, December 20, 1983.

215 *this matter involving Forrest*: Salituro, Chuck. "Gregg Shortened Parins' Search," *Milwaukee Journal*, December 25, 1983.

215 *He was the only person*: Salituro. "Gregg Shortened Parins' Search."

215 *I don't think I would have left*: Salituro. "Gregg Shortened Parins' Search."

215 *People in the office were sad*: Harlan with Hofmann. *Green and Golden Moments*, 67.

215 *I believe in discipline*: Salituro. "Gregg Shortened Parins' Search."

216 *Forrest will have full responsibility*: Gregg, Forrest, and Andrew O'Toole. *Winning in the Trenches: A Lifetime of Football* (Cincinnati: Clerisy, 2009), 248.

216 *If I could put my finger*: 1984 Packer Prospectus, 10.

216 *a move that probably cost us*: Gregg and O'Toole. *Winning in the Trenches*, 250.

217 *I'll never forget his answer*: Gentile with D'Amato. *Packer Tapes*, 121.

217 *winning seven of our last eight*: Gregg and O'Toole. *Winning in the Trenches*, 250.

217 *Before the start of the NFL's 1985 season*: Fortunato. *Commissioner*, 180–200.

218 *I'll just say this*: 1985 Packer Prospectus, 20.

219 *There are paper mills*: Pomerantz, Gary. "Lombardi: Packers Wallow for Years in Wake of the Golden Era Created by Vince," *Milwaukee Sentinel*, November 30, 1985.

219 *After every loss*: Pomerantz. "Lombardi: Packers Wallow for Years."

219 *even Forrest said he was tired*: Pomerantz. "Lombardi: Packers Wallow for Years."

219 *You knew it had to hurt*: Carlson, Chuck. *Tales from the Packers Sideline: A Collection of the Greatest Stories Ever Told* (Champaign, IL: Sports Publishing, 2003), 62.

220 *During my tenure as coach*: Gregg and O'Toole. *Winning in the Trenches*, 254.

220 *I don't think the rivalry*: Carlson. *Tales from the Packers Sideline*, 51.

220 *It's been that way for us*: Pomerantz. "Lombardi: Packers Wallow for Years."

220 *Winning another game or two*: 1986 Packer Prospectus, 10.

220 *after two years of mediocrity*: Gregg and O'Toole. *Winning in the Trenches*, 251.

220 *What I'm trying to do*: Sauerberg, George, and Vernon Biever. *The Pack Fights Back: Can Fresh Faces Turn Things Around? 1986–1987 Green Bay Packers* (Chicago: Bonus, 1987), 4.

221 *When the Extremely Honorable Robert J. Parins*: Bauman, Michael. "Packers' Woes Are at the Top," *Milwaukee Journal*, October 3, 1986.

222 *I hated to see us resort*: Gentile with D'Amato. *Packer Tapes*, 122.

222 *I don't think it was a coincidence*: Gregg and O'Toole. *Winning in the Trenches*, 256.

223 *Overshadowing our dismal performance*: Gregg and O'Toole. *Winning in the Trenches*, 252.

223 *For Packer players, life*: Gregg and O'Toole. *Winning in the Trenches*, 257.

223 *Some teams are astute enough*: Bauman, Michael. "Packers' Woes Are at the Top."

223 *I feel a little hurt and sadness*: Bauman, Michael. "Packers' Woes Are at the Top."

223 *Because Lombardi could do it*: Lea, Bud. "The Difference Was Holmgren," in *Heir to the Legacy: The Memorable Story of Mike Holmgren's Green Bay Packers*, ed. Francis J. Fitzgerald (Louisville, KY: AdCraft Sports Marketing, 1996), 66.

224 *I think it's a tremendous job*: Christl, Cliff. "Packers Are Interviewing for Football Director," *Milwaukee Journal*, January 19, 1987.

224 *Up to that point I had*: Gregg and O'Toole. *Winning in the Trenches*, 261, 269.

224 *I don't know how you feel*: Christl, Cliff. "Packers Want to Bury Woes," *Milwaukee Journal*, June 2, 1987.

224 *I think we've reached a saturation point*: Christl, Cliff. "Packers Want to Bury Woes."

225 *three-year agreements with ABC, CBS, and NBC*: Fortunato. *Commissioner*, 96.

225 *When the strike came*: Gregg and O'Toole. *Winning in the Trenches*, 265.

226 *Those three contests*: Gregg and O'Toole. *Winning in the Trenches*, 266.

226 *It was a very, very difficult season*: Harlan with Hofmann. *Green and Golden Moments*, 72.

226 *After four frustrating years*: Gregg and O'Toole. *Winning in the Trenches*, 269.

227 *the prospect of returning*: Gregg and O'Toole. *Winning in the Trenches*, 273.

227 *At the time, the organization*: Harlan with Hofmann. *Green and Golden Moments*, 74.

227 *At this point I was extremely worried*: Gentile with D'Amato. *Packer Tapes*, 123.

227 *Perles, it turned out*: Gentile with D'Amato. *Packer Tapes*, 123.

228 *That was probably the low point*: Carlson. *Tales from the Packers Sideline*, 47.

228 *they hinted that the board of directors*: Gentile with D'Amato. *Packer Tapes*, 110.

228 *We've got a long way to go*: 1988 Packer Prospectus, 10.

229 *the team had announced its second-largest profit*: "Packers Report Their Second-Largest Profit Ever," *Milwaukee Journal*, May 8, 1988.

229 *we've increased the quality*: Remmel, Lee. "Chapter Two: 'We Should Expect More of Ourselves,'" *1989 Green Bay Packers Yearbook*, 3.

229 *At that time, Infante and Braatz split*: Wolf, Ron, and Paul Attner. *The Packer Way: Nine Stepping Stones to Building a Winning Organization* (New York: St. Martin's, 1998), 19.

230 *His failure on the field*: Gulbrandsen. *Green Bay Packers*, 134.

230 *the team's smallest annual profit*: Butler, Vincent. "Packers Make Money but Profits Shrink," *Milwaukee Journal*, May 8, 1989.

230 *If you didn't have the free agent market*: Butler. "Packers Make Money but Profits Shrink."

230 *the franchise's net worth escalate*: Maier, Harry. "Retiring Judge Reviews His Tenure," *1989 Green Bay Packers Yearbook*, 24.

230 *that totally wiped out*: Hofmann, Dale. "Do-It-All Harlan Tackles Big Job," *Milwaukee Sentinel*, June 8, 1989.

231 *None of the young people*: McGinn, Bob. *The Road to Glory: The Inside Story of the Packers' Super Bowl XXXI Championship Season* (Louisville, KY: AdCraft Sports Marketing, 1997), 66.

231 *I thought we needed to find a way*: Harlan with Hofmann. *Green and Golden Moments*, 90.

231 *We had looked around*: Harlan with Hofmann. *Green and Golden Moments*, 97.

232 *that the league may soon*: Oriard, Michael. *Brand NFL: Making & Selling America's Favorite Sport* (Chapel Hill: University of North Carolina Press, 2007), 137.

232 *We're going to be more solid*: Remmel. "Chapter Two: 'We Should Expect More.'"

232 *I hope our record's even*: 1989 Packer Prospectus, 12.

232 *Those who jumped on*: Goska, Eric. *Green Bay Packers: A Measure of Greatness* (Iola, WI: Krause, 2003), 252.

233 *That 1989 season was the first year*: Carlson. *Tales from the Packers Sideline*, 65.

233 *There was real excitement*: Harlan with Hofmann. *Green and Golden Moments*, 94.

234 *An awful lot of people*: Miller, Ira. "New-and-Improved Packers Are the Pride of Green Bay," *Free Lance-Star*, August 16, 1990.

234 *This is what the city revolves around*: Miller. "New-and-Improved Packers."

234 *Lindy wanted to teach these guys*: Gentile with D'Amato. *Packer Tapes*, 125.

234 *[Infante] got rid of*: Poling. *Downfield*, 22.

235 *The situation had reached*: Wolf and Attner. *Packer Way*, 16.

235 *their net profit grew by more than*: Associated Press. "Profits Grow for Packers," *Telegraph-Herald*, May 30, 1991.

235 *I don't think I've ever been*: Mulhern, Tom. "Braatz Takes Heat as Team Struggles," *Milwaukee Sentinel*, October 31, 1991.

236 *Year after year of losses and excuses*: Gulbrandsen. *Green Bay Packers*, 109.

236 *I don't have the answers*: Goska. *Green Bay Packers*, 260.

237 *I think we're probably*: Silverstein, Tom. "Packers Mull Front-Office Restructuring: Braatz's Future Is Unclear," *Milwaukee Sentinel*, November 19, 1991.

237 *The franchise was floundering*: Isaacson, Kevin, with Tom Kessenich. *Return to Glory: The Inside Story of the*

Green Bay Packers' Return to Prominence (Iola, WI: Krause, 1996), 8.

237 *At that point*: Harlan with Hofmann. *Green and Golden Moments*, 91.

237 *I knew my timing was strange*: Harlan with Hofmann. *Green and Golden Moments*, 99.

237 *the handwriting was on the wall*: Gentile with D'Amato. *Packer Tapes*, 126.

237 *At the time of Lindy's firing*: Gentile with D'Amato. *Packer Tapes*, 129.

CHAPTER SEVEN

239 *strung along the Tampa Bay Buccaneers*: Gentile, Domenic, with Gary D'Amato. *The Packer Tapes: My 32 Years with the Green Bay Packers* (Madison, WI: Prairie Oak, 1995), 131.

239 *[Chiefs' head coach] Marty Schottenheimer*: Wolf, Ron, and Paul Attner. *The Packer Way: Nine Stepping Stones to Building a Winning Organization* (New York: St. Martin's, 1998), 66.

240 *Once I met him*: George, Thomas. "Taming the Legend That Haunts," in *Heir to the Legacy: The Memorable Story of Mike Holmgren's Green Bay Packers*, ed. Francis J. Fitzgerald (Louisville, KY: AdCraft Sports Marketing, 1996), 27.

240 *There was a kind of cocky confidence*: Harlan, Bob, with Dale Hofmann. *Green and Golden Moments: Bob Harlan and the Green Bay Packers* (Stevens Point, WI: KCI Sports, 2007), 131.

240 *We got an idea of the respect*: Harlan with Hofmann. *Green and Golden Moments*, 132.

240 *There never will be another*: George. "Taming the Legend That Haunts," 29.

241 *he came back to the press box*: McGinn, Bob. *The Road to Glory: The Inside Story of the Packers' Super Bowl XXXI Championship Season* (Louisville, KY: AdCraft Sports Marketing, 1997), 11.

241 *I told them not only*: Wolf and Attner. *Packer Way*, 48.

241 *I explained he was a third-string quarterback*: Wolf and Attner. *Packer Way*, 48.

241 *The opportunity to acquire Brett Favre*: Isaacson, Kevin, with Tom Kessenich. *Return to Glory: The Inside Story of the Green Bay Packers' Return to Prominence* (Iola, WI: Krause, 1996), 30.

241 *He wanted to win*: Wolf and Attner. *Packer Way*, 70.

242 *During the annual stockholders' meeting*: Mulhern, Tom. "Packers Show Profit Despite Infante Payoff," *Milwaukee Sentinel*, May 28, 1992.

242 *it was evident we soon would be*: Wolf and Attner. *Packer Way*, 34.

243 *The ability to improvise*: George, Thomas. "A Gunslinger with Swagger," in *Heir to the Legacy*, 43–45.

243 *What people don't remember*: Gutman, Bill. *Brett Favre: Leader of the Pack* (Brookfield, CT: Millbrook Sports World, 1998), 20.

243 *I never even saw it*: Carlson, Chuck. *Tales from the Packers Sideline: A Collection of the Greatest Stories Ever Told* (Champaign, IL: Sports Publishing, 2003), 67.

243 *That incredible comeback*: Cameron, Steve. *The Packers! Seventy-five Seasons of Memories and Mystique in Green Bay* (Dallas: Taylor, 1993), 210.

243 *What transpired over the next months*: Wolf and Attner. *Packer Way*, 88.

244 *I can't imagine any franchise*: Wolf and Attner. *Packer Way*, 91.

244 *I remember in the mid-80s*: McGinn. *Road to Glory*, 12.

244 *Total free agency without a salary cap*: Harlan with Hofmann. *Green and Golden Moments*, 187.

244 *the timing couldn't have been better*: Wolf and Attner. *Packer Way*, 192.

245 *You no longer can be*: Wolf and Attner. *Packer Way*, 243.

245 *The Packers' 1992 turnaround resulted in*: Associated Press. "Packers Fare Well Financially," *Telegraph-Herald*, May 27, 1993.

245 *in 1993 the average salary of an unrestricted free agent*: Oriard, Michael. *Brand NFL: Making & Selling America's Favorite Sport* (Chapel Hill: University of North Carolina Press, 2007), 143.

245 *I don't believe in pretenses*: Wolf and Attner. *Packer Way*, 108.

245 *Ron told Reggie he could go anyplace*: Harlan with Hofmann. *Green and Golden Moments*, 114.

246 *When it was finished*: Isaacson with Kessenich. *Return to Glory*, 52.

246 *His presence would do away with*: Wolf and Attner. *Packer Way*, 96.

246 *It started out as a murmur*: Isaacson with Kessenich. *Return to Glory*, 49.

247 *The guy they cut*: Isaacson with Kessenich. *Return to Glory*, 47.

247 *I'm sure the players came in every day*: Wolf and Attner. *Packer Way*, 186.

247 *In our early seasons, we were*: Wolf and Attner. *Packer Way*, 191.

247 *But I kept harking back to 1989*: Harlan with Hofmann. *Green and Golden Moments*, 134.

247 *I was sitting next to Wolf*: Harlan with Hofmann. *Green and Golden Moments*, 135.

247 *I don't want to say a hope*: Goska, Eric. *Green Bay Packers: A Measure of Greatness* (Iola, WI: Krause, 2003), 395.

248 *the Packers hadn't put together*: Wolf and Attner. *Packer Way*, 195.

248 *Fox, understanding that the NFL*: MacCambridge, Michael. *America's Game: The Epic Story of How Pro Football Captured a Nation* (New York: Anchor, 2004), 393.

248 *It's not bad when you consider*: Associated Press. "Pack in the Black," *Sarasota Herald-Tribune*, April 12, 1994.

249 *Every time John Underwood*: Harlan with Hofmann. *Green and Golden Moments*, 143.

250 *With no stadium on the horizon*: Harlan with Hofmann. *Green and Golden Moments*, 145.

250 *If anyone had told me*: Harlan with Hofmann. *Green and Golden Moments*, 142.

250 *wanted the league, not the Packers*: Harlan with Hofmann. *Green and Golden Moments*, 145.

250 *Buddy, it's your job*: Gutman. *Brett Favre*, 23.

251 *People throughout the league*: Silverstein, Tom. "Always a Winner," in *Heir to the Legacy*, 35.

251 *Ron always said*: Harlan with Hofmann. *Green and Golden Moments*, 114.

251 *When you've got your shot*: Dougherty, Pete. "Lions Weep Today," in *Heir to the Legacy*, 87.

251 *I think I saw something*: Dougherty. "Lions Weep Today," in *Heir to the Legacy*, 84.

252 *our fans' wish list had changed*: Wolf and Attner. *Packer Way*, 196.

253 *Nearly everyone else is threatening*: Murphy, Tom. "$24 Million Stock Sale Preserves 'National Treasure,'" *1998 Green Bay Packers Yearbook*, 68.

253 *in the days before our*: Wolf and Attner. *Packer Way*, 201.

253 *He's got to know that*: Isaacson with Kessenich. *Return to Glory*, 99.

253 *They're going to eat their words*: Isaacson with Kessenich. *Return to Glory*, 141.

254 *It just seemed like*: Carlson, Chuck. *Game of My Life: Memorable Stories of Packers Football* (Champaign, IL: Sports Publishing, 2004), 180.

254 *it was just one of those games*: Carlson. *Game of My Life*, 72.

254 *Winning the division means*: Isaacson with Kessenich. *Return to Glory*, 111.

254 *In terms of winning this game*: Goska. *Green Bay Packers*, 397.

254 *We knew we had to be aggressive*: Isaacson with Kessenich. *Return to Glory*, 155.

254 *You have to give all the credit*: Dougherty, Pete. "Defense Stars as Packers Dethrone Champs," in *Heir to the Legacy*, 118.

255 *We had one major obstacle*: Butler, LeRoy, and James J. Keller. *The LeRoy Butler Story: From Wheelchair to the*

Lambeau Leap (Neenah, WI: JJK Sports Entertainment, 2003), 136.

255 *Jerry Jones, who had purchased the team*: Associated Press. "It's Small-Town Packers vs. Cowboy Money Machine," *Toledo Blade*, January 12, 1996.

255 *We had them right there*: Myers, Gary. "Pack Up Marvelous Season Comes Up Short for Favre, Green Bay," *New York Daily News*, January 15, 1996.

255 *it was three minutes like an avalanche*: Dougherty, Pete. "Dream Dies in Dallas," in *Heir to the Legacy*, 129.

255 *Afterwards, Coach Holmgren*: Butler and Keller. *LeRoy Butler Story*, 137.

255 *that was three years in a row*: Harlan with Hofmann. *Green and Golden Moments*, 141.

256 *What people outside Green Bay*: Bauer, David, ed. *The Champions: Green Bay Packers 1996* (New York: Sports Illustrated, 1997), 18.

256 *[Wolf] always made it a point*: Harlan with Hofmann. *Green and Golden Moments*, 105.

256 *Almost every Packer of the old days*: Isaacson with Kessenich. *Return to Glory*, 175.

256 *Boy, I never thought*: Schaap, Dick. *Green Bay Replay: The Packers' Return to Glory* (New York: Avon, 1997), 27.

257 *When the corporation was formed*: Harlan with Hofmann. *Green and Golden Moments*, 183.

257 *Back when the Packers were reporting modest earnings*: McGinn, Bob. "Packers' Meeting Gets a New Twist," *Milwaukee Journal Sentinel*, May 30, 1996.

258 *During the 1995 season, the Packers received*: Kass, Mark. "Score Another Victory for Jerry Jones' Dallas Cowboys," *Business Journal*, December 22, 1996.

258 *eighty-four percent of the Packers'*: Fortunato, John A. *Commissioner: The Legacy of Pete Rozelle* (New York: Taylor Trade, 2006), 207.

258 *If we would ever lose that*: Associated Press. "Revenue Sharing Keeps Pack Thriving," *Beaver County Times*, January 15, 1997.

259 *What I saw tonight*: Dougherty, Pete. "Prime Time Pounding," in *Heir to the Legacy*, 137.

259 *In this league, very rarely*: Remmel, Lee. "Team Overview," *1996 Green Bay Packers Postseason Guide*, 4.

259 *The way it is right now*: Remmel, Lee. "Best Packer Defense Since 1962," *1996 Green Bay Packers Postseason Guide*, 29.

259 *Everybody will always talk about*: Carlson. *Game of My Life*, 98.

259 *I don't want to get to a certain age*: Carlson, Chuck. *Titletown Again: The Super Bowl Season of the 1996 Green Bay Packers* (Lenexa, KS: Addax, 1997), 69.

260 *I think everybody's scared*: Bauer. *Champions*, 45.

260 *The league really takes control*: Kass. "Score Another Victory."

260 *I heard the rain coming down*: Carlson. *Titletown Again*, 98.

260 *It's gotten to the point*: Goska. *Green Bay Packers*, 398.

260 *We made a point on the first play*: Carlson. *Game of My Life*, 98.

260 *There are so many things*: McGinn. *Road to Glory*, 118.

261 *we had a record crowd of 60,787*: Harlan with Hofmann. *Green and Golden Moments*, 159.

261 *The week before Carolina came*: Butler and Keller. *LeRoy Butler Story*, 138.

261 *we could hear the Carolina Panthers*: Havel, Chris. *A Year of Champions: The 1996 Green Bay Packers; Remembered by Gilbert Brown* (Green Bay: Petasek Promotions, 2006), 171.

262 *He still goes brain-dead every*: Green Bay Press-Gazette. *Titletown: The Unforgettable Story of the Green Bay Packers' Road to Super Bowl XXXI* (Louisville, KY: AdCraft Sports Marketing, 1997), 95.

262 *They had us on our heels*: Carlson. *Titletown Again*, 131.

262 *end zone to end zone*: Kramer, Jerry. "Everything Has Changed, Nothing Is Different," *Super Bowl XXXI Official Game Program*, 158.

262 *Our biggest motivation*: Havel. *A Year of Champions*, 170.

262 *As you sat in the stadium*: Green Bay Press-Gazette. *Lambeau Field: Green Bay's National Treasure* (Green Bay: Pediment, 2003), 110.

263 *our fans didn't rush the floor*: Butler and Keller. *LeRoy Butler Story*, 139.

263 *You can't imagine how emotional*: Harlan with Hofmann. *Green and Golden Moments*, 160.

263 *twenty-two of our draft choices*: Wolf and Attner. *Packer Way*, 206.

264 *When I was warming up*: Green Bay Press-Gazette. *Titletown*, 154.

264 *took off his helmet*: Harlan with Hofmann. *Green and Golden Moments*, 127.

264 *The Patriots came right back*: Butler and Keller. *LeRoy Butler Story*, 147.

264 *I don't know where he comes up*: Carlson. *Titletown Again*, 83.

264 *It's like we reinstated the legacy*: Carlson. *Titletown Again*, 137.

264 *Vince Lombardi would have to be*: Green Bay 1997 World Champions (Northbrook, IL: H&S Media, 1997), 18.

266 *That's why Ron Wolf is Ron Wolf*: Green Bay Press-Gazette. *Titletown*, 154.

266 *there's nothing like being*: Harlan with Hofmann. *Green and Golden Moments*, 166.

266 *People talk about ticker tape parades*: Harlan with Hofmann. *Green and Golden Moments*, 163.

266 *Our national fan phenomena*: Murphy, Tom. "Packers' Annual Economic Impact Surpasses Millions," *1997 Green Bay Packers Yearbook*, 71.

266 *The NFL reported sales*: Schaap. *Green Bay Replay*, 280.

267 *Commissioner Paul Tagliabue came*: Harlan with Hofmann. *Green and Golden Moments*, 152.

268 *started getting calls and letters*: Harlan with Hofmann. *Green and Golden Moments*, 178.

268 *I acknowledged to them*: Buss, Dale. "Got What It Takes for the 'Best Job in Sports'?," *Forbes*, September 7, 2007, www.forbes.com/2007/09/07/nfl-franchises-packers-lead-manage-cz_db_0907harlan.html.

268 *I never dreamed we'd reach*: Harlan with Hofmann. *Green and Golden Moments*, 182.

270 *we were strong favorites*: Butler and Keller. *LeRoy Butler Story*, 148.

270 *He was the best general manager*: Harlan with Hofmann. *Green and Golden Moments*, 167.

270 *I think winning it the first time*: Remmel, Lee. "Holmgren: A New and Bigger Challenge: To Repeat," *1997 Green Bay Packers Yearbook*, 6.

270 *we were humbled in a big way*: Butler and Keller. *LeRoy Butler Story*, 151.

270 *It really felt like we hadn't played*: Goska. *Green Bay Packers*, 400.

271 *They can say what they want*: Youngblood, Kent. "Packers Repeat for NFC Title in 'Our Weather,'" *1998 Green Bay Packers Yearbook*, 16–17.

271 *It was still pouring when*: Harlan with Hofmann. *Green and Golden Moments*, 172.

272 *the danger was that we were*: Butler and Keller. *LeRoy Butler Story*, 155.

272 *One thing that made the atmosphere*: Harlan with Hofmann. *Green and Golden Moments*, 175.

272 *we had to deal with rumors*: Wolf and Attner. *Packer Way*, 244.

272 *I remember thinking as I watched*: Harlan with Hofmann. *Green and Golden Moments*, 175.

272 *The Broncos had scouted us*: Butler and Keller. *LeRoy Butler Story*, 155.

273 *and for the first time I felt*: Harlan with Hofmann. *Green and Golden Moments*, 175.

273 *When it was over*: Harlan with Hofmann. *Green and Golden Moments*, 176.

273 *We felt that we were the best team*: Mulhern, Tom.

"Super Bowl XXXII Leaves—an Empty Feeling," *1998 Green Bay Packers Yearbook*, 18.

273 *You just have that empty feeling*: Mulhern. "Super Bowl XXXII Leaves—an Empty Feeling," 18.

273 *The most important thing*: Christopherson, Brett. "Homecoming: Return to Titletown II," *1998 Green Bay Packers Yearbook*, 22.

274 *the NFL announced that its new broadcast agreements*: Kass, Mark. "Packers Face Three Major Off-Field Test," *Business Journal*, June 27, 2004.

274 *It was the most disappointing loss*: Harlan with Hofmann. *Green and Golden Moments*, 166.

274 *The bottom line*: Dougherty, Pete. "Shrewd Money Policy Key to Packers' Cap Era Success," *2005 Green Bay Packers Yearbook*, 107.

274 *If you're a good football team*: Mulhern, Tom. "Wolf," *1998 Green Bay Packers Yearbook*, 24.

274 *Ever since the first year of free agency*: Mulhern. "Wolf," 27.

274 *When the salary cap was developed*: Dougherty. "Shrewd Money Policy Key," 107.

274 *It's the first time, I think*: Murphy. "$24 Million Stock Sale," 66.

275 *You could tell what they*: Harlan with Hofmann. *Green and Golden Moments*, 183.

275 *The beauty of the stock offering*: Silverstein, Tom. "Packers' Stock Continues to Rise," *Daily News*, April 9, 1998.

275 *It seemed to me that he knew*: Harlan with Hofmann. *Green and Golden Moments*, 192.

275 *we knew Coach Holmgren's time*: Butler and Keller. *LeRoy Butler Story*, 158.

275 *I'm sure he can handle*: Wolf and Attner. *Packer Way*, 244.

276 *This wasn't the Super Bowl*: Oates, Tom. "Packers Settle for Super Bowl 'Feeling,'" *1999 Green Bay Packers Yearbook*, 98.

276 *You just don't lose a game like this*: Oates. "Packers Settle for Super Bowl 'Feeling.'"

276 *If I had gone into the locker room*: Wolf and Attner. *Packer Way*, 270.

276 *I understood why he was leaving*: Nickel, Lori. "Holmgren Leaves for Seattle after '98 Season," *Milwaukee Journal Sentinel*, November 12, 2005, www.jsonline.com /sports/packers/45969457.html.

276 *When Mike left, he took*: Harlan with Hofmann. *Green and Golden Moments*, 198.

277 *Reinfeldt, meanwhile, was a very big loss*: Harlan with Hofmann. *Green and Golden Moments*, 198.

277 *I believe to this day*: Harlan with Hofmann. *Green and Golden Moments*, 164.

CHAPTER EIGHT

279 *When we looked at it*: Content, Thomas. "The Second 'Lambeau'?," *1999 Green Bay Packers Yearbook*, 75.

279 *the percentage of league revenues that went unshared*: MacCambridge, Michael. *America's Game: The Epic Story of How Pro Football Captured a Nation* (New York: Anchor, 2004), 427.

280 *We need to make money*: Content. "The Second 'Lambeau'?," 75.

280 *We all came in here together*: Mulhern, Tom. "Wolf." *1999 Green Bay Packers Yearbook*, 22.

280 *During the [1998] season*: Harlan, Bob, with Dale Hofmann. *Green and Golden Moments: Bob Harlan and the Green Bay Packers* (Stevens Point, WI: KCI Sports, 2007), 108.

280 *He had known almost that whole season*: Harlan with Hofmann. *Green and Golden Moments*, 199.

280 *When you look at the football team*: Associated Press. "Schottenheimer Resigns as Chiefs Coach; Rhodes Joins Pack," *Gettysburg Times*, January 12, 1999.

280 *It's been a factor*: Marvez, Alex. "Injured Favre Keeps Struggling to Get a Grip," *South Florida Sun-Sentinel*, November 21, 1999.

280 *We would be going through*: Harlan with Hofmann. *Green and Golden Moments*, 203.

281 *thought we should take responsibility*: Butler, LeRoy, and James J. Keller. *The LeRoy Butler Story: From Wheelchair to the Lambeau Leap* (Neenah, WI: JJK Sports Entertainment, 2003), 160.

281 *The team was dead*: Carlson, Chuck. *Tales from the Packers Sideline: A Collection of the Greatest Stories Ever Told* (Champaign, IL: Sports Publishing, 2003), 16.

281 *He had lost his authority*: Harlan with Hofmann. *Green and Golden Moments*, 203.

281 *I'd have made the same decision*: Carlson. *Tales from the Packers Sideline*, 16.

281 *I think we have to have*: Harlan with Hofmann. *Green and Golden Moments*, 203.

282 *the team's reserve fund*: Bahr, Kevin M., Ph.D. "The Business of Sports and Small Market Visibility: The Green Bay Packers and the Milwaukee Brewers," Central Wisconsin Economic Research Bureau, 2001, www4.uwsp.edu /business/cwerb/SR%20PDFs/The%20Business%20of%20 Sports%20and%20Small%20Market%20Viability.pdf.

282 *After making a profit*: Harlan with Hofmann. *Green and Golden Moments*, 205.

282 *As more and more teams play*: Lombardo, John. "Pack Cracks Books, and It's Not Pretty," *Street & Smith's Sports Business Journal*, July 17, 2000, www.sportsbusinessdaily .com/Journal/Issues/2000/07/20000717/No-Topic-Name /Pack-Cracks-Books-And-It146s-Not-Pretty.aspx.

282 *It's a slippery slope*: Lombardo. "Pack Cracks Books."

283 *We asked engineers to test*: Carlson. *Tales from the Packers Sideline,* 41.

283 *It's about money*: Stephenson, Crocker. "Wolf Say's It's about Money," *Milwaukee Journal Sentinel*, July 13, 2000.

283 *This is when John became famous*: Harlan with Hofmann. *Green and Golden Moments*, 205.

284 *The Green Bay Packers have come to us*: Mayers, Jeff. "Green Bay Packers Seeking Legislative Touchdown," *Stateline*, January 28, 2000, www.stateline.org/live /ViewPage.action?siteNodeId=136&languageId =1&contentId=13912.

284 *Hopefully, people will see*: McGinn, Bob. "Players: Poor Start Shouldn't Defeat Referendum," *Milwaukee Journal Sentinel*, September 11, 2000.

284 *One of the factors driving*: Gulbrandsen, Don. *Green Bay Packers: The Complete Illustrated History* (St. Paul, MN: Voyageur, 2007), 162.

284 *Marty was the one person*: Harlan with Hofmann. *Green and Golden Moments*, 207.

285 *Marty never showed*: Harlan with Hofmann. *Green and Golden Moments*, 207.

285 *Tell you what*: Carlson. *Tales from the Packers Sideline*, 18.

285 *I want some of Coach Lombardi*: Carlson, Chuck. *Green Bay Packers: Yesterday & Today* (Lincolnwood, IL: West Side, 2009), 135.

285 *most realized it was a worthwhile investment*: Gulbrandsen. *Green Bay Packers*, 166.

286 *We were playing our best football*: Harlan with Hofmann. *Green and Golden Moments*, 210.

286 *Then Brett Favre had made the comment*: Harlan with Hofmann. *Green and Golden Moments*, 111.

286 *I think one of the main things*: Harlan with Hofmann. *Green and Golden Moments*, 111.

286 *I believed that was*: Harlan with Hofmann. *Green and Golden Moments*, 111.

287 *You can hit him*: Connolly, Marc. "Green Makes Impact without Big Numbers," *ESPN.com*, December 4, 2001, http://espn.go.com/abcsports/mnf/s/2001/1203 /1289235.html.

289 *It's do or die*: Associated Press. "Favre Keeps Lambeau Streak Intact with 25–15 Win vs. 49ers," *SportsIllustrated .com*, January 13, 2002, http://sportsillustrated.cnn.com /football/2002/playoffs/news/2002/01/13/49ers _packers_ap/.

289 *It's not one of my better days*: Associated Press. "Rams Use Defense to Beat Packers, 45–17," *Altus Times*, January 21, 2002.

289 *people would do anything*: Harlan with Hofmann. *Green and Golden Moments*, 128.

289 *If the economics of professional football*: MacCambridge. *America's Game*, 423.

290 *NFL teams averaged just over*: Coenen, Craig R. *From Sandlots to the Super Bowl: The National Football League, 1920–1967* (Knoxville: University of Tennessee Press, 2005), 2.

291 *total NFL revenues had doubled*: MacCambridge. *America's Game*, 421.

291 *You look around*: Stapleton, Arnie. "Packers Left Numb after Cold-Weather Loss to Falcons," *Day*, January 6, 2003.

292 *There's a lot of guys*: Wood, Skip. "Vick, Falcons Make History with 27–7 Upset of Packers," *USA Today*, January 4, 2003.

292 *the NFL would not be what it is*: Green Bay Press-Gazette. *Lambeau Field: Green Bay's National Treasure* (Green Bay: Pediment, 2003), 141.

292 *We have the best of both*: Associated Press. "Lambeau Remodeled: New Amenities, Attractions Designed to Help Packers Remain Competitive," *SportsIllustrated.com*, August 27, 2003, http://sportsillustrated.cnn.com/2003 /football/nfl/08/27/new.lambeau.ap/.

292 *The Packers will be here*: Green Bay Press-Gazette. *Lambeau Field*, 142.

293 *Lambeau Field's increased economic impact*: "Hallowed Ground—Lambeau Field," *Gameday*, December 30, 2007, 110.

293 *I don't think facilities*: Stapleton, Arnie. "New Look This Fall for Lambeau Field," *Daily Union*, July 23, 2002.

294 *It was an unbelievable feeling*: Banks, Don. "You Gotta Believe: Favre, Packers Grateful for Unlikely Postseason Spot," *SportsIllustrated.com*, December 28, 2003, http:// sportsillustrated.cnn.com/2003/writers/don_banks /12/28/packers.broncos/.

294 *The way we're playing*: Banks. "You Gotta Believe."

294 *We want the ball*: Sports Illustrated. *Brett Favre: The Tribute* (New York: Sports Illustrated Books, 2008), 92.

294 *I was just praying*: Associated Press. "Packers Overcome Seahawks in Overtime," *Argus-Press*, January 5, 2004.

294 *I was just thinking*: Associated Press. "Packers Overcome Seahawks In Overtime."

295 *I guess we didn't have enough people*: Weisman, Larry. "Eagles Work Miracles, Alter Packers' Destiny," *USAToday .com*, January 12, 2004, http://www.usatoday.com/sports /football/nfl/2004-01-12-packers-sidebar_x.htm.

295 *I was as devastated*: Harlan with Hofmann. *Green and Golden Moments*, 221.

295 *I'm very disappointed*: Goldberg, Dave. "One Perfect Pass, Field Goal Sink Packers," *Ludington Daily News*, January 12, 2004.

295 *When you're the head coach*: Vandermause, Mike. "Confident Sherman Embarks on Sixth Season Tied with Belichick, Dungy Among NFL's Coaching Elite," *2005 Green Bay Packers Yearbook*, 10.

296 *We've been very pleased*: Kass, Mark. "A Small Market Scores Big: Success of Expanded Lambeau Boosts Packers' Finances," *Business Journal*, May 16, 2004.

297 *What we did was very unique*: Kass. "A Small Market Scores Big."

297 *we were running the risk*: Kass, Mark. "Renovated Lambeau Fuels Packers' Income Growth," *Business Journal*, June 19, 2004.

297 *We are exceeding the targets*: Kass. "Renovated Lambeau Fuels Packers' Income Growth."

297 *The whole purpose*: Kass. "A Small Market Scores Big."

297 *If you were to diagnose*: Imrie, Robert. "Publicly Owned Packers Hit Pay Dirt with Record Profit, *USA Today*, June 20, 2004.

298 *All Mike [Sherman] could talk about*: Harlan with Hofmann. *Green and Golden Moments*, 225.

298 *We had no motivation*: Sports Illustrated. *Brett Favre*, 98.

298 *It would be easy to walk off*: Stapleton, Arnie. "Vikings Avoid Packers Sweep," *Pittsburgh Post-Gazette*, January 10, 2005.

300 *is what I would have liked*: Harlan with Hofmann. *Green and Golden Moments*, 225.

300 *I got a copy*: Harlan with Hofmann. *Green and Golden Moments*, 227.

300 *I'm sure he took it personally*: Harlan with Hofmann. *Green and Golden Moments*, 230.

300 *I was probably as close to him*: Harlan with Hofmann. *Green and Golden Moments*, 230.

301 *The NFL's annual revenue*: MacCambridge. *America's Game*, 462.

301 *Television continues to this day*: Harlan with Hofmann. *Green and Golden Moments*, 184.

301 *League-wide revenues totaled*: Yost, Mark. *Tailgating, Sacks, and Salary Caps: How the NFL Became the Most Successful Sports League in History* (Chicago: Kaplan, 2006), 1.

301 *Even the Packers*: "NFL Team Valuations: #13 Green Bay Packers," *Forbes.com*, August 31, 2006, http://www .forbes.com/lists/2006/30/06nfl_Green-Bay-Packers_ 302814.html.

301 *[The reserve] allows us*: Kass, Mark. "WPS Executive Relishes His Second Job," *Business Journal*, October 9, 2005.

301 *it seems the Packers*: "Guard Packers' Bottom Line," *Green Bay Press-Gazette*, June 19, 2005.

302 *We had to evolve*: Kass. "WPS Executive Relishes His Second Job."

302 *We're proud we've had the best record*: Dougherty, Pete. "Shrewd Money Policy Key to Packers' Cap Era Success," *2005 Green Bay Packers Yearbook*, 106.

302 *I want to come back*: Havel, Chris. "Brett Favre Striving to Make Most of Stretch Run," *2005 Green Bay Packers Yearbook*, 22.

302 *You have to do what you think*: "Ted Thompson— Executive VP, General Manager & Director of Football Operations," *Gameday*, December 30, 2007, 24.

303 *We were a little surprised*: Remmel, Lee. "Ted Launches the Thompson Era," *2005 Green Bay Packers Yearbook*, 6.

303 *He can figure it out*: Carlson, Chuck. *Brett Favre: America's Quarterback* (Chicago: Triumph, 2007), 113.

303 *You make draft choices*: Korth, Todd. "Packers Draft for Future," *2005 Green Bay Packers Yearbook*, 34.

303 *I totally recognize*: Korth. "Packers Draft for Future," 34, 38.

303 *When you work in Titletown*: Vandermause. "Confident Sherman Embarks on Sixth Season," 11, 12.

304 *I don't know that anyone*: Harlan with Hofmann. *Green and Golden Moments*, 236.

304 *The system with free agency*: Harlan with Hofmann. *Green and Golden Moments*, 240.

304 *It started during free agency*: Harlan with Hofmann. *Green and Golden Moments*, 236.

304 *It's hard to imagine*: Nickel, Lori. "Packers Look for Positives in Losing Season," *Milwaukee Journal Sentinel*, January 2, 2006.

304 *He just said it hadn't worked out*: Harlan with Hofmann. *Green and Golden Moments*, 237.

305 *It was a sad end*: Gulbrandsen. *Green Bay Packers*, 177.

305 *I honestly felt*: Harlan with Hofmann. *Green and Golden Moments*, 239.

305 *What stood out to me*: Jenkins, Chris. "McCarthy Era Begins in Green Bay," *USA Today*, January 12, 2006.

306 *There will be an unconditional commitment*: Jenkins. "McCarthy Era Begins in Green Bay."

306 *People who don't think*: Carlson. *Brett Favre*, 123.

307 *What are they going to do?*: Carlson. *Brett Favre*, 119.

307 *estimates of unshared revenues*: Oriard, Michael. *Brand NFL: Making & Selling America's Favorite Sport* (Chapel Hill: University of North Carolina Press, 2007), 148.

308 *This agreement is not about one side*: Bell, Jarrett. "NFL Owners Accept Player Union Proposal with 30–2 Vote," *USA Today*, March 8, 2006.

308 *It seems odd that Green Bay*: Kass, Mark. "Packers' Revenue Increases, but Net Income Falls," *Business Journal*, June 17, 2006.

308 *When Tagliabue replaced Rozelle*: Oriard. *Brand NFL*, 140.

309 *He was someone I thought*: Kass, Mark. "Jones Looks ahead to a Packer Fan's Dream Job," *Business Journal*, September 25, 2005.

309 *The history of a new stadium*: Kass. "Packers' Revenue Increases."

309 *He's a good football player*: Korth, Todd. "Woodson Officially Signs; Thomas Dumped," *Packer Report*, May 1, 2006, http:/gnb.scout.com/2/526773.html.

310 *That's when Mike McCarthy*: Harlan with Hofmann. *Green and Golden Moments*, 241.

310 *If this is my last game*: Korth, Todd. "Packers Whip Bears in Season Finale, 26–7," *Packer Report*, December 31, 2006, http://gnb.scout.com/2/605597.html.

310 *The big thing with him*: Sports Illustrated. *Brett Favre*, 117.

310 *He's not only our leader*: Sports Illustrated. *Brett Favre*, 120.

310 *It's going to be a sad, sad day*: Harlan with Hofmann. *Green and Golden Moments*, 129.

311 *mutually beneficial for John*: "Packers' Harlan to Delay Retirement as CEO," *Minneapolis Star Tribune*, May 26, 2007, http://www.startribune.com/sports/vikings/11704821.html.

311 *The team's late surge in 2006*: "Packers Profit Rises 22 Percent," *Business Journal*, June 25, 2007.

311 *Back in 1993 the Packers' retail operation*: Kass, Mark. "Fans' Appreciation Adds Up to Big Bucks," *Business Journal*, September 16, 2007.

312 *Initially, you'll be remembered*: Kasan, Sam. "I Am Legend: A Personal View of Brett Favre's Iconic Status," *Gameday*, December 30, 2007, 8.

312 *When he got the opportunity*: "Grant Drops Ball, Then Drops Seattle," *Reading Eagle*, January 13, 2008.

313 *Did I ever think*: Sports Illustrated. *Brett Favre*, 136.

315 *Any season, when you're together*: Jenkins, Chris. "NFC Championship Loss to Giants Leaves Packers Coaches Looking for Answers," *USA Today*, January 22, 2008.

315 *We did not play our best football*: Jenkins, Chris. "Packers, McCarthy Moving on after Loss to Giants," *USA Today*, January 23, 2008.

CHAPTER NINE

317 *I've given everything*: Silverstein, Tom. "Tear-Drenched Favre Offers Weepy Farewell," *Times Herald-Record*, March 7, 2008.

318 *I'm not going to sit here*: Silverstein. "Tear-Drenched Favre Offers Weepy Farewell."

318 *I got to learn the offense*: Dillon, Dennis. "Super Bowl XLV: Worth the Wait," *Sporting News*, February 14, 2011, 60.

318 *I'm not opposed to moving up*: Korth, Todd. "Packers Draft for Future," *2005 Green Bay Packers Yearbook*, 34.

318 *There are a lot of general managers*: Mulhern, Tom. "Packers: Bob Harlan, Job Placement Expert," *Wisconsin State Journal*, February 2, 2011, http://host.madison.com/sports/columnists/tom_mulhern/article_fe48bbf0-2ca8-11e0-9f1c-001cc4c03286.html.

319 *We had a good year*: Kass, Mark. "Packers' Profits Less Than Hoped," *Business Journal*, June 22, 2008.

319 *We're looking at ways*: Kass. "Packers' Profits Less Than Hoped."

319 *I think we saw it a year before*: Dougherty, Pete. "Green Bay Packers Defeat Pittsburgh Steelers 31–25 to win Super Bowl XLV: Quotebook," *Green Bay Press-Gazette*, February 7, 2011.

319 *I think guys understood*: Dillon. "Super Bowl XLV: Worth the Wait," 60.

320 *The train has left the station*: Jenkins, Chris. "Favre Saga Over as QB Gets Fresh Start with Jets," *Peoria Journal Star*, August 6, 2008.

320 *When we went through*: Mulhern. "Packers: Bob Harlan, Job Placement Expert."

320 *You would like for all of them*: Vandermause, Mike. "Green Bay Packers GM Ted Thompson Has Team on Right Path," *Green Bay Press-Gazette*, February 13, 2011.

320 *I just think it's been part of my story*: Dillon. "Super Bowl XLV: Worth the Wait," 60.

321 *I mean, it's shocking*: McGinn, Bob. "Ax Falls on Defensive Staff: McCarthy, Packers Decide to Make Dramatic Changes," *Janesville Gazette*, January 6, 2009.

321 *However, the NFL remained unscathed*: Badenhausen, Kurt, Michael K. Ozanian, and Christina Settimi. "Recession Tackles NFL Team Values," *Forbes.com*, September 2, 2009, http://www.forbes.com/2009/09/02/nfl-pro-football -business-sportsmoney-football-values-09-values.html.

321 *The former Executive Director*: Brandt, Andrew. "The Meaning of the Green Bay Packer's Crop Report," *Forbes .com*, July 14, 2010, http://blogs.forbes.com/sportsmoney /?p=5764.

322 *We were still able to turn*: Kass, Mark. "Packers' Profits Drop Significantly," *Business Journal of Milwaukee*, June 20, 2009.

322 *when you really dig in*: Jenkins, Chris. "Green Bay Packers Address Favre, Finances with Shareholders," *Fox6Now.com*, July 31, 2009, http://www.fox6now.com /news/witi-090731-shareholders-packers,0,4817655.story.

322 *It is extremely important*: Kass. "Packers' Profits Less Than Hoped."

322 *I think that's one of our real advantages*: Associated Press. "Packers Turn $20.1 Million Profit," *ESPN.com*, June 21, 2009, http://sports.espn.go.com/nfl/news/story?id= 4275519.

323 *He says he's going to*: Mulhern. "Packers: Bob Harlan, Job Placement Expert."

323 *I thought, "I can't believe*: Mulhern. "Packers: Bob Harlan, Job Placement Expert."

324 *If you'd have told me*: Dougherty, Pete. "Green Bay Packers Lose to Arizona Cardinals 51–45 in NFC Playoff Game," *Green Bay Press-Gazette*, January 10, 2010.

324 *To get this award*: Associated Press. "Packers' Charles Woodson Wins Defensive Player of Year Award," *USA Today*, January 13, 2010.

326 *Every year as a head coach*: Green Bay Packers. *Green Bay Packers Super Bowl XLV Championship Commemorative*

Edition (Big Lake, MN: GameDay Sports Media & Marketing, 2011), 4.

326 *I disagree*: Reischel, Rob. "Packers on the Cusp of Greatness," *Milwaukee Journal Sentinel*, May 13, 2010.

327 *We're a better football team*: Reischel. "Packers on the Cusp of Greatness."

327 *I think a lot of people*: Pearson, Paige. "Packers Revenue Highest in Its History," *Fox11Online.com*, July 14, 2010, http://www.fox11online.com/dpp/news/packers -financials-due-today-.

327 *It's really the continuing growth*: Pearson. "Packers Revenue Highest in Its History."

327 *The report estimated that*: "Study: Packers, Lambeau Impact $282M in 2009," *Business Journal*, September 29, 2010.

328 *I think the guys upstairs*: Dillon, Dennis. "Bad News for the NFC: The Packers Will Be Even Better Next Season," *Sporting New*, February 14, 2011, 62.

328 *Success in the NFL is obviously*: Brandt, Andrew. "With No Salary Cap, Parity Is Alive and Well in NFL," *Forbes .com*, November 11, 2010, http://www.forbes.com/sites /sportsmoney/2010/11/11/with-no-salary-cap-parity-is -alive-and-well-in-nfl/.

328 *We've had a very difficult road*: Milwaukee Journal Sentinel. *The Pack Is Back! How the Green Bay Packers Won Their 13th NFL Championship* (Stevens Point, WI: KCI Sports, 2011), 79, 77.

328 *we spend more than we are reimbursed*: Ryman, Richard. "Green Bay Packers Lose Money during Playoff Run, but Increase National Exposure," *Green Bay Press-Gazette*, January 11, 2011, http://packersnews .greenbaypressgazette.com/article/20110111/PKR03 /301120133/Green-Bay-Packers-lose-money-during -playoff-run-increase-national-exposure.

329 *he didn't hurt us that much*: Milwaukee Journal Sentinel. *Pack Is Back!*, 83.

329 *That interception saved*: Milwaukee Journal Sentinel. *Pack Is Back!*, 81.

330 *You never feel invincible*: Milwaukee Journal Sentinel. *Pack Is Back!*, 87.

330 *That's one thing*: Silverstein, Tom. "Thompson Finds Path to NFL Success," *Milwaukee Journal Sentinel*, January 22, 2011, http://www.jsonline.com/sports/packers /114400979.html.

331 *I don't get paid to tackle*: Associated Press. "Defense Propels Packers into Super Bowl after Bears Lose Jay Cutler," *ESPN.com*, January 23, 2011, http://scores.espn .go.com/nfl/recap?gameId=310123003.

331 *B. J. has dropped a handful*: Milwaukee Journal Sentinel. *Pack Is Back!*, 100.

332 *Main thing is, we got the win*: Milwaukee Journal Sentinel. *Pack Is Back!*, 102.

332 *The President don't want to come*: Green Bay Packers. *Green Bay Packers Super Bowl XLV Championship*, 13.

332 *This was the path that was chosen*: Milwaukee Journal Sentinel. *Pack Is Back!*, 100.

332 *We loved it*: Green Bay Packers. *Green Bay Packers Super Bowl XLV Championship*, 7.

333 *he tried to give a pep talk*: McGinn, Bob. "Green Bay Holds on to Win Fourth Super Bowl Title," *Milwaukee Journal Sentinel*, February 7, 2011, http://www.jsonline .com/sports/packers/115382579.html.

333 *kind of defines our season*: Dougherty. "Green Bay Packers Defeat Pittsburgh Steelers."

333 *That's what we've been doing*: Green Bay Packers. *Green Bay Packers Super Bowl XLV Championship*, 8.

335 *The NFL is a quarterback's league*: McGinn, Bob. "Green Bay Holds on to Win."

335 *I'm thinking, Oh God*: King, Peter. "Last Men Standing," *Sports Illustrated*, February 14, 2011, 38.

336 *We just never gave Ben*: King, Peter. "Last Men Standing."

336 *I think people are going to write*: Merrill, Elizabeth. "Poised Aaron Rodgers Steadies Packers," *ESPN.com*, February 7, 2011, http://m.espn.go.com/nfl/story ?storyId=6097828&wjb.

336 *The organization stood by me*: Walker, Don. "Rodgers Repays Debt to Packer Organization," *Milwaukee Journal Sentinel*, February 7, 2011, http://www.jsonline.com /sports/packers/115458124.html.

337 *The smallest city in the league*: Cohn, Bob. "Packers' Resolve Brings Lombardi Back to Titletown," *Pittsburgh Tribune-Review*, February 7, 2011.

337 *Chasing perfection*: Milwaukee Journal Sentinel. *Pack Is Back!*, 5.

337 *We've got some difficult times ahead*: Pearson. "Packers Revenue Highest in Its History."

EPILOGUE

338 *You're expected to win here*: Vandermause, Mike. "Packers Craft Culture of Winning," *Green Bay Press-Gazette*, January 7, 2012.

338 *It's a culture*: Vandermause. "Packers Craft Culture of Winning."

338 *We saw a big jump*: Kass, Mark. "Super Bowl Run Helps Packers' Bottom Line," *Business Journal*, July 26, 2011.

338 *We are seeing a lot of interest*: Kass, Mark. "Murphy: Super Bowl Trumps Lockout for Packers," *Business Journal*, September 8, 2011.

338 *We are hoping to match*: Kass, Mark. "Packers Hope to Raise $22 Million," *Business Journal*, December 6, 2011.

339 *significant bragging rights*: Krantz, Matt. "Green Bay Packers Sell Stock, First Time since '97," *USA Today*, December 6, 2011.

339 *In Green Bay, Super Bowl definitely*: Kass. "Murphy: Super Bowl Trumps Lockout for Packers."

339 *We refuse to be hunted*: Silverstein, Tom. "McCarthy's Ability to Motivate Breeds Success," *Milwaukee Journal Sentinel*, January 7, 2012.

339 *I'm proud of the performance*: Dougherty, Pete. "Notebook: McCarthy Expresses Desire to Keep C Wells Around Next Year," *Green Bay Press-Gazette*, January 18, 2012.

340 *Everything that happened*: Reischel, Rob. "Packers Can't Wrap Heads around Loss," *Milwaukee Journal Sentinel*, January 18, 2012.

340 *That's the way the game goes*: Mihoces, Gary. "Eli Manning, Giants Stun Packers for NFC Title Berth," *USA Today*, January 16, 2012.

340 *we play to win championships*: Mihoces. "Eli Manning, Giants Stun Packers for NFC Title Berth."

340 *We have a lot to build on*: Froberg, Tim. "Red Smith Banquet: Green Bay Packers President Mark Murphy Expects Future Success," *Green Bay Press-Gazette*, January 18, 2012.

340 *You learn from things*: McGinn, Bob. "Packers' Super Bowl Plans Nixed by Giant Thud," *Milwaukee Journal Sentinel*, January 15, 2012.

340 *I think it all starts with the organization*: Vandermause, Mike. "Packers Craft Culture of Winning," *Green Bay Press-Gazette*, January 7, 2012.

INDEX

ABOUT THE AUTHOR

Wisconsin native William Povletich is the author of *Some Like It Cold: A Sheboygan Surfin' Safari* (Clerisy Press, 2010), *Milwaukee Braves: Heroes and Heartbreak* (Wisconsin Historical Society Press, 2009), and *Green Bay Packers: Legends in Green and Gold* (Arcadia Publishing, 2005) as well as many magazine articles on sports and entertainment. An Emmy Award–nominated and Peabody Award–winning documentary filmmaker whose works have received both international acclaim and audience success, he recently produced *Police Women of Broward County* for TLC, *Beach Patrol* for Court TV, and *A Braves New World* for PBS and Milwaukee Public Television. William lives in the Los Angeles area with his wife and two sons.